D1235663

THE CRUCIFIX ON MECCA'S
FRONT PORCH

DAVID PINAULT

THE CRUCIFIX ON MECCA'S FRONT PORCH

A Christian's Companion for the Study of Islam

IGNATIUS PRESS   SAN FRANCISCO

Cover images:
Crucifix, location and photographer unknown
and
Mosque in Old Town, Rhodes Greece
Vladj55/istock photos

Cover design by Enrique J. Aguilar

© 2018 by Ignatius Press, San Francisco
All rights reserved
ISBN 978-1-62164-232-9
Library of Congress Control Number 2018931252
Printed in the United States of America ∞

For Jody
with love always

and in memory of two companions

Paul George Pinault
1947–2011
friend and brother

Paul Kosloski
1982–2017
student, seeker, spiritual quester

CONTENTS

PREFACE

WHAT DISTINGUISHES THIS BOOK
FROM OTHERS IN THE FIELD

Serambi Mekkah: "Mecca's front porch". A title bestowed with affection and religious fervor, it is the nickname Indonesian Muslims give to Aceh, the part of the East Indies island chain that lies closest to the Arabian peninsula. Because of this geographic proximity, for centuries Aceh has been the departure point from which Muslim pilgrims of the archipelago have sailed to Arabia's sacred cities.

As you will see in a subsequent chapter, the Acehnese Muslims I met during my own travels in the region tend to have a strong sense of their collective adherence to Islam. "More devout than Muslims anywhere else in the country", boasted an Islamic cleric I met in Aceh. To prove his boast, he reminded me that Aceh is the only province in Indonesia to be governed by sharia law. It is a law that is applied, sometimes violently, not only to Muslims but also to Christians and other non-Muslim residents.

And yet, despite the harshness to which they are subjected, Aceh's minority Christian population survives and even flourishes under persecution. I will never forget one Sunday visit to an old Dutch colonial-era church in Banda Aceh (the district capital). I will describe the visit in more detail later. For now I will share with you a memory that lingers.

I arrived just in time for Mass. A procession was making its way along the center aisle to the altar—priests, acolytes, worshippers. Leading them all was a young girl. Proudly she held high a crucifix, big and bronze.

The cross bearing Christ's body: lovingly, and defiantly, visible on Mecca's front porch. One of many moments, in the course of a long career in Islamic studies, that have helped deepen my own self-understanding and strong sense of identity as a Catholic Christian.

Not that I anticipated such outcomes when I began work in this field. At the outset of my vocation as an Orientalist, several decades ago now, I was pulled by the intricate density of Arabic grammar, by the prospect of the sheer exotic splendor of the East. That was enough for starters.

If that sounds strange, try this experiment sometime. Roam about your own house of memories. Pause before a mirror in a half-lit room when the curtains admit a single beam of late-afternoon light—a moment when dust motes dance (as Rumi once sang) like dervishes in the sun.

Now glance at the glass. What ghosts do you glimpse, winking at you from behind your shoulder? Me, I am likely to spot the young T. E. Lawrence (teenage young, before "of Arabia" was affixed to his name), murmuring the self-description he jotted in a letter over a century ago while traversing Syria on foot. He called himself "an artist of sorts and a wanderer after sensations".[1]

A wanderer after sensations. Yes. I know that impulse. It carried me far, from Northwest Africa to Southeast Asia. Fascinating work; got paid for it, too. Clive Brook sums it all up well in *Shanghai Express*: "It was an active life, full of interest and excitement."

All very true. But Orientalist splendor can take you only so far. Looking back, I see now I would not have kept going if not for three things that happened along the way.

First, the growth of Islamic terrorist and militant groups. Gradually, this claimed more and more of my attention beginning in the late 1980s. It began to dawn: hey, my job is not just *Golden Road to Samarkand*. This stuff *matters*.

Second, the harm inflicted by Islamists on Christian minority populations. I had begun attending Church services in Muslim countries as early as 1982, while living as a graduate student in Cairo. But after the Islamic terrorist strikes of 9/11, I developed a special interest in Christian survival under Islamist oppression. This work led (as

---

[1] *The Home Letters of T. E. Lawrence and His Brothers*, ed. M. R. Lawrence (New York: Macmillan, 1954), p. 147. The letter in question dates from 1911.

mentioned above) to a heightened appreciation for my own identity as a Catholic Christian.

And third, *da'wah* (Islamic evangelizing) by Muslim missionaries. As I mention in subsequent chapters, over the years I have frequently escorted students in my Islam courses on field trips to neighborhood mosques. Our hosts often exploit this opportunity to proselytize and (obliquely or directly) encourage my students to convert to Islam. Many of my undergrads—unchurched and largely ignorant of their own Christian heritage, idealistic but spiritually adrift—are vulnerable to such pitches.

Seeing this vulnerability has heightened my own sense of mission. As a Catholic teaching courses on Islam at a Jesuit Christian university, I structure my courses from a comparative perspective. My goal: to ensure that even as students become acquainted with Islamic doctrines, they also learn what is distinctive and uniquely precious about the Christian tradition.

All of which has influenced the content of the book you are now reading. Of course I address topics you will find in any introduction to Islam: the life of Muhammad, Koranic scripture, the origins of Sunni, Shia, and Sufi forms of the faith. But in each case, I keep in mind what I think will interest a Christian reader.

For this reason, a figure of recurrent importance in this book is Jesus Christ. As you will learn in the following pages, the Koran trumpets Jesus as a Muslim and a prophet of Islam. Adherents of ISIS and *da'wah* missionaries claim him as a jihadist and an enemy of Christianity. Well-meaning but massively wrongheaded peacemakers on the interfaith dialogue circuit—both Christians and Muslims—try to minimize Christological differences between the two religions in hopes of achieving Islamic-Christian concord.

My argument in this book is that attempts at Christological rapprochement do a disservice to both religions. It is far wiser to admit that the Jesus of Christian faith differs radically from the 'Isa (Islamic Jesus) we see in the Koran.

Among the Arabic texts I examine in this book are Muslim treatises on Jesus ranging in date from the eleventh century to the twenty-first. You will see for yourself that a religion such as Islam—denying as it does divine Sonship, the Trinity, and the reality of the crucifixion—necessarily assigns Jesus a role that diminishes him and misses the main message of Christianity. I present such material precisely so as to highlight the Christian Gospel truth of a God-made-Man who suffers in solidarity with the beings he both created and loves—loves even to the point of death on a cross.

I think I will have done my job if this book helps you to a fresh appreciation of what it means to be Christian.

A note on the sources used in this book

For this investigation, I provide my own translation of various Islamic primary source materials in Arabic, Persian, and Urdu, as well as texts in Latin written by Christian eyewitness participants in the Crusades. A number of the passages I have translated appear here in English for the first time.

I also offer my own translation of selected verses from the Koran. No previously published Koran translation is satisfactory for the close reading I propose to do with you. Some Muslim translators euphemize, gloss over, or wish away Islamic scripture's most problematic passages. The translations I give are meant to shine a hard, harsh light on such texts. Might this make some individuals squirm? Good. The first step in dealing with a problem is admitting a problem actually exists.

Acknowledgments

Portions of chapters 13 and 14 appeared previously in articles I wrote for the magazines *America, Commonweal,* and *The National Catholic Reporter.* I thank the publishers for permission to use this material.

Help came from many quarters for the research for this book: in Indonesia, Pak Rosek Nursahid and Mas Bayu Sandi, of ProFauna Indonesia; in Pakistan, the Most Reverend Lawrence Saldanha, Diocesan Archbishop of Lahore, and Mr. Qamar Jalil, of the Berkeley Urdu Language Program; in Yemen, Mr. 'Ali 'Abdullah al-Kohlani, executive manager of the Imam Zayd ibn 'Ali Cultural Foundation in Sanaa, and Mr. 'Ali al-Sharei, member of the general secretariat of Hizb al-Haqq (also in Sanaa); and in Egypt, the congregation of the Mu'allaqah Church in Cairo, as well as Ms. Hebba Bakri and her staff at the delightful Longchamps Hotel in Zamalek. I thank them all. Many other individuals in these countries also provided assistance but prefer to remain anonymous. So I will simply add a special note of gratitude to the house-church communities of Sanaa and Banda Aceh. Their Christ-centered steadfastness is one of the main things I remember from this research.

Closer to home, grants from the Dean's Office in the College of Arts and Sciences at Santa Clara University and SCU's Markkula Center for Applied Ethics provided financial support that made possible my time overseas. I am grateful for this generous aid. Friendship and encouragement from colleagues here in SCU's Department of Religious Studies constituted a big boost. And I have learned a lot from the students with whom I have worked over the years, especially the undergraduates in my comparative Christology course, "Jesus in Islam and Christianity".

Shouldering the biggest burden in the making of this book was my wife (and Religious Studies colleague), Dr. Jody Rubin Pinault. Tough locales: she was there for many and beamed me prayers through all the rest. Lucky is what I call myself, and all of it thanks to her.

I also feel blessed in the support I have received from the members of Ignatius Press, especially founding editor Father Joseph Fessio, S.J., production editor Carolyn Lemon, and copy editor Anne Nash. They provided not only technical expertise but also a sense of community and shared vision. I am grateful to them all.

As for the final product. Mistakes and infelicities: the responsibility and blame are mine. And if you the reader find something good about this book, then with the Psalmist and Knights Templar I will simply say: *Non nobis Domine non nobis sed nomini tuo da gloriam.*

Santa Clara
January 2018

CHAPTER 1

INTRODUCTION: HOW STUDYING ISLAM CAN HELP MAKE US BETTER CHRISTIANS

I teach courses on Islam for a living. I also happen to be a Catholic Christian. People in my line of work get lots of free advice on how to do their job.

On one occasion, it happened like this. An anxious Muslim father stopped by my office to ask how his son was doing in class. But it turned out he had more than his son's academic performance in mind. Before our chat ended, he told me he could tolerate the idea of a Christian teaching courses on Islam as long as I understood that my job was to defend Islam.

I replied that, no, actually my job had nothing to do with defending Islam. My job, I explained, was to *investigate* Islam—sympathetically whenever possible, but nonetheless in a way that was rigorous, historically oriented, and critically minded. Hopefully, I added, such a scholarly investigation would give his son perspectives with which to evaluate the many difficulties and opportunities facing Islam in the twenty-first century.

"Critically minded": these were the words this anxious parent noticed, and they did little to reassure him.

But something else I said seemed to help. I noted that part of the course included group field trips in which I accompany my students to religious services at local mosques. This gives imams plenty of opportunity to lecture my undergraduates and present their own understandings of the faith.

Although the question did not come up in my chat with this particular Muslim father, the mosque trips I build into my courses present uncomfortable challenges to both my Muslim and non-Muslim students. The challenges differ for each.

Most of my Muslim students show at least some familiarity with Islam but have been raised with relatively insular world views: they know something about their own denomination but exhibit quite a few unexamined prejudices about differing forms of Islam. Our field trips involve expeditions to mosques representing very divergent forms of the faith: Sunni, Shia, Sufi, Ahmadi. For many of my Muslim students who happen to be Sunni (the denomination with which most of them identify), such trips are their first-ever close-up experience of alternative kinds of Islam.

The responses I hear—whether in private office-hour conversations or in the classroom the day after each visit—range widely. Some Muslims say they are grateful for the exposure to something new. Others voice disgust and shock (Sunnis expressing doubt whether Shias are really Muslim; Sunnis and Shias uniting sufficiently to agree that the Ahmadiyyah sect cannot possibly be part of Islam).

These field trips have a somewhat different range of effects on my non-Muslim students. Most of them are Christian, and many of them come from Catholic backgrounds (not surprising, considering that most of my years as a teacher have been spent at Jesuit universities— Santa Clara, in northern California, and Loyola, in Chicago).

Over the years, no matter the setting (and I have taught on the East Coast, in the Midwest, and in the San Francisco Bay area), and no matter how painstakingly I have explained to our Muslim hosts that these mosque visits are part of an academic exercise in comparative religion—helping students to encounter and develop respect for other cultures, et cetera—they generally cannot help but think of such outings as a not-to-be-missed chance for *da'wah*. This Arabic word (literally meaning "summons", "call", or "invitation") is the term used by English-speaking Muslims in North America and elsewhere to refer to missionary work: summoning unbelievers to embrace Islam.

Usually, of course, such work is presented more obliquely. Thus, on one mosque tour with my students to an Islamic community center in the Bay area, I saw beside the prayer hall an office door marked "Da'wah/Education Outreach".

And "education outreach", rather than evangelizing, is how our hosts have rationalized their presentations when they talk to my students about Islam. At one talk at a local mosque, the speaker began by summarizing the Koran's view of Allah but then proceeded to condemn "inaccuracies" in the Bible by noting discrepancies in details of New Testament accounts of the life of Christ.

He then compared Christianity's view of Jesus with that of Islam by claiming the latter is simpler and more logical: Jesus in Islam is a prophet and the son of the Blessed Virgin Mary, but he is not divine, not the Son of God, and not someone who ever experienced crucifixion. Before leaving the mosque, we were also given copies of a leaflet (to be discussed in a subsequent chapter) explaining the absurdities of the doctrine of the Trinity and the superiority of *tawhid* (monotheistic belief in Allah).

Education outreach: indeed.

On another occasion, at the beginning of Ramadan some years ago, a preacher asked if he could come to campus to explain the purpose of fasting during this holy season. The topic appeared straightforward, an opportunity for interfaith dialogue. I said sure.

The talk began predictably enough. Fasting as a form of spiritual discipline, a way of curbing one's appetite not only for food but for anger and other forms of indulgence. Sounded thoroughly unobjectionable.

But the lecture took a curious turn when he said that becoming Muslim and fasting during Ramadan constituted a superlative way to lose weight and look great.

Now keep in mind here, as you consider this preacher's approach, that he was speaking to a roomful of undergraduates, young people, all too many of whom might well have been harboring worries and anxieties about thinness, body image, and attractiveness. Islam-as-weight-cure seemed to be his evangelistic way of targeting a specific late-adolescent audience.

(What the speaker did not mention was that the Ramadan fast also includes dawn-to-sunset abstention from drinking even a sip of water, something that few nutritionists are likely to recommend. And at the first opportunity, I made sure to point out to my students that many Muslims I have known in the course of my career have complained about how much weight they actually *gain* during the month of Ramadan, because of the all-night binge eating in which many people engage in order to compensate for their fasting throughout the day.)

The proselytizing quality of this pitch was reinforced by a movie that accompanied the lecture. It featured testimony by several recent American converts to Islam (or "reverts", as many prefer to call themselves—meaning they have "reverted" to their original, prenatal, faith). They spoke fervently of how their lives had now acquired direction and meaning.

Heady stuff, if you consider the world view of many of my students. (I have some notion of this in part because I have them keep field journals throughout the academic quarter; and their first assignment is to write a reflection in which they define their own world view, however they construe the term.)

Most of my Christian students come from backgrounds I would call unchurched (in fact, to judge from their journal entries, their mothers and fathers all too often also grew up unchurched—which gives you some sense of the gravity of the difficulties facing Christianity in the United States). This means that my Christian undergrads had some vague exposure to Christian doctrine as children but as teens became skeptical of the faith and often cynical about organized religion in general. Many such students are ideologically adrift; they know they are supposed to be respectful to people of other faiths, but they tend to have a jokey and offhand—if not outright hostile—view of their own Christian background.

And yet these same students—like undergraduates in general—are idealistic, generous, and hungry for meaning.

Which in turn leads to their peculiar vulnerability when it comes to our field trips to Islamic places of worship.

For many of my unchurched Christian students, our mosque visits constitute their first experience as adults (for some, their first time *ever*) being exposed to ritual, to the use of chanted language in a liturgical setting, to the feeling of group solidarity that comes when row upon packed row of believers moves together in unison in a collective act of worship.

No question: impressive.

And it is precisely such young people, students who are idealistic and hungry for meaning, who are unmoored in our consumerist-- celebrity culture of infinite distractibility, who are targeted by Islamic proselytizers. To quote from the exhortatory preface to a *da'wah* book I picked up at the Muslim Community Association in the city of Santa Clara:

As the American culture becomes more and more materialistic, and loses the values and moral ideals and practices of its Judeo-Christian heritage, Islam is filling the spiritual void created by the overemphasis on the secular vision of reality (versus the sacred), the greed of corporations ..., and the superficiality and hypocrisy of the mass media.... Islam provides purpose, discipline, guidance and support to give meaning to a culture that is drowning itself in meaningless trivia.[1]

As you read this, you might well say in reply: Well, if you are so concerned about your students being targeted for Islamic evangelization, then why keep taking them on mosque field trips?

A good question. It reminds me of something once said to me by Ahmed Kobeisy, a Saudi-trained Egyptian cleric who in the early 1990s was the imam of a mosque in Syracuse, New York. At that time, I taught in a nearby town, in Colgate University's Department of Philosophy and Religion, and several times I took students to Imam Kobeisy's mosque to witness Friday prayers.

A curious exchange occurred at the end of the first visit. Following his Q&A session with my undergrads after the service, the imam took me aside to ask whether the university was requiring me to do these excursions.

When I said no, he frowned and then confessed that if these were *his* students, he would never let them out of the classroom to talk to anyone else about the faith. There would be too much danger, he explained, of their hearing something that was wrong and differed from his own interpretation and that might lead them astray.

I admitted such things could happen. But rather than insist on keeping total control, I preferred letting my students be exposed to the risks and thrills of the world of ideas.

The frown persisted. He did not look very convinced.

If there had been time that day, I might have added (though I am not sure it would have done much good) that, as someone who was born and raised in the state of Rhode Island, I took inspiration from Roger Williams. He was the seventeenth-century religious visionary and refugee from Puritan Massachusetts who established the region of "Rhode Island and Providence Plantations" as a haven for spiritual freethinkers of all sorts.

[1] Muzaffar Haleem and Betty Batul Bowman, *The Sun Is Rising in the West: New Muslims Tell about Their Journey to Islam* (Beltsville, Md.: Amana Publications, 1999), p. xv.

In his "Letter to the Town of Providence" (written in January 1655), Williams envisioned his colony as an ocean-faring vessel:

> There goes many a ship to sea, with many hundred souls in one ship, whose weal and woe is common, and is a true picture of a commonwealth, or a human combination or society. It hath fallen out sometimes, that both papists and protestants, Jews and Turks, may be embarked in one ship; upon which supposal I affirm, that all the liberty of conscience, that ever I pleaded for, turns upon these two hinges—that none of the papists, protestants, Jews, or Turks, be forced to come to the ship's prayers of worship, nor compelled from their own particular prayers or worship, if they practice any.[2]

To appreciate the unsettling force of Williams' vision, imagine the connotation of the word "Turk" for a European colonist of his day. "Turk" was used as a synonym for "Muslim" in seventeenth-century England and France precisely because the dominant and emblematic Islamic entity at that time was the Istanbul-based dynasty of the Ottomans. Sultans like Selim the Grim and Suleiman the Magnificent and their successors had no interest in interfaith dialogue save the kind that is delivered at the tip of a sword. Their janissaries ravaged Europe repeatedly in militantly jihadist campaigns that took the Turks to the very gates of Vienna.

Mind you, Williams' creation of the first pluralistic society in the American colonies does *not* mean he was indifferent to what people believed. A case in point is the Quakers. Under Williams' leadership, Rhode Island allowed a group from this much-persecuted sect to settle in Newport. In 1657, the British government tried to enlist Rhode Islanders in a campaign to repress the Newport Quaker community. Here is the Rhode Island General Assembly's answer: "We have no law among us whereby to punish any for only declaring ... their minds and understanding concerning the things and ways of God."[3]

Not that Williams agreed with Quaker doctrine. Far from it. Zealous Christian that he was, he felt morally compelled to attempt to show the Quakers all the errors in their faith. With this in mind,

[2] Anson Phelps Stokes, ed., *Church and State in the United States* (New York: Harper & Bros., 1950), 1:197–98.

[3] Edwin S. Gaustad, *Roger Williams* (New York: Oxford University Press, 2005), p. 60.

on one occasion he rowed himself in a small boat across Narragansett Bay from Providence to Newport—a distance of some thirty miles—in order to engage the Quakers in theological debate.

Does this mean the man was intolerant? Not at all. As the historian Edwin Gaustad puts it:

> See, some commentators say, he did not really believe in religious liberty, because he told the Quakers they were wrong! What a dreadful misunderstanding this is. Yes, Williams told the Quakers they were wrong and for several days debated their religious principles with them. But no, he did not prevent their moving to and thriving in Rhode Island. And he did not allow the hand of the state ever to be raised against them. Nor did he fine, jail, whip, or hang any Quakers, or permit others to do so.[4]

A willingness to engage in intellectual debate with doctrines that differed from his, while creating a colony where all residents might freely explore the widest range of beliefs and seek God however they thought best: this is why I as a teacher find Roger Williams an admirable model. Quakers, Papists, Jews, Turks, rogue thinkers of every stripe: thanks to him, Rhode Island had room for them all.

What Williams championed in seventeenth-century Providence, I want to see sustained throughout America today: a society where residents respect each other's forms of worship, no matter what a neighbor's faith might be. If Williams, who came from an ardently Puritan background, could find it in himself to honor the religious freedom of "papists . . . and Turks", then I as a latter-day Rhode Islander ought to find ways to encourage my students to explore Islam as freely as possible, the risk of Islamic evangelism notwithstanding.

Ah, but the word "risk", you might reply, reveals a bias. To which I would have to plead: guilty. And here is my bias: before seeing any of my unchurched Christian undergrads convert to Islam, I would first like at least to give them the chance to rediscover their own Christian tradition.

An anecdote by way of illustration. In graduate school at the University of Pennsylvania, I met a young American Muslim woman (I will call her 'Afifah) in my Persian language course. Occasionally we

[4] Ibid., pp. 107–8.

compared notes outside class as we translated the mystical poetry of Hafez, Rumi, and Farid al-Din 'Attar.

One evening she mentioned she had been born into a Catholic family and raised without any exposure to the Catholic tradition or to what Catholicism meant. At the age of seventeen, she said, she had converted to Islam.

Years later, long after we had graduated from Penn, we both happened to be in Philadelphia while she was visiting family members. At our reunion, 'Afifah filled me in on her intervening years: marriage to a Muslim, raising two children, a home in Saudi Arabia (her husband had found work in Riyadh). I mentioned the Persian poems we had once read together.

"Sufi mysticism", she said, and she smiled. That, she added, was what had attracted her to Islam in the first place. When she was seventeen, 'Afifah said, she had had no idea that any kind of mystical tradition existed in Catholicism. No one had ever told her about Teresa of Avila or John of the Cross or even Thomas Merton. If someone had let her know about such writers, she said, she might never have gone off into Sufism and become Muslim. "Now, of course," she concluded quietly, "my life is all set up."

My own take-away from this meeting: students should be free to make their own life choices, but—and this is essential—I would just like those choices to be as fully informed as possible.

Or, to put it another way: Haleem and Bowman, in the da'wah book I quoted earlier, claim that "Islam is filling the spiritual void" caused by the decay of America's Judeo-Christian heritage. But I would suggest that unchurched young Christians be encouraged first to explore the riches of the Judeo-Christian tradition that they have never really known.

Thus, in every course on Islam that I teach, I put my own bias into play by telling those who show up the first day that I am a Catholic and that my own study of Islam has deepened my faith and strengthened my attachment to the Christian tradition into which I was born. That statement—in an academic environment where all too many professors evince casual contempt for faith commitments and religious identity—succeeds in getting students' attention.

On the first day of class, I also explain that since so much of Islam and the Koran entails either a reinterpretation or outright refutation and condemnation of Christian doctrines and scripture, we will be studying the Koran and the Bible in tandem. That means, I tell my students, that we will engage with four faiths in our course—not only Islam and Christianity, but also Jahiliyah polytheism (the Arab tradition into which Muhammad ibn 'Abd Allah—whom Muslims identify as the prophet of Islam—was born) and Judaism (the monotheistic tradition that has so strongly influenced both Christianity and Islam).

All these traditions will be addressed in the book you are reading now, which has grown out of my experience of teaching courses on Islam and comparative religion since the 1980s. The perspective, as you can gather from the above, is personal and opinionated.

Let me be clear: this book is written by a Christian, for fellow Christians (though I hope non-Christian readers will find much to interest them here). And, writing as one Nazarene to another, may I draw special attention to the following:

The argument of this book is that the study of Islam can give Christians fresh appreciation for the distinctive beauties and strengths of their own religion. This is especially true with regard to understandings of Jesus. But—caveat lector!—such a study can accomplish this only if we avoid the trap of restricting ourselves to the banalities of a "common word"/we-are-all-children-of-Abraham approach.

Many an interfaith dialogue have I endured (and I use the word "endured" deliberately) where conversation partners limit themselves to emphasizing whatever Islam and Christianity share in common. Such an approach involves truly praiseworthy goals: mitigate bigotry, prevent religious violence (concerns of worldwide relevance and increasing urgency today, no question). But such an approach fails to bring out the distinctive doctrines characteristic of each faith. Only when differences are acknowledged and explored can the theological resources of each religion be appreciated. That is the point at which real dialogue begins.

This is especially true with regard to Islamic and Christian understandings of Jesus, which will be one of the principal topics I will investigate in the following chapters. Superficially, the two faiths agree in honoring Jesus and recognizing him as the son of the Blessed Virgin Mary. But in their Christologies, Islam and Christianity differ far more than they agree.

Another argument of the book before you is that studying Islamic texts dealing with Jesus (excerpts from which I translate and discuss in what follows), precisely because such texts deny and even mock essential Christian truths, will have the effect of inspiring you to go back to the New Testament to rediscover Christian teachings involving especially the Incarnation and the crucifixion.

I will draw particular attention to three areas where I believe Christianity strongly diverges from Islam: (1) the kenotic (self-emptying) experience of the second Person of the Trinity in becoming man; (2) God's solidarity with created beings in the suffering undergone by all those who are sent into this world; and (3) the redemptive Passion of Christ in his death on the Cross.

Over the years, my study of Islam has made these three topics ever more meaningful to me as a Christian. If reading this book helps achieve this for you as well, I will feel satisfied I have accomplished my goal.

CHAPTER 2

THE WORLD INTO WHICH MUHAMMAD WAS BORN—PAGAN ARABIA—AND ITS CONTACTS WITH THE JEWISH AND CHRISTIAN FAITHS

To begin to understand Islam, we need to learn about the tradition into which the prophet Muhammad was born in A.D. 570. The word used by the Koran to describe this pre-Islamic tradition is "Jahiliyah". The term encompasses the religion, society, and values of pagan Arabia.

Since Jahiliyah means "condition of ignorance", it is clearly not intended as a compliment (the implied ignorance in question is the state of being ignorant of Islam). But the word has wide currency today, not only to designate the pre-Islamic Arabia of antiquity, but also (in the minds of Islamist malcontents such as Sayyid Qutb, the intellectual godfather of al-Qaeda) to denigrate any present-day society that claims to be Muslim but is deemed "ignorant" of what true Islamic life should be.

There are three dimensions or components of Muhammad's Jahiliyah environment to which I will draw your attention here: what I will call the desert; the city; and the hermitage, or monastery.

The desert dimension of the Jahiliyah

Let's begin with the geographic setting. Jahiliyah society of the Arabian peninsula was characterized by tribalism. The harsh and arid environment fostered a mentality whereby the Bedouin nomads who wandered Arabia's wastelands felt that resources were always unreliable, water and food could not be counted on to last, and whatever a rival tribe acquired meant that there would simply be that much less available for one's own family and clan.

25

In such a world, a prime virtue was *'asabiyah*: group solidarity, in which one owed loyalty only to fellow members in the tribe. Morality was group-determined, personal identity and personal worth collectively defined: one's conduct was measured by the reputation one earned in the eyes of one's extended family.

With no central government or police force, and given recurrent competition for scarce resources, it is no surprise that violence, vendettas, and a hair-trigger readiness to defend the honor of one's tribe were prevalent motifs in Jahiliyah society.

Presiding over each tribe was a sheikh (literally, an "old man"; being aged was a mark of wisdom in traditional societies), who was a repository of knowledge concerning the sunnah, a term that can be translated as "exemplary tribal custom". Each tribe had its own collective memory concerning the behavior of outstanding individuals from previous generations whose actions were recalled as a model by which tribal members could shape their lives.

In the pre-literate society of the Jahiliyah, the sunnah was encoded and transmitted orally from one generation to the next by tribal poets. Jahiliyah poetry is well worth reading, because the surviving poems from this era are our best and most direct source for appreciating the values, world view, and moral system of pre-Islamic Arabia. True, both the Koran and early Islamic commentators have much to say about the Jahiliyah; but in reading this material, we have to allow for the severely judgmental tone in these post-pagan sources.

(Over the years, I have occasionally encountered pious students in my courses who object as soon as I announce that we will begin our study of Islam by examining the Jahiliyah. "Why waste our time?" is one way the challenge is voiced. "Jahiliyah people had no morals." Well, actually they did, is my reply. It might not be a set of standards with which we entirely agree today. But as the renowned Jahiliyah poet Labid ibn Rabi'ah al-'Amiri put it in verse, "We have leaders, noble and generous, men who come from a tribe that follows a sunnah, a way of life laid out for us by our fathers and their fathers before them. For every tribe, after all, has a sunnah and a model to follow.")[1]

---

[1] The Arabic text of Labid's *Mu'allaqah* can be found in Charles James Lyall, ed., *A Commentary on Ten Ancient Arabic Poems* (Calcutta: Dar al-Imarah, 1894), pp. 67–89; translated from the Arabic by D. Pinault.

Tribal poets were well known (and they were often viewed with a mixture of awe and fear as well) for their ability to improvise dozens or even hundreds of verses in honor of a heroic warrior. Such verses—recited, memorized, and transmitted orally for generations—secured a hero's reputation.

Reputation was all the more important given Jahiliyah views of the afterlife. Arabs of the pre-Islamic era seemed to acknowledge the existence of some kind of survival for the soul, but it was nothing to look forward to. The afterlife was imagined as a cheerless shadow--existence reminiscent of the gray underworld in the ancient Mesopotamian *Gilgamesh* epic, where the deceased inhabit a subterranean "house whose people sit in darkness. Dust is their food and clay their meat." Similar to this is the Old Testament's Sheol, "the Pit" from which the witch of Endor summoned the ghost of Samuel. Ecclesiastes, Ezekiel, and Job provide us with more details: Sheol is where souls subsist in subterranean gloom, with no company save massed piles of corpses and burrowing worms.[2]

Important to emphasize here is that—in Jahiliyah thought as in Mesopotamian speculation and early biblical renderings of Sheol—the good and the bad, the moral and the immoral alike, faced the same gloomy fate.

As in *Gilgamesh*, pagan Arabs likened the spirits of the dead to spectral birds. Jahiliyah poets sometimes described the human soul after death as an owl that haunts the grave. In this society, preoccupied as it was with vendettas and tribal honor, it was believed that the most restless of spirits were the owl ghosts of those who had been killed and remained unavenged. These phantom birds haunted the site where their corpses lay, hooting *Isquni, isquni:* "Give me a drink, give me a drink!" The drink such owls wanted, of course, was a long deep slurp of blood.[3]

Given such beliefs, genuine immortality, the kind worth striving for, consisted of an enduring reputation within one's tribe. And the way to secure this immortality was to do a deed worthy of a poem.

[2] *The Epic of Gilgamesh*, trans. N.K. Sandars (Harmondsworth: Penguin Books, 1964), p. 89; 1 Samuel 28:7–19; Ecclesiastes 9:10; Ezekiel 32:17–32; Job 7:9, 17:13–16.

[3] Charles James Lyall, *Translations of Ancient Arabian Poetry* (London: Williams & Norgate, 1930), p. 67.

Unsurprising, then, that poets were so important to the people of the Jahiliyah. So powerful were their words, so uncanny the ability to chant verses that conferred an approximation of eternal life, that many poets were believed to be paired with spirit helpers. Such spirits were known as jinns.

Since belief in jinns persists worldwide in Islam today (though with modifications to allow for monotheistic doctrine), and since jinns played significant roles in both the Koran and Muhammad's life (as we shall see), it is worth pausing here to assess notions about these beings in pre-Islamic Arabia.

Jinns of the Jahiliyah era can be understood as nature spirits: amoral, in that they are beyond human categories of good or evil. Fire can scorch us but also keep us warm; water can drown us but also ease our thirst. So, too, with the entities called jinns: they are capricious, able to help or harm us, depending on their mood.

And, in fact, some jinns were explicitly linked with natural phenomena such as dust storms, whirlwinds, or the sudden onset of disease. An eleventh-century Muslim scholar named 'Abd al-Malik ibn Muhammad al-Tha'alibi devoted an entire chapter of his book on famous literary "quotations and attributions" to the topic of "things related to, or attributed to, angels, jinns, and satanic demons".

Among the ancient sayings al-Tha'alibi preserved was this: "The Bedouin Arabs of the desert call plague 'lances of the jinns'. According to tradition, plague is the experience of being stabbed and pierced by your enemies from among the jinns."[4]

"Being stabbed and pierced" suggests that it is the jinns that have the advantage and can take the initiative in dealings with humans; and so, too, for those individuals who become poets. One ancient verse refers to poets as *kilab al-jinn* (dogs of the jinns), a metaphor that makes clear who is the master in such relations. Such poets were said to be majnun (possessed by a jinn).[5]

The scholar Tha'alibi has this to say about such relationships during the Jahiliyah: "Poets used to claim that the satanic demons would cast

---

[4] Abu Mansur 'Abd al-Malik ibn Muhammad al-Tha'alibi al-Nisaburi, *Kitab thimar al-qulub fi al-mudaf wa-al-mansub*, ed. Muhammad Abu Shadi (Cairo: Matba'at al-Zahir, 1908), p. 53; translated from the Arabic by D. Pinault. The book's Arabic title can be translated as "The Heart's Harvest of Quotations and Attributions".

[5] Ibid., p. 54.

poetry into their mouths. The demons inspired them, taught them, and helped them with poetry. The poets claimed that every master verse-maker had a Satan who spoke poems and placed them on his tongue. And the more defiant, rebellious, and evil a demon was, the better the poet's poems would be."[6]

You may have noticed how judgmental this comment is: the old poetry may have been good, but that is only because its source was so malevolently bad.

Which leads to another question. Why would a Muslim scholar writing centuries after the defeat of Jahiliyah paganism be so interested in the question of demon-infested poets? One reason surely is that the Koran itself, as we shall see, deals with the accusation by the prophet Muhammad's Meccan neighbors that he himself was a *sha'ir majnun* (a poet possessed by a jinn, as is mentioned in chapter 37:36 of the Koran). We will look more closely at passages like this when we come to our investigation of Islamic scripture.

Tha'alibi also notes that some famous Jahiliyah poets would give their demons names. One poet, al-Farazdaq, called his jinn 'Amr; the poet Bashar applied to his spirit companion the title "Shanaqnaaq" (Tha'alibi says that Shanaqnaaq refers to one of the "great and powerful leaders among the jinns"). And the poet al-A'sha referred to his jinn as "Musahhil" (which literally means "the one who makes smooth", or—perhaps more colloquially—"Smoothie").[7]

Our scholar Tha'alibi adds this comment and quotation:

> Concerning Smoothie, al-A'sha used to recite:
> "And there I'd be, I wouldn't have a thing to say;
> But then what would happen, as far as I could tell,
> Is that Smoothie would trim and shape my words for me,
> And all I had to do was speak.
> Friends, the two of us: between us, real love;
> Partners, jinn and man; we get along just fine."[8]

Tha'alibi quotes another verse by al-A'sha: "My brother, the jinn, salutes me. My soul is consecrated to him." And concerning the same

[6] Ibid., p. 55.
[7] Ibid.
[8] Ibid.

topic of demon-poet relations, our scholar adds a citation from an anonymous Jahiliyah poet: "My Satan is the prince of the jinns." Tha'alibi follows this with a verse by al-Zafayan al-'Awafi, who boasted that his teacher was "from the race of the jinns": "If anyone tries to come against me as a foe, then I will make him taste fast the quick signs of shame."[9]

Texts like these let us sense what it is like to be clasped in a jinn's embrace: an infusion of power, of unpredictability, a certain heady loss of volition and control. Again, we will have reason to refer to this evidence when we examine the Koran and Muhammad's response to the charge of being majnun.

At least one famous female Jahiliyah poet is mentioned in the context of jinns. This is Tumadir bint 'Amr ibn al-Sharid, better known by her nickname al-Khansa'—"the Snub-Nosed"—a name intended as a compliment. As one Arab commentator explained: "She was given the honorific title 'Snub-Nosed' because this is a way of referring to gazelles and to those in general who have a small and well-proportioned nose, something that is characteristic of gazelles." She was renowned for her rapid-fire way with words. (Her father warned one unsuccessful would-be husband, "This woman has a spirit like no other of her sex.")[10]

The ninth-century literary critic Ibn Qutaybah in his *Kitab al-shi'r wa-al-shu'ara'* (The book of poetry and poets) describes how al-Khansa' once entered a tournament of poets that was held at an annual fair near Mecca. The site was called 'Ukaz. The judge who heard her recite was a poet named al-Nabighah al-Dhubyani. Ibn Qutaybah offers us the scene:

> A great pavilion-tent, red in color and made of leather, had been set up for al-Nabighah at 'Ukaz Fair. The poets came to him and recited before him their poems. Al-A'sha Abu Basir recited, then Hassan ibn Thabit, then other poets.
>
> Then came al-Khansa' al-Salmiyah, and she too recited. At this al-Nabighah said to her, "By Allah, if Abu Basir had not just recited

[9] Ibid., pp. 55–57.

[10] Louis Cheikho, S.J., *Anis al-julasa' fi sharh diwan al-Khansa'* (Beirut: al-Matba'ah al-Kathulikiyah lil-Aba' al-Yasu'iyin, 1895), p. 7 (translated from the Arabic by D. Pinault); Lyall, *Translations*, p. 43.

for me, I would have said you are the best poet among both jinns and men!" ... Then he added, "Well anyway, at least I have never seen anyone equipped with a womb who is a better poet than you."

To which al-Khansa' replied, "True, by Allah—but I also happen to be better than anyone equipped with a pair of testicles."[11]

We will meet more such feisty female reciters, equipped with pride and quick wit, outstanding among poets, whether human or jinn, when we look at the prophet Muhammad and how he dealt with women and men who challenged him in verse.

Jahiliyah sources let us know that in addition to demonic entities that initiated relations with individual men and women, there existed other jinns that were territorial, residing in caves, desert rock formations, abandoned fortresses: any place empty and ruined. One Jahiliyah poem describes the experience of traversing "land like the flat back of a shield, wild, where jinn are overheard in the corners, rustling, that no one dares enter."[12]

"Where jinn are overheard": worth noting here is how often these beings are associated with noise and unseen voices. Arabic dictionaries offer words like these: "*Zajal*. A soft humming sound produced by the jinn at night." " '*Azif*. The low, or faint, or humming, sound of the jinn, or genii, that is heard by night in the deserts; or a sound heard in the night, like drumming: or the sound of the winds in the atmosphere, imagined by the people of the desert to be the sound of the jinn." The commentator al-Asma'i links such sounds to "the falling of grains of sand driven along by the wind, as they sweep over the wrinkled surface of the desert."[13]

Wind-driven sand; soft humming sounds; voices on the night air. The kind of thing we can dismiss while moving along in a crowd of friends but that can prey on us if we find ourselves straggling and

[11] Abu Muhammad 'Abd Allah ibn Muslim ibn Qutaybah, *Kitab al-shi'r wa-al-shu'ara'*, ed. Hasan Tamim and Muhammad 'Abd al-Mun'im (Beirut: Dar Ihya' al-'Ulum, 1987), pp. 218–19; translated from the Arabic by D. Pinault.

[12] *Desert Tracings: Six Classic Arabian Odes*, trans. Michael A. Sells (Hanover, N.H.: Wesleyan University Press, 1989), p. 64.

[13] Hans Wehr and J. Milton Cowan, eds., *A Dictionary of Modern Written Arabic*, 3rd ed. (Ithaca, N.Y.: Spoken Language Services, 1976), p. 434; Edward William Lane, *Arabic-English Lexicon* (London: Williams & Norgate, 1863). Online edition: http://www.tyndalearchive .com, s.v. " '*Azif* "; Lyall, *Translations*, p. 82.

suddenly alone. Notions of jinns can arise in times of isolation, when one is alone with the silence of one's own heart and thoughts—a moment that can be experienced as burdensome in any society where personality is group-determined and privacy is something rare and not always welcome.

This ubiquity of jinns among the ancient Arabs brings us to another insight. For as far back in time as we can peer, into the Neolithic and Paleolithic eras and beyond, we see traces unearthed by archaeological excavations that are highly suggestive. Carved figurines of lion-headed men; carefully arranged animal skulls grouped about an altar; grave goods laid beside the dead for their afterlife journey: the evidence indicates that we have always tended to be religious, have always tended to sense all about us the presence of divine forces.

Throughout human history and prehistory, then, the recurrent question has not been: *Do the gods exist?* I imagine Jahiliyah tribal folk would have laughed at anyone who brought up the thought as they huddled together after nightfall in some encampment and would have told such a skeptic: *Just take a walk on your own beyond the firelight, and sit among the dunes in the dark for an hour. You will be able to feel forces pressing in from all around you. They will resolve your doubts. Go ahead.*

No, the question has not been: *Do the gods exist?* Rather, the question for the Jahiliyah, as with most societies throughout history, has been: *Do the gods care? Do we matter to them?*

And the Jahiliyah reply to this question seems to have been: *No, not consistently, or at best only intermittently.*

We see this view reflected in the numerous pre-Islamic poems that provide vignettes of the lives of animals. In one of the most popular collections of verses in Arab antiquity, Labid al-'Amiri describes a herd of antelopes surprised by a pack of wolves and how the fawns and does that once peacefully fed on young green plants are torn apart and are fought over as dismembered corpses.

"For when it comes to al-Manaya [the goddesses of Fate, about whom more later]," remarks Labid moodily, "the arrows and darts the goddesses shoot forth never miss their targets." One antelope survives the wolf raid and hides alone at night in a thicket, while a storm drenches it and it keeps still in the mud.

With dawn and a clear sky, the antelope catches the scent of a foe far worse than wolves: man. It runs, pursued by hunting dogs, until, cornered, it wheels and lowers its head and fights back with its horns, "using them", the poet tells us, "as a man would a spear".[14]

Other poems suggest similar links in the condition of men and animals. Al-Khath'ami describes a tribe afflicted with plague: "They wander, a trembling herd, their herdsman Death."[15] Imru' al-Qays tells of a fierce storm and flood that swept away towers and other human habitations; but he dramatizes the incident by focusing on how the floodwaters rose up along the hills, driving forth "the white-- legged deer from the refuge they sought therein".

He then visualizes the storm's aftermath the following morning. "At earliest dawn ... the birds were chirping blithely, as though they had drunken draughts of riot in fiery wine." He contrasts this cheerful birdsong with the overnight fate of the desperately fleeing deer: "The drowned beasts lay where the torrent had borne them, dead."[16]

Wildlife and man: we share an existential solidarity, these ancient poets tell us, as we try to survive the same unforgiving and harshly indifferent environment. A bleak assessment.

But the Jahiliyah poets also tell us how to respond to such a world: we need to develop the quality of *al-sabr*—a stubborn, steadfast capacity to endure. We see this quality in the verses of the famed "outlaw poet" Shanfara, who was exiled from his tribe for some crime:

Three good friends I have:
A bold heart,
A knife unsheathed from its scabbard and ready for use,
And a long bow of yellow polished wood, with a fistful of
    arrows....

So if you catch sight of me
Like the snake, offspring of the desert sands,
Sun-scorched and blasted by the midday heat,
Barefoot and worn thin from what I have been through,
Then keep this in mind:
I am the master of endurance, and I wear endurance
Like a shirt over a heart that beats strong as a young wolf's....

[14] Labid, *Mu'allaqah*, pp. 67–89.
[15] Lyall, *Translations*, p. 37.
[16] Ibid., pp. 103–4.

I raid camps by night, crawl past the guards,
And knife men in my way, leaving their wives widows and
    their children fatherless.
Come morning, the tribesmen ask each other:
"Who—or what—was that? Our dogs howled and barked,
But whatever it was last night came and went unseen.
Human? No. Men cannot manage that. Maybe a jinn,
Ill-omened, leaving a trail behind of destruction as it
    passed."...

Many a wasteland, bare and blank, like the back of a shield,
Have I crossed, on my two feet, alone,
Deserts no one else dares cross.
But I made it, from one end to the other,
And finally came to a halt
On the summit of a sand-swept hill,
And rested at my ease.

Around me, close at hand, the wild goats came and went,
Their coats sweeping the earth, like gowns young women
    wear.
At twilight, they gathered motionless around me,
As if I, too, were a desert beast,
Long-horned, white-footed, making my way forever
Up a steep mountain path.[17]

Here human-animal solidarity is now complete. The outlaw Shanfara has found a new tribe: the company of goats in the wild. And the only time he mentions the spirit world is in a camp-raid boast that proves he can go toe-to-toe with the demons and show he is as destructive as any jinn.

The pride Shanfara takes in his weapons—his knife and bow and arrows—recalls the weaponry of a legendary figure from another ancient tradition: Hercules, hero of the Twelve Labors, the half-human, half-divine son of Zeus. The Athenian playwright Euripides

[17] Shanfara, *Qasidat lamiyat al-'Arab*, with a commentary in Arabic by Mahmud ibn 'Umar al-Zamakhshari (Istanbul: Matba'at al-Jawa'ib, 1883), pp. 4–7; translated from the Arabic by D. Pinault.

in his tragedy *Heracles Mainomenos*, known also by its Latin title, *Hercules Furens* (Hercules gone mad) describes how the goddess Hera, motivated by jealousy and resentment, sends a spell of madness upon Hercules. The enchantment compels him to use his bow and arrows—with which he once achieved his Labors—to kill his wife and the children whom he loves.

Only then does he awaken from his madness, realize the horrors he has wrought, and address the weapon he still holds in his hand: "My bow! Which I have loved, and lived with; and now loathe! What shall I do—keep it, or let it go? This bow, hung at my side, will talk: 'With me you killed your wife and children; keep me, and you keep their murderer!' Shall I then keep and carry it? With what excuse? And yet—disarmed of this, with which I did such deeds as none in Hellas equaled, must I shamefully yield to my enemies and die? Never! This bow is anguish to me, yet I cannot part with it."[18]

Like Shanfara, Hercules sees his bow as a token of the deeds he has accomplished, and, like Shanfara, he clings to his weapon as a way to stay alive in a hostile world. Hercules' bow is a thing of violence—but it is his link to past glory and very much a part of him as well as a link to his whole jagged, strife-torn, and heroic life. Abused by the gods, Hercules, like Shanfara, will choose to survive.

But only after overcoming the temptation to suicide: "Why do I not take my life? Leap from some bare cliff, aim a sword at my own heart, become myself the avenger of my children's blood?"[19]

What saves him is the fortunate entrance of an old comrade: "But see! To prevent these thoughts of death, here Theseus comes, my kinsman and my friend." When Hercules in his despair cries out, "Could I but stay here, changed to a rock that feels no sorrow!", Theseus replies, "Say no more. Give me your hand; I'll hold you.... Put your arm round my neck; lean on me as you go."[20] In a world where gods exist but do not care, it is the touch of human friendship and human company that helps Hercules get by.

So too with the world as envisioned by the Jahiliyah poet Labid. Listen, as he recites:

[18] Euripides, *Heracles Mainomenos*, trans. Philip Vellacott (Harmondsworth: Penguin Classics, 1984), p. 197.

[19] Ibid., p. 189.

[20] Ibid., pp. 189, 197–98.

See, you have no idea how many good times I have had,
Chatting away the night with pals,
Keeping off the chill with a stiff drink of wine,
Enjoying the view of the hired girls as they play their songs
    for me....
And when animals are to be slaughtered and offered as food,
I make sure there is enough for all guests—the wanderer
    and traveler,
The old woman and all the orphans.
We have leaders, noble and generous,
Men who come from a tribe that follows a sunnah,
A way of life laid out for us by our fathers and their fathers
    before them.[21]

On this I think the Greek playwright and the pagan Arab poet
might agree: any sunnah, any ancestor-based code of conduct, is a
purely human product. The gods are a presence—in fact, they press
in all around us—but they are too fickle, too likely to shoot us with
darts, to help us figure out how to live.

Such values are akin to the existentialism voiced by Albert Camus
in *The Myth of Sisyphus* and *The Plague*. If gods are there, they look
on in silence. It is up to us to create our own values, build our own
world, find our own cure for the plague.

But the Jahiliyah poets, to their credit, were less glum than the
French existentialist crowd. Listen to Sulmi ibn Rabi'ah:

Roast flesh, the glow of fiery wine,
To speed on camel fleet and sure,
As your soul inclines to urge the beast on
Through all the hollow's breadth and length;
Pale-skinned women statue-like that trail
Rich robes of price with golden hem;
Wealth, easy lot, no dread of ill,
To hear the lute's wailing string:
These are life's joys. For man is set
The prey of Time, and Time is change.

[21] Labid, *Mu'allaqah*, pp. 67–89.

> Life narrow or large, great store or nought,
> All's one to Time, all men to Death.
> Death brought to nought Tasm long ago,
> Ghadhi of Bahm, and Dhu Judun,
> The race of Jash and Marib, and
> The house of Luqman and al-Tuqun.[22]

The final four lines of this poem refer to lost cities and vanished civilizations of the Arabian peninsula. Even in the sixth century A.D. (when Sulmi composed these verses), these names were a source of mystery and awe. Bedouin wanderers and caravan masters passed by the still-visible ruins of such sites and speculated on what might have brought them low. The Koran, too, as we will see, also refers to—and interprets—the fate of some of these very same towns.

But for now let's note how Sulmi juxtaposes this list of long-dead great powers—each once a byword for the good life—with a catalogue of "life's joys". Bisecting the poem, like a wounded animal's blood trail, is a reminder: "Man is set the prey of Time."

The *carpe diem* motif here is like the scene in a literary composition from the early Roman Empire: Petronius' *Satyricon*. Amidst a lavish thronging banquet, the host, Trimalchio, has his slaves suddenly bring out for contemplation a jointed figurine in the shape of a human skeleton, its bones and skull made of silver. As the slaves abruptly fling the jangling *memento mori* onto the dinner table, Trimalchio exhorts his guests in verse: *Sic erimus cuncti postquam nos auferet Orcus; ergo vivamus dum licet esse bene*: "Thus we will all be", goes the lesson, "after Hades carries us off. So let's live it up while we can!"[23]

Common to such works is an awareness of Time as a force that destroys us (the Arabic term is *al-Dahr*, a word that also occurs in the Koran but that is used in Islamic scripture to convey a different kind of lesson—as we shall see).

Before concluding this section, consider one more poem, by the Jahiliyah poet Iyas ibn al-Aratt. It offers advice with which both Trimalchio and Sulmi might raise high their cups in agreement:

---

[22] Adapted with slight modifications from Lyall, *Translations*, 64.

[23] *The Satyricon of Petronius*, trans. William Arrowsmith (Ann Arbor: University of Michigan Press, 1962), p. 32.

Let's forget the blame others cast our way: let's have another
    drink,
And let's shut off all the bad things life brings,
By giving ourselves to pleasures and playing and anything
That will keep us from having to think.
If an hour comes your way, make it a good one,
For Time's jaws grin; its fangs sink deep; it brings unrest and
    cares.
You might get a moment's ease, but right after that,
You will meet afflictions and sorrows and fears.

A twelfth-century Arab commentator on the above poem offered
this thought: "The meaning is that whatever al-Dahr [Time] seizes
with its fangs cannot be snatched back or rescued, just as nothing can
be snatched back from tusks that are hooked and sharply curved."[24]

Such poems clarify the values created in response to the world
as experienced by the people of the Jahiliyah. It is a nontheocentric
world: the gods unquestionably exist but cannot be relied on for help.

What flourishes in such a world are the values of tribal solidarity,
fatalistic endurance, and why-not-have-another-round hedonism.
Just as well to have one more drink, before fang-tipped Time treats
us like beasts and hunts us all down.

*City and hermitage: The urban and Abrahamic
dimensions of the Jahiliyah*

But cities also played a vital role in Jahiliyah culture, as they did in
the life of Muhammad and the early history of Islam. Two in particular were important: Mecca, Muhammad's hometown, and Yathrib (later to be renamed Medinat al-nabi, "the prophet's city", or
simply Medina), some 280 miles to the north. Both were located in
the Hejaz, the coastal area of the Arabian peninsula near the Red
Sea. Among Medina's population were communities of Jews and

---

[24] Abu Tammam Habib ibn Aws al-Ta'i, *Diwan al-Hamasah* (Cairo: Bulaq, 1878), 3:137;
translated from the Arabic by D. Pinault. The commentary on Ibn al-Aratt's poem is by
Yahya ibn 'Ali al-Tibrizi (d. A.D. 1109) and is included on the same page as the poem in this
Egyptian edition of Abu Tammam's famous ninth-century anthology called *al-Hamasah*.

Christians. We will discuss this city more closely when we examine Muhammad's career. For now, let's concentrate on Mecca, the city where Muhammad first began to preach.

In the late sixth and early seventh centuries A.D., during the time when Muhammad grew up and began his career, Mecca was known especially as a center of commerce and pilgrimage. Business interests were dominated by a tribe known as the Quraysh (this was the tribe to which Muhammad belonged).

Members of the Quraysh were also custodians of Mecca's principal shrine, the Ka'ba. This site is renowned today as the focal point of the hajj, the pilgrimage all Muslims are required to make at least once in their lifetime if they are able to. Less well known is that for centuries preceding the historical advent of Islam, Jahiliyah Arabs had made the hajj and—just as Muslims do today—had performed the *tawaf* (ritual circumambulation) around the Ka'ba, which in pre-Islamic times was a center of polytheistic worship. Since the annual hajj brought in thronging crowds of pilgrims—as it does today—and since such visitors also constituted business opportunities for local merchants, it is understandable that the Quraysh—who were both shrine caretakers and business leaders—might well be wary of disruptive religious messages that threatened Mecca's traditional forms of worship.

By way of comparison, think of the silversmiths of Ephesus and their reaction when Saint Paul arrived to teach the Ephesians about Jesus Christ. The New Testament's Acts of the Apostles (19:23–41) tells us what happened. These silversmiths, who made miniature souvenir copies of the temple of the goddess Artemis to sell to the numerous pilgrims that visited her shrine, understood at once that the Christian message would disturb their trade. Thus a smith named Demetrius cried out to his fellow workers,

> Men, you know that from this business we have our wealth. And you see and hear that not only at Ephesus but almost throughout all Asia this Paul has persuaded and turned away a considerable company of people, saying that gods made with hands are not gods. And there is danger not only that this trade of ours may come into disrepute but also that the temple of the great goddess Artemis may count for nothing, and that she may even be deposed from her magnificence, she whom all Asia and the world worship. (Acts 19:25–27)

Demetrius succeeded in stirring up a mob of protesters who ran through the streets yelling "Great is Artemis of the Ephesians!"

For generations before the time of Muhammad, the Ka'ba was surrounded by a circle of 360 idols. But the principal divinity worshipped at this shrine was a deity known as Allah (a name probably derived from *al-ilah al-akbar*, "the great god"). It is important here to draw attention to the fact that Muhammad did not introduce the worship of Allah; this was a deity already well known to the Jahiliyah. During the pagan era, Allah was venerated as a creator and a sky god that held the power of bestowing rain. One of his early titles was Rabb al-ka'bah, "Lord of the Ka'ba".

The pagan Arabs also worshipped a triad of goddesses—Allat, Manat, and al-'Uzza—that they called *banat Allah*, "the daughters of Allah". Allat (the grammatically feminine form of "Allah") was associated with childbirth and the fertility of the soil. Manat was revered by the Arabs as the goddess of destiny (the name is related to Manaya, "the goddesses of Fate", whom we encountered in Labid's poem, firing darts that cut life short).

Particularly popular among the Quraysh and other Arabs living in the vicinity of Mecca was the third goddess, al-'Uzza, "the Mighty One", who was venerated in association with Venus, the Dawn Star (the inhabitants of Petra, in what is today southern Jordan, equated her with Aphrodite). Individuals prayed to her for cures from afflictions of sickness. Her sanctuary at Nakhlah, east of Mecca, featured three acacia trees that were consecrated to her as well as "a place of slaughter for al-'Uzza, where visitors sacrificed their gifts for her".[25]

At one point in his life, Muhammad, too, participated in such rituals. Abu Mundhir Hisham ibn al-Kalbi, an eighth-century Muslim scholar who made a specialty of collecting information about religious practices among the Jahiliyah Arabs of earlier generations, tells us this:

> Among the desert Bedouins and the Quraysh, there were some that were given the name 'Abd al-'Uzza [servant of al-'Uzza] in her honor.

---

[25] Yaqut ibn 'Abd Allah al-Rumi, *Mu'jam al-buldan* (Beirut: Dar Sadir, 1957), 4:185, s.v. "al-Ghabghab".

She was the greatest of the idols among the Quraysh. They would visit her and make offerings to her and draw near to her by means of ritual slaughter.

And word has reached us that Allah's messenger—may Allah's blessings and prayers be upon him—mentioned her one day, for he said, "While I was following the religion of my people, I made an offering to al-'Uzza, an offering of a sheep that was the color of red desert sand."[26]

Ibn al-Kalbi's report is important for helping us reconstruct Muhammad's early life before he began preaching Islam. Given al-'Uzza's popularity among the Quraysh, and given the fact that this was the tribe to which Muhammad belonged, it is unsurprising that he, too, in the early stages of his life, engaged in animal sacrifice to this goddess.

But be careful where you mention this. Linking Muhammad to pagan worship, no matter what the sources say, can get you into trouble. Even the merest reference to such a topic may suffice. Just ask Younus Shaikh.

Younus Shaikh is a Pakistani Muslim who taught at a college in Islamabad. In 2001, he was tried in court and found guilty under the terms of Pakistan's blasphemy law. According to Dr. Shaikh's students, who filed the complaint, "He had told them that the Prophet had not become a Muslim until age 40 [the age at which, according to Muslim biographers, Muhammad received Allah's summons to preach Islam] and that before then, he had not followed Muslim practices."[27] This alleged statement was enough to earn Younus Shaikh a death sentence.

We will examine Muhammad's career and Pakistan's blasphemy law in subsequent chapters. But for now, let's return to Ibn al-Kalbi's description of pre-Islamic Arabia. Immediately after mentioning Muhammad's sacrifice of a sheep to al-'Uzza, he tells us more about the rituals engaged in by Muhammad's fellow tribesmen in Mecca:

---

[26] Abu Mundhir Hisham ibn Muhammad ibn al-Kalbi, *Kitab al-asnam*, ed. Ahmed Zeki Basha (Cairo: Imprimerie Nationale, 1914), pp. 18–19; translated from the Arabic by D. Pinault.

[27] Celia W. Dugger, "Pakistani Sentenced to Death for Blasphemy", *The New York Times*, August 20, 2001.

When the Quraysh performed the *tawaf* around the Ka'ba,
   they would say:
"By Allat, and al-'Uzza, and the third one, Manat!
In truth, they are the cranes that fly high,
And their intercession may be hoped for!"
They used to say, "The daughters of Allah intercede with
   him."[28]

Let's examine this intriguing passage. The word I translate "cranes"
is *gharaniq* in the original Arabic (the singular form would be *ghurniq*,
ghurnuq, or *ghirnawq*). A detailed philological discussion of this term
can be found in the Arabic-English lexicon of the famed nineteenth--
century Orientalist scholar Edward William Lane, who notes that the
term can refer in general to "a certain aquatic bird, long in the neck".

So *ghurniq* might be rendered as "swan", "stork", or "crane". In
this context of the Quraysh and their recitation at the Ka'ba, however,
Lane favors translating *ghurniq* as the *ardea virgo* or "Numidian crane"
(Numidia is the ancient Mediterranean kingdom comprising coastal
Algeria and Tunisia). He offers this justification: "For the Numidian
crane is remarkable in the East for its superlatively high flight; referring, as Ibn al-'Arabi says, to the idols, which were asserted to be
intercessors with God, wherefore they are likened to the birds that
rise high into the sky."[29]

The three goddesses as birds that plead for us with a Supreme
Force overhead: an imaginative soaring with which one can sympa-
thize. Huddled over Lane's dictionary, I remembered a trip of my
own, to northern California's marshland delta, where I saw a flight of
sandhill cranes at sunset. Massive wingspans, cries echoing across a
red winter sky as darkness came on fast: easy enough to ask these
creatures to snatch up one's prayers and forward them skyward.

But the prayers uttered by the Quraysh to these goddess birds had
a carefully patterned, formal structure to them. This becomes noticeable if we look at the Arabic wording of the text. Here it is, in
transliteration:

---

[28] Ibn al-Kalbi, *Kitab al-asnam*, p. 19; translated by D. Pinault. The pious-minded Ibn al--
Kalbi inserts into his report the reproof: "May Allah be exalted far above all that!"
[29] Lane, *Arabic-English Lexicon*, s.v. "Ghurniq".

> *Wa'l-lati wa-l-'Uzza*
> *Wa-Manata al-thalithati al-ukhra*
> *Fa-inna-hunna al-gharaniq al-'ula*
> *Wa-inna shafa'ata-hunna la-turja.*

'Uzza/ukhra/'ula/turja: this is what the ancient Arabs called *saj'*. The word is usually translated as "prose rhyme", but the literal meaning of *saj'* is "pigeon cooing", because the recurrent rhymes reminded Jahiliyah audiences of the rhythmic trilling of doves. Here is my attempt at a version of the above lines in English-language *saj'*:

> By al-'Uzza and Allat,
> By the third one named Manat!
> These goddess cranes fly high
> May they bring their blessings nigh!

Saj', much favored by poets of the pre-Islamic era, is one of the oldest types of traditional Arabic recitation, and it was used especially for curses and incantations: enlisting the unseen forces that exist all around us. Thus Jahiliyah poetry and magic were closely bound together; and, given the fact that a significant portion of the Koran, especially its early Meccan verses, are composed in *saj'* prose rhyme, it is not surprising that Muhammad's neighbors wondered whether he was a majnun poet and a sorcerer—charges to which he responded, as we shall see, with increasing irritation.

Remarkable, too, about the Qurayshi prayer to Allah's daughters is that it accompanied a specific action; as Ibn al-Kalbi tell us, these words were recited "when the Quraysh performed the *tawaf* around the Ka'ba". This means that worshippers walked repeatedly in a circle around the shrine. (Muslims who do the hajj today are required to circumambulate the Ka'ba seven times to complete the ritual.)

Jahiliyah *tawaf* has its analogue in the ancient Egyptian practice called *sa' per* (protecting the house) or "cultic encirclement", whereby worshippers and chanting priests walked about a temple. This popular ritual, attested from remotest pharaonic antiquity through the Ptolemaic dynasty of the first century B.C., served to demarcate, purify, and protect a sacred space.

But *sa' per* did more. Such acts linked men to gods via rituals that imitated and conjured ancient myth. Just as the sun god Ra established his universal sovereignty through his circuit around the earth and sky, so too did worshippers in their processions hope to evoke, enchant, and in some measure control the forces resident within their own temple circuit.[30]

So, too, with the Jahiliyah combination of *tawaf* and *saj'*-incantation at the Ka'ba. The monotonous rhyme, the repetitive chant, the continuous encircling: all are meant to have the hypnotic effect of reducing the target—whether human, divine, or animal—to a state where it is lulled and susceptible as the enchanters strive to impose their will.

Ritual and rhymed verse, encirclement and chant: powerful pairings, as Samuel Taylor Coleridge attested in *Kubla Khan*, his own opium-dream evocation of the pleasure dome in Xanadu and the joys and terrors of being a poet:

> Weave a circle round him thrice,
> And close your eyes in holy dread,
> For he on honey-dew hath fed,
> And drunk the milk of Paradise.

Weaving a Coleridge-esque circle, chanting *saj'* dove-rhymes, asking for intercession as they called on the three daughters of Allah: all these elements were involved in Jahiliyah rituals at the Ka'ba. Since the Koran explicitly names and condemns these goddesses, we will return to this triad when we discuss Muhammad's life in more detail. For now I will conclude this section with one more observation.

Each of these three goddesses originally had her own shrine in the regions neighboring Mecca. Al-'Uzza's was in Nakhlah (as we have learned); Manat's, in Qudayd; Allat's, in Ta'if. In the time period immediately before Muhammad began his preaching, greater commercial traffic and greater wealth poured into Mecca (for reasons we will examine below). Arranging these goddesses—who had originally been venerated independently of each other—in a triad and calling them "daughters of Allah" was a way of systematizing their worship

---

[30] Robert Kriech Ritner, *The Mechanics of Ancient Egyptian Magical Practice* (Chicago: Oriental Institute, 1993), pp. 57–67.

and fitting them within a hierarchy linked to the sky god's cult at the Ka'ba, the chief deity at the increasingly important city of Mecca. And this is one of the pragmatic strengths of polytheism: rather than claim a rival town's deity does not exist, one can simply incorporate it into the structure of a divine family.

The lute, the song, and the hermitage: Cultural change and the Abrahamic dimension of the Jahiliyah

As a center of both pilgrimage and trade, Mecca was subject to outside cultural influences, especially those of the two great rival political superpowers of the time, the Constantinople-based Byzantine Empire and the Zoroastrian Sassanid dynasty of Persia. These states were heirs to a long tradition of war. For centuries, Romans had fought Parthians for domination of the Near East. In an earlier age at Thermopylae, Xerxes had led the Immortals of his imperial guard against Leonidas and the hoplites of Sparta.

War broke out anew between Persia and Byzantium in sporadic conflicts throughout the sixth and early seventh centuries, during Muhammad's youth and early years of prophethood. This violence disrupted traditional trade routes connecting East and West. Consequently, Mediterranean-based merchants found it safer to travel from Syria to Arabia's Hejaz coast, where ships could transport goods through the Red Sea and the Gulf of Aden and out into the Indian Ocean.[31]

Situated as it was along this vital trade corridor, Mecca was a beneficiary of these political-military developments. New wealth flowed into Muhammad's hometown, and with it came fresh influxes of both people and ideas.

The cultural changes in Mecca underway at this time are reflected in the experiences of a contemporary of Muhammad named al-Nadr ibn al-Harith. Nadr came from a prominent Hejazi family and had a reputation as a storyteller, merchant, and traveler. Of particular interest are his journeys to the city of al-Hirah in southern Iraq, which

[31] Bernard Lewis, *The Arabs in History*, rev. ed. (New York: Harper & Row, 1966), pp. 33–34.

at that time was under the influence of the Sassanid shahs of Persia. Famous for its palaces and castles, the region around al-Hirah was also a center of Nestorianism (a form of Christianity that emphasized Christ's human nature at the expense of his divinity).[32]

The tenth-century historian 'Ali ibn Husain al-Mas'udi records a story about Nadr in the city of al-Hirah that suggests the changes underway in Meccan society shortly before the advent of Islam:

> Among the desert Arabs, the *hida'*—the chant used by camel-drivers—preceded all other forms of song.... The *hida'* was thus the first form of singing and of chanting refrains among the Arabs. Among the songs derived from the *hida'* are the lamentations of longing and yearning sung by the Bedouin women for their dead.... The Bedouin style of singing is called "nasb"....
>
> The tribe of the Quraysh was familiar only with the "nasb" style of singing until al-Nadr ibn al-Harith ibn Kaldah ibn 'Alqamah ibn 'Abd Manaf ibn 'Abd al-Dar ibn Qusayy returned from Iraq, where he had been a member of a delegation to the court of the Persian shah Chosroes in the city of al-Hirah. There he had learned to play the lute and how to sing in accompaniment to this instrument. He returned from Iraq to Mecca and taught its people these arts. Then they began to acquire for themselves slave-girls that had been trained as professional singers.[33]

From simple camel chants to imported arts involving lutes and melodies sung by singing slave girls: this anecdote illustrates what happened in Mecca as new wealth and political contacts triggered cultural change. There is more to tell about al-Nadr ibn al-Harith—especially because he and the future prophet of Islam became rivals and then bitter enemies—but that is a story I will save for our next chapter.

I mentioned above that al-Hirah was home to a community that belonged to the Nestorian form of Christianity; and this region was one of many that served as a conduit providing the Hejazi cities of Mecca and Yathrib (later renamed Medina) with what I call Jahiliyah Arabia's Abrahamic dimension. A significant Jewish minority population lived in and about Yathrib. Many of these Arabian Jewish

[32] For a discussion of Nestorian Christology, see Richard P. McBrien, *Catholicism: New Edition* (San Francisco: Harper, 1994), pp. 470–72.

[33] 'Ali ibn Husain al-Mas'udi, *Muruj al-dhahab*, ed. C. Barbier de Meynard (Paris: l'Imprimerie Nationale, 1874), 8:92–95.

families probably originated in the diaspora that resulted from the Roman conquest of Jerusalem, the destruction of the Second Temple in A.D. 70, and unsuccessful attempts to win Jewish independence from Rome in the first and second centuries.

Christians, too, were present in the world of the Jahiliyah. Particularly impressive to the pagan Arabs of the time were the monks inhabiting the desert wastelands, who sometimes welcomed travelers at their hermitage dwellings. According to the earliest Muslim biography of Muhammad, when he was a young man—years before becoming the prophet of Islam—Muhammad traveled in a merchant caravan to Syria. There, in the vicinity of Busra, a Christian monk named Bahira emerged from his monastery cell to offer food to the travelers and engage Muhammad in conversation.[34]

Christianity was encountered by Jahiliyah-era Arabs not only in Syria but also in the Hejaz. Christians as well as Jews lived among the pagans of Yathrib. And Christians made their presence felt even in the vicinity of polytheistic Mecca. The nearby annual fair of 'Ukaz—where, as we have already learned, poets like al-Khansa' recited verses in public competitions—was a place of pagan-Christian encounter. Among those thronging 'Ukaz, according to the ninth-century Muslim scholar Abu al-Faraj al-Isbahani, was a Christian ascetic named Quss ibn Sa'idah ibn 'Amr. (The name "Quss" means "priest", a mark of his clerical rank.) A Christian Arabic source describes him: "He dressed in coarse woolen robes and followed the life-style of a wanderer in imitation of Christ."[35]

Quss' wanderings occasionally took him to the fair at 'Ukaz. There he sometimes borrowed a camel that served as a living pulpit. Perched high atop the beast, he would address the crowds in cadenced prose rhyme, preaching to them on mortality and life's fleeting quality. They should take heed, he urged them, of how quickly all things on earth pass away.

Our ninth-century source tells us that one person in the fairground crowd listened with particular attention to this priest's rhymed sermon:

[34] Muhammad ibn Ishaq, *The Life of Muhammad: A Translation of Ibn Ishaq's Sirat Rasul Allah*, ed. and trans. A. Guillaume (Karachi; New York: Oxford University Press, 1968), pp. 79–81.

[35] Louis Cheikho, S.J., *Kitab shu'ara' al-nasraniyah fi al-jahiliyah* (Cairo: Maktabat al-Adab, 1982), 2:211.

Before he became the prophet of Islam, Allah's messenger—God's blessings and prayers be upon him—noticed Quss and saw him at 'Ukaz. While listening to him, Muhammad was impressed by Quss with regard to what he said. Later, when Muhammad was asked about him, he said, "On Judgment Day, that one will step forward in a class of his own, in a community of one."[36]

Sometime later, Muhammad met kinsmen of Quss ibn Sa'idah. They told him that the preacher had died. Muhammad exclaimed, "It's as if I can still see him now at the 'Ukaz Fair, seated on that camel of his—it was ash-grey in color—giving a speech, speaking with refinement and grace."

One of Quss' kinsmen then offered an anecdote, recalling how he had once spotted the priest alone in the wilderness, seated beneath a tree near a spring of water, keeping company with a group of lions. As each thirsty lion took its turn to lap up water, Quss reprimanded the others that roared with impatience, telling them, "Stop and wait until the one that's ahead of you finishes drinking."[37]

This story may remind you of an incident from the life of Francis of Assisi: how the saint tamed the ferocious wolf of Gubbio and made a pact of friendship between the animal and the local townspeople.[38] The ability to live peaceably among God's creatures in nature is a mark of piety and a longstanding motif in tales of ascetics and mystics. The tradition goes back to the origins of Christianity: recall from the Gospel of Mark (1:13) how after Jesus was baptized in the river Jordan, the Spirit drove him to the desert, where "he was with the wild beasts; and the angels ministered to him."

The swordsmith's chant: Encounters with an enslaved Christian in Mecca

Another account—this one linked to Islamic scripture—attests to an ancient Christian presence in Mecca itself. Here is what the Koran

---

[36] Abu al-Faraj al-Isbahani, *Kitab al-aghani*, ed. Ahmad al-Shinqiti (Cairo: Matba'at al--Taqaddum, 1905), 14:40–41. Translated from the Arabic by D. Pinault.

[37] Ibid., p. 41.

[38] Adrian House, *Francis of Assisi: A Revolutionary Life* (Mahwah, N.J.: Hidden Spring/Paulist Press, 2001), pp. 180–81.

states, in an intriguing but obscure verse (16:103): "We know that they [the pagan Quraysh] say, 'It is simply a man who has been teaching him.' But the man they are maliciously referring to: *his* tongue is foreign [*a'jami*], not Arabic. Whereas *this* [the Koran] is in a clear Arabic tongue."

Who is this man who is being referred to so cryptically? The fourteenth-century Koran commentator Nasir al-Din al-Baydawi provides a helpful clarification of this verse: "They [the pagan Quraysh] are referring to Jabra the Greek, the slave of 'Amir ibn al-Hadrami. It is said that Jabra and Yasara [another slave] used to make swords in Mecca and recite the Torah and the Gospel. The prophet—may Allah bless him and grant him salvation—used to drop in on them and listen to what they recited."[39]

You can imagine the scene: two slaves hammering hot metal, keeping up their spirits in exile and servitude by reciting to each other favorite verses from the Bible. And there is Muhammad, listening to it all, enraptured.

You may have noticed that the Koran does not deny that Islam's prophet visited such men and learned from them. Rather, it implies that Muhammad deserves credit for taking what he heard and rendering it into a composition that would be intelligible for his local Arab audience: "in a clear Arabic tongue".

King Solomon's jinns: Biblical references in pre-Islamic poetry

Accounts of Bahira the monk, Quss the preacher, and Jabra the swordsmith slave all amount to a kind of implicit Islamic acknowledgment of Christianity's significant presence within the Jahiliyah world in which the young Muhammad came to maturity. Not that the pagan Arabs of Mecca were likely to have been intimately acquainted with the details of Judeo-Christian doctrine or scripture. Rather—as we will see when we examine the Koran in the next chapter—they seemed to have heard stories about the most horrific calamities and heroic feats to be found in the Jewish and Christian Bible: the kind of thing, in other words, that travels well and makes for a terrific tale.

[39] Nasir al-Din Abu Sa'id al-Baydawi, *Anwar al-tanzil wa-asrar al-ta'wil* (Beirut: Dar al-Kutub al-'Ilmiyah, 1988), 1:557, commentary on Koran 16:103; translated from the Arabic by D. Pinault.

An example can be found in the verses of the sixth-century pre--
Islamic poet al-Nabighah al-Dhubyani, whom we met earlier serving
as a judge in the recital competitions at 'Ukaz. In one of his poems
he states:

> The god said to Solomon:
> "Rise up among the creatures, and prevent them from error.
> Bring the jinns low; I have permitted them
> To build Tadmur with stone slabs and columns."[40]

Nabighah's reference to Tadmur (the Syrian desert city known
to the Greeks and Romans as Palmyra) is derived from two sources.
The Bible tells us (in 2 Chron 8:3–8) that King Solomon, in addition to constructing the great Temple in Jerusalem, "built Tadmor
in the wilderness and all the store-cities which he built in Hamath".

But another source is reflected as well in al-Nabighah's poem: the
Haggadah, or oral folklore tradition of the Jews, legendary material
that dates back to at least the second century A.D. and that is in all
likelihood derived in turn from yet earlier sources. The Haggadic
stories relating to Solomon that have been collected by the scholar
Louis Ginzberg state that when the Israelite king sought to build the
Temple in Jerusalem, the archangel Michael gave him an enchanted
seal-ring. With this, Solomon called up hordes of demons, learned
their names, and compelled them to serve him. Some he put to work
digging foundation trenches; others were made to cut massive stones;
a third set of demons prepared gold, silver, and precious gems for
ornamenting the Temple's walls. This story is emblematic of Haggadic tales, which tend to elaborate in richly imaginative ways their
biblical sources.[41]

In reciting his poem, the poet al-Nabighah seems to have assumed,
in mentioning Solomon, that his Arab audience had some acquaintance with this Jewish legendary tradition involving Solomon and
his conscript-labor jinns. And some echo of this tradition will subsequently be found in the Koran as well, which mentions (in chapter

---

[40] Al-Nabighah al-Dhubyani, *Diwan al-Nabighah al-Dhubyani*, ed. Muhammad Abu al-Fadl
Ibrahim (Cairo: Dar al-Ma'arif, n.d.), pp. 20–21; translated from the Arabic by D. Pinault.

[41] Louis Ginzberg, *The Legends of the Jews* (Philadelphia: Jewish Publication Society of
America, 1942), 4:149–52.

34:12–13) that the jinns were put to work on massive construction projects for this same king (whom Islamic scripture identifies as an Islamic prophet).

Trophies of war: The loss—and recovery—of the True Cross

Before concluding this discussion, there is one more incident relating to the Abrahamic and Judeo-Christian presence in the Near East that is vital to know about in relation to Muhammad's early career. In A.D. 611, just one year after Muhammad began to preach Islam, the Sassanid Persians under the leadership of Emperor Chosroes II invaded Syria. Successful there, they then attacked the Byzantine province of Palestine and besieged Jerusalem. In 614, the Persian army conquered the city, destroyed many of its Christian shrines, and set fire to the church of the Holy Sepulchre.

Rumors of war reached all the way to Mecca, where Muhammad received news of the Sassanid victory and pondered its implications for his own emergent mission. "The Romans", announced the Koran (30:2–4), "have been defeated in a nearby land." (Al-Rum, "the Romans", is the word used in the Koran and in medieval Arabic texts to designate the Greeks of the Byzantine Empire.)

Among the plunder that the Persians took from the Sepulchre was one of the most revered relics of Christendom: the True Cross, revered as the cross on which Jesus himself had been crucified. Discovered in the early fourth century by Saint Helen, mother of Emperor Constantine, it had for centuries been a focus of devotion and pilgrimage.

A nun named Egeria who visited Jerusalem sometime in the 380s wrote a description of the rituals performed by pilgrims at the Sepulchre. According to her account, each year on Good Friday, the True Cross was lifted from its "silver-gilt casket" and exposed for veneration. "And as all the people pass by, one by one, all bowing themselves," Egeria tells us, "they touch the Cross ... first with their foreheads, and then with their eyes; then they kiss the Cross and pass through."[42]

---

[42] M. L. McClure and C. L. Feltoe, eds. and trans., *The Pilgrimage of Etheria* (London: Society for Promoting Christian Knowledge, 1919), pp. 74–75.

The loss of this relic was only one of the disasters to strike the Byzantines—Chosroes and his armies had captured not only Syria and Palestine but also Egypt and much of Asia Minor—but it acquired enormous symbolic importance. The Persian shah and his forces installed the True Cross as a trophy in the Sassanid province of Iraq, in the imperial city of Ctesiphon.

Popular outcries in Christendom called for rescuing the Cross and recovering the lost and damaged shrines. Sergius, patriarch of Constantinople, placed "the treasures of the churches" at the disposal of the Byzantine emperor Heraclius to help him in the savage wars that lay ahead.[43]

And savage they were. The Persian-Byzantine conflict lasted for years, devastating cities in Egypt, Palestine, Syria, Asia Minor, and Iraq. Finally, Heraclius succeeded in defeating Chosroes and rescuing the sacred relic. With the war finally concluded, he set out to fulfill a vow he had made. In thanksgiving for this God-given victory, the emperor made a pilgrimage on foot from Edessa (in what is now Turkey) to Jerusalem. There he presided over the restoration of the True Cross to the church of the Holy Sepulchre.[44]

A contemporary of Heraclius, the Armenian chronicler Sebeos, evoked the feeling of celebration attending this event:

> There was much joy at their entrance to Jerusalem: sounds of weeping and sighs, abundant tears, burning flames in hearts, extreme exaltation of the emperor, of the princes, of all the soldiers and inhabitants of the city; and nobody could sing the hymns of our Lord on account of the great and poignant emotion of the emperor and the whole multitude. The emperor restored [the Cross] to its place and returned all the church objects, each to its place; he distributed gifts to all the churches and to the inhabitants of the city, and money for incense.[45]

Peace was restored. The True Cross was safe. But the superpowers had exhausted each other. As Edward Gibbon noted in his *Decline*

[43] B.J. Kidd, *The Churches of Eastern Christendom from A.D. 451 to the Present Time* (London: Faith Press, 1927), p. 105.

[44] Sir William Muir, *The Life of Mahomet: From Original Sources*, 3rd ed. (London: Smith, Elder, & Co., 1894), p. 357.

[45] Cited in A.A. Vasiliev, *History of the Byzantine Empire* (Madison: University of Wisconsin Press, 1973), 1:198.

and Fall of the Roman Empire, the prolonged duel between Heraclius and Chosroes was "a war which had wounded the vitals of the two monarchies". Much of the Near East lay in ruins.[46]

The year was 630. And in that same year, Muhammad ibn 'Abd Allah, prophet of Islam, completed his conquest of Mecca and turned his attention to campaigns against the unbelievers who filled the world beyond Arabia.

[46] Edward Gibbon, *The Decline and Fall of the Roman Empire* (New York: Heritage Press, 1946), 2:1550.

CHAPTER 3

MUHAMMAD AND THE KORAN

An introductory thought

Many piously minded Muslims I have met in the course of my career seem accustomed to thinking of Islam and the pre-Islamic Jahiliyah in antithetical terms. Some of the students I have taught over the years become impatient with my insistence that we study pagan Arab poetry before we begin reading Islamic scripture. They are eager to get to the "good stuff"—the Koran and the prophet's life—and away from what Muhammad rejected.

But my argument—one that I make every semester—is that Islam does not involve simply a rejection of the Jahiliyah tradition in which Muhammad ibn 'Abd Allah was raised or a repudiation of the Jewish and Christian faiths that caught his interest as a young man. Rather, the message he presented in the Koran is one that I characterize as "selective appropriation". By this I mean that he incorporated into his Islamic message whatever conformed to his ideology, while he discarded whatever was incongruent with his doctrine of *tawhid* (strict monotheism).

In comparing Islam with the culture and religion of ancient Arabia, it is worth noting how many elements of the Jahiliyah were preserved (even if reinterpreted) in the Muslim faith. The conservatism of Islam with regard to the Jahiliyah makes sense if we keep in mind what I consider one of the primary characteristics of any successful religious reformer: such a person, rather than introduce new teachings ex nihilo, retains as much as possible of the preexisting religious tradition to which his audience adheres.

You may have already noticed that my phrasing here—"he incorporated into his Islamic message whatever conformed to his

54

ideology"—might well be construed as a violation of basic tenets of this faith. Muslims agree in viewing Allah, not Muhammad, as the author of the Koran. According to this doctrine, any talk of Muhammad's "incorporating" or "discarding" points of doctrine would be incorrect, since such words impute far too much agency to a mere human.

Instead, Islamic doctrine presents Muhammad as a pure and empty vessel; this is the theological meaning behind the tradition that insists he was illiterate. Illiteracy, so goes the argument, means that he could not possibly have written the Koran; the author is Allah, and Allah alone. (In this sense, the doctrine of Muhammad's illiterate status is comparable to the Christian belief in the virgin birth of Jesus. Jesus in Christianity is the divine and eternal Word of God the Father, as the Koran in Islam is the divine and eternal word of Allah.)

Which brings me to an important disclosure. Everything I present here is shaped by the fact that I personally regard the Koran as a human artifact: in my view, Muhammad is the author of Islam's scripture. This judgment affects how I write about the Koran in what follows; and you will need to take that into account as you read.

I am aware this is—to put it mildly—a sensitive issue. Let me illustrate.

In 1988, my wife, Jody, and I visited various Arabic manuscript archives in Tunisia and Morocco. While in the city of Tunis, I was invited to give a public lecture on my research. After the talk, tired but happy to have gotten through the long evening, we returned to our hotel.

The lobby was filled with men who stood about talking and smoking. One of them—a man I had never seen before—came up to us, hailed me in a loud voice, and said he recognized me from the talk. He offered what sounded more or less like a compliment. "For a Christian," he said, "you seem to know a lot about Islam."

I smiled but said nothing, not sure what direction this chat of ours would take.

"So could you tell us," he added, and his voice was good and loud, "with regard to the prophet Muhammad: Was he a liar, or not?" (The Arabic term he used here—*kadhdhab ibn kadhdhab*—literally means "liar, son of a liar", which is a particularly emphatic way of making sure the words are to be understood as an insult.)

Muhammad: Was he a liar, or not? The lobby suddenly went quiet.

I might have been tired, but I was bright enough to understand: here comes a volatile hand-grenade question, forcefully lobbed at a Christian in a Muslim social setting.

Luckily, people had asked me similar questions in the past (although not quite so rudely or so publicly), which meant my mind did not go altogether blank. First, I said, I'm a Christian, so I'm not required to believe what Muslims believe. Second, I think Muhammad was sincere in what he preached in Mecca, and I acknowledge his sincerity (more on this point below).

But third (and here I looked around at the men who stood about listening), Islam emphasizes the importance of *al-niyyah* (intentionality) in the things we say and do. So now, I asked my questioner, what is *your* intention in asking such questions of me, a foreigner and a guest in your country?

He's right, exclaimed a bystander. He's a guest. Leave him alone.

Murmurs of agreement from the onlookers.

That broke the tension. Quick thank-yous and good-nights all around, and Jody and I headed with silent sighs of relief to our room.

Had I wished to linger in that lobby (I did not), I might have added this:

When I say I think Muhammad was sincere, I mean that he believed himself to be inspired and the recipient of Allah's message (though he also experienced intense and recurrent self-doubts, especially in his early Meccan phase of prophethood, as we shall see).

Although I do not regard the Koran as Allah's eternal word, here is a point where pious Muslims and I might be able to agree. First, Koranic verses refer repeatedly to the Koran itself as *kitab mubin* or *al-kitab al-mubin*, "a clear book" or "the clear book", clear in the sense of "plain", "evident", "manifestly understandable" (for example, Koran 5:15, 12:1, 27:1). Second, every word that Muhammad presented as a Koranic utterance came to his audience through the medium of his lips and his consciousness.

Hence, if we take seriously the claim that these scriptural verses were manifestly understandable (rather than, say, meaningless, alien, or obscure), then these words must have made sense and been accessible in terms of the thought world and cultural identity of both the speaker (Muhammad) and those to whom he spoke (the Quraysh of

Mecca as well as the Jews and Christians of Yathrib/Medina). For this reason, it is fair to argue that the Koran is one of our very best guides for understanding Muhammad's mentality and the emotional and spiritual stages of his life experience. Thus, in what follows I will make considerable use of Islamic scripture as a biographical resource in the survey of Muhammad's career I will present to you now.

Angel or jinn? The cave, the call, and the visit from the stranger

As a Qurayshi, Muhammad ibn 'Abd Allah was a member of the tribe that dominated Mecca's commerce and its Ka'ba-centered religious traffic. It is not surprising, then, to learn from Muhammad's earliest biographer that as a young man, he, like his fellow tribesmen, had the habit of visiting the Ka'ba and performing the *tawaf*, circling the shrine seven times on each visit, amid the crowds of pilgrims and the circle of 360 idols.[1] Like other Quraysh, he, too—as we learned in the previous chapter—offered an animal sacrifice to the goddess al-'Uzza. Growing up in a cultural crossroads like Mecca also meant that he was exposed from his youth to bits and snatches of the Judeo--Christian tradition—folklore references to King Solomon in pagan poetry, sermons given by a priest at the fair in 'Ukaz.

Orphaned at the age of six, Muhammad was raised by his uncle Abu Talib and lived with his cousin 'Ali ibn Abi Talib (a point to which I will return in our discussion of Shiism). As a young man, Muhammad was employed by a wealthy widow named Khadija bint Khuwaylid, who ran a business that operated caravans from Mecca to Syria and Yemen. Such work as a merchant shaped Muhammad's mentality (business imagery recurs in the Koran) and widened his experience of the Near East's landscapes and cultures (recall how Muhammad encountered the monk Bahira on a caravan trip to Syria).

When Muhammad was twenty-five, his employer (who was wealthier than he and fifteen years his senior) proposed marriage. During the twenty-five years of their marriage, he remained

---

[1] Muhammad Ibn Ishaq, *The Life of Muhammad: A Translation of Ibn Ishaq's Sirat Rasul Allah*, ed. and trans. A. Guillaume (Karachi; New York: Oxford University Press, 1968), pp. 105–6.

monogamous. (His practice of polygamy—he accumulated a total of thirteen wives—began only after Khadija's death, in the year 620.)

Much of what has been presented so far about Muhammad's life conforms to what must have been the life and work of many Jahili-yah Meccan men. More unusual was his habit of retreating to a cave on the heights of nearby Mount Hira' for solitary prayer. It was there, in the year 610, when he was forty years old, that Muhammad experienced the *da'wah*: the "call", that is, the divine summons to preach Islam.

Not that Muhammad understood at first what was happening to him. According to the early Muslim biographical sources, Muham-mad was alone in the cave when a stranger suddenly approached and uttered a one-word command: *Iqra'* (Recite!). Muhammad could only stammer in confusion, asking what he was supposed to recite. Again and again, the stranger voiced the command; again and again, the Qurayshi merchant confessed he was at a loss as to what he should say.

> Finally the stranger said:
> Recite, in the name of your lord who created,
> Created men from a clot of blood;
> Recite, and your lord the most generous,
> Who taught by means of the pen,
> Taught men that which they did not know.

These words are considered the first revelation received by Muhammad. They comprise the initial five verses of chapter 96 of the Koran. (The Koran is not arranged in chronological order, a fact that has led to many interpretive challenges over the centuries.) And it is from the first word of command articulated by the stranger—*iqra'*/recite!—that Islamic scripture's title is derived: the word Koran (also spelled Qur'an) simply means "recitation".

Muhammad did what he was told. He recited the words; the stranger disappeared. After this came the merchant's emotional reac-tion, and it was not positive: "Now none of God's creatures [said Muhammad later] was more hateful to me than an (ecstatic) poet or a man possessed: I could not even look at them. I thought, Woe is me poet or possessed—Never shall Quraysh say this of me! I will go to the top of the mountain and throw myself down that I may kill myself and gain rest."[2]

But as he rushed from the cave, tormented by thoughts of suicide, a voice hailed him, telling him he was Allah's prophet. The speaker identified itself as Gabriel. Muhammad raised his eyes skyward and saw "the form of a man, with feet astride the horizon". Once more the voice told Muhammad he was Allah's prophet.

Not at all reassured by what he had been told, the merchant made his way down the mountain, back to Mecca and the familiarity of his own home. As soon as Khadija caught sight of him, she asked him where he had been, telling him she had sent out messengers to look for him. One of our early Muslim biographical sources tells us that Muhammad's anguished reply was the cry, "Woe is me poet or possessed!"[3]

What was it about the stranger's words in the cave that made Muhammad react with such fear? We begin to glimpse an answer if we look at the original Arabic phrasing of the Koranic words that Muhammad had been commanded to recite:

> *Iqra' bismi rabbik alladhi khalaq*
> *Khalaq al-insan min 'alaq*
> *Iqra' wa-rabbuk al-akram*
> *Alladhi 'allama bi'l-qalam*
> *'allama al-insan ma lam ya 'lam.*

Look at the words that end each line—*khalaq / 'alaq*, followed by *akram / qalam / ya 'lam*—and you will understand right away that the stranger's recitation is in the form of *saj'*. This, you will recall, is the "dove-cooing" prose rhyme so popular among Jahiliyah poets. And Muhammad was well aware that many of these poets had a reputation for being *majnun*—possessed by jinns, in a relationship that both empowered and literally bedeviled the humans who served as hosts for these spirits. He was understandably afraid that the same thing was overtaking him.

How he felt about such demon-human pairings can be seen from the Koran's twenty-sixth chapter, which is entitled "The Poets". It

[2] Ibid., p. 106.
[3] Ibid.

includes a discussion of what the Koran calls *shayatin*, which is the plural of *shaytan* or "Satan". Sometimes the Koran uses the word *shayatin*/Satans as a generic synonym for jinns (see Koran 21:82, 34:12–13, and 38:37). More often, however, Islamic scripture employs *shayatin* to designate a particularly harmful and malevolent subspecies of jinn. Here is what chapter 26 (verses 221–25) says about these baleful creatures and their relations with certain humans: "Shall I tell you people who it is on whom the Satans (*al-shayatin*) repeatedly descend? They descend upon everyone who does wicked things and makes a habit of lying. It is people like this who listen to the Satans; and most such people are liars. The poets: the only ones who follow them are those who go astray! Have you not seen these poets, wandering about in every desert gorge?"

The notion of condemnation and hostility is reinforced in Koran 6:112: "And thus for every prophet We created enemies: Satans from among humans and jinns, inspiring each other with ornamented speech as a means of deception."

Here the implication is that "Satans" can be found among both humans and jinns. Such beings are drawn together. The result: a babbling hybrid-mutant entity, what the Koran (37:36) calls *sha'ir majnun* (a jinn-possessed poet). Verse-maker and demon, gibbering their pigeon talk, inciting each other with "ornamented" rhymes: twinned snakes hissing through a sun-bleached skull.

No, Muhammad knew he loathed their kind. And now, coming out of that cave, he worried he might be turning into one of them.

Luckily for him, his wife, Khadija, knew whom to consult. She hurried off to visit her cousin, Waraqa ibn Naufal ibn Asad ibn 'Abd al-'Uzza ibn Qusayy, who had embraced the Christian faith. (Her cousin's genealogy displays his pagan heritage: Waraqa's great-grandfather had been named "Slave of al-'Uzza", in honor of one of the divine "Daughters of Allah".) According to the early Muslim biographers of Muhammad, Waraqa reassured Khadija that the stranger who had visited her husband was none other than the angel Gabriel.[4]

Let's pause to consider the implications of this claim. Verses chanted by majnun poets tended to be limited with regard to their

[4] Ibid., pp. 106–7.

audience. Poets were tribally minded, and jinns were for the most part territorial in that they haunted specific localities. As the great Jahiliyah poet Labid ibn Rabi'ah al-'Amiri stated, every tribe had its own sunnah and way of life to follow. These tribally specific sunnahs were encoded in the rhymes created by the verse-makers of each tribe.

But Muhammad became convinced—although he underwent recurrent doubts for some years—that he was being visited by an angel rather than a jinn. The angel in question—Gabriel—is part of the faith system of both Judaism and Christianity, religions that are universal and not limited in their territoriality or geographical reach. Thus, identifying Gabriel as the stranger in the cave at Mount Hira' was the first step in shaping Islam as a religion oriented toward world-wide evangelism.

So Muhammad began to preach. His first audience was comprised of inhabitants of his hometown, Mecca, and nearby towns. Islamic doctrine states that he received revelations via Gabriel throughout his prophetic career. These Koranic revelations are grouped chronologically as Meccan and Medinan. The Meccan revelations begin with the first verses Muhammad believed he received in the year 610 in the cave at Mount Hira' and continue up through the hijrah (Muhammad's exodus from Mecca to Yathrib/Medina) in 622. The chronologically later verses date from immediately after the hijrah until shortly before his death in 632. In general, the Meccan and Medinan verses differ significantly from each other in tone, style, and content—a reflection of the very different circumstances Muhammad encountered in each city at varying stages of his prophetic career.

"I will stuff hell full": The moral choices faced by demons

Before moving on to the next section, let's see how the Koran reinterprets the status of a class of beings that caused Muhammad noticeable anxiety during the Meccan phase of his career—the jinns.

Useful to read in this context is surah 72, which describes an occurrence from A.D. 620, two years before the hijrah. Having been rejected by so many of his Qurayshi kinsmen, Muhammad decided to journey to the town of Ta'if (located near Mecca) to offer his tawhidic message there. But the elders insulted him, and the children of the streets threw stones at him, so he had to flee in a hurry. Discouraged, he made his way toward home, and he paused for the evening at a desert ravine in the vicinity of Nakhlah, not far from the shrine of al-'Uzza (the "daughter of Allah" whom Muhammad once worshipped). And it was there, while he was comforting himself by reciting his Koranic verses aloud, that he had unexpected visitors. Here is how surah 72 (verses 1–2, 4, 6, 11) presents the scene:

> Say: It has been revealed to me that a group of jinns listened and said, "We have heard a wonderful recitation! It guides one along the right way, and so we believe in it. We will not associate any divine partners with our Lord.... There were some insolent and shameless individuals among us who told extravagant lies about Allah.... And there were also some individuals from among mankind who took refuge with certain members of the jinns; but those jinns simply caused them to increase in folly and go astray.... Among us jinns, there are some that are righteous and some that are not. We follow paths that diverge from each other."

The themes articulated here are reinforced by a verse from another Meccan surah (32:13), in which Allah makes the following promise: "I will stuff hell full with jinns and men all together."

From these verses you can see how radically the Koran reinterprets old Jahiliyah understandings of the jinns. Pagan Arabs viewed them as demons, often territorially based, independent in their power, capricious in their whims to help or harm, capable of initiating relationships with individual men and inspiring them with powerful poetic verse.

The Islamic teachings preached by Muhammad regard the jinns as being akin to men in that both are created by Allah and both are classed as volitional beings—that is, creatures that are capable of making moral choices that will earn them either heaven or hell. The group of jinns that visited Muhammad at Nakhlah on his way home from Ta'if demonstrated this capacity to choose. They heard him reciting the Koran and decided at once to become Muslims: "We will not associate any divine partners with our Lord."

But surah 72 also shows those aspects of Jahiliyah belief that Muhammad retained—specifically, the possibility of personal relationships between men and jinns. It is clear he disapproved of such relations: too many of these demonic beings spread "extravagant lies about Allah", which is precisely what many jinns—and their protégés the poets—are said to do as a way of distracting people from the message of Islam. This is one reason why hell is going to be stuffed full "with jinns and men all together".

Given the fact that the Koran acknowledges their existence, it is understandable that Muslims throughout the Islamic world believe in jinns today. "There are some that are righteous, and some that are not", scripture says of these creatures; but Muslim folklore and popular belief seem to insist that most jinns fall into the category of the decidedly unrighteous.

Muslim sorcerers I met in the course of research during visits to the Pakistani city of Lahore told me that their city was infested with jinns. These jinns, they assured me, were not only kuffar (unbelievers) but Hindu—which, in Muslim-majority Pakistan, was a term that was not meant as a compliment.[5]

"You alone do we worship": The doctrinal challenge of tawhid

Now let's examine Muhammad's Meccan preaching in more detail by beginning with the surah (Koranic chapter) called al-Fatihah (the opening—chapter 1 of the Koran). Here is my translation:

> In the name of Allah, the gracious, the merciful.
> Praise Allah, lord of the worlds, the gracious, the merciful,
> Master of the Day of Judgment.
> You alone do we worship, and from you alone do we seek help.
> Guide us along the straight path,
> The path of those you have blessed,
> Not those who are the object of your anger,
> Nor those who go astray.

Prominent in this surah is the emphasis on Allah, a god already familiar both to Meccans and to pilgrims from all over the Arabian

[5] For more information on the sectarian identity of jinns in the Islamic world, see D. Pinault, *Notes from the Fortune-Telling Parrot: Islam and the Struggle for Religious Pluralism in Pakistan* (London: Equinox Publishing, 2008), pp. 122–60.

peninsula as "Lord of the Ka'ba". But Muhammad goes further, insisting on *tawhid*—the assertion of strict monotheism: "You alone do we worship."

Here is where Muhammad's problems began. His Meccan neighbors had no difficulty with the idea of worshipping Allah—they had already been doing that for generations. The sticking point was that the Islamic *shahadah* (testimony of faith) stipulates: *ashhadu anna la ilaha illa Allah*: "I testify that there is no god except Allah." (By the way, I will just note here that translating the *shahadah* as "There is no god but God", as some scholars have done, is misleading and vague, since it omits the Meccan historical context and the very pointed specificity of this Islamic creedal claim.)[6]

The Koran itself, in a verse (39:38) dating from the Meccan period, records the kind of response Muhammad got when he began preaching to the Quraysh: "And if you ask them, 'Who created the heavens and the earth?' they will certainly say, 'Allah did.' Say to them: 'Well, in that case, do you not see? Those beings that you people invoke besides Allah: If Allah wanted to do me harm, would they be able to lift that harm from me?'"

Here Allah—via Gabriel—coaches Muhammad on how he should deal with his recalcitrant neighbors. What is clear from this verse is that the people of Mecca had no problem with the notion of worshipping Allah and acknowledging him as a creator god. No, their problem was with the exclusivist monotheism associated with the word *tawhid*. They wanted to continue invoking other beings besides their creator god Allah.

The issue can be illustrated via an ancient Athenian drama entitled *Hippolytus* (authored by Euripides, a playwright we have already encountered). The protagonist is Hippolytus (son of the Greek hero Theseus), a young huntsman who consecrates himself to Artemis, the divine archer and virgin goddess of nature, wildlife, and the forest.

But his vow of perpetual chastity excites jealousy in the love goddess Aphrodite: Hippolytus dishonors her by shunning sexual activity and neglecting to leave offerings at her shrine. Aphrodite retaliates

---

[6] Consider, for example, the reference to the *shahadah* in the title of Reza Aslan's book on Islam: *No God but God*.

by setting in motion a cascade of ruinous events that cause him to be cursed by his father and expelled from his native land.

Persecuted by one deity, he turns for comfort to another—the nature goddess to whom he dedicated his life. "Dearest of the gods to me," he cries, invoking her, "comrade and partner in the hunt, behold me, banished from famous Athens.... O divine fragrance! Even in my pain, I sense it, and the suffering is lightened. The goddess Artemis is near this place."

"She is", Artemis reassures him, as she appears at his side, "the dearest of the gods to you."[7]

Here we see the comfort to be found in a world where the air is thick with Presences we may invoke. If we irritate one deity, we can call on another, so that, like the huntsman Hippolytus, we too can find that our "suffering is lightened".

"The cranes that fly high": The satanic verses, the Daughters of Allah, and the question of divine intercession

The scandal involving the notorious "satanic verses" illustrates the problem further. This incident is recorded by the ninth-century Muslim historian Abu 'Abd Allah Muhammad ibn Sa'd. One day, during the Meccan phase of his preaching, Muhammad was seated with his fellow Qurayshi tribesmen at the Ka'ba. These men were influential. He wanted to please them, have them on his side, convince them of his message.

He began reciting Koranic verses (53:19–23) concerning the three "Daughters of Allah"—Allat, Manat, and al-'Uzza—verses that in their present-day form, in the Koran as we now have it, strongly condemn their worship and dismiss them as follows: "These females are nothing but names that you and your fathers before you invented!"

But on that particular day at the Ka'ba, Muhammad, who was eager to win over the Quraysh if he could, found himself tempted by Satan. The devil whispered to him verses we have already encountered,

---

[7] Euripides, *Hippolytus*, trans. David Grene (Chicago: University Press, 1966), pp. 208, 217–18.

verses that the Quraysh themselves liked to recite as they circled the Ka'ba:

> By Allat, and al-'Uzza, and the third one, Manat!
> In truth, they are the cranes that fly high,
> And their intercession may be hoped for!

Muhammad in turn recited these satanic *saj'*-rhymes aloud, and as soon as he did so, his clansmen let him know they were delighted. "All were greatly pleased with the Prophet, and said to him: 'We know that Allah killeth and giveth life, createth and preserveth, but these our goddesses pray to Him for us, and since you have now permitted them to share divine honors with Him, we therefore desire to unite with you.' "[8]

But at night, at home, alone, a troubled Muhammad found himself confronted by Gabriel, who reprimanded him and instructed him to recant. Which Muhammad did, publicly, the next day, thereby antagonizing his would-be followers. The verses hailing the goddesses as intercessors were cancelled and replaced by verses of denunciation. Under no circumstances was this female triad to be worshipped or considered divine or labeled "daughters" of Allah. Allah simply has no offspring (a point to which we shall return when we consider how the Koran responds to Jesus).

Of course many of the pious insist that no such incident involving faulty Koran verses could ever have occurred. (One example is from the staunchly Islamic and anti-Christian website Answering--Christianity.com, where an article on this topic begins, "There is no greater lie than the Satanic verses lie. The Prophet never said those verses.")[9] You might recall how the novelist Salman Rushdie got *fatwa'ed* in 1989 and had to go into hiding for years when he wrote a story inspired by this occurrence.

But one could offer an "argument from embarrassment" to make the case that devout Muslim historians like Ibn Sa'd would hardly be inclined to take the risk of fabricating a tale such as this. As the scholar

---

[8] Cited in Tor Andrae, *Mohammed: The Man and His Faith* (New York: Harper Torchbooks, 1960), p. 19.

[9] Bassam Zawadi, "Prophet Muhammad (peace be upon him) and the Satanic Verses", http://www.answering-Christianity.com/bassam_zawadi/satanic_verses.htm.

Tor Andrae puts it, "In my opinion it is unthinkable that the men ... of the later tradition, who regarded Mohammed in every respect as a perfect example for the faithful, would have deliberately invented a story so seriously compromising their Prophet."[10]

But there is also evidence within the Koran itself that hints at the historical reality of such an incident. These are verses relating to a scriptural doctrine called *al-nasikh wa-al-mansukh* (that which cancels, and that which gets canceled). What this means is that in cases of doubt, where verses appear to contradict each other, the chronologically later verse takes precedence.

The justification for this doctrine is derived from two passages in Islamic scripture, 2:106 and 22:52. In the first passage, Allah is made to speak (as he often does in the Koran) in the first person plural (the "royal We"): "Whenever We cancel a verse or cause it to be forgotten, We replace it with another verse that is better or similar."

The second passage asserts (again, Allah is presented as the speaker, addressing Muhammad directly): "In the past, before your time, whenever We have sent a messenger or a prophet, if that messenger or prophet desires something, then Satan casts something into that desire of his. But Allah cancels whatever Satan throws in, and then Allah confirms His verses."

It is fascinating to read the *tafsir* (Koran commentary) on this particular passage of scripture. Let's look at a widely circulating example of the genre, a commentary entitled *Tafsir al-jalalayn*, authored by a fifteenth-century Egyptian authority named Jalal al-Din 'Abd al--Rahman al-Suyuti (the work is still popular in North Africa today). Here is Suyuti's explanatory comment on the Koranic passage you just read:

> "Satan casts something into that desire of his": that is, he casts something into his recitation that is not in the Koran, something that will please the prophetic messenger. Now, on one occasion the prophet— may Allah bless him and grant him salvation—was seated with a group of the Quraysh while he was reciting the "Surah of the Star" [that is, chapter 53 of the Koran]. After he recited the Koranic verse "Have you seen Allat, and al-'Uzza, and the third one, Manat?",

---

[10] Andrae, *Mohammed*, pp. 20–21.

Satan—without the prophet's knowledge—placed upon his tongue the following words:

> "In truth, they are the cranes that fly high,
> And their intercession may be hoped for!"

So the Quraysh were delighted, and they rejoiced in this. But later Gabriel informed the prophet as to what Satan had cast upon his tongue, and then he felt grief. But thereafter he was granted this verse [that is, Koran 22:52] as a consolation, in order to give him peace of mind.[11]

In other words, this Koran commentator accepted the historical validity of the "satanic verses" incident and used it to explain what Muslim scholars call the *asbab al-nuzul* (the reasons for revelation or the circumstances of revelation) underlying the scriptural verse "Allah cancels whatever Satan throws in."

A similar account appears in another popular Koran commentary, this one by the renowned fourteenth-century scholar Nasir al-Din Abu Sa'id al-Baydawi:

> In his eagerness for his tribe to acquire the faith, it is said that the prophet desired to receive a revelation that would draw them near to him. This desire stayed with him until one occasion when he was with a group of them. Then there descended upon him the "surah of the Star", and he began reciting it. But when he pronounced the words "and the third one, Manat", Satan whispered to him, until, in a state of inattention, his tongue spontaneously uttered the words:
>
> > "In truth, they are the cranes that fly high,
> > And their intercession may be hoped for!"
>
> The polytheists were delighted at this, with the result that, when the prophet prostrated himself in prayer at the end of his recitation, they joined him in prostration. Thus it was that everyone in that place, believer and polytheist alike, prostrated himself in prayer. Thereafter Gabriel warned the prophet, and he felt distressed at this, so Allah comforted him with this verse [that is, the Koranic verse concerning

---

[11] Jalal al-Din 'Abd al-Rahman al-Suyuti, *Tafsir al-jalalayn*, ed. Marwan Sawar (Beirut: Dar al-Ma'rifah, n.d.), p. 440, commentary on Koran 22:52; translated from the Arabic by D. Pinault.

satanic interference and Allah's cancellation of "whatever Satan throws in"].[12]

This doctrine of "cancellation" has had a long afterlife, resurfacing recently in two very different contexts—justifications for violence by Islamic terrorist groups such as al-Qaeda and attempts by reformers to reinterpret the Koran in the service of interfaith pluralism and peace. We will want to return to this topic when we examine twenty-first--century Islam.

"He frowned and turned away": Struggling with the demands of prophethood

Aside from what Islamic scriptural commentaries tell us, what evidence can we find to determine whether this "satanic verses" scandal ever actually occurred? I think we can use additional verses from within the Koran itself to argue that it is likely this incident happened, if we bear in mind that Muhammad's short-lived endorsement of Allah's daughters was motivated by an understandable eagerness to please his Qurayshi kinsmen and win them over to Islam.

This eagerness did not last—in fact, it was replaced by a mood of all-out war—but in his initial phase of evangelism, Muhammad did what he could to ingratiate himself when possible with his fellow Meccans. This is reflected in a tense encounter that took place one day while the prophet was talking with influential Qurayshi leaders, only to be interrupted by the insistent approach of an impoverished blind man named 'Abd Allah ibn Umm Maktum. Surah 80 (vv. 1–10) describes the encounter, referring to Muhammad initially in the third person and then addressing him directly:

> He [Muhammad] frowned and turned away because the blind man had come up to him. But what made you think you should act that way? Perhaps he [the blind man] was striving to be pious and holy; perhaps he was striving humbly to be admonished, and perhaps that

[12] Nasir al-Din Abu Sa'id al-Baydawi, *Anwar al-tanzil wa-asrar al-ta'wil* (Beirut: Dar al-Kutub al-'Ilmiyah, 1988), 2:93, commentary on Koran 22:52; translated from the Arabic by D. Pinault.

admonishment might benefit him. As for the individual who regards himself as self-sufficient and in need of no one, he was the one you were paying attention to, even though it is not your fault if he does not become pious. But as for the person who hurried over to you earnestly and in a state of fear: you did not pay any attention to him.

Suyuti's commentary provides us with this clarification:

"The blind man": that is, 'Abd Allah ibn Umm Maktum, who inter-rupted him [Muhammad] while he was busy; he [Muhammad] was hoping that the nobility and leaders of the Quraysh would accept Islam, and he was eager for them to do so. The blind man did not know that he was busy with this, and so he cried out to him, "Teach me what Allah has taught you!" So the prophet—may Allah bless him and grant him salvation—withdrew and went to his home. There-after, he was reprimanded for that via what was revealed in this surah. After this, whenever the blind man came up to him, he would say, "Welcome to the one through whom my Lord reprimanded me", and then he would spread out for him his cloak.[13]

For me, this is the most psychologically compelling and emotion-ally honest passage in the whole Koran. Here we see Muhammad at his most appealing: conscience-stricken, self-critical, willing to hold himself to the same moral standards he proclaimed in his preaching. After all, if he had wanted to, he could have suppressed this incident, could have chosen to tell no one that he felt the presence of Gabriel in his home chastising him for privileging the elite over the poor. Instead, he allowed this incident of the blind man to become part of the canon of the Koran.

Unfortunately, the themes that come to predominate in the later, Medinan, surahs will tend to be confrontational rather than concil-iatory, which is why I find my favorite verses in the Meccan portion of the Koran. The Medinan phase will take us on a dark journey—killings of helpless prisoners; vengeance, violence, and blood. But it is good to remember there was a time when Muhammad humbled himself before a blind man who reminded him of what was truly important and good.

[13] Suyuti, *Tafsir*, p. 791, commentary on Koran 80:2.

We will return to this subject when we come to the twenty-first century and the possibilities for Muslims to bring about a reformation within Islam.

"Master of the day of judgment": Pagan responses to the resurrection of the dead

Let's return to the theological claims made in chapter 1 of the Koran. Besides insisting on tawhid, the assertion of exclusivist monotheism, with worship to be given only to Allah, this surah also characterizes Allah as "Master of the day of judgment". Here Muhammad introduced to his Meccan neighbors doctrines of the afterlife: the resurrection of the dead, the rewards of heaven, and the punishments of hell.

The Koran vividly records for us (in surah 44:34–37) how his tribal peers responded to such teachings:

> These people [the Quraysh] say: "There is nothing but this first life of ours. We are not going to be raised from the dead! So bring back our forefathers, if you are telling the truth!"
>
> But are these people any better than the people of Tubba' and all the others who came before them? We destroyed them because they were guilty of sin.

Another cluster of verses (45:24–26) that likewise dates to Muhammad's early preaching in Mecca similarly indicates how members of the Quraysh reacted:

> But they say: "There is no life except our life in this world! We die and we live, and nothing destroys us except al-Dahr [Time]."
>
> Yet they do not really know anything about this. They are just speculating. And when Our clear verses are recited to them, the only argument they offer in response is that they say: "Bring back our forefathers, if you are telling the truth!"
>
> Say: "Allah gives you life. Then he puts you to death. Then he will gather you together for the day of resurrection. There is no doubt about this."
>
> But most of the people simply do not know.

Here we get a snapshot glimpse of how the crowd at the Ka'ba responded to Muhammad. "Nothing destroys us except al-Dahr"—a name we have already encountered in pagan Arab poetry: fang-tipped Time, the big-jawed Devourer, who treats us all like prey. Muhammad replies that it is Allah who does the slaying, not Time.

But rather than accept this, hecklers in the throng challenge him to work a miracle on the spot: "Bring back our forefathers, if you are telling the truth!"

The word that follows this challenge, "Say", is an imperative directed personally to Muhammad, instructions that are supposed to have been delivered via the angel Gabriel telling the prophet what to say in reply. We can well imagine Muhammad going home bitter and frustrated after public encounters like this.

A tone of anger is suggested in the reference to Tubba', a vanished kingdom of Yemen well known to the Jahiliyah: like Muhammad's Meccan neighbors, the Yemenis, too, were once wealthy and prosperous; but Allah struck them down for their sins. This use of legend and history to deliver Islamic teachings is a theme we will look at more closely below.

There is something intriguing and curious about the Koranic passages we have just seen. The you-are-there-in-Mecca feel of these verbal exchanges, the snippets of back-and-forth taunts and pious threats that we overhear as we stand in the crowd: these suggest what I would call the dialectic between eternity and contemporaneity that is discernible in Islamic scripture.

I say this because, on the one hand, surah 85:21–22 describes the "glorious Koran" as something that is inscribed on *lawh mahfuz*, "a preserved tablet". This is supposed to be located "above the seventh heaven", according to the commentator Suyuti. This inscribed Koranic tablet predates the creation of the world; Suyuti links this with surah 68:1, which begins with the invocation "By the reed--pen!" Our commentator explains that the pen in question is the one with which Allah "wrote the things that are in the preserved tablet".[14]

The tenth-century historian and scriptural commentator Abu Ja'far al-Tabari provides further detail, stating that the Koran "is inscribed on a preserved tablet near God". The scholar Aliza Shnizer notes an

---

[14] Ibid., p. 802, commentary on Koran 85:22; p. 757, commentary on Koran 68:1.

additional sacred legend recorded by al-Tabari: "In the same spirit another tradition maintains that the preserved tablet is inscribed on the forehead of Israfil, the most senior of the angels of revelation, who stands by the divine throne."[15]

Popular traditions like these are a folkloric illustration of the Islamic doctrine that the Koran is eternal, the uncreated Word of Allah. Hence it predates by eons the lifetime of Muhammad, who was simply the recipient and transmitter of this scriptural message.

The notion of Islamic scripture as something that Allah inscribed with a pen is also suggestive. As in many cultures, so too in the ancient Near East, writing was associated with that which is permanent, fixed, irreversible, and possessed of a predetermined quality. Such notions endure to this day. Consider the Egyptian Arabic proverb *Illi maktuub 'ala al-gibiin lazim tishuuf al-'ayn*: "What is written on the brow will eventually have to be seen by the eye", reflecting the notion that our individual fate, although inscribed where we cannot see it, will nonetheless irresistibly come about.[16]

As was proven on at least one occasion with my own inscribed fate. In graduate school, I prepared for months for a particularly difficult set of Ph.D. exams. One evening, dispirited, grimly crossing campus, I encountered a Saudi friend and fellow student named Ahmed.

Ma-lak? he called out. *What is bothering you?* I explained I was discouraged and would never make it through all those tests.

Yes you will, he told me firmly; and when I asked him how he could be so sure, Ahmed laughed and pointed at my forehead. *Because it is maktuub,* he smiled, *written right there, even if you cannot see it.*

And, in fact, I did survive. Maktuub: written; fated.

So that is one quality of Koranic verses: eternal and possessed of a predestinarian quality. But I also mentioned contemporaneity. Here I am referring to the Islamic belief that these scriptural revelations were meant to comfort and encourage Muhammad personally in all the trials he faced (such as the jeers voiced by Meccans who rejected the idea that they would be resurrected from the dead). So

---

[15] Aliza Shnizer, "Sacrality and Collection", in *The Blackwell Companion to the Qur'an*, ed. Andrew Rippin (Oxford: Blackwell Publishing, 2006), p. 160.

[16] El-Said Badawi and Martin Hinds, eds., *A Dictionary of Egyptian Arabic* (Beirut: Librairie du Liban, 1986), p. 734, s.v. "maktuub".

too today: if the inscribed Tablet is eternal, then it applies to us all right now, casting a long heaven-sent shadow from the seventh century to the twenty-first and beyond.

Affliction, deliverance, and the "chain of the prophets"

The Koran's chronologically earliest surahs—those dating from Muhammad's initial preaching in Mecca—give us clues to his emotional state as he struggled with his newly found sense of himself as a prophet.

Doubts persisted. In various Meccan verses, Allah addresses Muhammad directly to reassure him, as in 68:1–2: "You are not, by the grace of your Lord, possessed by a jinn." Again, in chapter 52: "So proclaim [O Muhammad]! For you are not, by the grace of your Lord, a fortune-teller or someone possessed by a jinn" (52:29–30). And yet once more, in surah 34: "Say [O Muhammad]: '... Your companion is not in a state of jinn-possessed madness'" (34:46).

Muhammad's fear of being majnun was not helped by what his neighbors had to say. Islamic scripture provides us with a kind of transcript of their replies to his message. As we have seen already, the Koran is a hall of echoes, reverberating with the Meccan taunts that lingered in Muhammad's mind.

Let's listen in. Here is chapter 21, verse 5, of the Koran: "'No', they say, 'this is all just a jumble of dreams. No, he has just made it all up. No, he is simply a poet.'" Chapter 37 lets you know how the Quraysh responded to their kinsman's enunciation of Islam's central tenet: "And they, when they were told, 'There is no god except Allah', became prideful and said: 'Are we going to abandon our gods on the say-so of a poet who has been possessed by a jinn?'" (37:35–36).

Muhammad argued back: "This is the word of a noble prophet, and definitely not the word of some poet!" (Koran 69:40–41).

Not majnun and not a poet: he rejected these old identity markers that were linked with pagan tribes. Instead, he embraced a different but equally ancient identity: he classed himself as belonging to *silsilat al-anbiya'*, "the chain of the prophets", the historical sequence of messengers associated with Judaism and Christianity.

The Meccan surahs of the Koran refer repeatedly to stories from the biblical tradition. They demonstrate the workings of sacred history as understood by Islam: that is, a history that is made meaningful because of divine interventions when humans go astray.

And going astray is something we do frequently. One of Islam's earliest scriptural references to human nature states, "Mankind transgresses, in that it sees itself as self-sufficient"—an assertion about our tendencies that is reminiscent of Christian teachings on original sin (Koran 96:6–7).

Besides being transgressive, we also tend to be negligent and forgetful of our obligations. In response to these tendencies of ours, the Koran emphasizes that two of Allah's primary attributes are justice and mercy. If Allah's justice were to predominate, then almost all of us, being transgressors, would be hell-bound; but luckily Allah's mercy takes the fore.

Allah showers us with blessings; all he asks of us in return is *islam*—a word that literally means submission. The Arabic language, like Hebrew, is structured around trilateral root clusters, whereby each triad of root-letters is associated with a specific range of meanings. The S-L-M cluster is linked to notions of submission and the peace and security that come in the wake of this submission (from this same root we get *salam*, "peace", which is cognate with the Hebrew word "shalom").

The prefix "mu-" in Arabic indicates "someone who does the action associated with the root-cluster". So a Muslim in that case is simply anyone who submits to Allah. It is for this reason that Islamic theology claims that its faith is the world's oldest and that Muhammad, rather than founding a new religion, was simply purifying the original and ancient faith of tawhid.

According to Muslim belief, Muhammad is simply the last in a long "chain of prophets". (One tradition states that there have been a total of 124,000.)[17] Each prophet preached the same Islamic message, and each was a manifestation of Allah's mercy, as a way to compensate for our recurrent forgetfulness and transgressions.

The seventh chapter of the Koran is one of the most useful for illustrating the doctrine of Islamic prophethood in relation to

---

[17]Baydawi, *Anwar*, 2:92–93, commentary on Koran 22:52.

sacred history. Here is how chapter 7 presents the story of the great flood:

> We sent Noah to his people. He said, "O people! Worship Allah. You do not have any god except him. I fear for you the punishment of a day to come that will be full of disaster." The leaders from among his people said, "We see that you have obviously gone astray!" He said, "O people! There has been no going astray on my part. But I am a messenger from the lord of the worlds."... Yet they called him a liar. So We saved him and those who were with him in the Ark, and We drowned those who said that our verses were lies. They were a people who were blind! (7:59–64)

Jews and Christians reading the Koran's account of the flood story will notice important variations from the version found in the biblical Book of Genesis. First is that the Koran turns Noah into a prophet. In Genesis, Noah is a virtuous man who builds an ark in obedience to God's command; but he does not preach to his people. Second, the Koran presents Noah not only as a prophet but specifically as a prophet of Islam. He proclaims tawhid and the worship of Allah; finds himself rejected by his own people, who brand him a liar; and is rescued in the ark with a righteous remnant, while all his detractors are vindictively drowned.

The third big difference has to do with brevity. The Koran's version is a great deal shorter than the Bible's. These verses, which were originally recited in Mecca, suggest that Muhammad's audience had ample previous acquaintance with this story. Muhammad was apparently reminding his listeners of a tale they had already heard while he reshaped the flood narrative to conform to his own Islamic themes.

Relevant here is an observation by the scholar Hamilton Gibb concerning one of the chronologically earliest surahs, which refers disapprovingly to the attitude of the Quraysh. The Koran states, "Have you seen the one who turns away?... Has he not already been told about what is in the scriptures of Moses and of Abraham?" (53:33, 36–37). Gibb comments:

> The obvious inference is that the "Scriptures of Moses" were so familiar in Mecca that one could scarcely imagine any Meccan being

ignorant of them.... But of course Muhammad was not preaching to the converted; the assumption from the context, supported by the known general course of events, is that the Meccans in general were rather cold, even contemptuous, towards these religious ideas, and their first attitude was probably one of surprise that one of their own people should take them so seriously.[18]

"Contemptuous" is an apt word to describe the attitude encountered by the prophets described in chapter 7 of the Koran. According to this surah, after Allah drowned Noah's people, he allowed another prosperous civilization to arise, that of 'Ad, a legendary realm said to have been situated in parts of southern Arabia extending from Oman to Yemen. Prosperity is a test and a challenge, whereby one is expected to show gratitude for Allah's blessings through the act of submission to him. 'Ad's test came in the form of the prophet Hud (a nonbiblical figure derived from indigenous Arab traditions).

Hud's message to the people of 'Ad was identical to the message given by Noah to an earlier generation: he preached tawhid and submission to Allah. After the inhabitants of 'Ad rejected Islam and called Hud a liar, punishment came in the form of "a wind bearing a painful punishment" that left 'Ad and all its prosperity and riches in ruins (Koran 7:65–72, 46:24).

Chapter 7 likewise briefly mentions in succession several other legendary events associated with natural catastrophes. Salih (another nonbiblical figure from Arabian myth) brings the message of tawhid to the people of Thamud. Considerable archaeological remains attest to this civilization, which once extended from northern Arabia into southern Jordan, including the Nabataean desert city of Petra, famous for the many funerary chapels and tombs chiseled into the cliffs that surround its urban center. Salih's address to the people of Thamud suggests that Muhammad was personally acquainted with the region: Salih's reference (Koran 7:74) to how these people "carve the mountains into dwellings" is evocative of Petra. Here history and Islamic myth converge: after the leaders of Thamud reject Salih's tawhidic

[18] Hamilton Gibb, "Pre-Islamic Monotheism in Arabia", *Harvard Theological Review* 55, no. 1 (1962): 272–73.

message, Allah triggers an earthquake that destroys their civilization. And, in fact, the city of Petra was leveled in the year A.D. 363 by an earthquake that devastated its houses and temples.

Chapter 7 goes on to mention Moses' confrontation with Pharaoh in Egypt. Here the Koran incorporates components of the biblical account from the Book of Exodus but modifies the tale to conform to Islamic themes. Moses preaches about Allah; the sorcerers who are defeated by Moses in displays of magic fall prostrate in prayer, announcing themselves to be Muslims; and Allah drowns "Pharaoh's people" in the Red Sea because "they referred to Our verses as lies, and because they were negligent and heedless about them" (Koran 7:103–36; cf. 2:50).

Thus the Koran's "chain of the prophets" consists of two entwined strands, biblical and Arab. Chapter 7 presents the patterns of sacred history: prosperity, tested by the opportunity to show gratitude to Allah; the message of tawhid offered by a prophet; rejection of the message; and finally, subsequent punishment, whether in the form of flood, wind, or quake.

The Koran inserts into this interpretive matrix tales relating to the lost cities and vanished civilizations of Yemen, Oman, and Jordan. You may recall that Jahiliyah poets like Sulmi ibn Rabi'ah had also evoked long-dead realms of the past, but for a very different purpose: if even the wealthy and mighty become the helpless prey of Time, then we might as well seize the day and comfort ourselves with another drink before we are swallowed whole.

Muhammad's purpose in reciting sacred history is to point it like a dart at the present moment. The thematic culmination of chapter 7 comes in verses 184–85, after the catalogue of disasters visited upon the various peoples who rejected Muslim prophets such as Noah, Hud, Salih, and Moses: "Have they not given this any thought? Their companion is not in a state of jinn-possessed madness. He is simply a clear warner. Have they not looked at the kingdom of the heavens and the earth and what Allah has created? Have they not considered that it could well be that their own predetermined end has now drawn to a close?"

The "they" in question here are the Meccans of Muhammad's own time: the past has now caught up with the present. What happened to others for rejecting Allah's prophets is about to happen to the pagans of Muhammad's hometown. And a characteristic tic (one that disappears with his subsequent relocation to Medina) reasserts itself: Muhammad, we are told once again, is not in fact majnun.

But, the Koran asserts, Muhammad is not the only messenger to face this accusation. Surah 26 (which, like chapter 7, is a Meccan surah) offers a slightly different version of Moses' appearance at the Egyptian court, in which Pharaoh cries out, in a defiant reaction to the admonitions offered by the Israelite prophet: "Your messenger, who has been sent to you, has become possessed by a jinn!" (Koran 26:27).

Two other Meccan surahs have something similar to say about another prophet. Chapter 54 states, "The people of Noah made accusations of falsehood, and they called our servant [Noah] a liar. They said, 'He is possessed by a jinn!', and he was driven away." So, too, chapter 23: "We sent Noah to his people, and he said, 'O people! Worship Allah! You have no god except him.' But the crowd among his people who were unbelievers said, '. . . He is only a man in whom is jinn-possessed madness'" (Koran 54:9, 23:23–25).

My own interpretation is as follows. During the dispiriting years of his early preaching in Mecca, Muhammad gazed into the well of prophethood and saw reflected in its waters the likeness of his own personal circumstance. What was happening to him must have happened to the prophets who came before him. It was consoling to think that they, too, had been called liars and majnun. And it was heartening to recall that they had ultimately been rescued and their enemies brought low.

I mention this interpretive pattern because I think it will help serve as a key to unlock some challenging and cryptic verses in the Koran surrounding the life and crucifixion of Jesus Christ, as you and I will see in subsequent chapters.

As a footnote to this section, it is worth pondering the present-day implications of a theme underlying the sacred history presented in surah 7, namely, the assertion that natural disasters are caused by our human moral failings. This same assertion resurfaced in the aftermath of the 2004 Indian Ocean earthquake and tidal wave that devastated coastlines in South and Southeast Asia. "In Banda Aceh, Indonesia," reported the *Washington Post* at that time, "the hardest-hit area in the world's most populous Muslim country, imams blamed the Dec. 26

tsunami on lay Muslims who were shirking their daily prayers and
following a materialistic lifestyle."[19]

In the eyes of those who adhere to such a view, Allah is always
ready to unleash natural catastrophes against those who are slack in
their belief.

"In the end We rescue our messengers": Abraham, the fire, and the claims of family versus faith

There is yet another biblical figure whom the Koran presents as a
prophet of Islam, someone who helps shed light on what I think of
as the "career path" of Muslim prophets. I have in mind Abraham,
whose story as recounted in Islamic scripture differs markedly from
what we read in the Bible.

According to surah 21 (a chapter that also dates to the Meccan
period of Muhammad's preaching), Abraham grew up among idol-
worshippers. As a young man, he audaciously confronted his own
family: "He said to his father and his people, 'What are these statues,
to which you are so continuously devoted?'" He then tried to turn
his father and family away from idolatry to tawhidic worship of Allah,
to no avail.

So, the Koran tells us, the young Abraham devised a plan. While
his family was away, he broke the statues into pieces—all except the
biggest idol. When his family returned, they confronted their son and
asked what had happened. He turned to the surviving statue, said,
"Here is the biggest one of them", and suggested flippantly that his
family members ask it what had happened. When they said in reply,
"You know these things do not talk", he then expressed intense dis-
pleasure, exclaiming, "Then why are you people worshipping things
other than Allah? Don't you have any sense?"

The result of this maddening show of disrespect to his father and
family elders: they cast him into a blazing fire. But Allah intervened,
commanding the flames, "O fire! Do you be cool and a place of safety
for Abraham." The story concludes with Allah's pronouncement:

---

[19] Bill Broadway, "Divining a Reason for Devastation", *The Washington Post*, January 8,
2005, p. B09.

"We made them [Abraham's family members] into the ones who were the biggest losers, and to him [Abraham] we gave deliverance" (Koran 21:51–71).

If you are familiar with the Old Testament, you are probably aware that no such story about Abraham can be found there (although the episode about his being cast into a fire recalls the Book of Daniel (3:1–30), where King Nebuchadnezzar orders three young men who refuse to worship a giant golden statue to be cast into a fiery furnace). But in this Islamic scriptural tale about Abraham, we find evidence for what seems to have been an important source for Muhammad in his Koranic recitations: the Haggadah.

You may recall that this term refers to the ancient Jewish folkloric tradition surrounding figures from the Bible, a tradition predating the Koran by centuries. The Haggadah (much like the post-New Testament apocryphal gospels in the Christian tradition, as we will see) often served the function of "fan-fiction". Storytellers filled in chronological gaps in the biographies of beloved biblical heroes by inventing episodes that were crammed full with action even if they were not always characterized by theological precision.

And, in fact, the ancient Haggadah includes a tale about the young Abraham, who is distressed because his father is an idol-carver. As in the Koran, Abraham secretly destroys the family idols, offers a flippant and sarcastic explanation when his father returns and demands an explanation, and then is cast into a blazing fire as punishment, only to be saved, as he himself piously notes, by "the God of heaven and earth in whom I trust".[20] Thus it is entirely possible that Muhammad in his early preprophetic travels encountered Jews—or, for that matter, Christians or Jahiliyah Arabs—who told him this vivid and memorable tale.

But what particularly interests me here is the use to which Muhammad put such material. Within the context of the Koran, the story of young Abraham in the fire conforms to a pattern we can label "the eleventh-hour rescue" as part of the career path of the prophets. Allah's messengers will be rejected and threatened and called liars and jinn-crazy; but they and their attendant righteous remnant will be

---

[20] Louis Ginzberg, *The Legends of the Jews* (Philadelphia: Jewish Publication Society of America, 1968), 1:209–17.

plucked safely from flood and quake and flame. "In the end," Allah reassures Muhammad in the Koran, "We rescue our messengers and those who believe" (10:103).

"Tales of the Ancient Ones": Competitive storytelling and threats of "painful punishment"

How familiar all these Koranic stories were to Muhammad's original Meccan audience can be gauged by an accusation that was apparently flung at him repeatedly—and that must have irritated him intensely, to judge from the frequency with which it is mentioned in the Meccan surahs of the Koran.

Consider the following:

> Those who are unbelievers say, "These are nothing but tales of the ancient ones!" (Koran 6:25)

> They say, "What? When we die and we turn into dust and bones, we are going to be raised from the dead? We and our forefathers have been promised this before. But these are nothing but tales of the ancient ones." (Koran 23:82–83)

> Those who are unbelievers say, "This is nothing but a lie that he has invented. Other people have helped him with it." But they are the ones who have come forward with wrong and false things. They say, "Tales of the ancient ones, which he has had some people write down for him. Then, morning and evening, these tales are dictated and repeated for him." Say: "The One who sent this down is the One who knows that which is secret in the heavens and the earth." (Koran 25:4–6)

Most intriguing of all such passages, however, is the following, which carries an all-too-believable tone of professional competitiveness: "When Our verses are recited to them, they say, 'We have heard this before. If we wanted to, we could tell tales like this. These are nothing but tales of the ancient ones'" (Koran 8:31). The Koran scholar Suyuti offers an explanation for the above verse: "It was Nadr ibn al-Harith who said this, because he used to go to al-Hirah as a merchant and buy books containing accounts and information concerning the Persians. Equipped with this material, he had the custom of telling stories to the people of Mecca."[21]

Nadr ibn al-Harith: an individual we have encountered before. We met him on the road to al-Hirah, that Iraqi frontier town and listening post on the rim of the Persian Empire, where a traveler could hear much about the doings of Byzantine traders, Arab Bedouins, and the magi and fire priests of Iran. It was Nadr, you may recall, who brought back to Mecca the strange new melodies and the art of lute playing that he had learned on his trips far from home.

There is a pair of Meccan verses in the Koran that target this man directly. The first states: "There is one person who purchases frivolous stories so as to lead people away from the path of Allah. Ignorant, he mocks Allah's path. For persons such as him there will be a humiliating punishment" (31:6).

In his scriptural commentary, Mahmud ibn 'Umar al-Zamakhshari (d. A.D. 1143) explained the context of the above verse:

> "Frivolous stories": such as evening conversations dealing with legends, tales lacking any basis of truth, the telling of fairytales and jokes, excessive talk in general, unseemly popular poems; also singing and acquaintance with musicians, and so forth.
>
> It is said that this passage was revealed concerning al-Nadr ibn al--Harith, who had the custom of traveling as a merchant to Persia. He would purchase books of the Persians and then recite tales from them to members of the Quraysh tribe. He would say, "If Muhammad has been reciting for you tales of 'Ad and Thamud, well then *I* am going to recite for you tales of Rustam and Behram, and of the Persian shahs and the monarchs of al-Hirah!"
>
> They found his tales very amusing and began to give up listening to the recitation of the Koran.[22]

Allah's prophet was not about to tolerate this kind of competition. The subsequent verse in the same surah warns: "When Our verses are recited to him, he turns away, thinking himself something big, as if he had not heard these verses, as if there were a deafness in his

---

[21] Suyuti, *Tafsir*, p. 232, commentary on Koran 8:31.

[22] Mahmud ibn 'Umar al-Zamakhshari, *al-Kashshaf 'an haqa'iq al-tanzil* (Beirut: Dar al-Ma'rifah, n.d.), 3:210; translated from the Arabic by D. Pinault.

ears. So announce to him this: a punishment that will be painful"
(Koran 31:7).

Easy to sense the resentment smoldering within these words. Frivolous storytelling during recitations of Allah's verses: this feud would
lead to a showdown after Muhammad's move to Medina. But that is
a tale I will save for our next chapter.

CHAPTER 4

THOSE WHO SELL THEIR SOULS TO GOD: VIOLENCE AND "THE PATH OF ALLAH"

Uproar over Jesus: Rejection, opportunity, and emigration

If you want a quick glimpse of the challenges Muhammad faced in his hometown as he tried to present himself as a biblical-style prophet of monotheism, consider the following late Meccan verse. It records how members of the Quraysh tribe reacted when he tried discussing with them the figure of Jesus: "And when the son of Mary is mentioned as an example, look at how your people laugh and make an uproar at this! And they say, 'Which is better, our gods or Jesus?' They put this question to you only for the purpose of quarreling and disputing with you. They are a very contentious people!" (Koran 43:57–58).

No wonder Muhammad was ready to try a new venue.

Opportunity came in the form of an encounter in Mecca during the annual pilgrimage season of the year 620, when Medinan travelers visiting the Ka'ba initially met Muhammad. Impressed with his message, his speaking skills, and his potential as a leader, they spoke with him several times and eventually invited him to emigrate to their city and serve a much-needed function as arbitrator.

The situation in Medina at that time certainly cried out for arbitration. Unlike Mecca, an arid desert setting celebrated for its caravan trade and religious shrine, Medina consisted of settlements built around an oasis some twenty square miles in extent. A number of semi-sedentarized tribes—largely unaccustomed to living in continuously close proximity to each other—competed for control of the region's fertile land and its resources: water, cereal crops, and date-palm groves. Intertribal blood feuds were frequent, sometimes taking the form of open daylight large-scale battles, sometimes manifesting themselves in the form of individual stabbings by night.[1]

Amidst this largely pagan Jahiliyah population lived a scattering of Christians and a more substantial minority community of Jews—most notably the three clans of the Qaynuqa', the Banu Nadir, and the Banu Qurayzah. Some members of these clans could probably trace their ancestry to the destruction of Solomon's Temple and the diaspora that resulted from failed attempts to gain independence from the Roman Empire. Others were the descendants of Arab converts to Judaism.

Violence-burdened Medina, in other words, was a complex and volatile place to which to emigrate—but as such it also offered opportunities. Muhammad planned carefully and took full advantage of this new setting.

He himself undertook his hijrah (exodus or emigration) in the year 622 (which is counted as year 1 of the Islamic or "hijri" calendar, the moment when Islam's prophet established the *ummah*, or community of believers). But Muhammad was not the first *muhajir* from Mecca to Medina. (You may recall that the Arabic language is organized around triliteral root clusters, and that the prefix "mu-" indicates someone who undertakes the action associated with the verbal root; if the root meaning of "Islam" is submission, then a "Muslim" is simply someone who submits (to Allah). Thus a *muhajir* is someone who undertakes the hijrah: a pious emigrant.) Before he himself abandoned Mecca, Muhammad sent ahead some seventy Muslim converts, who established themselves in Medina and provided their prophet a base of support in his new home.

He arrived by invitation as an arbitrator but within a few short years managed not only to end Medina's feuds but also to become by acclamation a civic leader, warlord, and recognized prophet of Islam. He united the Muhajir emigrants from Mecca with the Ansar (helpers or protectors, a term used to denote those residents of Medina who accepted Muhammad and helped bring about Allah's ultimate victory).

Not all the people of Medina accepted him or his message; some were tepid in their support or made only a show of supporting

---

[1] W. Montgomery Watt, *Muhammad: Prophet and Statesman* (New York: Oxford University Press, 1961), pp. 83–87.

Islam because they felt constrained to. The Koran refers to them as *munafiqun*, "hypocrites". Over time, Muhammad coopted, neutralized, or eliminated them.

His civic accomplishment was to introduce a new form of *'asabiyah* (group solidarity). Membership in the Islamic *ummah* was defined, not by bloodline, clan, or tribe, but rather by collective religious identity. To join this community, all one had to do was to announce one's monotheistic submission to Allah and acknowledgment of Muhammad's role as Allah's messenger. Prestige and social rank within this *ummah*—at least in theory—were to be determined, not by ancestry or wealth, but by religious fervor. "The noblest of you in the sight of Allah", a Medinan surah tells us, "is the most pious" (Koran 49:13).

Since Allah was the one who knew best whether individual Muslims were hypocrites or sincere believers, and since Allah entrusted such divine insights to his messenger, this meant that Muhammad became the supreme earthly leader of the *ummah*, while tribal sheikhs found their traditional authority eroded and subordinated to the new religious order. The theocratic structure of this Islamic hierarchy is summed up in the following Medinan verse: "O you who believe! Obey Allah, and obey the prophet, and obey those who have been put in authority over you" (Koran 4:59).[2]

Jihad: Holy struggle, holy war, and the question of religion and violence

Having begun to create this Islamic *ummah*, Muhammad then faced the question of selecting activities and projects that would heighten a sense of unity in his newly emergent community. His decision: launch raids on wealth-laden Meccan caravans. His justification? These camel trains belonged to the people who had rejected tawhid and the bearer of the tawhidic message.

Important to bear in mind here is that Islam from its inception was never pacifist. Muhammad ordered his converts not to engage in combat against fellow Muslims, as reflected in this Medinan verse: "If

[2] Bernard Lewis, *The Arabs in History*, rev. ed. (New York: Harper & Row, 1966), pp. 43–44.

two groups of believers are fighting each other, make peace between them ... for the believers are brothers. So make peace among your brothers, and fear Allah" (Koran 49:9–10). But Muhammad did not forbid them from fighting altogether. Rather, he took this aggressive energy and directed it outward, against the kuffar (plural of kafir: the unbelievers or infidels).

This helps to explain the Islamic *ummah*'s rapid political and military expansion. William Montgomery Watt, the noted twentieth-century biographer of Muhammad, commented as follows: "If members of the pagan tribes raided by the Muslims professed Islam, they at once became exempt from further Muslim raids. Consequently, as the Islamic community grew, the raiding propensities of the Muslims had to be directed ever further outwards."[3]

Here we enter the realm of jihad, a word that has become the object of much controversy as apologists and critics try to define to what extent violence is inherent in the faith. The root meaning is "struggle", "striving". (From this root are derived the verb *jahada*, "to strive", and the noun *mujahid*, "one who strives" or "holy warrior".)

Much has been made of the fact that jihad can mean the struggle to purify oneself (sometimes labeled the "greater jihad"), or (as the Sufi mystics would say) the battle to annihilate one's appetite-driven self. All true. But jihad also means combat in defense of Islam: in short, holy war.

Noteworthy in this context is that one of the foremost manifestations of jihadic striving during Muhammad's Medinan phase was violence against the kuffar—the unbelievers who opposed Muhammad and his Islamic message. We can see the term deployed in this militant sense in surah 5, verse 54 of the Koran, where the ideal community of Muslims is described as "humble toward the believers, harsh against the unbelievers, striving in the path of Allah (*yujahiduna fi sabil Allah*)."

Surah 9 (which, like chapter 5, is a Medinan surah) also uses this verbal root as Allah addresses Muhammad directly: "O prophet! Struggle (*jahid*) against the kuffar and the hypocrites, and treat them harshly and ruthlessly" (Koran 9:73). Chapter 16 refers to Muslims "who made the hijrah after having been oppressed, and then strove

---

[3] Watt, *Muhammad*, p. 109.

(*jahadu*) and endured" (16:110). Watt comments on this verse in his study of Muhammad's time in Medina: " 'Strove' here implies 'went on *razzias*' [raiding for the purpose of plundering an enemy]."[4]

Vendors, weighing-scales, and beautiful loans:
Holy business, holy war

I have stated previously my conviction that we can read the Koran as a historical and quasi-autobiographical document that offers us glimpses of Muhammad's life. Here I want to draw your attention to recurrent metaphors that illustrate both his early preprophetic career as a businessman and his attitude toward violence in the service of Islam. I am thinking here of the Koran's mercantile imagery.

Not that all such images are violent. An important example occurs in surah 55, an early Meccan chapter that targets Muhammad's fellow tribesmen in the city's business community:

> The gracious One has provided instruction in the Koran. He has created men and taught them eloquence. The sun and moon are arranged according to computation and exact reckoning. The grasses and the trees prostrate themselves in prayer. And the sky: he has raised it up and put in place the balance that weighs things out precisely, so that you people will not transgress the balance. So then, when you weigh things, do so justly, and do not shortchange customers when you use the balance. (Koran 55:1–9)

Dominant in these verses is an image the prophet's neighbors would have recognized at once: *al-mizan*, the "weighing-scale" or "balance". This evokes for us an instrument that must have been frequently used in Mecca's marketplace.

The balance here is twofold. One is in the sky, placed there by Allah, reflected there in the balanced and circumscribed way that sun and moon, grasses and trees, behave in a harmonic and submissive fashion. The other is on earth, among us in our business lives, giving us the chance to demonstrate to Allah that we will weigh and give

[4] Ibid., p. 107.

due measure here below just as he does on high: a pleasing vision of cosmic order.

Mercantile imagery reappears after the hijrah, in the Koran's Medinan chapters, after Muhammad has put together a combined force of Muslim emigrants and Medinan "helpers" that will launch attacks on Muhammad's former Meccan neighbors.

Let's read the following Medinan verses. The first is from surah 61:

> O you who believe! Shall I guide you to a piece of business that will rescue you from a painful punishment?—Namely, that you believe in Allah and his prophet and that you strive in the path of Allah (*wa-tujahiduna fi sabil Allah*) by means of your worldly wealth and your lives. (61:10–11)

The second is from chapter 2:

> Then fight in the path of Allah, and know that Allah is all-hearing, all-knowing. Who will lend unto Allah a beautiful loan at a favorable rate of interest, for which Allah will repay him at double the original amount, and then double it again many times over? (2:244–45)

Business transactions and beautiful loans at favorable interest rates: Muhammad's personal background in the caravan trade provided him with the conceptual vocabulary with which to address the faithful as he prepared his followers for war.

Among the Medinan verses that blend merchandizing and militancy, there are two in particular that have been influential up to the present day in justifying acts of religious violence. Both depict Allah as a purchaser of souls:

> Among the people are those who sell their lives seeking to please Allah. (Koran 2:207)

The other Medinan verse in question reads as follows:

> Allah has purchased from the believers their worldly goods and their lives (*anfusahum*), on the condition that in exchange they get the Garden of Paradise. They fight in the path of Allah; they kill and are killed.... So rejoice in the sale that you have made. (9:111)

(The Arabic term *anfusahum* you have just seen is derived from the consonantal triad n-f-s, with the root meanings "soul/self/life--breath". *Anfusahum* can be validly translated as "their lives", "their selves", "their persons", or "their souls"—a point useful to know as we explore various interpretations of this verse in what follows.)

The popular scriptural commentary by Suyuti offers a clarification about the verse just quoted with regard to the phrase "their worldly goods and their lives": "in that they expend these things [their worldly goods and their lives] as jihad in obedience to him [i.e., to Allah]."[5]

The transactional view of divine-human relations in these verses—we sell something to Allah; we get something from Allah in exchange—provided a kind of marketing tool and branding device for a group known as the Kharijites, which arose in the seventh century, during the caliphate of 'Ali ibn Abi Talib. This was the first organized militant movement in Islamic history after the death of Muhammad.

Known—and feared—for their ferocity and readiness to die as they killed fellow Muslims they deemed deficient in faith, the Kharijites were notorious for their practice of *isti'rad* (critical inspection, examination). This involved waylaying individual Muslims, quizzing them on the orthodoxy of their beliefs concerning Islam and political leadership, and killing them if they gave the wrong answer.[6]

The Kharijites called themselves *shurat*. The word means "vendors" or "those who sell", and it echoes the verses of the Koran just quoted above. The *shurat* believed they were the beneficiaries of a good business bargain: in performing jihad in its most violent form, they sold their souls to Allah and got the Garden in return.

Militants as vendors who get a great afterlife deal: the violent influence of such Koranic verses has continued beyond the time of the Kharijites. This can be seen in the writings of Yusuf al-Qaradawi, an Egyptian religious authority, prominent social-media personality, and widely respected mufti (a cleric trained in sharia law who issues *fatwas* or decrees on specific topics relating to Islam and contemporary

---

[5]Jalal al-Din 'Abd al-Rahman al-Suyuti, *Tafsir al-jalalayn*, ed. Marwan Sawar (Beirut: Dar al-ma'rifah, n.d.), p. 260, commentary on Koran 9:111.

[6]Jeffrey T. Kenney, *Muslim Rebels: Kharijites and the Politics of Extremism in Egypt* (New York: Oxford University Press, 2006), p. 34.

life). In 2003 Qaradawi published a *fatwa* justifying the use of suicide bombers against Israel, even in instances when the perpetrators know that nonmilitary bystanders will be killed: "The martyrdom operations carried out by the Palestinian factions to resist the Zionist occupation are not in any way included in the framework of prohibited terrorism, even if the victims include some civilians."

Qaradawi goes on to explain why he prefers the term "martyrdom operation" (the politically correct term among Islamist militants for such acts of self-destructive savagery): "Those who oppose martyrdom operations and claim that they are suicide are making a great mistake. The goals of the one who carries out a martyrdom operation and of the one who commits suicide are completely different." Suicides, he proclaims, are individuals who are failures and have been defeated by life. But individuals who detonate themselves in the name of Islam: such persons earn the name of martyr:

> What weapon can harm their enemy, can prevent him from sleeping, and can strip him of a sense of security and stability, except for these human bombs—a young man or woman who blows himself or herself up amongst their enemy? This is a weapon the likes of which the enemy cannot obtain, even if the U.S. provides it with billions [of dollars] and the most powerful weapons, because it is a unique weapon that Allah has placed only in the hands of the men of belief.[7]

Qaradawi rounds off his argument with the Koranic vendor verse we have just seen:

> The one who carries out a martyrdom operation does not think of himself. He sacrifices himself for the sake of a higher goal.... He sells himself to Allah in order to buy Paradise in exchange. Allah said: "Allah has bought from the believers their souls and their properties for they shall inherit Paradise."[8]

Such logic would have made the seventh-century Kharijites proud.

---

[7] Yusuf al-Qaradawi, "Suicide Bombers Are Martyrs", July 24, 2003, http://www.memri .org. The text is available in John J. Donohue and John L. Esposito, *Islam in Transition: Muslim Perspectives*, 2nd ed. (New York: Oxford University Press, 2007), 469–71.

[8] Donohue and Esposito, *Islam in Transition*, pp. 470–71.

Qaradawi is not only anti-Israeli but also virulently anti-Shia. Consequently, in recent years he has served as an ideologue rallying those Sunnis of the Middle East who oppose Syria's Bashar al-Assad and Iran's grand ayatollah Sayyid 'Ali Khamenei (both Assad and Khamenei are adherents of various denominations of Shiism). In 2015 Qaradawi appeared on a TV talk show sponsored by Al Jazeera, in which he was asked, in his capacity as a Muslim cleric and mufti, to answer the question, "Is it permissible—in the Syrian context—for an individual to blow himself up to target a group that owes allegiance to the Syrian regime, even if this causes casualties among civilians?"

Anyone familiar with this cleric's earlier *fatwa* can guess that the answer came out as a big affirmative. But Qaradawi was careful to stipulate that spiritual strivers should not operate solo. They must submit themselves to the discipline and decisions of the organization that sponsors their efforts: "If the need arises, individuals should only blow themselves up if a group (*jamaa*) decides that it is necessary.... These are matters that are not to be left to individuals.... Individuals should surrender themselves to the *jamaa*, and it is the *jamaa* that determines how to utilize individuals according to its needs." As noted in 2016 by Yasser Reda, Egypt's ambassador to the United States, Qaradawi's reply "effectively condones and blesses the fanaticism of Osama bin Laden, al Qaeda in Iraq's Abu Musab al-Zarqawi, Islamic State's Abu Bakr al-Baghdadi and the leaders of Boko Haram."[9]

On dealing with troublesome storytellers and poets:
The fate of Nadr ibn al-Harith

Encouraging believers to think of themselves as vendors who sell their souls to Allah and who seal the deal by killing and being killed in Allah's path: to urge such things on one's followers requires considerable confidence. And this is one thing that marks the Medinan phase of Muhammad's career. Compared with his days in Mecca, Muhammad in Medina—to judge from the Koranic verses dating from that period—showed much less evidence of uncertainty or

[9] Yasser Reda, "Countering the Pontiff of Terror", *The Wall Street Journal*, August 24, 2016, p. A13.

hesitation. No longer ridden by jinn-doubts—or at least no longer voicing such doubts or needing reassurance that he was not majnun—Allah's prophet now proved himself to be both decisive and frequently ruthless.

This is reflected in the campaigns he initiated against Meccan camel caravans shortly after his hijrah to Medina. The first raids he authorized were largely unsuccessful or inconclusive. But matters changed early in the year 624. Muhammad ordered a dozen Muhajirs to travel south to Nakhlah (not far from the ancient shrine to the goddess al-'Uzza) and intercept a Meccan caravan that was on its way back from Yemen.

The Muslims did as they were ordered. Pretending to be pilgrims to the idol-encircled shrine of the Ka'ba, they received permission to join the caravan. None of the Meccan pagans in the lightly guarded camel convoy feared robbery, for they were traveling during one of the "forbidden months". The term indicated a time of year in the ancient Arab calendar when inter-tribal fighting was forbidden so as to facilitate both pilgrimage and trade.

Nonetheless, at an opportune moment, Muhammad's men attacked their unsuspecting hosts, killed one of the guards, and escaped triumphantly with the loot.[10]

William Montgomery Watt, Muhammad's twentieth-century biographer, describes this ambush as "the first bloodshed" initiated by the prophet.[11] Once the successful raiders returned to Medina, a number of the city's inhabitants apparently let the prophet know they were troubled both by the timing of the event and the likelihood that the Meccans would retaliate. The Koran informs us what Allah ordered Muhammad to tell the Medinans in reply: "They are asking you about the forbidden month and fighting during that time. Say: 'Fighting during that time is a serious thing. But hindering people from Allah's path, and being a kafir with regard to Allah, and hindering people from the Sacred Mosque, and driving its people from there: that is a more serious thing as far as Allah is concerned. Oppression is worse than killing'" (2:217).

This verse made it clear that more conflict was on the way. And, in fact, Muhammad authorized further attacks on Meccan caravans. Finally, later in the same year 624, hundreds of Muslims and polytheist

---

[10] Watt, *Muhammad*, pp. 109–11.
[11] Ibid., p. 109.

Meccans fought each other at the battle of Badr, which resulted in
the first major military victory for the newly emergent *ummah*. The
defeated pagans fled back to Mecca. Dozens of wounded men were
captured on the battlefield.

Now came a moral challenge for the Muslims. Longstanding
Jahiliyah custom encouraged victors not to kill prisoners of war but
instead hold them for ransom; their families would gladly pay to rescue them. But Muhammad surprised his followers by singling out
two of the captives. He insisted on having them beheaded.

The scriptural commentator Suyuti states that "when they were
arranging to take ransom for the prisoners of Badr", a Koranic verse
was revealed to Muhammad, which he then proclaimed to his followers: "It is not appropriate for a prophet to take prisoners of war
until he has made a great slaughter in the land" (8:67). Just to make
sure readers understand the implications of this revelation, Suyuti
adds this clarification: " 'Until he has made a great slaughter in the
land': that is, until he has done his utmost and gone to great lengths
in killing the *kuffar* [unbelievers]."[12]

And the two prisoners who were singled out for killing?

One was named 'Uqbah ibn Abi Mu'ayt. Not only had he composed poetic verses insulting Muhammad; on one occasion in Mecca,
he had crept up on Muhammad while the prophet was at prayer
beside the Ka'ba and dumped camel dung and intestines on his
head. Bystanders laughed. In reply, Muhammad called upon them
all a curse, crying aloud three times, "O Allah, take revenge on the
Quraysh!" He then named those who particularly deserved punishment, including 'Uqbah ibn Abi Mu'ayt.[13]

Now here they were in the aftermath of the battlefield of Badr.
One account describes how the prisoners were confined: hands
tied to the neck with a rope. 'Uqbah the captive faced Muhammad
the victor.[14]

According to Muhammad's eighth-century biographer, the prisoner made a plea for mercy. "When Allah's prophet ordered him

[12] Suyuti, *Tafsir*, p. 238, commentary on Koran 8:67; translated from the Arabic by D.
Pinault.

[13] *Sahih al-Bukhari*, ed. Muhammad Muhsin Khan (Ankara: Hilal Yayinlari, 1978), vol. 1,
chap. 20, p. 295, no. 499; Watt, *Muhammad*, p. 123.

[14] *The History of al-Tabari*, ed. and trans. W.M. Watt and M.V. McDonald, vol. 7, *The
Foundation of the Community* (Albany: SUNY Press, 1987), p. 66.

to be killed, 'Uqbah asked, 'But who will look after my children, O Muhammad?' He replied, 'Hellfire.' "[15]

And the other POW who was executed after Badr by command of the prophet? This is someone we have met already: Nadr ibn al-Harith, the Meccan storyteller and traveler who had brought back from al-Hirah the art of playing the Persian lute. You may recall that he had competed with Muhammad by telling tales of ancient heroes while the prophet was reciting verses of the Koran. Victory at Badr gave Muhammad the chance to settle this score.

As we learned in a previous chapter, the Koran had condemned Nadr for his "frivolous stories", threatening him with "a humiliating punishment ... a punishment that will be painful". In these verses, we sense lingering resentment and rage.

This rage was vented at a site in the wasteland called Uthayl, near the desert ravine of Wadi Safra', where the prophet of Islam halted his triumphant march back to Medina long enough to have the story-teller pulled from the column and killed on the spot. His corpse lay abandoned on the sand as the victors marched away.

Observing Muhammad's behavior, I am reminded of this truth: anger is a form of pleasure. The risk for all of us is nurturing such pleasures until they well up into violence.

Disturbing, this lack of mercy on the prophet's part with regard to his two helpless foes. Worth noting, too, is that the early Muslim biographers voice no objection. Far from it. The fourteenth-century biographer Abu al-Fida' ibn Kathir, after citing Ibn Ishaq's account of these two killings, adds a personal note: "I say: These two men were among the most evil of Allah's creations, and the worst of them, in terms of pagan unbelief, obstinate resistance, wrongdoing, envy, and insulting Islam and its adherents. May Allah curse the both of them!"[16]

A somewhat softer note is sounded by Ibn Ishaq in describing the aftermath of Badr. He quotes a poem composed in the slain story-teller's honor by his sister, who is identified as Qutaylah bint al-Harith.

"Qutaylah" is a curious name. A ninth-century collection of poetry makes note of this woman and includes the following commentary:

[15] Ferdinand Wüstenfeld, ed., *Kitab sirat rasul Allah* (Göttingen: Dieterichsche Universitäts-Buchhandlung, 1860), p. 458; translated from the Arabic by D. Pinault.

[16] Abu al-Fida' al-Hafiz ibn Kathir, *al-Sirah al-nabawiyyah*, ed. Ahmad 'Abd al-Shafi (Beirut: Dar al-Kutub al-'Ilmiyah, n.d.), 1:493.

" 'Qutaylah' might have been used as a term of contempt and humiliation." The reason is that the word literally means "a little female thing that has been killed"—a dismissive way of referring to the loss this woman suffered in the death of her brother.[17]

Nonetheless, we are fortunate that Ibn Ishaq preserved the poem. Here is a portion of it:

> O Rider, I think you will reach Uthayl [the site where
>   Nadr's corpse was left]
> At dawn of the fifth night if you are lucky.
> Greet a dead man there for me.
> Swift camels always carry news from me to thee.
> (Tell of) flowing tears running profusely or ending in a sob.
> Can al-Nadr hear me when I call him,
> How can a dead man hear who cannot speak,
> O Muhammad ... 'twould not have harmed you had you
>   spared him.
> (A warrior oft spares though full of rage and anger.)
> Or you could have taken a ransom,
> The dearest price that could be paid.[18]

On first reading these verses, I thought at once of the Greek epitaph composed in the fifth century B.C. by Simonides of Ceos: "O stranger, go tell the Spartans that here we lie, obedient to their commands."

The two memorials share in common a certain structural feature. The three hundred dead of Thermopylae, adhering to their city's command to hold the coastal pass at all costs against Xerxes and his hordes from the East, hail a passerby at their burial site and ask him to convey a message to those they safeguarded.

But where Simonides' verse is addressed from the dead to the living, Qutaylah's poem has a survivor speak to the slain. As in the Greek composition, she calls out to a passerby—here, a camel-mounted rider—and asks him to bridge the worlds of the living and the dead.

---

[17] Abu Tammam Habib ibn Aws al-Ta'i, *Diwan al-Hamasah*, with a commentary in Arabic by Imam al-Bara' (Cairo: Bulaq, 1878), 3:13; translated by D. Pinault.

[18] Ibn Ishaq, *The Life of Muhammad: A Translation of Ibn Ishaq's Sirat Rasul Allah*, ed. and trans. Alfred Guillaume (Karachi; New York: Oxford University Press, 1968), p. 360.

What heightens the sense of sorrow in Qutaylah's poem is the knowledge that Muhammad could have chosen to follow the Jahili-yah custom of accepting a ransom for her brother's life. She acknowl-edges her adversary's vindictive fury while suggesting how he could have risen above it: "A warrior oft spares though full of rage and anger." But since this was not to be, all she can do is beg the passerby to salute the slain at the wasteland site of Uthayl: "Tell of flowing tears running profusely or ending in a sob."

"Men who overthrew mountains and never submitted": Poetry as resistance to the message of Islam

But Nadr and 'Uqbah were not the last to die for speaking out against Allah's prophet and blocking his message. Early Islamic sources describe what happened to various poets and singers who defied Muhammad.

We have already seen the religious underpinnings of the prophet's hostility to pagan poets: they tended to be jinn-ridden, taking sugges-tions from satanic spirits. In what follows, we can glimpse the politi-cal dimension of poetic resistance to Muhammad. Consider here the fate of five who spoke out.

The first was an elderly pagan named Abu 'Afak of the Bani 'Ubayda clan. He composed a poem in which he defied the prophet and mocked the language of the Koran, referring to Muhammad in his poem as "a rider who came to them [i.e., Abu 'Afak's tribe] [and] split them in two (saying) 'Permitted', 'Forbidden' of all sorts of things." Abu 'Afak also tried to rally his tribe against Islam and praised his fellow tribesmen as "men who overthrew mountains and never submitted".

In response to the reciting of this poem, Muhammad said, "Who will deal with this rascal for me?" Immediately, one of Muhammad's followers, Salim ibn 'Umayr, went out and killed Abu 'Afak. A poem by another Muslim celebrated this killing with a verse that taunted the dead pagan: "A hanif [monotheist] gave you a thrust in the night saying, 'Take that, Abu 'Afak, in spite of your age!'"[19]

[19] Ibid., p. 675.

The second defiant poet was a woman named 'Asma' bint Marwan, of the Bani Umayya clan. According to the biographer Ibn Ishaq, after the Muslims' murder of Abu 'Afak, she composed a poem "blaming Islam and its followers". Among the verses she recited was this: "You obey a stranger [i.e., Muhammad] who is none of yours, one not of Murad or Madhhij. Do you expect good from him after the killing of your chief?... Is there no man of pride who would attack him by surprise?"

Here is a clear instance of the use of poetry to rally public opinion. Muhammad understood at once that this constituted yet another challenge to his ascendancy. His response, as recorded by Ibn Ishaq, reminds me of Henry II's exasperated outburst to his courtiers once he conceived the desire to be rid of his rival Saint Thomas of Canterbury. This is what Ibn Ishaq tells us:

When the apostle heard what she had said he said, "Who will rid me of Marwan's daughter?" 'Umayr ibn 'Adiy al-Khatmi who was with him heard him, and that very night he went to her house and killed her. In the morning he came to the apostle and told him what he had done and he [Muhammad] said, "You have helped God and His apostle, O 'Umayr!" When he [i.e., 'Umayr] asked if he would have to bear any evil consequences, the apostle said, "Two goats will not butt their heads about her" [i.e., No one will do anything about it].[20]

My third example, also from Ibn Ishaq, involves "two singing girls", one named Fartana, the other unnamed:

The apostle had instructed his commanders when they entered Mecca [during the conquest of the year 630] only to fight those who resisted them, except a small number who were to be killed even if they were found beneath the curtains of the Ka'ba. Among them ... was 'Abdullah ibn Khatal [an apostate said to be guilty of murder].... He had two singing girls, Fartana and her friend, who used to sing satirical songs about the apostle, so he [i.e., Muhammad] ordered that they should be killed with him.... Another [person whose death was ordered by Muhammad at the time of the Meccan victory] was ... Sara, freed slave of one of the Bani 'Abdu'l-Muttalib.... Sara had insulted him

[the prophet] in Mecca. . . . As for Ibn Khatal's two singing girls, one
was killed and the other ran away until the apostle, [when] asked for
immunity, gave it to her.[21]

My fourth example involves an impulse-killing—yet it is nonetheless presented in the early Islamic sources as an act worthy of divine
blessing. In the year 626, in the midst of his war against the pagan
Quraysh, Muhammad commissioned one of his followers, a Muslim
named 'Amr ibn Umayya, to go to Mecca and kill Abu Sufyan (a
preeminent Jahiliyah leader). 'Amr seemed a good choice for a chore
involving premeditated murder; he was already known for his history
of killings.[22]

But 'Amr failed in his assassination attempt and had to flee the city.
Desperate, he took refuge from his Meccan pursuers in a cave.

Ignorant of what was going on, a one-eyed Bedouin shepherd
leading his sheep also entered the cave, introduced himself in a
friendly way, and sat down beside the assassin to relax. The shepherd
was apparently unaware of who 'Amr was or what was the nature of
'Amr's religious-political loyalty.

Here is 'Amr's report of what happened next:

Then he [the shepherd] lay down beside me and lifting up his voice
began to sing:

> "I will not be a Muslim as long as I live,
> Nor heed to their religion give."

I ['Amr] said to myself, "You will soon know!" and as soon as the
badu [Bedouin] was asleep and snoring I got up and killed him in a
more horrible way than any man has been killed. I put the end of my
bow in his sound eye, then I bore down on it until I forced it out
at the back of his neck. Then I came out like a beast of prey and took
the highroad like an eagle hastening.

Later 'Amr reported to the prophet Muhammad. "Then he
[Muhammad] questioned me and I told him what had happened.
'Well done!' he said, and prayed for me to be blessed."[23]

[21] Ibid., pp. 550–51.
[22] Ibid., p. 673.
[23] Ibid., pp. 673–75; *History of al-Tabari*, 7:149–50.

The murders listed above targeted Jahiliyah pagans. My last example has to do with a member of the Bani al-Nadir, one of the Jewish communities that lived in and around Medina. His name was Ka'b ibn al-Ashraf, and he was one of Muhammad's opponents who refused to convert to Islam. After the defeat of the Meccans at Badr, Ka'b composed a poem lamenting the Muslims' victory: "At events like Badr you should weep and cry.... How many noble handsome men, the refuge of the homeless, were slain, generous when the stars gave no rain, who bore others' burdens."

A ninth-century collector of *hadiths* (sayings attributed to the prophet of Islam) named Muhammad Isma'il al-Bukhari tells us how Allah's messenger reacted to this poem: "The Prophet said, 'Who is ready to kill Ka'b ibn al-Ashraf, who has really hurt Allah and His Apostle?'" A group of Muhammad's followers then went to Ka'b's house at night and killed him. They severed Ka'b's head and brought it to the prophet.[24]

W.M. Watt (who overall is extraordinarily sympathetic in his biography of the prophet) discreetly observes that "throughout his career Muhammad was specially sensitive to intellectual or literary attacks of this kind."[25]

"Specially sensitive" rates, I think, as an understatement. Grim accounts, these; unpleasant and bloodstained reading. Nonetheless, I have summarized these killings for you because the details of Muhammad's life are considered paradigmatic in Islam: they provide examples for the pious to follow in structuring their own lives as faithful believers.

And in Muslim-majority countries like Pakistan, where a significant portion of the Islamic population may be said to be "specially sensitive" to issues involving the prophet's honor, even the suspicion of dishonoring Muhammad or questioning some aspect of his revered prophetic status can land one in jail or worse. As we shall see in subsequent chapters, freedom of speech, freedom of conscience, and freedom to criticize are all under threat in societies where intimidation is used to prevent Muslims from challenging the exemplary value of incidents in their prophet's life.

---

[24] *Sahih al-Bukhari*, 4:167–69; Ibn Ishaq, *Life of Muhammad*, pp. 364–69; *History of al-Tabari*, pp. 94–98.
[25] Watt, *Muhammad*, p. 123.

CHAPTER 5

DEPICTIONS OF JEWS AND CHRISTIANS IN THE KORAN

Which way to pray?: The qiblah *question*

Thus far in discussing Muhammad's time in Medina, I have concen-
trated mostly on his relations with the Jahiliyah Quraysh of Mecca
and other pagan Arabs of the region. Now let's see how he dealt with
the Jews and Christians of the city to which he emigrated.

After his hometown disappointments, Muhammad had high
hopes for the "people of the Book"—a term frequently used in the
Koran for addressing Jews and Christians (see, for example, surah
3:64–71). As you noticed in the last chapter, Muhammad had tried
to discuss biblical figures like Jesus with his Meccan neighbors. The
Koran records how scornfully they responded: "And when the son
of Mary is mentioned as an example, look at how your people laugh
and make an uproar at this!" (43:57).

True, the Quraysh acknowledged Allah, but—as discussed earlier—
they also ranked Allat, Manat, and al-'Uzza as goddesses and worshipped them accordingly. Because of this, Muhammad proclaimed
the Meccan polytheists to be guilty of *shirk* (literally, associationism): the
sin of associating divine partners with Allah. Anyone who commits
shirk is labeled a *mushrik* (someone who ascribes partners to the sole
true god).

This is a serious matter. Surah 4:48 warns that "Allah will not forgive this if partners are associated with Him. He will forgive anything
else, to whomever He wishes; but anyone who associates partners
with Allah: such a person has devised a monstrous sin."

And it was precisely this sin of which the pagan Quraysh were
guilty, according to surah 30 (a Meccan chapter): "Allah is the one

who created and nurtured you people; thereafter He will give you death and then give you life again. But can any of your 'divine partners' do anything like that in any way? Glory unto Allah! He is exalted high beyond the partners they associate with Him" (Koran 30:40).

The same chapter uses the term *mushrikin* (the plural of *mushrik*) to describe the inhabitants of previous civilizations and lost cities: "Say: 'Travel throughout the earth and see what was the fate of those who came before. Most of them were people who ascribed partners to Allah (*Kana aktharuhum mushrikin*)'" (Koran 30:42).

In moving to Medina, with its minority population of Jews and Christians, Muhammad hoped for a fresh start, hoped to win over a people who were not guilty of idol worship and pagan *shirk*. After all, years earlier, before receiving his summons from Gabriel, Muhammad as a young man had enjoyed contact with "people of the Book", had listened to the priest Quss ibn Sa'idah, and wondered at the sermons he heard at the 'Ukaz fair. It was the Jews and the Christians, after all, who believed in one God and His prophets, in resurrection and judgment, in heaven and hell—all beliefs incorporated by Muhammad into Islam.

So he was optimistic: if anyone would accept his Islamic message, it would be Medina's Christians and Jews. A mark of this optimism: during the early stages of his residence in Medina, Muhammad directed his followers that their *qiblah* (the direction they faced in prayer) should be toward Jerusalem.

This city is important for the sacred history of both Judaism and Christianity, and it resonates in the prayer life of heroes of the Bible. When King Solomon dedicates the Temple in Jerusalem that is to house the Ark of the Covenant, he addresses God and notes the orientation in worship stipulated for the people of Israel: "They pray to the LORD toward the city which you have chosen and the house which I have built for your name" (1 Kings 8:44).

Even after the fall of the kingdom and the destruction of Solomon's Temple, Jerusalem continued to play a vital role in Jewish rituals, as is reflected in the Book of Daniel, with its tale of a young Israelite who stays true to his faith throughout his exile in Babylon. Despite the interdict of the Persian shah Darius ("Whoever makes petition to any god ... except to you, O king, shall be cast into the den of lions" [Dan 6:7]), Daniel, visionary and interpreter of dreams, "went to his house where he had windows in his upper chamber open toward Jerusalem; and he got down upon his knees three times a day and prayed and gave thanks before his God, as he had done previously" (Dan 6:10). Muhammad's Jerusalem-oriented *qiblah* followed this biblical tradition.

Muhammad's conciliatory period in his dealings with people of the Book is reflected in Medinan verses such as 2:62: "Those who are Muslim believers, and the Jews, and Christians, and Sabians—those who believe in Allah and the Last Day and who do good works—they shall have their reward with their Lord. No fear will come upon them, nor shall they feel sorrow."

This verse is generously inclusive. Four different religious denominations are identified as qualified to "have their reward with their Lord". The criteria seem oriented toward "people of the Book" rather than Jahiliyah polytheists: belief in the Last Day implies acceptance of judgment in the afterlife, heaven, hell, and personal accountability—all of which are doctrines that would have been familiar to Medina's Jews and Christians.

The least familiar name on this list: the Sabians. Islamic scriptural commentary offers a range of speculations: that they were a people whose beliefs and practices were "halfway between the Christians and the Magians [Zoroastrians]"; that "the origin of their religion was the religion of Noah"; that they worshipped angels, or perhaps the stars and planets. Even more intriguing is the theory that they belonged to a Gnostic sect that had taken refuge in the marshlands of southern Iraq, whose religious practices involved wearing white garments and presiding over baptisms that entailed "frequent immersions in water". Whether because of their link with Noah or their impressive ritual life, Muhammad listed the Sabians along with the other people of the Book as those who would be delivered from fear and sorrow.[1]

A similarly expansive and generous note is sounded in Medinan verse 5:48: "If Allah had wanted to, He could have made you people one single *ummah* [religious community]. But He did otherwise, so as to test you concerning that which He brought you. So compete with

---

[1] Nasir al-Din Abu Saʻid al-Baydawi, *Anwar al-tanzil wa-asrar al-taʼwil* (Beirut: Dar al-Kutub al-ʻIlmiyah, 1988), 1:66, commentary on Koran 2:62; ʻAbdullah Yusuf ʻAli, *The Meaning of the Holy Qurʼan* (Beltsville, Md.: Amana Publications, 1999), p. 33.

each other in good works. Unto Allah will you return, all of you. Then He will inform you about those things concerning which you used to disagree with each other."

As with the other verse, here, too, the emphasis is on that which unites people rather than that which divides us. If we insist on distinguishing ourselves from each other, let it be through the good works we do. Rather than sweat the little stuff—"those things concerning which you used to disagree"—let's leave such matters to Allah. We are all on a journey that will take us back to Him, and when we reach our destination, He will satisfy our all-too-human curiosity about the distinguishing denominational details that seemed so important to us here below.

Both verses are heartening. I make a point of citing them every time I read the Koran with my students. They are also cited frequently at interfaith dialogue sessions I have attended over the years. They embody what I call the upbeat mood of the Jerusalem *qiblah*.

But that mood did not last. Some sixteen and a half months after arriving in Medina, Muhammad abruptly announced a change in *qiblah*. No longer were believers to pray toward Jerusalem; now they were to face Mecca and its Ka'ba.

Here is the Koran's explanation for the switch: "The fools among the population are going to say, 'What has turned them away from their *qiblah* that they used to follow?' Say: '... We appointed the *qiblah* you used to follow only so that We might know who would follow the prophet.... Now We will turn you toward a *qiblah* that will please you. So turn your face toward the Sacred Mosque'" (2:142–44).

Islamic scripture presents the switch as a straightforward test of obedience: Who is willing to follow Allah's commands—and by extension His prophet's—without hesitation or question? But I think we can push the inquiry further. I would put it to you that abandoning Jerusalem as the *qiblah* was Muhammad's way of demonstrating—publicly and liturgically—that he had reached a breaking point in his withered hopes and mounting frustrations with Medina's people of the Book.

He had expected the Jews and Christians to accept his message; instead, most of them refused to convert to Islam. This is reflected in the actions of Ka'b ibn al-Ashraf, a member of the Jewish Bani

al-Nadir tribe. You may recall that he defied the Muslims by com-
p'osing a poem lamenting the Islamic victory at Badr. Muhammad
retaliated by having him beheaded.

Another example of unexpected defiance from people of the Book
can be pieced together from what Muslim authors tell us about an
individual named Abu 'Amir al-Rahib. He was a Christian living in
the vicinity of Medina before the time of the hijrah. Ibn Ishaq tells
us that Abu 'Amir "had practiced the monastic life during the time
of the Jahiliyah. He wore coarse woolen fabric and sackcloth. People
called him al-Rahib [the monk]."[2]

It is clear Muhammad did not like him. He told his followers,
"Don't call him 'the Monk'. Call him 'the Sinner'."[3]

The fourteenth-century biographer Ibn Kathir obeys these instructions, referring to Abu 'Amir as "the Sinner, may Allah disfigure
him!" Ibn Kathir also tells us this:

> When Allah's messenger summoned him to Islam, he refused. Then
> he went to Mecca and tried to rouse its people to battle [against
> Muhammad].... When this matter did not advance satisfactorily, he
> went to the king of the Greeks, the Byzantine emperor, in order to
> try to help him attain victory against Allah's messenger. Abu 'Amir
> belonged to the religion of [the emperor] Heraclius: he was among
> those Arabs who embraced Christianity.[4]

The conflict between Abu 'Amir and Muhammad is illustrated by
a conversation reported to us by Ibn Ishaq:

> Before he departed for Mecca, Abu 'Amir approached Allah's messen-
> ger at the time when Muhammad came to Medina. He asked, "What
> is this religion that you have brought?"
>
> Muhammad replied, "I have brought the hanif religion, the reli-
> gion of Abraham."
>
> Abu 'Amir said, "Why, that is the religion that I am following."
>
> Allah's messenger said to him, "No, you are not! That is not what
> you are following."

[2] Ferdinand Wüstenfeld, ed., *Kitab sirat rasul Allah* (Göttingen: Dieterichsche Universitäts--
Buchhandlung, 1860), p. 411; translated from the Arabic by D. Pinault.
[3] Ibid., p. 411.
[4] Abu al-Fida' al-Hafiz ibn Kathir, *al-Sirah al-nabawiyyah*, ed. Ahmad 'Abd al-Shafi (Beirut:
Dar al-Kutub al-'Ilmiyah, n.d.), 2:283; translated from the Arabic by D. Pinault.

Abu 'Amir replied, "Yes, I am. Muhammad, you are the one who has introduced into the hanif religion things that do not belong to it."

Muhammad said, "No, I have not! What I have brought is white and pure and unmixed with anything else."[5]

This intriguing dispute might lead you to ask: So what is this hanif religion that the two men were quarreling about? The linkage of this word with the phrase "the religion of Abraham" guides us to a Medinan surah that states: "Abraham was not a Jew or a Christian. But he was a hanif, a Muslim. And he was not one of the *mushrikin* [those who ascribe divine partners to Allah]" (Koran 3:67).

Baydawi's commentary on this Koranic verse interprets hanif Muslim as "someone who turns away from those creeds that are deviant and false, submitting to Allah". Suyuti offers this: "someone who turns away from all the other religions to the true religion, declaring Allah's oneness".[6]

The term hanif is derived from the Syriac word *hanpa* (Syriac is a dialect of Aramaic associated with the ancient Christian communities of much of Mesopotamia and Syria). *Hanpa* can mean "pagan" or "gentile". (The plural is *hanpe*: "pagans", "gentiles".) The scholar Gabriel Said Reynolds points to its use in the Peshitta (the Syriac text of the Bible) to translate a term in Paul's Letter to the Romans (1:16): "For I am not ashamed of the gospel: it is the power of God for salvation to every one who has faith, to the Jews first and also to the Greeks [*hanpe*]." *Hanpa* is how the Peshitta renders the notion of a Gentile, a non-Jew.[7]

With this in mind, note how the Koranic passage about Abraham we have just read states that he is a hanif Muslim but *not* a Christian or a Jew. In addition, the same passage pointedly asserts, Abraham was not one of those who associate partners with Allah. The same pattern appears in chapter 2 (another Medinan surah): "They say: 'Be a Jew or a Christian; you will be guided.' Say: 'No! I prefer the religion of Abraham the hanif! He was not one of the *mushrikin*'" (Koran 2:135).

---

[5] Wüstenfeld, *Kitab*, pp. 411–12; translated by D. Pinault.

[6] Baydawi, *Anwar*, 1:164; Jalal al-Din 'Abd al-Rahman al-Suyuti, *Tafsir al-jalalayn*, ed. Marwan Sawar (Beirut: Dar al-ma'rifah, n.d.), p. 75.

[7] Gabriel Said Reynolds, *The Qur'an and Its Biblical Subtext* (London: Routledge, 2010), pp. 84–85.

Likewise, surah 3:95 presents "Abraham the hanif" as part of a contrastive pair with the word *mushrikin*: "So follow the religion of Abraham the hanif; he was not one of the *mushrikin*." This Medinan verse occurs in the context of a rebuke delivered to the *Bani Isra'il* (the "children of Israel", the Jews).

Keeping in mind the story of Abraham as told elsewhere in the Koran, you may recall that Abraham was someone who broke the pagan idols of his family and was saved by Allah when he was cast into a fire. Thus Muhammad's fundamental understanding of the term hanif seems to have been: a gentile from a Jahiliyah background who turned away from false worship and became a Muslim before Muhammad began his preaching and thus before the formal organization of Islam as a world religion. To judge from the Koranic verses just quoted, such a definition excludes Jews and Christians from the circle of hanifs.

But I would argue that the reason for the quarrel between Abu 'Amir and the prophet of Islam is that Abu 'Amir—and, I suspect, other Arabs as well—understood the word hanif somewhat differently and more inclusively. Perhaps Abu 'Amir understood it this way: a hanif is anyone from a Jahiliyah background who leaves tribal polytheism and seeks out the one God of Abraham; and a valid path for such a seeker might be not only Islam, but also Judaism, Christianity—or even an improvised monotheism that is free of any denominational label.

Evidence for this broader definition of hanif can actually be found, I would argue, in Ibn Ishaq's biography of Muhammad himself. We are told of four Qurayshi clansmen—all of them contemporaries of the prophet of Islam—who one day gathered with their tribe to hold a religious festival. Amid the celebrations—animal sacrifices to deities, circumambulating idols—these four found themselves dissatisfied with their ancestral faith. And so they "drew apart secretly and agreed to keep their counsel in the bonds of friendship.... 'Find for yourselves a religion,' they said [to each other]; 'for by God you have none.' So they went their several ways in the lands, seeking the Hanifiya, the religion of Abraham."[8]

---

[8] Ibn Ishaq, *The Life of Muhammad: A Translation of Ibn Ishaq's Sirat Rasul Allah*, ed. and trans. A. Guillaume (Karachi; New York: Oxford University Press, 1968), pp. 98–99.

The biographer tells us what befell each of them. The first, Waraqa ibn Naufal, is the most famous. He "attached himself to Christianity and studied its scriptures until he had thoroughly mastered them." A cousin of the caravan owner and businesswoman Khadija bint Khu-waylid, he was on hand to provide advice, as we saw in a previous chapter, when her husband came home one night from a solitary prayer session on Mount Hira' in a state of emotional tumult. Kha-dija's husband was afraid he would become jinn-infested, majnun. It was Waraqa who reassured him: You have been visited, not by a jinn, but by an angel, Gabriel.

The name of Khadija's husband is of course Muhammad ibn 'Abd Allah, the prophet of Islam. Thus Waraqa's name is vital in the his-tory of hanifs.[9]

Less well known is the second name in Ibn Ishaq's account: 'Ubay-dullah ibn Jahsh. After Muhammad began his public preaching in Mecca, 'Ubaydullah embraced the Islamic faith and joined a group of Muslim emigrants who settled in East Africa. Thereafter "he adopted Christianity, parted from Islam, and died a Christian in Abyssinia [Ethiopia]."[10]

The third person in this circle of friends was named 'Uthman ibn al-Huwayrith. We are told that he "went to the Byzantine emperor and became a Christian. He was given high office there."[11]

The fourth, Zayd ibn 'Amr ibn Nufayl, underwent a particularly challenging odyssey: "Zayd ibn 'Amr stayed as he was: he accepted neither Judaism nor Christianity. He abandoned the religion of his people and abstained from idols ..., saying that he worshipped the God of Abraham.... Then he went forth seeking the religion of Abraham, questioning monks and rabbis until he had traversed al--Mausil and the whole of Mesopotamia."[12]

Although he never submitted to Muhammad's summons to Islam, Zayd preached in front of the Ka'ba ("O God, if I knew how You wished to be worshipped I would so worship You; but I do not know") and lingered on Mount Hira'—actions that would have been

[9] Ibid., p. 99.
[10] Ibid.
[11] Ibid.
[12] Ibid., pp. 99–103.

familiar to Muhammad himself. Zayd died as he had lived, a wanderer and a solo spiritual quester.

The lives of these four friends as described by Ibn Ishaq illustrate
the broader definition of what it means to be a hanif. One embraced
Islam; two became Christian; the fourth journeyed endlessly without
adopting a formal label. But all were Jahiliyah Arabs "seeking the
Hanifiya, the religion of Abraham".

I think it was in accord with this broader definition that Abu 'Amir
"the Monk" protested when Muhammad told him he did not qual-
ify for the title of hanif. After all, Abu 'Amir followed a monastic
life-style, engaged in ascetic discipline ("he wore coarse woolen fabric and sackcloth"), and embraced Christianity. But the prophet of
Islam said no, he did not make the grade. From Muhammad's point
of view, Abu 'Amir did not accept his preaching, did not become
Muslim, and thus did not rate the name hanif. And in any case, a
Medinan verse from the Koran (57:27) makes clear Muhammad's
disapproval of the kind of life followed by individuals such as Abu
'Amir: "Monasticism is something they devised for themselves as an
innovation; We did not prescribe it for them."

As a result, the two men came into open conflict with each other.
Abu 'Amir sided with the Meccans, fled with ten disciples from
Medina, and eventually settled into life as an exile in Christian Syria.

He was one of the lucky ones. Less fortunate were the three Jewish tribes of Medina. Like Ka'b ibn al-Ashraf, many of their leaders
apparently sided with the Meccans against Muhammad.

Once Muhammad consolidated his Meccan Muhajirs with the
Ansar of Medina into one unified Islamic *ummah*, he turned against
the Jews of his host city. Two of the tribes he expelled, plundering their lands and goods. The third, the Banu Qurayzah, became
the object of even harsher treatment. In 627, after an unsuccessful
attack by the Quraysh against Medina, Muhammad accused the Banu
Qurayzah of secretly supporting his enemies. The prophet ordered
his Muslims to surround the barricaded homes in which the Jews had
taken refuge.

After a twenty-five-day siege, they surrendered. The Koran
(33:26–27) alludes to what happened: "And as for those people of
the Book who had helped them [i.e., the Quraysh]: Allah took them
down from their fortified dwellings and cast terror into their hearts.

Some of them you killed; some you took prisoner. And so He made you heirs of their land, their homes, and their possessions."

"Some of them you killed": the early Muslim histories and scriptural commentaries provide additional detail concerning what befell the Jewish tribe of the Banu Qurayzah. Muhammad's followers beheaded all the men; the women and children were sold into slavery. The twentieth-century commentator 'Abdullah Yusuf 'Ali justifies this violence against the Banu Qurayzah by arguing that the Muslims "applied to them the Jewish law of the Old Testament", citing ancient campaigns of extermination described in the Bible.[13]

The same logic surfaced more recently—and much closer to home. In 2016 I obtained a copy of a textbook that instructors use at the South Bay Islamic Association in San Jose, California, for the purpose of introducing young American Muslims to Muhammad's life and exemplary accomplishments. This textbook deals succinctly with the fate of the Jews of the Banu Qurayzah: "After the battle, the Muslims decided to deal with Banu Qurayzah for their treachery.... Banu Qurayzah was punished according to Jewish law." The text is silent concerning the precise details of what the Muslims actually did with these Medinan prisoners. The student reader is given only two bits of data: the notion of "treachery" and of punishment "according to Jewish law".[14]

What I see at work in such argumentation is a clever rhetorical twist of the knife in seeking to justify this atrocity that was inflicted on the Jews (and I use the word atrocity deliberately, because that is precisely what the Muslims under Muhammad's command perpetrated). The implication is that the Banu Qurayzah adhered to the biblical tradition, and so they deserved the worst things that could be conjured from the biblical text.

But what is disturbing for me, in observing such behavior and such rationales, is the lack of mercy shown to these prisoners by Muhammad and his followers. I am aware, of course, of the historical-contextual defense offered by apologists. Watt (consistently ardent in

---

[13] 'Ali, *Meaning of the Holy Qur'an*, p. 1063; Ibn Ishaq, *Life of Muhammad*, 461–69; Suyuti, *Tafsir*, p. 553, commentary on Koran 33:26.

[14] Mansur Ahmad and Husain A. Nuri, *Islamic Studies: Level 5* (Columbus, Ohio: Weekend Learning, 2012), p. 36.

explaining away the prophet's behavior) lectures us on this point: "It has to be remembered, however, that in the Arabia of that day when tribes were at war with one another or simply had no agreement, they had no obligations towards one another, not even of what we would call common decency."[15]

True enough. But one would hope—or at least so it seems to me—that someone who repeatedly describes Allah as merciful and who believes himself to be Allah's prophet would in turn exert himself to show mercy toward defenseless prisoners of war. Instead, we are treated to the Koran's gloating spectacle of how Allah "cast terror into their hearts".

This is all the more important to note since twenty-first-century Sunni and Shia Muslims, regardless of their sectarian differences, all agree in regarding Muhammad as a moral exemplar whose behavior is to be imitated (a point to which we will return in subsequent chapters).

A theology of estrangement: Koranic depictions of Jews and Christians as practitioners of tahrif (scriptural distortion) and shirk (ascribing divine partners to Allah)

What I find fascinating and sad is how the Koran's *theological* depictions of Judaism and Christianity changed and darkened over the years as Muhammad's *political* relations worsened with the Jews and Christians of Medina.

The likes of Ka'b ibn al-Ashraf and Abu 'Amir the Monk had rejected Islam; Muhammad in turn rejected the religions to which they belonged. One very visible manifestation of this split was the change of *qiblah* from Jerusalem to Mecca, as we have seen.

But Islam's prophet went further. You will recall the Medinan verse (2:135) that asserts, "They say: 'Be a Jew or a Christian; you will be guided.' Say: 'No! I prefer the religion of Abraham the hanif! He was not one of those who associate divine partners with Allah.'" Such language seeks to sequester Abraham from the other two

---

[15] W. Montgomery Watt, *Muhammad: Prophet and Statesman* (New York: Oxford University Press, 1961), p. 173.

Abrahamic faiths. According to this argument, the only authentically monotheistic religion is that of Abraham the hanif; and that religion is Islam. The other faiths that claim Abraham have disqualified themselves because they have tried to "associate divine partners with Allah" (more on this allegation below).

This same Medinan chapter of the Koran further alienates Abraham from Judaism and Christianity by claiming that he and one of his sons initiated a unique construction project in the heart of the Arabian peninsula: "And behold! Abraham and Ishmael raised the foundations of the House, praying, 'Our Lord! Accept this from us. You are the one who hears, the all-knowing. Our Lord! Make us Muslims, submitting to You; and make our descendants a Muslim community, submitting to You'" (Koran 2:127–28).

The "House" in question, of course, is the Ka'ba; and what strikes me as remarkable—and curiously appropriate, given the geographic setting of this shrine—is the identity of Abraham's helper.

You will recall from the biblical Book of Genesis that Abraham fathers two sons: Isaac (whose mother was Sarah) and Ishmael (whose mother was Hagar, the Egyptian slave woman). Isaac is revered as the ancestor of the Hebrews and the Israelite nation; but from Ishmael (Isma'il, in the Arabic text of the Koran) descended the twelve tribes and "twelve princes" of Arabia (Gen 25:12–18). These descendants played a role in subsequent biblical history, as in the story of Joseph and his jealous brothers. When Joseph is sold into slavery, it is a "caravan of Ishmaelites" on their way to Egypt who purchase him (Gen 37:25–28).

Muhammad was certainly familiar with this tale. Chapter 12 of the Koran focuses on Joseph, and verses 19–21 mention the caravan that sold him into slavery in Egypt. This does not mean that Muhammad was necessarily influenced directly by the Book of Genesis. Numerous homilies and prose narratives about Joseph survive in Christian Syriac texts from the fourth and fifth centuries A.D., and some oral version of these stories may have reached Muhammad in his own youthful caravan travel before he began preaching Islam.[16]

---

[16] Joseph Witztum, "Joseph among the Ishmaelites: Q 12 in light of Syriac Sources", in *New Perspectives on the Qur'an: The Qur'an in Its Historical Context 2*, ed. Gabriel Said Reynolds (New York: Routledge, 2011), pp. 425–48.

Given Muhammad's familiarity with the tales of Abraham's off-spring, why does the Koran identify Ishmael rather than Isaac as co--builder of the Ka'ba? Here we have a good match between Ishmael, ancestor of the Arabs, and the most famous Jahiliyah shrine of the Arabian peninsula. In one stroke, Muhammad lays claim to the distinctively Arab strand of the Abrahamic legacy while entwining it with an Arabian religious monument that is independent of the Bible.

So far we have seen the use of ritual (shifting the *qiblah* from Jerusalem to Mecca) and story (Abraham and Ishmael as Muslims and partners in building the Ka'ba) to estrange Islam from the other Abrahamic traditions. But the Koran deploys theology as well—specifically, a pair of theological claims that are intended to finesse a conceptual challenge faced by Muhammad in Medina.

The conceptual challenge was as follows. From his early days in Mecca, Muhammad had been disenchanted with his own Jahiliyah tradition but strongly attracted to the values linked to Judaism and Christianity. This is symbolized, as you will remember, in the account of Muhammad listening wonderstruck to the sermons of the priest Quss ibn Sa'idah at the 'Ukaz fair. But some sixteen months into his stay in Medina, he also became frustrated with the people of the Book who failed to accept him as their prophetic messenger.

What to do? He wanted to spurn Medina's Christians and Jews; but clearly he did not want to abandon the attractive doctrines to which they laid claim—monotheism, personal moral accountability, heaven and hell. Out of this nettle, disillusion, he wished to pluck the flower of Abrahamic tawhid. The way he accomplished this was via an accusation known as *tahrif* (corruption, distortion). The following Medinan verses (Koran 2:75, 101) demonstrate what is meant by this accusation:

> Can you possibly hope that they will believe in you, considering that a group of them in the past heard the word of Allah, understood it, and then deliberately and knowingly distorted and corrupted it? . . . And when a messenger from Allah came to them, confirming what was with them, a group from among the people of the Book threw away the Book of Allah behind their backs, as if they had no knowledge!

The theological implication of these verses is as follows. We have already examined the idea of the "chain of the prophets". That is, because of our recurrent human tendency to forget our obligation to submit to Allah and accept Islam, throughout history He has sent us prophets to warn us to become Muslims before it is too late. All of these prophets—Noah, Abraham, Lot, and so on—were Muslims. Certain of these messengers—most notably Moses and Jesus—were also entrusted with scriptural revelations that they were then commanded to share with their people, just as was the case with Muhammad, the last in this chain of prophets.

According to Islamic theology, unto Moses was revealed the Torah, and some at least of his followers were faithful Muslims. But the story of the golden calf (the Koranic version of this narrative can be found in surah 20:80–97) represents how the Israelites fell away from tawhidic monotheism into idol worship. The Torah that Moses conveyed to his people reflected perfectly the pure teachings contained in the "preserved tablet" that has existed from before all time in heaven; but the people of Israel distorted this Islamic Torah just as they distorted monotheistic worship by creating a golden calf.

This necessitated Allah's dispatching of another messenger with another iteration of the tawhidic teachings preserved in the heavenly tablet. So the Muslim prophet Jesus was sent to the Jews, and unto him was revealed the Gospel (the Arabic term that appears in the Koran is "Injil", which is a loanword derived from the Greek *Evangelion*, or "good news"). Jesus' original followers, the apostles (who are mentioned collectively in the Koran, although not individually by name), were good disciples, according to surah 3:52: "When Jesus perceived unbelief among them [that is, the Jews], he said, 'Who will be my Ansar [helpers, supporters] to help achieve Allah's victory?' The apostles replied, 'We are Allah's Ansar. We believe in Allah, so give witness that we are Muslims.'"

The word Ansar is resonant, since it is also the term used to describe those residents of Medina who supported Muhammad and became Muslim. Here we have a blending of ancient past and Medinan present.

The content of the Injil revealed to Jesus was—as was the case with Moses' Torah—supposedly identical to the contents of the eternal tablet residing with Allah in heaven. But over time, Jesus' faithful followers distorted and corrupted this scriptural message, introducing notions such as trinity, incarnation, and crucifixion (as will be seen in the next chapter). In short, these followers degenerated into Christians.

This *tahrif*-doctrine of scriptural distortion was useful on several counts. First, it explained away any discrepancy between the Bible and the Koran. Second, it showed how the "people of the Book" (a term originally intended as a compliment to indicate that the Jews and Christians ranked higher than Jahiliyah pagans because they had originally been entrusted with authentic scriptures) had failed in their scriptural trust. And third, it provided a theological justification for Muhammad's political estrangement from the Jews and Christians of Medina.

In addition to *tahrif*, Muhammad also deployed against his erstwhile Abrahamic peers another theological accusation that justified this political breach: *shirk* (the sin of ascribing divine partners to Allah). We have seen this word before. During his time in Mecca, Muhammad used the term to denounce the polytheists who gave divine honors to the triad of Allah's daughters. But in the Medinan period, after his rupture with the city's uncooperative Jews and Christians, Muhammad offered this indictment (surah 9:30–31):

> The Jews call Ezra "son of Allah", and the Christians call Christ "son of Allah". That is what comes out of their mouths! What they say resembles the talk of those who were unbelievers in ancient times. May Allah curse them! How they have been led into lies! They consider their rabbis and their monks to be divine lords at the expense of Allah; and they make the same claim with regard to Christ, the son of Mary. And yet they were ordered to worship no one except one sole God. There is no god except Him. May He be glorified and exalted far beyond the partners they associate with Him (*'amma yushrikuna*)!

It is unsurprising that the Koran speaks so harshly of Christian belief: doctrines concerning the Trinity and Jesus as the Son of God could easily lead to a charge of *shirk* by someone who had only a glancing acquaintance with Christian theology. Skeptics have launched similar attacks for centuries.

Much more startling, however, is that the Koran lumps Judaism together with Christianity in making this charge, and it does so by claiming that "the Jews call Ezra 'son of Allah'." Judaism, after all, is just as strict as Islam in its monotheistic doctrines (a point to be developed when we explore Christological statements in Paul's epistles and the four Gospels). And anyone familiar with Jewish belief will be aware that its adherents do not ascribe to Ezra, or to any other human, a status comparable to that assigned to Jesus by Christians. So what is going on in this passage of the Koran?

To reconstruct Muhammad's polemic, we will need to review Ezra's role in ancient Jewish history. The Bible describes him as both a priest and "a scribe skilled in the law of Moses" (Ezra 7:6). He lived in Babylon during the Exile after Nebuchadnezzar's army destroyed the kingdom of Judah and ravaged the capital and Solomon's Temple: "They burned the house of God, and broke down the wall of Jerusalem, and burned all its palaces with fire, and destroyed all its precious vessels" (2 Chron 36:19). The Babylonian monarch led away thousands of Jews into captivity in Iraq.

But the Babylonians in turn were overthrown by the Persians under the shah Cyrus. The Persian Empire instituted a policy of keeping order in its many provinces by allowing subject populations limited political autonomy and a relative degree of freedom in observing their own local religious customs and laws.

It was in keeping with this imperial policy that in the fifth century B.C., one of Cyrus' successors, the shah Artaxerxes, authorized Ezra the scribe to bring large numbers of Babylonian Jews to the land of Judea in order to rebuild Jerusalem and reestablish the region as a Jewish homeland. Artaxerxes also authorized Ezra to promulgate the Torah as the law of the land for all Jews living in the provinces of the Persian Empire.

The Old Testament reproduces the text of the letter of authorization in which the shah addressed the Jewish scribe: "And you, Ezra, according to the wisdom of your God which is in your hand, appoint magistrates and judges who may judge all the people in the province Beyond the River, all such as know the laws of your God; and those who do not know them, you shall teach" (Ezra 7:25).

The Bible tells us how, under the leadership of the Jewish governor Nehemiah, the newly released population rebuilt the walls and gates of shattered Jerusalem. Thereafter we are told in detail of the day on which Ezra proclaimed the Torah as the binding code of conduct for all who identified themselves with the Jewish faith:

And when the seventh month had come, the children of Israel were in their towns. And all the people gathered as one man into the square before the Water Gate [beside the walls of Jerusalem]; and they told Ezra the scribe to bring the book of the law of Moses which the LORD had given to Israel. And Ezra the priest brought the law before the assembly, both men and women and all who could hear with under-standing.... And Ezra the scribe stood on a wooden pulpit which they had made for the purpose.... And Ezra opened the book in the sight of all the people, for he was above all the people; and when he opened it all the people stood. And Ezra blessed the LORD, the great God; and all the people answered, "Amen, Amen," lifting up their hands.... Also Jeshua, Bani,... Pelaiah, the Levites, helped the people to under-stand the law, while the people remained in their places. And they read from the book, from the law of God, clearly; and they gave the sense, so that the people understood the reading. (Neh 8:1–8)

This act of interpretation was vital to the success of what Ezra and his peers were attempting. Much of the Jewish population at that time spoke Aramaic, the lingua franca in many of the provinces of Persia's Achaemenid dynasty, whereas the language of the biblical Torah was Hebrew, a classical tongue beyond the comprehension of the untutored. So scriptural authorities such as Ezra were on hand to provide a translation and commentary.

The subsequent biblical verses evoke the drama and emotional intensity of this moment:

And Nehemiah, who was the governor, and Ezra the priest and scribe, and the Levites who taught the people said to all the people, "This day is holy to the LORD your God; do not mourn or weep." For all the people wept when they heard the words of the law. Then he said to them, "... Do not be grieved, for the joy of the LORD is your strength." ... And all the people went their way ... to make great rejoicing. (Neh 8:9–12)

Thus, biblical tradition credited Ezra with a leading role in pro-mulgating, teaching, and thereby preserving the Torah of Moses among the newly repatriated exile community in and around Jeru-salem. And it was precisely the commandments, ethical values, and ritual observances encoded in this scripture that helped ensure com-munal survival for the Jews under centuries of foreign domination.

So it is understandable that the scribe Ezra was honored by suc-
ceeding generations for safeguarding Jewish collective identity—
though if he was in fact ever called a "son of God", it was surely not
in the sense intended by any Christian understanding of the phrase.

A legendary version of this historical event is preserved in Baydawi's fourteenth-century commentary on the relevant verses from
the Koran:

> "And the Jews say Ezra is the son of Allah": This was said by some
> of their ancestors or some of those who were in Medina. They said
> this because after the devastation of the time of Nebuchadnezzar, no
> one remained who had preserved the Torah in memory. When Allah
> brought Ezra back to life after a hundred years, he dictated the Torah
> to them from memory. They marveled at this and said, "This can only
> be because he is the son of Allah!"[17]

With the exception of this complaint regarding Ezra, the Koran
has relatively few theological arguments to make against Judaism,
aside from the passing complaint about rabbis being venerated as lords
"at the expense of Allah". But here the gripe is basically political in
nature. Muhammad disapproved in general of any form of priesthood
or ecclesiastical hierarchy that might compete with his own preferred
form of theocracy: Allah imparts commands directly to His prophet,
who in turn imparts these commands to His people, without recourse
to any intermediary—or rival—religious authorities.

As you might imagine, the Koran has a larger stock of theological
indictments against Christianity than against Judaism, especially with
regard to the sin of *shirk*. Here is a Medinan verse (5:72) that targets
Christians directly: "Those who say that Allah is Christ, the son of
Mary, are guilty of unbelief (*la-qad kafara*). But Christ said, 'O sons of
Israel! Worship Allah, my Lord and your Lord.' If anyone associates
divine partners with Allah (*man yushrik bi-llah*), then Allah will forbid
him the Garden, and his place of abode will be the Fire."

There will be more about Koranic Christology for us to explore
in the next chapter. For now, let's simply note that according to
the verses we have just read, both Jews and (especially) Christians
are *mushrikun* (those guilty of *shirk*). We have already come across

---

[17] Baydawi, *Anwar*, 1:402, commentary on Koran 9:30.

one Medinan verse (4:48) that warns infidels how serious a sin *shirk* is. Here is another (4:116) that repeats the warning with some variation in wording: "Allah will not forgive it if divine partners are ascribed to Him. He will forgive anything other than that to anyone He wishes. Anyone who associates partners with Allah has strayed and in fact gone very far astray (*wa-man yushrik bi-llah fa-qad dalla dalalan ba'idan*)."

The repetitive use of stray/astray (*dalla/dalalan*) is reminiscent of the most prominent verse in the Koran where this same verbal root occurs: the Fatihah, chapter 1 of the Koran, which forms the basis of daily ritual prayer in Islam. We encountered it earlier; it concludes with this plea to Allah: "Guide us along the straight path, the path of those You have blessed, not of those who are the object of Your anger, nor of those who go astray (*wa-la al-dallin*)." Suyuti's commentary offers the following explanation: "'Those who are the object of Your anger': These are the Jews.... 'Those who go astray': These are the Christians."[18]

Jihad sermons, sword verses, Bengal lancers: Dealing with scriptural assaults in an age of terror

Guilty of *shirk*; denied forgiveness; irredeemably astray: for Jews and Christians, grim prospects for the afterlife. But the penalties and punishments also pertain to the present life as well. Consider surah 9:5: "When the sacred months are past, kill those who ascribe divine partners to Allah (*al-mushrikin*) wherever you find them. Seize them, and besiege them, and lie in wait for them in every place of ambush."

This is one of the Koran's notorious *ayat al-sayf* (sword verses), divine commands to slay infidels. Apologists have tried to soften the impact of such words, often by reminding readers of the Koran's historical context. For example, Sheikh Jamal Rahman, member of an interfaith dialogue group that has been meeting at intervals since the 9/11 Islamic terrorist attacks, says with regard to another of these sword verses, surah 2:191 ("Slay them wherever you find them"): "This 7th century revelation came at a time when the Islamic

---

[18] Suyuti, *Tafsir*, p. 2, commentary on Koran 1:7.

community in Arabia was a tiny embryonic group in Medina under constant attack by the Quraiysh tribe and their allies."[19]

One could additionally note that surah 9:5, immediately after ordering believers to kill *mushrikin* wherever they find them, also tells Muslims to relent if the infidels "repent, observe the salat [the mandatory five-times-a day prayer], and pay the zakat [charity tax]". Baydawi's commentary on this verse clarifies what is meant here by "repent": "Repent for having committed *shirk* with regard to the faith."[20] So, in other words, in light of the reality that salat and zakat are mandatory for all Muslims, this verse effectively commands the following: kill, seize, and ambush the *mushrikin* until they abandon *shirk* and embrace Islam.

Sword verse 9:5 and 9:30–31 (the pronouncements cursing Jews and Christians as *mushrikin*) belong to what Muslim scholars regard as one of the very last Koranic revelations received by Muhammad. You might recall the exegetical principle we encountered before—in the context of the satanic verses—known as *al-nasikh wa-al-mansukh* (that which cancels and that which is canceled). This means that wherever Koranic revelations appear to contradict each other, the chronologically later passage "cancels" or takes precedence over verses that came earlier in Muhammad's prophetic career.

So with Muhammad's utterance of surah 9, we are a long way from the reassuringly feel-good quality of chronologically earlier verses such as 2:62, where Christians and Jews are grouped with Muslim believers as those who will receive their reward from Allah and who will neither grieve nor sorrow. Instead, surah 9 plucks Jews and Christians from among the believers and lumps them together with the pagans of Mecca as accursed *mushriks*—those whose sins will never be forgiven.

Given the fact that surah 9 classifies Jews and Christians as *mushriks* and that the same chapter also commands believers to slay *mushriks* "wherever you find them", it is not surprising that sword verse 9:5 has been used at various points in history as a rallying cry to initiate jihad against populations associated with the people of the Book.

---

[19] Jamal Rahman, "Making Peace with the Sword Verse", http://www.yesmagazine.org /blogs/interfaith-amigos.

[20] Baydawi, *Anwar*, 1:396, commentary on Koran 9:5.

An example can be found in the memoirs of Francis Yeats-Brown, who, in the days of British India, served as an officer with a Bengal lancer regiment on the Afghan-Indian frontier. Yeats-Brown tells of his arrival as a nineteen-year-old second lieutenant at the garrison of Bannu in the year 1905. He received a fast introduction to the threat posed by Muslim *mujahideen*:

> My companion loaded his revolver; for there was a Garrison Order that we were always to be armed near cantonments, he told me. A fanatic had recently murdered our Brigade Major.
>
> At the city walls stood a sentry with fixed bayonet. He opened a barbed wire gate for us, and we drove on to the house where my regiment and two battalions of the Frontier Force Infantry messed together....
>
> At dinner that night I sat between the Adjutant and an elderly Infantry Major.... The port and madeira described constant ellipses over the long mess table, and the elderly Major helped himself at each round.
>
> I questioned the Adjutant about *ghazis* [warriors engaged on a "ghazwah", or raid, in the name of the Islamic faith]. He told me that a certain Mullah of the Powindahs was preaching to the tribesmen from the fateful 5th verse of the 9th chapter of the Koran: "And when the sacred months are past, kill those who join other gods with God wherever ye shall find them; and seize them and slay them and [lie] in wait for them with every kind of ambush."
>
> The murder of the Brigade Major had been a bad business. The *ghazi* hid in some crops at the roadside, waiting for the General, presumably, who was leading a new battalion into cantonments. The General had dropped behind for a moment, so the Brigade Major, who was riding at the head of the troops, received the load of buckshot intended for his chief. It hit him in the kidneys and killed him instantly. The *ghazi* tried to bolt, but was brought down wounded in the crops by a Sikh sergeant.[21]

That was over a century ago. Yet it also feels like just yesterday, doesn't it, in light of the wave of twenty-first-century jihadist events?

For a much more recent example of the sword verse as a weapon of holy war, we have only to consult the *fatwa* issued in February

[21] Francis Yeats-Brown, *The Lives of a Bengal Lancer* (New York: Bantam, 1946), pp. 6–7.

1998 by Osama bin Laden to provide the justification for al-Qaeda's ongoing terror attacks on the West. It is entitled "The World Islamic Front's Declaration to Wage Jihad against the Jews and Crusaders". Here are key passages in the decree as translated by the historian Raymond Ibrahim:

> Praise be to Allah, who revealed the Book [Koran], controls the clouds, defeats factionalism, and says in His Book: "Then, when the sacred months have passed, slay the idolaters [al-mushrikin] wherever you find them—seize them, besiege them, and be ready to ambush them" [9:5]. And prayers and peace be upon our Prophet, Muhammad bin Abdullah, who said: "I have been sent with the sword between my hands to ensure that no one but Allah is worshipped"....
>
> On that basis, and in compliance with Allah's order, we hereby issue the following decree to all Muslims:
>
> The ruling to kill the Americans and their allies—civilians and military—is an individual obligation incumbent upon every Muslim who can do it and in any country.[22]

For anyone who remembers September 11—smoking Towers, the Pentagon aflame, the struggle on Flight 93—this sword verse opens old wounds: a dagger to the heart.

Death of a goddess: Crushing paganism, chopping trees

With Medina as the capital of his new *ummah*, Muhammad fought for some eight years against his various enemies—both the Meccan Quraysh and the uncooperative Jews and Christians of Medina, whom (as we have seen) he eventually classified with the pagans as accursed *mushriks*. Meccans who attacked Medina were defeated in battle; Jews who resisted were expelled, enslaved, or beheaded; Christians, like the monk Abu 'Amir, fled—if they were lucky—to Syria.

Finally, in January of the year 630, a mere eight years after the hijrah, Muhammad amassed an army of ten thousand believers and conquered Mecca. Apologists have hailed the conquest as largely

---

[22] Text in Raymond Ibrahim, ed. and trans., *The Al Qaeda Reader* (New York: Broadway Books, 2007), pp. 11, 13.

bloodless. No more than two or three dozen combatants were killed in the conflict.[23]

But—as we learned earlier—the prophet of Islam, as he prepared to enter the city, also ordered the retaliatory killing of various individuals who had mocked and defied him or sung satirical songs about him. He was well aware that some targets of his wrath might try to take refuge at the Ka'ba, which for centuries had been venerated as a sanctuary where the prosecution of feuds and indulgence in other forms of violence were prohibited. The Koran itself (2:125, 3:97) announced its respect for this ancient custom of forbidding bloodshed at the Ka'ba: "Recall that We made the House a gathering place and a place of safety for people.... Whoever enters it is safe."

But on the day of conquest, Muhammad had little patience for such distinctions. "The apostle had instructed his commanders when they entered Mecca", Ibn Ishaq informs us, "only to fight those who resisted them, except a small number who were to be killed even if they were found beneath the curtains of the Ka'ba." Among those on the hit-list were 'Abdullah ibn Khatal, an ex-Muslim accused of murder, and his two singing girls, "who used to sing satirical songs about the apostle". As a result, Muhammad added them to the list: "He ordered that they should be killed with him."[24]

The biographer Ibn Kathir tells us what happened. Accompanied by his triumphant Muslims, the prophet entered Mecca, "riding a camel and reciting the surah of Victory [chapter 48 of the Koran]". In the midst of this celebratory entrance, "A man came up to him and said, 'Ibn Khatal is clinging to the curtains of the Ka'ba!' He [Muhammad] replied, 'Kill him.'" Which his followers did, the sanctity of this ancient place of refuge notwithstanding.[25]

His conquest complete, the prophet ordered that the site be purified. His followers gathered up the 360 tribal idols that had surrounded the Ka'ba, broke them, smashed them into pieces, and cast them into a fire.

But Muhammad was not finished with his iconoclasm. His mind was on al-'Uzza, one of Allah's three daughters, venerated in association with the planet Venus, whom he had worshipped years ago by

[23] Watt, *Muhammad*, 204–5; Ingrid Mattson, *The Story of the Qur'an: Its History and Place in Muslim Life* (Oxford: Blackwell, 2008), pp. 66–67.

[24] Ibn Ishaq, *Life of Muhammad*, pp. 550–51.

[25] Ibn Kathir, *al-Sirah al-nabawiyyah*, 2:181–82.

consecrating to her an animal sacrifice. Her shrine was near Mecca, at a place called Nakhlah.

At once he dispatched one of his lieutenants, Khalid ibn al-Walid, together with a group of fighters, with orders to destroy the site at Nakhlah. The ninth-century Muslim scholar of Jahiliyah customs, Ibn al-Kalbi, provides a description of this sacred place and what happened when Khalid arrived on his mission of destruction.

"Al-'Uzza", Ibn al-Kalbi tells us, "was a female Satan (*shaytanah*) that used to come and go, inhabiting three acacia trees in the valley of Nakhlah. Now when the prophet conquered Mecca, he sent forth Khalid ibn al-Walid, saying to him, 'Go to the valley of Nakhlah. There you will find three acacia trees.'" Muhammad ordered him to cut down each of these trees in succession.

Khalid followed his orders. Nothing extraordinary happened when he and his men felled the first two trees. But when he was about to cut the third, "suddenly an Abyssinian woman appeared, her hair wild and disordered, her hands on her shoulders, gnashing her teeth." Ibn Kathir, who also tells this story, describes her as "a black woman, her hair wild and unruly. She was howling and wailing.... She was naked."[26]

Khalid let nothing deter him: "He struck her and split her skull asunder. And behold!: she was nothing but ashes. Then he cut down the tree and killed Dubyatah, the custodian of the shrine. Thereafter he went to the prophet and gave him his report. The prophet said, 'That was al-'Uzza, the Mighty One, and there will be no mighty one after her for the Bedouins! After today she will never be worshipped again.'"[27]

I am confident you will agree with me: these accounts are fascinating and also disturbing. A foreign Abyssinian, a woman, naked and black, her hair unruly and wild: here was a symbolic antithesis of the carefully regimented patriarchal order these men meant to impose on their world.

Also of interest is that al-'Uzza is described here as *shaytanah*, "a female Satan". And "satans" is one term used repeatedly in the Koran, as we have seen, to describe jinns that lead men into sin.

[26] Abu Mundhir Hisham ibn Muhammad ibn al-Kalbi, *Kitab al-asnam*, ed. Ahmed Zeki Pacha (Cairo: Imprimerie Nationale, 1914), pp. 25–26; Ibn Kathir, *al-Sirah al-nabawiyyah*, pp. 204–5. Translated by D. Pinault.

[27] Ibn al-Kalbi, *Kitab al-asnam*, p. 26.

But—and here I will draw on my own perspective—reading about this wretched raid was an unsettling experience. Partly because of the gloomy spectacle as I sat at my desk, translating these Arabic texts, envisioning the scene: a trio of divine acacias, an ancient sacred site, cut down along with the priest—and the goddess—who once guarded the place.

But also because of personal memories. I have visited many localities in Indonesia—forests, villages, pilgrimage shrines, places I have loved—where local inhabitants, both Muslim and non-Muslim, venerate *penunggu* ("watchmen", resident nature spirits) that are said to take up their dwelling in trees that receive offerings and veneration from nearby populations.

But lately a worrisome trend has been at work. Such forms of nature worship and tree-rooted religion have recently begun to be denounced—as we will see in a subsequent chapter—by Islamist preachers who want to "purify" Indonesia. They are dead-set on extirpating from their nation any traces of Southeast Asia's pre-- Islamic Jahiliyah.

Jihad, expansion, endless conquest: Dealing with Jews, Christians, and kuffar

Even before completing his conquest of Mecca, Muhammad had begun expansionist military campaigns against the territory of the Christian Byzantine Empire. In September 629 he commissioned his adopted son Zayd ibn Harithah to lead an expedition of three thousand Muslims against the city of Busra in southern Syria. But at the village of Mu'ta, near the shores of the Dead Sea, they were intercepted by a combined force of Greek soldiers and Christian Arab tribesmen.

Seeing they were outnumbered, the Muslims hesitated to launch an attack, but 'Abd Allah ibn Rawaha, one of Zayd's lieutenants, spurred them on with these words: "Men, what you dislike is that which you have come out in search of, namely, martyrdom. We are not fighting the enemy with numbers or strength or multitude, but we are confronting them with this religion with which God has honored us." So they charged and were defeated by the Byzantines. Zayd was killed in the battle, along with 'Abd Allah and another lieutenant, Ja'far ibn Abi Talib.

When Muhammad heard of this defeat, he claimed he had just had an afterlife glimpse of Ja'far's soul: "Ja'far went by yesterday with a company of angels making for Bisha in the Yemen. He had two wings whose fore-feathers were stained with blood"—a mark of Ja'far's status as a *mujahid*-martyr guaranteed Paradise.[28]

In October 630, shortly after consolidating control over Mecca and the surrounding region in the Hejaz, the prophet launched his last major military campaign, this time against Byzantine territory in the region around the oasis town of Tabuk, not far from the Gulf of Aqaba, near the present-day boundary between Jordan and Saudi Arabia. He assembled an army of 30,000 Muslims.

But at least some conflict-weary believers preferred to stay home rather than launch a new war against foreign realms. It is the stay-at--home Muslims who refused to join the march against Tabuk who are chastised in surah 9:81–82:

> Those who were left behind have been rejoicing in the fact that they have been sitting this one out against the wishes of Allah's prophet. They hated the idea of striving in jihad in the path of Allah with their worldly goods and their souls. They have been saying, "Do not hurry forth in the heat!" Say [in reply]: "The fire of Gehenna is a lot fiercer in heat!" If only they understood! So let them get in a little bit of a laugh now. They will be doing a lot of weeping later. That will be the reward they have earned!

After so many years of jihad, it is understandable that many of Muhammad's men lacked enthusiasm for the quest to seek out new enemies. But the prophet wanted to keep the aggressive energies of his freshly founded state firmly focused outward—against non--Muslims who declined to submit to Islam. Such defiance could then be labeled justification enough for the *ummah* to declare a campaign of holy war.

These jihad campaigns entailed a two-tiered system for how to deal with subjugated populations. Those who were labeled kuffar

---

[28] Ibn Ishaq, *Life of Muhammad*, pp. 531–35.

(the plural of kafir: pagan unbelievers) faced a harsh choice: convert or be killed. People of the Book (Jews and Christians) were treated more leniently. They had permission to retain their faith as long as they acknowledged the authority of the Islamic State and paid the jizyah (an annual discriminatory tax, generally assessed at a far higher rate than the zakat, or compulsory almsgiving mandated for Muslims).

Worth emphasizing here is that the jizyah has never been simply a financial transaction but is also meant to penalize Jews and Christians socially for their willful stubbornness in refusing to embrace Islam. As surah 9:29 stipulates, Muslims are to "fight against those from among the people of the Book who do not accept the religion of truth, until they pay the jizyah submissively and feel themselves humiliated and made small."

The experience of paying the jizyah and enduring life as second-class citizens is not merely a historical datum from bygone times. It is very much part of our twenty-first century, as can be attested by non-Muslims living under Taliban rule in Afghanistan or the Islamic State's caliphate in Syria and Iraq.

Are Jews and Christians kuffar? Lessons from a California mosque

Given the sharply drawn distinctions described above—people of the Book are allowed to retain their religious identities under Islamic rule, whereas kuffar cannot—it might strike you as unlikely that the categories would get blurred. But I assure you it happens. I myself have occasionally had the experience—in venues as varied as the Indonesian island of Java and Pakistan's North-West Frontier Province—of individuals accosting me and referring to me as a kafir. Muslim friends who have been with me on such occasions have hurried to my defense with words to the effect of "Leave him alone. He's a Christian!" They have understood that calling someone a pagan infidel is an insult that can metastasize into confrontations of a most unpleasant kind.

Once, such an accusation came wrapped in a theological rationale. It happened in 1983, when I was studying Arabic in Cairo. One morning, while shopping for vegetables in the Bab al-Luq neighborhood, I made the acquaintance of a seminary student from al-Azhar University. The conversation went pleasantly enough until he asked whether I was Muslim or studying Arabic so as to prepare for becoming a Muslim. I answered no on both counts, and then, under further questioning, pleaded guilty to being a Christian.

"Christian; kafir; no difference", he pronounced, and then proceeded to justify the allegation with a verse from the Koran (one we have seen before, 5:72): "Those who say that Allah is Christ, the son of Mary, are guilty of unbelief (la-qad kafara)." To deify Christ the way Christians do, he told me by way of summary, is to be guilty of unbelief, just as the holy Koran says; and to be guilty of unbelief is to be a kafir. End of story.

I thanked him for his insights, paid for my veggies, and beat a quick retreat.

But I have also seen this blurring of Christian/kafir distinctions in settings closer to home. It happened once at a mosque in Santa Clara, California, only a few miles from the university where I teach; and it involved an individual whose name you might recognize: Anwar al--Awlaki. He is the American preacher whose sermons inspired some of the 9/11 hijackers as well as the Muslim militants responsible for terrorist attacks in Orlando, San Bernardino, and the Boston Marathon. Awlaki's work was interrupted in September 2011 when he was killed in Yemen by a U.S. Hellfire missile.

Interrupted, but not terminated. Thanks to sermons still circulating on YouTube and other Internet sites, Awlaki continues even in death to wield influence in cyberspace. Ahmad Khan Rahami, an Afghan-born immigrant charged in September 2016 with setting off homemade bombs in New York and New Jersey, "allegedly wrote that his guidance came from radical jihadist cleric Anwar al-Awlaki, who 'said it clearly: attack the kuffar in their backyard.'"[29]

Awlaki has also been cited as an inspiration by Major Nidal Malik Hasan, indicted as the self-confessed shooter who opened fire at fellow soldiers at Fort Hood. Hasan has referred to Awlaki as his "teacher, mentor and friend", adding, "I hold him in high esteem for trying to educate Muslims about their duties to Allah." Immediately after the Fort Hood killings, Awlaki, while in hiding in Yemen, praised Hasan as "a hero" and "a man of conscience".[30]

---

[29] Devlin Barrett and Pervaiz Shallwani, "Terrorism Charges for Bomb Suspect", *The Wall Street Journal*, September 21, 2016, pp. A1–A2.

[30] Daniel Greenfield, "Nidal Hasan on Anwar al-Awlaki," *Front Page Magazine*, August 1, 2013, http://www.frontpagemag.com.

But it was not only in Yemen that Awlaki set about his militant agenda of "trying to educate Muslims". While in America, he delivered similar messages at mosques in our country. I know, because I saw him preach one day at a mosque in Santa Clara called the Muslim Community Association. This was in the fall of 2002, before Anwar al-Awlaki became known as an ideologue of terror.

As mentioned in a previous chapter, since I happen to be a Christian whose area of research is Islamic studies, I take a particular approach in teaching courses on Islam: I look for ways to blend my own take on Islam as a non-Muslim with the views of Muslim insiders.

That is why I arrange field trips: I go with my students to visit local mosques—Sunni, Shia, Sufi—located near our campus. The students witness Friday prayers and interview practitioners who follow various denominations of Islam. We are greeted with hospitality; we are often offered food. (Such offerings are part of the da'wah-evangelizing come-on that is presented by Muslim missionaries. More on that later.) Despite the proselytizing, the experience is usually positive.

Usually, but not always.

On the day we attended services at the Muslim Community Association, my undergraduates filed as usual into their gender-segregated spaces. The female students sat at the rear of the building in the women's section; the male students and I sat at the very back of the men's section, in a hall that was filled with over a thousand worshippers.

Two of the young men in my course were Muslim—one Kuwaiti, the other Egyptian—and as they sat beside me in the crowded room, they confided to me how happy and excited they were that their classmates would get to experience Islamic practice firsthand.

Their happiness did not last long.

From the back I could not see the preacher well. He was young, bearded, and wore glasses. A guest speaker, the manager had told me: an American of Yemeni descent, named Awlaki. Not a regular at the mosque.

The preacher caught my attention at once when he announced his theme: Avoid the kuffar. My students knew this Arabic word because we had discussed it in class: "unbelievers"; "infidels". Progressive--minded Muslims do not use this term for Jews or Christians, referring to them instead as *ahl al-kitab*, "people of the Book", individuals who have in common with Muslims a shared reverence for Abraham as a distinguished spiritual ancestor.

Awlaki made clear he was having none of this. He began by condemning the Reverend Jerry Vines and Franklin Graham for their criticisms of Islam and the prophet Muhammad. "But when you spit at the sky," he warned, "the spit just falls back on your face", saying that their verbal attacks could never hurt the faith. The longer he preached, the angrier he got. My students, seated on the floor beside me, shifted and began to look uncomfortable.

They became even more uncomfortable as Awlaki warned the congregation that such attacks by Christians should remind the faithful of the Koran's injunction (from surah 5:51), "O you who believe! Do not take the Jews and Christians as friends." All Americans who are non-Muslim—Jew, Christian, it does not matter—are kuffar and must be avoided. All persons who are truly faithful—by now Awlaki was shouting as he concluded his sermon—should be loyal, not to America or any other country, but only to the *ummah*, the global community of Islam.

That did it. As soon as the service ended, my two Muslim students complained to the management, saying that this preacher, whoever he was, had done a real disservice to Islam and to the chance for positive relations with members of other faiths.

Something good came out of this. The next time my students and I met, we had our liveliest discussion of the quarter, as students argued over Awlaki's points and anxiously searched out the various Koran verses that advocate peace and that speak positively of Jews and Christians who "do works of righteousness".

If nothing else, this militant's sermon reminded all of us that the theological points we study in the classroom make a real and visceral difference in the world at large. Educational help can come even from unexpected sources—even hostile ones that denounce fellow Americans as infidel kuffar.

A glimpse of the True Cross—and a hint of holy wars to come

Before concluding this chapter, I want to share with you an incident from the year 630—the same year as Muhammad's conquest of Mecca and his last expedition against the Greeks of Byzantium, before his death in 632. Ibn Ishaq, the prophet's biographer, tells us that as warfare wound down between the Muslims and the pagan

Quraysh, a group of Meccan merchants set out for Syria, hoping to take advantage of this interval of peace to renew business ties in Syria. And this is what they reported concerning the Byzantine emperor:

> We got there when Heraclius had conquered the Persians who were in his territory and driven them out and recaptured from them his great cross which they had plundered. When he had thus got the better of them and heard that his cross had been recovered, he came out from [the city of] Hims, which was his headquarters, walking on foot in thanks to God for what He had restored to him, so that he could pray in the holy city. Carpets were spread for him and aromatic herbs were thrown on them. When he came to Aelia [Jerusalem] and had finished praying there with his patricians and the Roman nobles he became sorrowful, turning his eyes to heaven; and his patricians said, "You have become very sorrowful this morning, O king."[31]

Ibn Ishaq then goes on to explain the cause of this sorrow: the Christian emperor, "in a vision of the night", had glimpsed the kingdom of a mysterious and unknown "circumcised man" who would become victorious. And immediately after voicing his sorrow, Heraclius is provided the glimmering of an explanation. A messenger appears, "from the Arabs, people of sheep and camels". He tells the emperor of a great prophet who has arisen and who has lately succeeded in attracting a large following of believers.[32]

Pious Muslim readers of Ibn Ishaq would understand at once the point of this hagiographic Islamic legend. At the very height of the Byzantine emperor's triumph—after decades of war, after having recaptured the relic of the Cross on which Jesus himself had been crucified—at this very moment, Heraclius is presented as suddenly realizing that his newly recaptured Jerusalem and the whole Byzantine province of Syria will soon fall to the newly emergent forces of an Arab prophet.

Fascinating, to catch a glimpse of the True Cross in this early Islamic biographical text. In a subsequent chapter, we will glimpse the Cross again and see it become the object of both devotion and dishonor, as we venture into the time of the Crusades.

---

[31] Ibn Ishaq, *Life of Muhammad*, p. 654.
[32] Ibid., pp. 654–55.

CHAPTER 6

SPEECH FROM THE CRADLE, BIRDS MADE FROM CLAY: CHRIST IN THE KORAN

Jesus in Islamic and Christian scriptures: (Deceptive) similarities and (significant) differences

In attempts to motivate Christians to embrace the Muslim faith, *da'wah* (Islamic missionary) writings often emphasize points of convergence between Christianity and Islam with regard to Jesus. Thus, among the "sample *da'wah* handouts" in a book entitled *How to Tell Others about Islam* is a pamphlet-style essay called "Who Was Jesus?" Among the things this Islamic pamphlet tells Christian readers is that Jesus "healed the sick, enheartened the distressed and revived those thought dead.... He led a simple and pious life. Soon he attracted an inner circle of devoted followers who listened to his teachings with fervor and humility."[1]

All this sounds comfortingly familiar for potential converts. But what seem to be points of convergence can prove to be misleading.

It is true of course that Islamic scripture generally assumes a reverent tone in its references to Jesus; and this fact alone can be startling for Christians who have no prior knowledge of Islam. Out of the approximately 6,200 verses in the Koran, ninety-three refer in some way to Jesus.[2] That is a significant number (although vanishingly small when compared to the number of verses discussing Jesus in the New Testament). But—as we shall see—many of these verses are negative—or, more precisely, polemical—in content, in that what they offer is a condemnation and refutation of Christian beliefs about Jesus.

---

[1] Yahiya Emerick, *How to Tell Others about Islam* (Beirut: Noorart, 2004), p. 210.
[2] Geoffrey Parrinder, *Jesus in the Qur'an* (London: Sheldon Press, 1965), p. 166.

133

In fact, the most useful introductory statement I can offer about Islamic scriptural representations of Jesus is this: how the Koran portrays Jesus is a function of how Muhammad saw himself and defined himself as a prophet. The Koranic Jesus served largely as a shadowy reflection of Muhammad, mirroring Muhammad's own preoccupations, self-image, and anxieties as the Arab prophet gazed into the glass of the past.

Let's review what we have learned so far about Jesus in Islamic scripture. You may recall that he is identified as a Muslim and a prophet, part of a historical sequence of divinely appointed messengers. The disciples of Jesus are called Ansar (helpers, those who help to achieve Allah's victory), the same name given in the Koran to those residents of Medina who welcomed and supported Muhammad (surahs 3:52 and 9:117).

Like Muhammad, Jesus is said to have received a scriptural revelation that Allah commanded him to preach to those around him. The revelation given to Muhammad is called the Koran; that given to Jesus is identified as the Injil (a loanword derived from the Greek *evangelion*: "good news", or gospel).

Here we run into one of many points where we have to distinguish between Islamic and Christian understandings of a term. Muhammad seems to have assumed that whatever was happening to him in his own life must also have befallen the great prophets who came before him. Muhammad believed he himself had received via Gabriel an oral revelation from Allah, the Koran (literally, the "recitation"); and he knew from his talks with local Christians that Jesus was associated with something called the Injil. Muhammad apparently surmised that this Injil—like Muhammad's Koran—must likewise have been an oral revelation from Allah that Jesus had been commanded to recite.

Christian doctrine, however, understands the word gospel in several ways. First, it refers to the good news preached by Jesus himself. We see this in Mark 1:14–15: "Jesus came into Galilee, preaching the gospel of God, and saying, 'The time is fulfilled, and the kingdom of God is at hand; repent, and believe in the gospel.'"

Second, it refers to post-Resurrection preaching by Christ's disciples *about* Jesus himself, the eternal Word of God made flesh, who inaugurates the "kingdom of God" through his voluntary self-sacrifice. We see this, for example, in Saint Paul's Letter to the

Romans (1:9): "For God is my witness, whom I serve with my spirit in the gospel of his Son" (which can also be translated as "the good news concerning his Son"). Paul uses the word *evangelion* with a similar meaning later in the same epistle (15:19): "I have fully preached the gospel of Christ."

Third, the term gospel also refers to the four canonical texts (as well as many apocryphal ones) about Jesus and his kerygma: the proclamation of salvation and God's love for our world.

As noted above, certain aspects of Jesus' life as presented in the Koran will be recognizable to Christian readers. He is acknowledged as the son of the Virgin Mary and as a miracle worker. But even these recognizable points come to feel less reassuringly familiar when we see the Islamic doctrine underlying them. Jesus is called "son of Mary" as an implicit rejoinder to those who would call him "son of God" (as in surah 5:72). As for the Koranic references to Jesus' miracles, surah 3:49 provides a good representative example; he is depicted as saying, "I heal those born blind, and the lepers, and I bring the dead back to life, with Allah's permission." The phrase *b'idhni Allah* (with Allah's permission) recurs throughout the Koran's references to Jesus' deeds as a way of emphasizing that he was not divine and could accomplish nothing on his own.

Even more striking—at least to me as a Christian who grew up hearing Gospel readings at Mass—is the *brevity* of Koranic references to Christ's life and work. Nowhere does Islamic scripture present a sustained narrative or story about any aspect of Jesus and his mission. Altogether missing from the Koran are the drama, the human longing, and above all the compassion Jesus felt and expressed as he responded to the brokenness of life in our world—an emotional dimension that we find so amply documented in the Christian Gospels. What the Koran gives us of Christ's ministry—"I heal those born blind, and the lepers, and I bring the dead back to life"—is no more than a quick drive-by flash-blur.

Such brevity, of course, implies that Muhammad's audiences in Mecca and Medina already knew something about the life of Christ, just as they also were apparently familiar with stories about Abraham and Moses (we have seen this in previous chapters). But the Koran's omission of any reference to the subjective emotional dimension of Jesus' earthly existence will affect both Islamic theological understandings of Christ and the entire course of anti-Christian polemics throughout Islamic history (as we will discover), from the Crusades up through the twenty-first century.

"You breathed into it, and it became a bird": Koranic miracles of Christ from the apocryphal gospels

Two of the Koran's most vivid references to Jesus come not from the Bible but from the apocryphal tradition—gospels that were composed centuries after the time of the New Testament. The particular text I have in mind here is "The Arabic Gospel of the Infancy of the Savior", also known as the Arabic Infancy Gospel (AIG). This text, dating from the mid-fifth to mid-sixth century, was originally composed in Syriac and later translated into Arabic. Oral versions of some of the stories contained in this text seem to have circulated in the market towns of the Arabian peninsula during the Jahiliyah.

I consider the AIG a good example of what I call religious pulp fiction, intended for a mass-market Christian audience eager for legends about Jesus' childhood. After all, the New Testament tells us little about his years as a boy or time as a teen in Nazareth, and fans abhor any vacuum in the lives of their heroes. The AIG fills the gap.

And the way it does so is to cram the miraculous into Christ's life at every turn it can. The trend begins with his nativity. Here is how the AIG renders the scene: "Jesus spoke, and, indeed, when He was lying in His cradle said to Mary His mother: I am Jesus, the Son of God, the Logos, whom thou hast brought forth, as the Angel Gabriel announced to thee; and my Father has sent me for the salvation of the world.'"[3]

The historical Jesus of the Bible of course makes no such speech at birth. But the doctrine coming from the infant's mouth here in the AIG is orthodox enough and recognizably Christian, identifying him as Logos, Savior, and Son of God.

The nativity is also dramatized with a speech in the Koran; but its content—as you might expect in this transposed Islamic context—is

---

[3] *The Arabic Infancy Gospel of the Saviour*, trans. Alexander Walker in *Ante-Nicene Fathers*, vol. 8, *Fathers of the Third and Fourth Centuries* (Peabody, Mass.: Hendrickson, 1995), 405.

different. In Muhammad's version, Mary's relatives accuse her of sexual promiscuity as soon as they catch sight of the baby Jesus. By way of defense, she points to the child in the cradle, who speaks up on her behalf by announcing his miraculous mission: "I am Allah's servant. He has given me the Book and made me a prophet" (19:30). Any reference to his status as Savior or Son of God is studiously avoided. Thus the AIG's infant-cradle scene has been put into the service of Muslim teachings.

The New Testament of course differs from both these texts by omitting any such baby talk. Which brings us to an important distinction. The Jesus we find in the AIG and Islamic scripture is a static figure, lacking any trace of spiritual growth or intellectual development as he ages. From infancy, he is fully cognizant and begins sermonizing from the cradle.

Whereas the Gospel of Luke tells us concerning the young Jesus that he "increased in wisdom and in stature, and in favor with God and man" (2:52). We will return to this point when we explore kenotic theology as a way of understanding some of the most important Christological differences between the New Testament and the Koran.

Another story from the AIG is worth our attention here. It features Jesus at the age of seven, playing with a group of neighborhood boys. "They were making images of asses, oxen, birds, and other animals," the AIG tells us, "each one boasting of his skill." But Jesus goes them one better:

> He had made figures of birds and sparrows, which flew when He told them to fly, and stood still when He told them to stand, and ate and drank when He handed them food and drink. After the boys had gone away and told this to their parents, their fathers said to them: My sons, take care not to keep company with him again, for he is a wizard: flee from him, therefore, and avoid him, and do not play with him again.[4]

Like the cradle-pronouncement scene, this episode does not appear in the New Testament but is picked up by the Koran. Muhammad makes use of it by imagining how on Judgment Day Allah will ask his

---

[4] Ibid., p. 412.

various messengers how they did in their prophetic missions. Surah 5:110 (a Medinan chapter) shows Allah reminding Jesus of the miracles He allowed him to perform: "And behold! You created out of clay the figure of a bird, with My permission. Then you breathed into it, and it became a bird, with My permission.... But those among them [the 'Children of Israel'] who were unbelievers said, 'This cannot be anything but obvious sorcery!'"

The first time I read this Koran verse, I was struck by the pleasing snapshot it offered—the child Jesus, breathing life into clay birds. Then I wondered: out of the many Christ stories available from the biblical and apocryphal traditions, why did this one in particular appear in the Koran?

I think the link has to do with black magic. The AIG says the fathers of the neighborhood boys ordered them to shun Jesus, "for he is a wizard." The Koran reproduces this motif by summarizing the bird miracle and then quoting the reaction of the "unbelievers": "This cannot be anything but obvious sorcery!"

Now, it will intrigue you to know that the Koran repeatedly uses precisely this same exclamation to indicate how Muhammad's neighbors responded to his own *da'wah*, especially when he tried to preach to them about the doctrine of Judgment Day and the resurrection:

> If you say, "You people will be raised from the dead", those who are unbelievers will be sure to reply, "This cannot be anything but obvious sorcery!" (Surah 11:7)

> And, when they see a sign, they make fun of it, and they say, "This cannot be anything but obvious sorcery! You mean, when we die, and we are just dust and bones, that we are going to be raised up again?" (Surah 37:14–16; see also surahs 6:7 and 34:43)

That this accusation was a sore point with Muhammad is evidenced also by the following early Meccan verse: "Likewise, whenever in past times a messenger came to them, they always said, 'He is a sorcerer!' or 'He is possessed by a jinn (majnun)!'" (51:52).

Muhammad had to fend off such taunts many times. But the Arabic Infancy Gospel's mention of sorcery apparently helped him feel there was a bond between himself and Jesus. Any reference to bygone prophets being wrongly accused of practicing the dark arts of wizardry: that was something Muhammad would want to remember and want to recite.

Messiah, Spirit, Table, Word: New Testament terms linked to Christ's life that resurface in the Koran

Another term that the Koran links to the lives of both Jesus and Muhammad is *ruh al-qudus*. The literal meaning of this Arabic phrase is "the spirit of sanctity" or "the spirit of holiness". Let's look first at a verse (2:253) where it appears in conjunction with the name of Jesus. Here, Allah speaks of him as a prophet: "We gave Jesus son of Mary the clear proofs, and We supported him with the spirit of sanctity" (*ruh al-qudus*; see also surahs 2:87 and 5:110 for other examples where the phrase is applied to Jesus).

In surah 16:102, the same phrase is used to describe how the Koran was given to Muhammad: "Say: 'The spirit of sanctity (*ruh al-qudus*) has brought it [i.e., the revelation] down from your Lord in truth, to strengthen those who believe.'"

But in lieu of "the spirit of sanctity", various Koran translators (such as 'Abdullah Yusuf 'Ali, Mohammed Pickthall, and A.J. Arberry) have chosen instead to render *ruh al-qudus* as "the Holy Spirit".[5] Christian readers might then immediately—and understandably— think of this as a reference to the same Holy Spirit that is revered in Christian doctrine as part of the divine Trinity.

This, in fact, was the exegetical move made by Geoffrey Parrinder, a twentieth-century British Christian missionary and Methodist minister who was also a professor of religious studies. He likened this Koranic *ruh al-qudus* to the Spirit in the Gospel of Mark that descends "like a dove" upon Jesus at his baptism in the River Jordan (Mk 1:10). Parrinder's interpretation was part of his affirmative reply to the hopeful question he raised in the conclusion of his book *Jesus in the Qur'an*: "Can Islam and Christianity be brought closer together?"[6]

---

[5] See, for example, how surah 2:87 is translated in 'Abdullah Yusuf 'Ali, *The Meaning of the Holy Qur'an* (Beltsville, Md.: Amana Publications, 1999), p. 40; A.J. Arberry, *The Koran Interpreted* (New York: Collier Books, 1955), p. 39; and Mohammed Marmaduke Pickthall, *The Meaning of the Glorious Koran* (New York: New American Library, n.d.), p. 40.

[6] Parrinder, *Jesus in the Qur'an*, pp. 49, 168.

This well-meaning question, together with its underlying agenda of Muslim-Christian theological rapprochement, is in my opinion both wrongheaded and unproductive. I will return to it later in discussing interfaith relations.

But for now let's return to *ruh al-qudus*. John Penrice, the nineteenth-century compiler of a still-useful work entitled *A Dictionary and Glossary of the Koran*, translates the phrase as "Holy Spirit", but then adds, "by which name the Mohammedans designate the Angel Gabriel".[7] Muslim scriptural commentators such as 'Abdullah Yusuf 'Ali, Mohammed Pickthall, and Jalal al-Din 'Abd al-Rahman al-Suyuti all concur, stating that *ruh al-qudus* refers specifically to the angel Gabriel.[8]

Confirmation for this argument can be seen in surah 16:102, the verse just quoted above, where *ruh al-qudus* is identified as the one who "has brought it [i.e., the revelation] down." You will recall from previous chapters that Muhammad's biographer Ibn Ishaq identifies the angel Gabriel as the entity that brought the Koranic revelation to Allah's prophet.

Further confirmation can be found in Islamic scripture itself. Surah 2:97 announces: "Gabriel: it is he who has brought it [i.e., the revelation] down." The verb *nazzala* (to bring down, to make descend) that appears in both these verses is used in the Koran specifically to refer to how Islamic revelation is made to descend from heaven to earth.

Nonetheless, Gabriel, the *ruh al-qudus*, or "spirit of sanctity", is a Koranic link between the second-to-last and very last messengers to be commissioned by Allah in the Islamic chain of the prophets: Muhammad believed that the same angel that appeared to him also supported Jesus.

There is another Koranic passage where the word *ruh* (spirit) appears in connection with Jesus. I have in mind surah 4:171. It is a verse densely coiled with deceptively familiar Christological terms—but the coil comes with a polemical sting in its tail:

---

[7] John Penrice, *A Dictionary and Glossary of the Koran* (London: Curzon Press, 1873), p. 116.

[8] 'Abdullah Yusuf 'Ali, *Meaning of the Holy Qur'an*, p. 104; Pickthall, *Meaning of the Glorious Koran*, p. 40; Jalal al-Din 'Abd al-Rahman al-Suyuti, *Tafsir al-jalalayn*, ed. Marwan Sawar (Beirut: Dar al-Ma'rifah, n.d.), p. 55, commentary on Koran 2:253. Here Suyuti identifies *ruh al-qudus* as "Gabriel, who traveled with him [Jesus] wherever he traveled".

O people of the Book! Do not go to extremes in your religion, and do not say anything about Allah except the truth. The Messiah, Christ Jesus son of Mary, was a prophet of Allah, and His word, which Allah cast upon Mary, and also a spirit from Him. So believe in Allah and His messengers. But do not say "Three"! Stop this! That will be better for you. Rather, Allah is one God. He is exalted far beyond the notion that He could have a son.

Setting aside for a moment the peremptory anti-Trinitarian language at the end of this verse (to be discussed later), right now I will note that in this passage Jesus is described as "a spirit" (*ruh*) from Allah. The precise meaning here with regard to Jesus is not entirely clear. The word "spirit" is used in variable ways within the Koran to refer to aspects of his life. To describe how Jesus was conceived, surah 21:91 states concerning the Virgin Mary, "We breathed into her of Our spirit (*min ruhina*)", which recalls the Annunciation scene presented in the Gospel of Luke (1:35): "The angel said to her, 'The Holy Spirit will come upon you, and the power of the Most High will overshadow you; therefore the child to be born will be called holy, the Son of God.'" But elsewhere in Islamic scripture (19:17), "spirit" is employed to refer to Gabriel in the Koran's version of the Annunciation.

So, too, with the Koran's designation of Jesus as Allah's "word": the term is employed without clarification, as it is in surah 3:45, where there is another brief reference to the Annunciation: "O Mary, Allah announces to you a word from Him; his name will be Christ Jesus, son of Mary."

The obscurity surrounding Jesus as word and spirit pertains also to his designation as al-Masih (Christ or Messiah) in the Koran. Parrinder notes that of the eleven Koranic references to Jesus as Christ, all are in Medinan surahs.[9] This makes sense, since in Medina Muhammad dealt with a more substantial Christian audience than he had in Mecca. But as with "word" and "spirit", the Koran calls Jesus al-Masih without discussion of what the term might mean. Baydawi's fourteenth-century scriptural commentary offers us this:

Al-Masih, Jesus son of Mary: al-Masih [Christ] is his honorific title, which is among the various noble titles such as al-Siddiq, "the truthful

---

[9] Parrinder, *Jesus in the Qur'an*, p. 30.

one". Its origin is from the Hebrew *Mashiha* [Messiah], and its meaning is "the blessed one". Both the Arabic and Hebrew words are derived from *al-mash*, "anointing", because both words mean "the act of anointing with blessings" or "the act of purifying someone from sins"... or because Gabriel anointed him.[10]

Baydawi is etymologically correct when he identifies al-Masih with a verbal root meaning "anointing". He errs, however, in claiming that al-Masih means "the blessed one", since the name (as with the Greek word *Christos* and the Hebrew *Mashiach*) literally means "the anointed one".

Moreover, missing from both Baydawi's commentary and from the Koran is any reference to the connotation of the term Messiah/Christ as it would have been known to the Jews of Roman Judea who originally encountered Jesus in the first century A.D. For this population, "messiah" had rich historical associations, evoking coronation ceremonies in which a ruler would be anointed with sacred oil as a mark of his divinely appointed right to reign. (See, for example, 1 Samuel 10:1, where Samuel declares to Saul that the Lord has "anointed you to be prince over his people Israel".) Jewish hopes for political liberation in Jesus' time focused on the prospect of a messiah who would also be a "son of David", someone descended from the royal line that had governed Israel when it was a united and independent kingdom.

But what the Koran does with "messiah" is similar to what it does with "word" and "spirit". It uses all three terms as reverent but vague epithets for Jesus, as—to use Baydawi's phrase—the "various noble titles" by which to designate one of Allah's prophets. My hypothesis is that Muhammad in his early years in the caravan trade heard these titles from the Christians he encountered who are mentioned in Islamic sources, whether Bahira the monk, Quss the preacher, or Jabra the slave-swordsmith. He was not conversant with the theology underlying these terms, but he accepted them as pious designations for a prophet he honored.

Not that he accepted every title associated with Jesus by Christians. "Son of God", for one, must have struck Muhammad as next-of-kin

---

[10] Nasir al-Din Abu Sa'id al-Baydawi, *Anwar al-tanzil wa-asrar al-ta'wil* (Beirut: Dar al-- Kutub al-'Ilmiyah, 1988), 1:159–60, commentary on Koran 3:45; translated by D. Pinault.

to the "daughters of Allah" he condemned in Mecca. But—perhaps as a way to win over as many Medinan Christians as he could—Muhammad retained every epithet for Jesus that did not offend him as a violation of tawhidic monotheism.

The same ambiguity-suffused reverence seems evident in the Koran's presentation (in surah 5:112–15) of an object linked to Christ's life that it calls the "table from heaven":

> Behold! The disciples said, "O Jesus son of Mary! Can your Lord send down to us a table from heaven?" He said, "Fear Allah, if you are believers." They said, "We wish to eat from it, so that our hearts may be satisfied, so that we will know that you have told us the truth, and so that we may be witnesses to it." Jesus son of Mary said, "O Allah our Lord! Make a table from heaven descend to us, that it may be for us a festival, for the first of us and for the last of us, and that it may be a sign from You. Provide for us, for You are the best of those who provide."

For Christian readers, this evokes several different passages from the Bible. Upon first coming across this text, I thought at once of the Last Supper. Altogether missing from the Koran's "Table", however, is any evidence of what is most precious to followers of Christ in the New Testament's rendering of this moment: Jesus' Eucharistic consecration of the bread and wine, as well as the words "This is my body, which is given for you"—words that link the Jewish Passover sacrifice with his own voluntary self-sacrifice on the Cross.[11]

The fact that the Koran's food-bearing table descends from heaven, however, also suggests to me some trace of Peter's vision in Joppa as recorded in the Acts of the Apostles (10:1–16). While at prayer on a rooftop, Peter becomes hungry. Suddenly he sees a sheet being lowered from heaven. It contains "all kinds of animals and reptiles and birds of the air". A voice reassures Peter that—contrary to traditional Jewish dietary laws—he may regard all these animals as permissible to eat.

Contrary to the themes of these New Testament passages—reassurance and the divine gift of self-sacrifice—what the Koran does with these source stories is altogether different. For immediately after

---

[11] Luke 22:19; cf. 1 Corinthians 11:23; Matthew 26:26; Mark 14:22.

the Islamic Jesus prays for a "table from heaven", he receives this response from Allah: "Allah said: 'I will send it down to you; but after this, if anyone among you is guilty of unbelief, I will punish him with a punishment such as I have never inflicted before on anyone from among the worlds'" (Koran 5:115).

Harsh words. The phrase "guilty of unbelief" (*yakfur*) comes from the same root as kafir: infidel. Worth noting here is that this Table passage is late-Medinan in date; Islam's prophet had long since given up on converting Medina's "people of the Book". These verses occur a number of years after Muhammad changed the *qiblah* (direction of prayer) from Jerusalem to Mecca, and they occur in the same time period in which—as you may recall from previous chapters—Muhammad told Medina's Christians they were kuffar and *mushriks* for considering Christ divine (cf. surah 5:72).

So in the Koran's telling, the Muslim disciples of the Islamic Jesus get their wish for food, but it comes salted with a warning of unprecedented punishment from Allah. *Bon appétit.*

On the Trinity: "Was it you who told people: 'Consider me and my mother as gods, in addition to Allah'?"

The Koran has already scolded us: "Do not say 'Three'!" To sharpen its warning, Islamic scripture (in surah 5:116–18) also visualizes a confrontation to take place on Judgment Day, when Christ will be called before the throne of Allah to answer for the promulgation on earth of Trinitarian doctrine:

> And behold! Allah will say: "O Jesus son of Mary! Was it you who told people, 'Consider me and my mother as gods, in addition to Allah'?" Jesus will say: "May You be glorified! I could never say what I have no right to say. If I had ever said that, You would already know it. You know what is in my soul, but I do not know what is in Yours. For You are the Knower of that which is hidden. I never said anything to them except what You commanded me to say: namely, 'Worship Allah, my Lord and your Lord.' And I was a witness over them for as long as I was among them. When You took me up to yourself, You were the one who was the Watcher over them. And

You are the witness of everything. If You punish them, well, they are Your servants; and if You forgive them, You are the one who is powerful and wise."

Remarkable for Christian readers is how this passage presents the Trinity as consisting of Allah, Jesus, and the Virgin Mary. No mention is made here of the Holy Spirit. The question naturally arises: How could Muhammad have mistaken the Christian doctrine he condemns?

That this is potentially a very embarrassing question is something I can attest personally. In January 1980, while studying in the Swiss city of Zürich, I attended an interfaith gathering sponsored by the Jesuit Student House, situated near the local university. The well-intentioned goal of the priests who organized the event was to bring together Christians and Muslims to learn about each other's faiths.

The event came at a tense time. Iranians had been holding American diplomats hostage at the U.S. embassy in Teheran since the previous November; and in December the Soviet Union had invaded Afghanistan. My memory of the time was that few people came to the Jesuit House that night in what looked like a relaxed frame of mind; and that was before the evening got started.

The hall was packed. Most attendees were Swiss-German undergraduates; but—to judge from the conversations I overheard as I looked for a seat—a sizable number of Arab and Iranian guests were in attendance as well.

The first speaker was a Muslim gentleman who began by lecturing us about *i'jaz al-Qur'an*: the Koran's inimitability in terms of its literary excellence and formal composition. From that point, he went on to speak of Islamic scripture's inerrancy, and how even today it serves as an unfailing source of knowledge on every conceivable subject.

Pretty standard stuff, I would say in retrospect, looking back now over a long distance in years. One can hear such points declaimed in some form in Friday mosque sermons all over the world; and in such pious congregations, pronouncements like those would simply be met by nods or affirmative silence.

But this was no pious mosque. No sooner had the speaker finished than he hurried away from the podium. Before he could leave the stage, however, a man in the audience stood up and asked if he might pose a question. I recognized him as someone I knew from Masses I attended at the Catholic Liebfrauenkirche in town.

The Jesuit moderator coaxed the speaker back to the podium. An instant later came the question: "If the Koran is inerrant, why does it claim that Christians worship the Blessed Virgin as part of a Trinity, when in fact it should have said the Holy Spirit?"

The speaker gulped, blinked, fumbled for words. But words were supplied for him, and fast. Within seconds, over a dozen Muslim men were on their feet. Several near me held aloft copies of the Koran. Angry shouts came from many of them, with accusations to the effect of "You have insulted Islam" or "This is an insult to our faith."

Our Jesuit moderator grabbed the microphone from the podium, thanked the questioner for his question, and nervously announced that in the interest of communal good will, it might be best to move on to the next speaker. The mood in the hall for the rest of the evening? Sullen watchfulness; mutual suspicion.

But my fellow Catholic's question was a good one. I am asked some version of it whenever I offer courses on Islam. Here is my own attempt at an answer.

First, what the Koran states about Christianity seems to reflect Muhammad's personal experience of Christian faith and practice in those regions of Arabia and the Near East that he visited in his business travels. As mentioned earlier, Islamic doctrine insists he was illiterate; he made no formal study of Christian doctrine. He was aware of Christians' worship of the Trinity; and he knew that Christians venerate the Virgin Mary. The fervor of Christian devotion to Mary in Muhammad's time is reflected in his assumption that she must have formed the third member of this Trinity.

Second, although he knew the word "Spirit" was associated with Christianity, he seemed uncertain of its role in Christian doctrine. Rather than assign it to the Trinity, Muhammad spoke of it variously, using it sometimes for Gabriel and sometimes, in other Koran passages (as we have seen), for Jesus Christ.

Third—and this is a remarkable rhetorical tactic—the Koran uses the figure of Christ himself to condemn Christian Trinitarian doctrines. Muhammad wanted to claim Jesus as part of Islam, as a Muslim prophet; to do so, he made Jesus a proclaimer of tawhid. From Muhammad's point of view, Christian belief in the Trinity could be lumped with Jahiliyah worship of Allah's three daughters as an example of *shirk*: ascribing partners to Allah. In other words, as noted by Gabriel Said Reynolds (a professor of Islamic studies at the University of Notre Dame), "The Qur'an makes Jesus an opponent of Christianity." (Reynolds also quotes the scholar Tarif Khalidi to similar effect: "The Qur'an turns Jesus into an anti-Christian figure.")[12]

Anti-Christian statements tend to be late-Medinan in date, eclipsing the sunnier pronouncements we saw earlier about how people of the Book will be exempted in the afterlife from fear or sorrow. The verse we have just read condemning the Trinity has a harsh tone to it; but even harsher is this, another late-Medinan verse:

> Guilty of unbelief are those who say Allah is Christ son of Mary. Say: "Well, who would have power over Allah in any way if He wished to destroy Christ son of Mary, along with his mother and everyone on earth all together? It is Allah who has power over the heavens and the earth and everything in between. He creates whatever He wishes. And Allah holds power over everything." (Koran 5:17)

Stunning, this verse, with its slap-in-the-face impact. In speaking of Jesus and Mary, the Koran's tone is normally reverent. But here Muhammad has become sick and tired of Christians and their beliefs; here the talk is of destruction. Son of God, Mother of God: the followers of Jesus have gone too far in their worship, and this verse comes as a lesson concerning who it is that really holds the power. My own lingering impression of this verse: a frustrated gamemaster sweeps helpless pawns from a board.

"All that I withheld from Jesus and gave him no power over it": How Muhammad dealt with the Christians of Najran

Who holds power? Who lacks it? The importance of this issue for Muhammad is reflected also in a visit he received from a delegation of sixty Christians while he was at the height of his political success.

---

[12] Gabriel Said Reynolds, "Alternate Ending: Lebanese Christians and a Muslim Film about Jesus", *Commonweal*, February 18, 2011, http://www.commonwealmagazine.org.

They were inhabitants of Najran, an oasis in southwestern Arabia near the frontier of Yemen. This was in the year 631, after the prophet's conquest of Mecca.

In meeting with them, Muhammad tried to induce these Christian Arabs to convert to Islam. They refused but were allowed to retain their identity as Christians in exchange for paying the annual jizyah-- tax and accepting political domination by the new Islamic State.

What interests me about this encounter is the kind of arguments Muhammad used in his attempt to induce his visitors' conversion. Here is how he began his address to the leaders of the Christian delegation: "The apostle said to them, 'Submit yourselves.' They said, 'We have submitted.' He said: 'You have not submitted, so submit.' They said, 'Nay, but we submitted before you [did].' He said, 'You lie. Your assertion that God has a son, your worship of the cross, and your eating pork hold you back from submission.' "[13]

Important to understand here is that Muhammad and the Christians of Najran each understood differently the verb *aslama* (to submit). *He* understood it in the specific denominational sense of submitting to Allah and converting to the Islamic religion Muhammad had been promulgating for over twenty years. *They* understood it in the generic universalist sense of submitting to the one God and articulating that submission in the form of Christian worship. And since a Christian population had existed in Najran for well over a century before the birth of Muhammad, they felt justified in reminding him that their community had "submitted" before he ever did.

This was not good enough for Muhammad. He abruptly called them liars and then enumerated their shortcomings: in Christology ("your assertion that God has a son"), in ritual ("your worship of the cross"), and in dietary habits ("your eating pork"—something forbidden in Islam as it is in Judaism).

After condemning these Christians' veneration of the Cross, the prophet of Islam continued his theological assault by intoning two of Allah's "beautiful names" as listed in the Koran and then contrasting them with Christian claims about Christ: "The 'Living,' the 'Ever-- existent,' the Living Who cannot die, whereas Jesus died and was

---

[13] Ibn Ishaq, *The Life of Muhammad: A Translation of Ibn Ishaq's Sirat Rasul Allah*, ed. and trans. A. Guillaume (Karachi; New York: Oxford University Press, 1968), p. 272.

crucified according to their doctrine."[14] The Cross and the crucifixion: sheer foolishness, a scandal and stumbling block for Muhammad, just as they had been for those people centuries earlier who first
heard of "Christ crucified" from Saint Paul (as Paul himself tells us in
I Corinthians 1:18–24).

Islam's prophet then issued a warning to the Christian delegation
by quoting a Koranic verse (3:4): "There will be a harsh punishment
for those who engage in unbelief with regard to Allah's signs. Allah is
mighty, the Lord of Vengeance."

Muhammad furthered his argument by reverting to the topic of
Jesus. At this point, Ibn Ishaq presents the prophet as speaking with
the voice of Allah:

> Though I gave Jesus power over those matters in virtue of which
> they [i.e., the Christians] say that he is God, such as raising the dead,
> healing the sick, creating birds of clay, and declaring the unseen.…
> [Nonetheless] some of My majesty and power I withheld from him,
> such as appointing kings by a prophetic command and placing them
> where I wished, and making the night to pass into day and the day
> into night, and bringing forth the living from the dead and the dead
> from the living, and nurturing whom I will without stint, both the
> good and the evil man. All that I withheld from Jesus and gave him no
> power over it. Have they not an example and a clear proof that, if he
> were a God, all that would be within his power, while they know that
> he fled from kings and because of them he moved about the country
> from town to town.[15]

If he were a God, all that would be within his power: with these words,
Muhammad reverts to a preoccupation that recurs in his pronouncements. The display of force, the ability to compel, the pleasure of
commanding kings rather than having to flee from them: all these
concerns come into view when Muhammad thinks about Jesus—
thereby giving us glimpses of how differently Christ is understood in
the Muslim and Christian faiths. We will revisit this issue of Jesus,
divinity, and divine power when we look at Christian theological
responses to Islamic polemical assaults on the Trinity and crucifixion.

[14] Ibid.
[15] Ibid., p. 274.

"O dog of a Nazarene": The long afterlife of Koranic names for Christians

We saw earlier that Islamic scripture presents Jesus as "an anti--Christian figure" and "an opponent of Christianity". This theological hostility, I would argue, is also expressed in the word the Koran uses to designate the followers of this fallen faith. That word is *Nasara*—the plural of *Nasrani*, "Nazarene".

This nomenclature is curious and intriguing. Why did Muhammad prefer to call these people "Nazarenes"? After all, textual evidence suggests that Christians of the Levant and the Arabian peninsula in Muhammad's time used altogether different terms to designate themselves. They described themselves with linguistic variations on the Greek *Christianoi* (a word whose pedigree goes back to the Acts of the Apostles (11:26): "In Antioch the disciples were for the first time called Christians"), the Syriac-Aramaic *mashihaye* (followers of the Messiah/Christ), and the Arabic *masihiyun* (the self-designation still preferred by Christian Arabs today).[16] These Greek/Syriac/Arabic names all mean the same thing: followers of Christ, the Messiah.

A study published by Sidney Griffith (a professor of Semitic studies at the Catholic University of America) argues that the Koran's use of *Nasara*/"Nazarenes" to designate Christians makes sense given the polemical history of this word, dating all the way back to the New Testament itself. Saint Paul's preaching of the gospel met with so much hostility in Jerusalem that the high priest Ananias and other elders of the Jewish community filed a complaint against Paul with the Roman authorities, labeling him a disturber of the peace.

Paul was put on trial in Caesarea, in the presence of the imperial procurator of Judea, Antonius Felix. The prosecuting attorney had this to say about Paul and those who were attracted to his preaching: "We have found this man a pestilent fellow, an agitator among all the Jews throughout the world, and a ringleader of the sect of the Nazarenes" (Acts 24:5; Christian Bible commentaries

---

[16] Sidney Griffith, "Al-Nasara in the Qur'an: A Hermeneutical Reflection", in *New Perspectives on the Qur'an: The Qur'an in Its Historical Context 2*, ed. Gabriel Said Reynolds (New York: Routledge, 2011), pp. 301–22.

indicate that this name was meant to designate "followers of Jesus of Nazareth").[17]

Thus, even in the first century, the word Nazarene was used in a pejorative sense by those opposed to the Christian message. As convincingly demonstrated in Griffith's research, Syriac texts (including some dating from the fifth century) indicate that pagans and other non-Christians of the Levant and Mesopotamia used the term *Nasraye* (Syriac for "Nazarenes") when they wished to refer to Christians in an insulting and hostile manner.[18]

The prophet Muhammad on his travels appears to have learned both the word and its connotations. Griffith says this of the nomenclature used in Islamic scripture: "The Arabic name *Nasara*, as we have it in the Qur'an, is etymologically in all probability a calque on the Syriac name *Nasraye*, which in Syriac texts, as in Greek in Acts 24:5 and elsewhere, occurs mainly as a name used for Christians by non-Christian adversaries.... In other words, the name has an anti-Christian ring to it."[19] Griffith also draws attention to the Medinan date of the Koranic verses in which the word *Nasara* is repeatedly used—precisely at a time when Muhammad had tired of the city's Christians and their Trinitarianism.[20]

Aside from this very convincing etymological and historical argument, there is another factor to consider in asking why the Koran designates Christians as Nasara rather than Mashihaye/Masihiyun (the latter terms, you will recall, were those used by Christians themselves). Mashihaye, after all, means "followers of the Messiah/the Christ". But al-Masih (the Messiah) is precisely one of the words used in the Koran to name Jesus and claim him as a Muslim prophet. In refusing to call Christians by the name they themselves preferred, and instead referring to them as Nazarenes (a name weighted with a long history of hostility and insult), Muhammad linguistically segregated Christians from the very Christ they followed.

[17] Bruce M. Metzger and Roland E. Murphy, eds., *The New Oxford Annotated Bible* (New York: Oxford University Press, 1991), p. 197; Donald Senior and John J. Collins, eds., *The Catholic Study Bible*, 2nd ed. (New York: Oxford University Press, 2006), p. 1484.

[18] Griffith, "Al-Nasara in the Qur'an", pp. 303–304.

[19] Ibid., p. 314.

[20] Ibid., p. 309.

From the seventh century up through the twenty-first, Western travelers have had this word flung at them in contempt. Testimony to this can be found in the writings of the Victorian poet Charles Doughty, who in 1876 set out on his own from Damascus to wander for years among the villages and wastelands of Arabia. (The product of this adventure, his two-volume *Travels in Arabia Deserta*, is the best travel writing about the Near East I have ever read, and I recommend it to you warmly.)

Making no secret of his religious identity (Doughty frequently refers to himself in the third person as "the Nasrany" and "the Christian stranger"), he encountered both hostility and hospitality from the tribes among whom he traveled. Doughty notes how "the name of Nasrany was yet an execration in this country, and even among nomads a man will say to another, 'Dost thou take me for a Nasrany! that I should do such an [iniquitous] thing.'"[21]

This solitary "Christian stranger" records how, journeying by camel on a "breathless sultry day" of "deadly heat" when, as he confesses, "I could hardly maintain myself in the saddle", he came upon "a small watering place of shallow pits". The Bedouins clustered at the site had just finished providing drink for their animals but were not at all inclined to receive the Nazarene kindly:

> I alighted as they were ready to depart again, and would bathe my head in a little water which remained in a waterer's leather after the cattle drinking; but the savage wretch forbade me, saying, 'Nay!— he feared Ullah [Allah];' and taking up his gear, he cast out the water, crying, with the dreary eyes of his ignorant fanaticism fastened upon me, 'Should he draw for a Nasrany, one that was accursed of Ullah? Was the sun hot to-day, and I fainted? He would God that I died also.'[22]

After this cruel treatment, Doughty pushed on until he reached the town of Hayil, where he received a much more generous welcome from the local emir, who asked him about his religion: "The Emir said further, 'So you are Mesihy?'—that was a generous word!

---

[21] Charles M. Doughty, *Travels in Arabia Deserta*, 3rd ed. (London: Butler & Tanner, 1921), 1:584.
[22] Ibid., 1:376.

He would not call me by the reproachful name of Nasrany.... Christians of the Arabic tongue in the great border lands name themselves Mesihiyun."[23]

As you read this passage, you can sense the relief Doughty felt (as well as the nervous strain he must have been under) as he records his gratitude for the emir's "generous word"—being addressed as "Mesihy" (Christian) rather than the customary—and derogatory—"Nasrany" (Nazarene).

European travelers in Doughty's time sometimes found themselves accosted by unflattering salutations that combined their religious identity with a species of animal that is regarded unfavorably in Islamic tradition.

To cite one example: in the 1850s, a British clergyman named Robert Buchanan traveled about the Levant and wrote up his experiences in a book called *Notes of a Clerical Furlough, Spent Chiefly in the Holy Land*. He remarked on his interactions with Arab beggars in Jerusalem: "When the customary cry of such a rabble for Buksheesh [alms] is not answered ... it is very apt to be exchanged for the favourite salutation of the fanatic Moslem—'dog of a Nazarene.'"[24]

Something similar was noted in nineteenth-century Egypt by Richard Francis Burton, the English explorer best known for having successfully disguised himself as an Afghan Muslim pilgrim in order to make the hajj to Mecca. He recorded a popular insult frequently shouted on the streets and alleys of Alexandria: *Ya Nasrani, Kalb awani!*—that is, "O Nazarene! O dog obscene!"[25]

In the West, writers of sword-and-scimitar fantasies have savored this insult as a way to depict verbal clashes between Crusaders and Saracens. One tale (first published in the magazine *Collier's Weekly* in 1928) by action-adventure storyteller Harold Lamb involves a Scottish knight named Sir Bruce of Famagosta. He encounters a band of heavily armed Muslim Tatars, "part of Tamerlane's horde", who are led by one Subai Ghazi. The Christian knight refuses to surrender to them a beautiful young woman who is traveling with him under his

[23] Ibid., 1:590–91.

[24] Robert Buchanan, *Notes of a Clerical Furlough, Spent Chiefly in the Holy Land* (London: Blackie & Son, 1859), p. 149.

[25] Richard F. Burton, *The Book of the Thousand Nights and a Night* (London: Burton Club for Private Subscribers, n.d.), 1:258n3.

protection. At this one of the Tatars menaces him with the words, "Subai Ghazi, the Emir of emirs, gave the command. Is his word smoke, O dog of a Nazarene?"[26]

In reply, the knight suddenly—but rather than spoil this story, I urge you to read it yourself (it has been republished by the University of Nebraska Press). You will enjoy it.

But back to Nazarene K-9s: to appreciate this taunt fully, you need to know that Islamic tradition defines dogs as *najis* (ritually unclean). This means that if a dog brushes, licks, or presses a wet nose against a believer, that person's prayers will be invalid until he performs a thorough *wudu'* (ablution). The religious disdain directed against dogs is reflected in a saying attributed to the prophet Muhammad: "Angels [of mercy] do not enter a house wherein there is a dog or a picture of a living creature [a human being or an animal]."[27]

Nazarenes as objects of contempt: some might be inclined to dismiss the above samples of old travelers' tales and pulp fiction as no more than historical curiosities, things we have thankfully left behind in this twenty-first century of ours. Not so.

Since 2014, the Koranic terms *Nasrani* and *Nasara* have been revived and put to violent use by the terrorist group that styles itself *al-Dawlah al-Islamiyah* (also known as the Islamic State or ISIS). Shortly after conquering the Iraqi city of Mosul in June of that year, ISIS announced it would impose on resident "people of the Book" the Koranically prescribed jizyah-tax mandated in surah 9:29.

Most of Mosul's Christians fled at once. Those who remained were confronted with an ultimatum: "Convert to Islam, pay a fine [the jizyah], or face 'death by the sword'." But the leaders of ISIS went further, using the Islamic jizyah-concept to justify expropriating buildings and other properties belonging to Mosul's non-Muslims. Christine Sisto of the *National Review* describes what they did: "The Islamic State, formerly known as ISIS, had marked homes and businesses owned by Christians with a red, painted ن (pronounced "noon"), the 14th letter of the Arabic alphabet and the equivalent to the Roman letter N. The ن stands for Nasara or

---

[26] "The Red Cock Crows", *Collier's Weekly*, June 9, 1928, reprinted in Harold Lamb, *Swords from the West* (Lincoln: University of Nebraska Press, 2009), p. 12.

[27] *Sahih al-Bukhari*, hadith 4:448, cited on the website http://www.islamhelpline.net/node/6233.

Nazarenes, a pejorative Arabic word for Christians."[28] And thus the whirligig of time—to paraphrase Shakespeare's *Twelfth Night*—brings in its old hatreds.

But this was not the end of the matter. Photographs began circulating online of the doors and walls of Iraqi Christian homes that ISIS militants had spray-painted with the letter ن and the grim words *'Aqarat al-Dawlah al-Islamiyah*: "Property of the Islamic State". Jeremy Courtney, founder of an Iraq-based charitable organization called the "Pre-emptive Love Coalition", responded to this situation in a way that had unexpectedly far-reaching results. As CBS News reported, Courtney "grabbed a marker in mid-July [2014] and marked his hand with the Arabic letter "n" to stand in solidarity with the Christians who were also being marked. He posted the photo on Twitter with the hashtag #WeAreN." Courtney commented, "When I started the #WeAreN hashtag, I certainly didn't know or envision that this was going to be a rallying cry for Christians and others around the world."[29]

But a rallying cry is in fact what it has become, so that the ancient words *Nasrani* and *Nasara*, for centuries Islamic terms of contempt for Christians, have now become a way to draw attention to the ongoing persecution undergone by religious minorities in Syria and Iraq. The Catholic website Rorate Caeli has issued a statement of defiance to signal how "people of the Book" worldwide must stand united against totalitarian tyrannies such as ISIS. It is exactly the wakeup call we need:

> In their genocidal physical elimination of Christians from the Mesopotamian city of Mosul, Muslim terrorists marked each Christian-owned institution and building with this letter, for the extermination of hold-outs and expropriation of their belongings.
>
> They mean it as a mark of shame; we must then wear it as a mark of hope: Yes, we are in the army of the Resurrected Nazarene, the Master and Lord of the Universe, the Man who is God Almighty, the Second Person of the Most Holy Trinity. You may kill our brethren and expel them, but we Christians will never go away.[30]

[28] Christine Sisto, "A Christian Genocide Symbolized by One Letter", *National Review*, July 23, 2014. Accessed online at http://www.nationalreview.com/article/383493.

[29] Heba Kanso, "Symbol of ISIS Hate Becomes Rallying Cry for Christians", *CBS News*, October 20, 2014. Accessed online at http://www.cbsnews.com/news/for-christians-symbol-of-mideast-oppression-becomes-source-of-solidarity.

[30] "Nun: The Sign of Genocide", *Rorate Caeli*, July 19, 2014. Accessed online at http://www.rorate-caeli.blogspot.com/2014/07/nun-sign-of-genocide.html.

CHAPTER 7

"BUT A LIKENESS WAS MADE TO APPEAR TO THEM": THE ENIGMA OF CHRIST'S CRUCIFIXION IN THE KORAN

The reality of Christ's Cross as a stumbling block for Islam

As noted earlier, many of the Koran's statements about Jesus focus on denying Christian beliefs. Thus we have seen how Islamic scripture condemns those who believe that Jesus is divine, that he is the Son of God, or that he is a member of some Trinity (however membership in that Trinity might be defined).

Another Koranic denial involving Jesus—one that marks a radical parting of the ways with Christianity—involves the crucifixion. The passage discussing this topic, surah 4:157–58, comes in the context of Allah's condemnation of the Jews for a variety of offenses, including worshipping the golden calf and "refusing to believe in Allah's signs". What the Koran proclaims about the crucifixion constitutes one of the more cryptic assertions in Islamic scripture:

> They said, "We killed Christ Jesus son of Mary, Allah's messenger." But they did not kill him, nor did they crucify him. But a likeness was made to appear to them (*walakin shubbiha la-hum*). And those who disagree about this are in a state of doubt concerning it. They do not know for sure; they merely follow supposition. No, they certainly did not kill him. Instead, Allah raised him up to Himself. And Allah is mighty and wise.

The most mysterious pronouncement here—and the subject of much speculation over the centuries—is the assertion, "But a likeness was made to appear to them." Suyuti's popular Koran commentary summarizes the prevailing Islamic interpretation: "'They did not kill him, nor did they crucify him. But a likeness was made to appear to them': that is, a likeness of the one who was killed and crucified. And this was one of their associates [i.e., one of the Jews] who was with Jesus. That is, Allah cast upon this person the likeness of Jesus, and so they supposed that he was Jesus."[1]

Thus the Koran presents us with what is called a docetic crucifixion (from the Greek word *dokeo*, "to appear", "to seem", as opposed to the reality of a thing or an occurrence). Islamic scripture claims that Jesus was never really crucified; instead, "a likeness was made to appear" to onlookers of the Cross.

The Koran's brief reference to a docetic crucifixion was elaborated into a full-scale story by the eleventh-century scholar Abu Ishaq Ahmad ibn Muhammad al-Tha'labi. His book *Qisas al-anbiya'* (Tales of the prophets) belongs to a long-lived genre of narratives that were designed to combine pious edification with entertainment for the Muslim masses. Tha'labi drew on Islamic scripture, *hadith* (non-Koranic sayings of Muhammad), and biblical texts as well.

What follows is Tha'labi's account of the docetic crucifixion. Worth noting is how he makes use of Koranic surah 5:60, which mentions "those whom Allah cursed or who became targets of His anger, and He turned some of them into apes and pigs." The twentieth-century commentator 'Abdullah Yusuf 'Ali, like others before him, assumes that the accursed individuals in question must have been Jews.[2] Here is how Tha'labi employs this verse in concert with the docetic account of Christ on the Cross:

> Al-Kalbi reports, on the authority of Abu Salih, who derived it from Ibn 'Abbas, that Jesus—peace be upon him—approached a group of the Jews; and when they saw him, they said, "Here comes the sorcerer, the son of the sorceress; the wizard, the son of the witch!" Thus they slandered both him and his mother.
>
> So when Jesus saw this, he cursed them and said, "Allah, you are my Lord, and I have come forth from your spirit. It is only through

[1] Jalal al-Din 'Abd al-Rahman al-Suyuti, *Tafsir al-jalalayn*, ed. Marwan Sawar (Beirut: Dar al-Ma'rifah, n.d.), p. 130, commentary on Koran 4:157; translated by D. Pinault.

[2] 'Abdullah Yusuf 'Ali, *The Meaning of the Holy Qur'an* (Beltsville, Md.: Amana Publications, 1999), p. 1742.

your word that I have made anything; and I have never imagined that I could do anything on my own. Allah, curse those who have insulted me and my mother!"

So Allah responded to his prayer and transformed into pigs those who had insulted Jesus and his mother.

When the chief priest and the leaders of the Jews saw this, they became frightened and afraid of his curse. A consensus grew among the Jews to kill Jesus.

So one day they came together in a group against him and began questioning him. So he said, "O community of the Jews, Allah hates you!"

They became very angry at what he had said, and they were stirred up against him to kill him. Then Allah most exalted sent to him Gabriel—peace be upon him—and Gabriel made him enter the window of a house. Gabriel concealed him in the rafters. For God most exalted raised him up.

The head of the Jews ordered one of his men (whose name was Philtiyanus) to go inside and kill Jesus. But when Philtiyanus entered, he did not see Jesus. The Jews outside were kept waiting for a long time, and they imagined that Philtiyanus was inside, trying to kill Jesus.

But then Allah cast upon Philtiyanus the likeness of Jesus (*fa-alqa Allah 'alayhi shibh 'Isa*). When he came out, they thought he was Jesus, so they killed him and crucified him.[3]

Then Tha'labi offers an alternative explanatory scenario, one that draws on a source that shows great familiarity with the details of the Passion account in the Gospel of John: Jesus summons his disciples for a meal and announces, "One of you will deny me before the cock crows three times, and one of you will sell me for a handful of dirhams." The disciple Peter (called Shim'an in this Arabic text) is seized and denies Jesus.

Christ's betrayal by Judas is also described. Here is Tha'labi's description of what happens after Judas is paid thirty dirhams to betray Jesus:

He guided them [the Jews] to him [i.e., to Jesus]; but he had already been "made to appear so to them" before that (*wa-kana shubbiha*

---

[3] Abu Ishaq Ahmad ibn Muhammad ibn Ibrahim al-Tha'labi, *Qisas al-anbiya' al-musamma 'ara'is al-majalis* (Beirut: al-Maktabah al-Thaqafiyah, n.d.), p. 360; translated from the Arabic by D. Pinault.

la-hum qabla dhalika). So they took him and verified his identity and bound him with cords and led him about by a halter, saying to him, "And you were the one who used to raise the dead and heal the blind and the lepers? Why don't you unbind yourself from these cords?" Then they spat on him and placed thorns upon him. Thereafter they erected a piece of wood for him in order to crucify him upon it.

And when they brought him to the piece of wood to crucify him, the earth grew dark. Allah sent the angels, and they intervened between them [i.e., the Jews] and Jesus. And the likeness of Jesus was cast upon the one who had guided them to him. And his name was Judas (*wa-ismuhu Yahudha*).

So they crucified Judas instead of Jesus, while they thought that it was Jesus. And Allah took Jesus unto himself for three hours and then he raised him to heaven. And that is His utterance—may He be exalted—"In truth I take you unto myself, and I raise you up to myself and free you from the impurities of those who are unbelievers" [Qur'an 3:55].

So when the one who had been made to look like Jesus had been crucified, Mary, the mother of Jesus, came, as well as a woman for whom Jesus had prayed and whom he had cured of possession by jinns. The two women were weeping in the presence of the one who had been crucified. Then Jesus came up to them and said, "For whom are you weeping?"

They said, "For you." He said, "Allah has raised me up, and nothing but good has befallen me. And this here is someone who 'was made to appear so to them'" (*wa-inna hadha shakhs shubbiha la-hum*).

And Muqatil has said: The Jews assigned a man to spy on Jesus and go wherever he might go. Then Jesus went to the top of a mountain, and the angel came and raised him to heaven. And Allah most exalted cast the likeness of Jesus on the spy, and the Jews thought he was Jesus.

So they seized him, while he kept saying to them, "I am not Jesus! I am So-and-So, the son of So-and-So!" But they did not believe him, and they killed him and crucified him.[4]

Thus Tha'labi stitches together verses from various chapters of the Koran and combines them with biblical and apocryphal material to make a coherent and superficially plausible story. Jesus was accused of being a sorcerer (as we have seen earlier in the Koran and in the Arabic Infancy Gospel). So he cursed those Jews who uttered the slander, and *that* is why Allah transformed some of these Jews into pigs. Jewish

[4] Ibid., pp. 360–61.

fear and anger, according to Tha'labi, in turn led to their attempt to kill Jesus. In other words, the author of *Tales of the Prophets* created out of various disparate Koran-verses a *motive* for the attempted crucifixion of Christ.

Speaking from my own perspective as a Christian, I will note briefly here (we will return to this later) what I find particularly disturbing in Tha'labi's account: the vindictive and violent behavior of both Jesus and Allah, and how this vindictiveness targets the population among whom Jesus lived and prayed ("O community of the Jews, Allah hates you!"). Missing from this account—as it is also missing from the Koran—is any acknowledgment that Jesus himself was a member of this community and was himself a practicing Jew. And of course by displacing Christ's Passion and death onto another person, Islamic sources such as Tha'labi nullify the possibility of developing a theology of meaningful and salvific suffering in connection with the Cross.

"The knowledge of who we were": The triple dungeon of Gnostic cosmology

Now that we have surveyed the outlines of Muslim belief about Christ and the Cross, we are faced with the question: How and why did this docetic account of the crucifixion make its way into the Koran? The *how* entails an inquiry into the historical and theological antecedents on which Muhammad could have drawn for his version of the crucifixion. The *why* is even more interesting: What motivated him to insist that Jesus never underwent death on the Cross?

The first thing to note here is that the doctrine of Christ's docetic crucifixion existed for centuries before Muhammad in the pre-Islamic Near East. Docetism itself is a quasi-Christian subset of Gnosticism—an ancient religious world view you will want to know about so as to have a context for appreciating what motivates the notion of a crucifixion that Jesus supposedly never underwent.

Gnosticism is based on an attempt to address a question every religion tries to answer: Why do created beings suffer? For Jahiliyah pagans, the answer was simple. Gods exist but cannot be counted on to care. The jinns are capricious; men and animals alike are hunted down and eaten up by spike-toothed Time.

Under such circumstances, what can we do? The Jahiliyah's response: Stick with your tribe, and grab whatever comforts come your way.

But what about faiths that posit the existence of a loving God who cares about His creation? How Islam and Christianity deal with suffering is a topic I will postpone until a later chapter. For now, let's consider the Gnostic response. (And one reason it is worth having some acquaintance with this tradition is that for the first five centuries A.D., Gnosticism presented itself as one of Christianity's chief rivals.)

And a quick acknowledgment as an aside: I say "the Gnostic response" but also must confess I am simplifying the system. Dozens of competing sects flourished and withered in antiquity, some of them surviving into the medieval and modern eras to take root anew in various mystical and theosophical movements. What I am presenting now is no more than an introduction to recurrent motifs in Gnostic thought.

So: Gnosticism claims that the reason why we suffer in this world is as follows. Yes, God is good, and, yes, God is benevolent; *but the world was not created by God.* Rather, it was created by an ignorant and prideful entity identified in some Gnostic texts as the Demiurge (the creator of people). The good God has nothing to do with our world; scholars Hans Jonas and Adolf von Harnack describe this deity as "the alien God" to emphasize how estranged our cosmos is from him.[5]

Various Gnostic writings, radically dualist in their orientation, account for how our world came to be. Common to many is that the Demiurge, an eternally existent principle of darkness, envied the radiance of the alien God. It captured some of this radiance in the form of sparks of light. Each spark (in Greek, the *pneuma* or spirit) was then imprisoned within a triple-walled dungeon. The innermost tier of this dungeon was the human body, a prison equipped with enough destructive appetites, angers, and lusts to distract the spirit forever and deflect any possible remembrance of its origin in the realm of light.

The second wall of this dungeon is the earth, a world where we are perpetually surrounded by other created beings, all of whom are

---

[5] Hans Jonas, *The Gnostic Religion: The Message of the Alien God and the Beginnings of Christianity* (Boston: Beacon Press, 1963); Adolf von Harnack, *Marcion: The Gospel of the Alien God* (Durham, N.C.: Labyrinth Press, 1990).

likewise ridden by the same bodily drives that imprison us individually. The result is a constant chaos of greed and blind harm.

The earth itself, composed of dross material (and Gnostic systems posit that the material world is radically evil), is encased within crystalline planetary spheres. (Thus, Gnosticism made use of the ancient geocentric Ptolemaic model of the universe.) Each sphere is associated with one of the planets. The Gnostic variation on this Ptolemaic model was to claim that each sphere is ruled by an Archon (a "ruler" or a planetary god) whose job it is to serve the Demiurge as a prison warden and prevent divine pneuma-sparks from escaping.

Ignorant, captives of our distracting appetites, we lack knowledge of our origin, of the radiant deity—the "alien God"—that exists beyond the crystalline spheres of our prison. We have forgotten the noble spark within us. In ignorance we die, and, because of this, at death we are flung once more into another prison-body and are reborn to serve another sentence.

So that is why we suffer.

It is a compelling explanation, one that takes into account many frustrating features of life as we know it. But no religion this grim could have lasted for centuries unless it offered a way out, a means of salvation.

And Gnosticism did. Salvation, it claimed, had to do with gnosis (knowledge, from which this religion derived its name). The kind of knowledge to which I am referring here is not the product of discursive logic or the result of our own rational initiative. Instead, it is illuminationist: within our darkness comes a lightning-burst that reveals to us strange new horizons, vistas that promise escape from the triple dungeon.

This illumination originates with the alien God, who feels compassion for the numberless spirits that are immured in imprisoning flesh. This compassion motivates him to send an emissary, who descends through the crystalline spheres, eludes the vigilant Archons, and alights on the gross materiality of the earth's surface.

For the purpose of communication with stranded souls, this emissary puts on a "robe" or garment—the likeness of a human body—so as to blend in with the population of unenlightened prisoners. But this likeness is no more than a phantom; for the coarseness of flesh must never taint the essence of the alien emissary.

The emissary then wanders the earth, selecting individuals it deems ready for gnosis. These chosen few (and Gnostics throughout history have tended to view themselves as an elite) then undergo an initiatory process of spiritual instruction. A statement survives from an Egyptian Gnostic sect known as the Valentinians that sums up this instruction: "What liberates is the knowledge of who we were, what we became; where we were, whereinto we have been thrown; whereto we speed, wherefrom we are redeemed; what birth is, and what rebirth."[6]

Haloed with this gnosis, at death we slip loose of all imprisoning rebirths. Free of the body, the earth, and the Archons, our pneuma ascends through the spheres for an eternal reunion with the Light from which we were once abducted.

The crucifixion as a stumbling block for Gnostics: The docetic solution

By now you have probably noticed how different Gnosticism is from all the Abrahamic faiths. Unlike Judaism, Christianity, and Islam, which teach that our world in its foundation is good because it was created by a benevolent God, Gnosticism is radically dualist in its insistence on the fundamentally evil quality of our corporeal prison-- world and its estrangement from the "alien God" of light.

Nonetheless, in antiquity there were Gnostics who regarded them- selves as Christians, at least insofar as they revered Christ as a savior. The fact that so many religions have claimed him for themselves is a testimony to the charismatic attractiveness of Jesus that has lingered through the centuries.

But the Gnostics' attraction to Jesus posed them a problem. Haters of the body—that inner wall of our cosmic dungeon—they looked hopefully to an individual who had assumed human flesh out of love for us in our fallen condition. They wished to be rescued from their exis- tence as humans; yet they were drawn to someone who had immersed himself in precisely this human condition of ours. They wished to escape the world and its suffering; yet here was a man who had freely surrendered himself to scarcely imaginable suffering on a cross.

[6]Jonas, *Gnostic Religion*, p. 45.

Suffering on a cross: a true stumbling block for Gnostics, just as it was for Jews and Greeks (and as it would subsequently prove to be for Muslims). The idea was repugnant to followers of Gnosis. What they wanted was a hero powerful enough to outwit the Archons and blast an escape path up and out through the encircling spheres. What they *did not* want was some helpless victim writhing in pain on a piece of wood.

Power and a secret display of superiority: this is what was craved by those who saw themselves as the chosen, the few, the Gnostic elite. But at the same time, they had to deal with a stubbornly resistant fact: the troublesome specificity of the Cross as a historical event. For the execution of Jesus of Nazareth by the Roman state is something that is attested not only in the New Testament but also in ancient non-Christian sources. The Roman historian Tacitus, for example, confirms that the procurator Pontius Pilate put Christ to death during the reign of the emperor Tiberius. The second-century Greek satirist Lucian of Samosata makes the following remark in one of his letters: "The Christians, you know, worship a man to this day—the distinguished personage who introduced their novel rites, and was crucified on that account.... [I]t was impressed on them by their original lawgiver that they are all brothers, from the moment that they are converted, and deny the gods of Greece, and worship the crucified sage, and live after his laws."[7]

Especially intriguing is an inscription dating from either the first or second century A.D. known as the "Alexamenos graffito". It consists of a crude picture and a few words roughly scratched in Greek on the wall of a room near the Palatine Hill in Rome. The room functioned as part of a boarding school for boys who served in the imperial court.

The picture shows a human figure on a cross, its arms outstretched— but the figure's head is that of a donkey. It looks downward, gazing upon a man who stands beside the cross. This bystander looks up at the hybrid figure on the cross and raises one arm as if to salute or hail the crucified donkey-man. The inscription states, "Alexamenos worships his god."

[7] Tacitus, *The Annals*, trans. and ed. A.J. Church and W.J. Brodribb (London: Macmillan & Co., 1906), bk. 15, chap. 44, pp. 304–5; *The Works of Lucian of Samosata*, ed. and trans. H.W. Fowler and F.G. Fowler (Oxford: Clarendon Press, 1905), 4:82–83.

This donkey-headed crucifix is clearly intended as mockery. But in its own sarcastic way, it also provides a kind of testimony. It attests that non-Christians were well aware of an individual who had been crucified and who was worshipped by his followers as a god.

Followers who were willing to proclaim their faith. The room adjacent to the one containing the donkey-god cartoon bears a Latin graffito that may have been a riposte. *Alexamenos fidelis*, it says simply: "Alexamenos is faithful."[8]

What all this non-Christian evidence suggests is this: any religion that wanted to claim Jesus for itself had to deal with the vast presence of the Cross on every skyline.

Those Gnostics who were hungry to add Christ to their list of emissaries from the alien God dealt as follows with the historical datum of the crucifixion. Yes, they argued, Jews and Roman soldiers and faithful followers of Christ all saw a crucifixion take place; but the figure they saw crucified was not the person they thought it was. It only seemed as if Jesus was crucified; someone else was nailed in his place.

This docetic crucifixion is described in an ancient Coptic text entitled *The Second Treatise of the Great Seth*. It is part of what is known as the "Nag Hammadi Library", a collection of Gnostic manuscripts dating from the late fourth century A.D. that was discovered in Egypt in the mid-1940s.

As the translators of *Great Seth* note, this text consists of "a revelation dialogue allegedly delivered by Jesus Christ to an audience of 'perfect and incorruptible ones,' that is, gnostic believers."[9] In this dialogue, Jesus describes how he descended through the imprisoning celestial spheres, evading the Archon-wardens in his descent: "And I subjected all their powers. For as I came downward no one saw me. For I was altering my shapes, changing from form to form. And therefore, when I was at their gates I assumed their likeness. For I

[8] Graydon F. Snyder, *Ante Pacem: Archaeological Evidence of Church Life before Constantine* (Macon, Ga.: Mercer University Press, 1985), pp. 27–28; Everett Ferguson, *Backgrounds of Early Christianity*, 2nd ed. (Grand Rapids, Mich.: Eerdmans, 1993), pp. 559–61.

[9] "The Second Treatise of the Great Seth", trans. Joseph A. Gibbons and Roger A. Bullard, in *The Nag Hammadi Library in English*, ed. James M. Robinson, rev. ed. (San Francisco: Harper Collins, 1990), p. 362.

passed them by quietly, and I was viewing the places, and I was not afraid nor ashamed, for I was undefiled."[10]

"Changing from form to form": this reference to Christ's chameleon qualities attests to the docetic doctrine that the body Jesus inhabited was no more than a phantom, for their savior could never have been tainted by the weakness of human flesh.

This text also presents the Gnostic version of the crucifixion:

> The plan which they devised about me to release their Error and their senselessness—I did not succumb to them as they had planned. But I was not afflicted at all.... And I did not die in reality but in appearance, lest I be put to shame by them.... For my death which they think happened, (happened) to them in their error and blindness, since they nailed their man unto their death.... It was another, their father, who drank the gall and the vinegar; it was not I.... It was another, Simon, who bore the cross on his shoulder. It was another upon whom they placed the crown of thorns. But I was rejoicing in the height over all the wealth of the archons and the offspring of their error, of their empty glory. And I was laughing at their ignorance.[11]

"Laughing at their ignorance": this savior is triumphalist and vindictive, quite satisfied to let others suffer while from above he rejoices in his own safety. A gulf gapes between the docetic world view and the truly Christian. What the Gnostics envision in Jesus is a shell, no more than a simulacrum of the Christ we know from John, the Christ whose love for his friends is so great that he gladly lays down his life for them.

"The light suffered harm and was hurt by the darkness": Muslim contact with Gnostic sects in the time of Muhammad?

Now that we have outlined the beliefs of Gnostics who considered themselves Christian, let's consider the question of whether Muhammad might have had contact with Gnostic teachings in his preprophetic travels in Arabia and Syria.

---

[10] Ibid., p. 365.
[11] Ibid.

The first possibility has to do with a group that is cited in the Koran: the Sabians. You may recall that they are mentioned favorably in early Medinan surahs. These Koranic verses state that Sabians, along with Jews and Christians, will be exempted from fear and sorrow in the afterlife. Islamic scripture does not describe them at all, and the word "Sabians" has been applied to various minority religions in the course of Islamic history. But the Sabians Muhammad himself had in mind are most likely to have been members of a sect that was also designated by the name Mandaeans.

Their origins go back at least to the fourth century. The Mandaean--Sabians endured for centuries, living in the marshlands of southern Iraq, and were tolerated as non-Muslim "people of the Book" during the Islamic caliphal period. In recent years, militant Islamist groups have subjected them to persecution and kidnappings for ransom, but the Sabians survive today in a diaspora that extends from Baghdad to Kurdistan.[12]

What may have drawn Muhammad's favorable regard is that the Sabians conducted impressive baptismal rituals involving full immersion in river waters and claimed as their prophet John the Baptist (who is also honored in the Koran).[13] It is unlikely that Muhammad was closely acquainted with the Sabian teachings that are recorded in the scripture called *Ginza Rba* (the great treasure), but the Gnostic elements contained therein are evident to those who study dualist religions. As one summary states, "Humans contain a particle of divine light in their material bodies; salvation is gnosis of its celestial origin, and redemption is its escape at death to rejoin the world of light." The planetary Archons are ruled by Shamish (the sun), "the Blind One who is in charge of the spheres".[14]

Evidence for other Near Eastern Gnostic sects that survived from antiquity into Muhammad's time can be found in a twelfth--century work entitled *Kitab al-milal wa-al-nihal* (The book of religious

---

[12] Kurt Rudolph, *Gnosis: The Nature and History of Gnosticism* (San Francisco: Harper & Row, 1983), pp. 343–66; Zaid Sabah, "Sabian Sect Keeps the Faith", *USA Today*, September 28, 2007.

[13] The Koran makes brief references to John the Baptist. See, for example, surahs 3:39, 19:12–15, and 21:90.

[14] Michael G. Morony, *Iraq after the Muslim Conquest* (Princeton: University Press, 1984), pp. 411–14.

communities and sectarian creeds). Its author, Abu al-Fath Muhammad al-Shahrastani, was of Iranian origin but wrote in Arabic, the lingua franca for scholars throughout the Islamic world (a role comparable to that played by Latin in Western Christendom).

Shahrastani's introduction to this book announces his goal:

> When Allah most exalted made it possible for me to examine written works by masters of various religions and faith communities from throughout the world,... then I conceived the wish to gather all this into a digest that would contain everything that the pious have professed and the faithful have followed, as a warning for those who have insight and as a source of insight for those willing to take warning.[15]

He begins by describing the dozens of denominations that claim adherence to Islam, both Sunni and Shia. Then Shahrastani presents the religions considered to be closest to the Muslim creed: the people of the Book—Jews and Nasara (Nazarenes)—as well as "those who have the likeness of a book" (such as *al-Majus*, "the Magians" or Zoroastrians). He goes on to give careful thought to Greek philosophy (thereby reflecting his sympathetic understanding that Hellenic wisdom also constituted a form of religious life). He includes discussions of Brahminic Hinduism and Buddhism as well. The result is a text that is fair-minded in approach and encyclopedic in its range of interests: an astounding intellectual achievement.

Shahrastani's discourse on dualism comes just after the section on Zoroastrianism. Here he summarizes a Gnostic creation myth that provides a slight variation on the cosmogony I summarized for you earlier:

> Some dualists tell the story that light and darkness have always been eternally existent. But light is sensitive and knowledgeable, whereas darkness is ignorant and blind.... The uppermost reaches of the darkness attacked the lower fringes of the light. Thus the darkness swallowed up a piece of the light, not deliberately or knowingly, but out of ignorance, like a child who cannot tell the difference between a

---

[15] Abu al-Fath al-Shahrastani, *Kitab al-milal wa-al-nihal*, ed. Muhammad Sayyid Kilani (Cairo: Maktabat Mustafa al-Babi, 1976), 1:11; translated from the Arabic by D. Pinault.

hot coal and a dried date. [Here the Arabic text offers a nicely phrased prose rhyme: *la yafsil bayna al-jamrah wa-al-tamrah*].[16]

Shahrastani gives us detailed descriptions of a number of Gnostic systems that came to his attention. Here I will briefly mention three. All of them originated in the Near East before Muhammad's time and survived for centuries after the beginning of the Islamic conquests.

The first, and the best known, is Manichaeism, the religion that Saint Augustine discovered as a teen and adhered to for some years before embracing the Christian faith. Manichaeism arose in third-century Iraq; the scholar Michael Morony characterizes it as "an ecumenical syncretism of pagan, gnostic, Magian, Judaeo-Christian, and Indian traditions".[17] Its founder, identified by Shahrastani as Mani ibn Fatik, was of ethnic Iranian origin and grew up in the vicinity of the Iraqi city of Ctesiphon, at that time the capital of the Persian Empire.

For centuries the region had been a crossroads for spiritual wanderers and visionaries from east and west, a reality reflected in the geographical breadth of Mani's own testimony. He preached that a variety of prophets had been commissioned to go to a variety of lands. The Buddha had been sent to India, he proclaimed, and Zoroaster to Persia; Hermes had been dispatched to Egypt, Plato to Greece, and Jesus to "the land of the Byzantines and the West; and after Christ, Paul had been sent to them as well." After this list of messengers, Shahrastani appends an addition that may reflect attempts by Manichaean preachers in his own day to appeal to Muslim audiences: "Then there came to the land of the Arabs the 'seal of the prophets'" (a Koranic title for Muhammad).[18]

And what message, according to Mani, did all these prophets preach? Like other Gnostics, Mani believed that pneuma sparks of divine light had been captured and entangled by darkness. But he propounded a distinctive vision of salvation and why our world was created: the "king of radiance" ordered his angels to create the cosmos for the purpose of extricating the "various species of light" from the darkness in which it had become mired. Shahrastani tells us that,

---

[16] Ibid., 1:253.
[17] Morony, *Iraq*, p. 404.
[18] Shahrastani, *Kitab*, 1:248; Morony, *Iraq*, p. 404; Koran 33:40.

according to Mani, when the light particles have finally been delivered from the darkness, "This will be the resurrection, and the return, and the life to come" (a very Christian turn of phrase).[19]

Shahrastani then summarizes Mani's explanation of how the cosmos can function as a mechanism of celestial salvation:

> This is what Mani prescribes to achieve liberation and the raising up of the particles of light: prayers of praise, a life of holiness and sanctification, good speech, and pious deeds. Through this, the radiant particles ascend on columns of light at dawn to the sphere of the moon. The moon continues to receive these from the beginning until the middle of the month, at which point it is filled and becomes a full moon. Thereupon, until the end of the month, it channels these particles to the sun, which in turn propels them to the Light above itself. This flow continues throughout the cosmos until it reaches the highest Light, that which provides deliverance and salvation.[20]

Crystalline globes surrounding our world; Christian vocabulary of "resurrection and the return"; Gnostic imagery of souls escaping at dawn "on columns of light": a compellingly poetic vision of salvation. No wonder it enchanted Augustine.

Manichaeans survived for centuries under Islamic rule. At the time of the early Muslim conquests, they were classed along with Zoroastrians, Jews, and Christians as "people of the Book": they could retain their faith in exchange for paying the discriminatory jizyah tax and acknowledging Muslim political dominance. The tenth-century encyclopedist and polymath Muhammad ibn Ishaq al-Nadim personally knew some three hundred Manichaeans who were resident in Baghdad "during the days of Mu'izz al-Dawlah" (who reigned from A.D. 946 to 967). Subsequently, however, they were persecuted by the caliphs of the 'Abbasid dynasty and took refuge in Central Asia.[21]

The second dualist system presented to us by Shahrastani is that of the Daysaniyah, "the disciples of Bardesanes" (in Arabic, Ibn Daysan), a Christian Gnostic of the early third century. Bardesanes lived

---

[19] Shahrastani, *Kitab*, 1:247.

[20] Ibid.

[21] Al-Nadim, *The Fihrist of al-Nadim: A Tenth-Century Survey of Muslim Culture*, ed. and trans. Bayard Dodge (New York: Columbia University Press, 1970), 2:802–3.

in Edessa, a Mesopotamian city located in what is today southeastern Turkey near the Iraqi border. Edessa was an early center of Syriac Christianity. Since ancient times it has been linked to legends about the biblical patriarch Abraham and the revered relic later known as the Shroud of Turin.

Gnostic influence can be seen in Bardesanes' acknowledgment of the reality and stern power of the planetary spheres, which weigh heavily on our individual existences in the form of cosmic fate. But (and here, I think, we see his Christian identity asserting itself) this does not excuse us from fighting back. "Human life", as one summary of his teaching states, "is limited by natural laws and further by fate; human freedom consists in taking up the battle with fate and limiting its power as far as possible." Bardesanes, in other words, emphasizes our dignity as created beings and our ability to wrestle with the world into which we have been flung.[22]

Surviving textual evidence suggests that Bardesanes' Christology— like that of many other Christian Gnostics—was docetic: he "denied the suffering of Jesus".[23] The blend of Gnosticism and Christianity in Bardesanes' world view can be discerned in Shahrastani's presentation of his cosmology:

> The companions of Bardesanes affirm the existence of two elemental principles—Light and Darkness. Light generates goodness, intentionally and by choice. Darkness generates evil, by the compulsion of its nature. . . .
>
> The disciples of Bardesanes differ concerning the mixture of Light and Darkness and the question of salvation. Some claim that the Light entered the Darkness and mingled with it. But the Darkness received it crudely and with harshness. Consequently, the Light suffered harm and was hurt by the Darkness. The Light wanted to refine and calm the Darkness and then deliver itself from this dark realm. . . .
>
> Other disciples say: Rather, the Darkness used deceitful stratagems until it managed to adhere to the lowest levels of the realm of Light. Then the Light struggled to free itself and repel the Darkness. In this

---

[22] Claude Huart, "Ibn Daisan", in *Encyclopaedia of Islam*, ed. M. Houtsma, A.J. Wensinck et al., 1st ed. (repr., Leiden: Brill, 1993), 3:370.

[23] Nicole Kelley, *Knowledge and Religious Authority in the Pseudo-Clementines: Situating the "Recognitions" in Fourth-Century Syria* (Tübingen: Mohr Siebeck, 2006), p. 185.

struggle, the Light propped itself against the Darkness below it but became even more immersed.

This is like the situation of people who want to climb out of the mud into which they have fallen. They put their weight on their legs and try to get out but only become more mired in the mud.

Thus the Light needs time to try to undertake its liberation from the Darkness and withdraw to its own world.

And still other disciples of Bardesanes say: In fact, the Light entered certain regions of the Darkness as a voluntary choice to reclaim and reconcile those regions and to extract from them those portions that are suitable for its own world.[24]

"The Light entered ... the Darkness." Christian readers will be reminded of the opening of John's Gospel. But Bardesanes blends Christian themes of compassion and salvation with grimmer motifs of the world as prison and mud pit.

Followers of Bardesanes survived in the marshlands of southern Iraq until at least the late seventh or early eighth century. The medieval *Fihrist* (catalogue of knowledge) of Muhammad al-Nadim indicates that "scattered communities" of this Gnostic sect still existed in the tenth century in Khorasan (the region comprising much of northeast Iran, Afghanistan, and Central Asia).[25]

Finally, the third of the Gnostic systems mentioned by Shahrastani is a sect affiliated with a Christian of the second century named Marcion of Sinope, a native of Pontus on the southern shores of the Black Sea. Although his teachings were condemned as heresy by his Christian contemporaries, Marcionite communities persisted in the Near East well into the tenth century and perhaps later.[26]

What distinguished Marcion was his fierce hatred of the God of the Old Testament, whom he equated with the Demiurge, the creator of our prison-dungeon world. According to Marcion, this God enforced a punitive and repressive "Law" and was utterly distinct from the deity of Light, whom Marcionites equated with the loving God of the New Testament. This approach to the Bible led Marcion to a radical rereading of the Old Testament, whereby disruptive,

---

[24] Shahrastani, *Kitab*, 1:250–51.
[25] Morony, *Iraq*, p. 404; Nadim, *Fihrist*, 2:806.
[26] Morony, *Iraq*, p. 402; Nadim, *Fihrist*, 2:807.

sinful, and violent figures such as Cain were honored as heroes who had tried to defy the tyrannical lord of our world. The Garden of Eden story is also reinterpreted in this light: "Marcionite sub-sects honored ... even the Serpent who had tried to give Adam and Eve the knowledge denied to them by the Creator." That is, the Serpent gave the first humans the Gnostic illumination that would lead them to defy the Demiurge and seek out the alien God.[27]

Marcion was denounced as a heretic not only for depicting our created world as radically evil but also for his Christology. A fourth-century Christian source summarized Marcion's view of Jesus as follows: "That he [Christ] appeared as (ὡς) man but was not man, and as enfleshed but (was) not enfleshed, and suffered in appearance (δοκήσις), but did not undergo birth/becoming (γένεσις) or suffering, except in semblance (δοκειν)."[28]

Christ "did not undergo ... suffering, except in semblance": this is a key element of Gnostic doceticism. For Marcion as for other Gnostics, Jesus could not have had a truly physical body, nor could he have truly experienced earthly life; for this would have tainted our Savior with both the agonies and fleshly weaknesses of our evil dungeon-world.

Shahrastani's description of Marcionite dualism characterizes the realm we are forced to inhabit as a "world of mixture" (that is, one in which—as in other cosmologies we have glimpsed—light has become trapped by darkness). His presentation combines vocabulary from both Christian and Islamic scripture: "The Light sent to the world of mixture a Christ-spirit (*ruhan masihiyah*). It is the spirit of Allah and His son (*huwa ruh Allah wa-ibnuhu*)."[29]

The reference to the "Christ-spirit" as the "spirit of Allah" sounds very Islamic, of course, recalling for us surah 4:171, a Koranic verse we have encountered earlier: "Christ Jesus son of Mary was Allah's prophet, and His word, which He cast upon Mary, and a spirit from Him." But characterizing Jesus as Allah's "son" reminds us that Marcion regarded himself as Christian.

[27] Morony, *Iraq*, p. 402.

[28] Ps.-Hippolytus, *Refutation* X.19.3, cited in Judith M. Lieu, *Marcion and the Making of a Heretic: God and Scripture in the Second Century* (Cambridge: University Press, 2015), p. 377.

[29] Shahrastani, *Kitab*, 1:252.

The Marcionite plan of salvation presented by Shahrastani combines Christian and Gnostic motifs. A cosmic primordial "element" had "fallen into the net of the accursed darkness" and become trapped in our prison world. It was "out of pity" for this entrapped element, Shahrastani tells us, that the "Christ-spirit" was sent down to the world, "in order to liberate it [the captive element] from the snares of the demons."[30]

It is telling in this context that the savior who is sent into our darkness is described as a "spirit", with no reference to a human envelope of flesh of any kind. This ethereal and incorporeal quality of the docetic Christ is characteristic of Gnostic thought.

"Do not consider dead those who have been killed in Allah's path": Is it possible the Koran does not really deny the crucifixion after all?

So: what we have established thus far—with Shahrastani's very able assistance—is that Christian Gnostic sects were active in the Near East in the time of the prophet Muhammad and were also well known to Muslims of subsequent generations. Gnostic motifs were present among certain Christian and quasi-Christian sects in Coptic Egypt, Syriac Mesopotamia, and Sassanid Iraq. It strikes me, then, as highly likely that Muhammad in his early travels had heard stories that described Jesus as a docetic savior who only seemed to undergo the torments of crucifixion.

But that still leaves the question of motivation. *Why* did Muhammad choose to depict Christ's crucifixion as docetic rather than actual?

Before tackling this question, I will draw your attention to the following. Although the overwhelming majority of Muslim theologians and scriptural commentators through the centuries have accepted the Koran's presentation of Christ's docetic crucifixion, there have been some scholars in recent years—both Muslim and non-Muslim—who have tried to deny that the crucifixion portrayed by the Koran is actually docetic.

[30] Ibid.

What seems to be a factor motivating such scholars is a desire to keep open the possibility for constructive interfaith relations between Muslims and Christians. For example, Suleiman Mourad, in the introduction to an article published in 2011 entitled "Does the Qur'an Deny or Assert Jesus' Crucifixion and Death?", notes how Islamic scripture's portrayal of the crucifixion has been a recurrent issue for "scholars concerned with religious dialogue". He then goes on to note: "One reason for this interest is the perception that the Qur'an refutes the crucifixion and death of Jesus; this perception ... places Islam's scripture in direct opposition to the foundational doctrine of Christian faith."[31]

Note Mourad's use of the word "perception". He recognizes that Christians might well be put off by what the Koran says about the crucifixion, since, as he himself acknowledges, it stands "in direct opposition to the foundational doctrine of Christian faith". His approach is to try to remove this barrier to interfaith dialogue by arguing that the Koran does not really say what it seems to be saying.

This is a tall order. After all, as we have seen earlier, the Koran states flatly, "They said, 'We killed Christ Jesus son of Mary, Allah's messenger.' But they did not kill him, nor did they crucify him. But a likeness was made to appear to them." This Koranic assertion amounts to an attempt to refute the bedrock of Christian faith.

Mourad deals with this by claiming the words "they did not kill him" should be understood only metaphorically. To support this argument, he cites a Medinan verse recited by Muhammad after a large number of his *mujahidin* (holy warriors) were killed fighting Meccan pagans at the battle of Uhud: "Do not consider dead those who have been killed in Allah's path. Rather, they are alive and are being provided with sustenance in the presence of their Lord" (Koran 3:169). True, these holy warriors were killed; but since they are now in heaven, says the scripture, they should not be considered dead.

With this as a paradigm, Mourad reminds readers that the Koran tells us Allah raised Jesus up to heaven. "[F]or someone to be considered killed," states Mourad, "he must remain dead!" Therefore, so his argument goes, the Koranic statement "They did not kill him" simply means Jesus is now alive in Paradise. Mourad's conclusion: "There is no denial of the act of crucifixion here" in Islamic scripture.[32]

A more complex argument that reaches fundamentally the same conclusion is developed by Todd Lawson in his book *The Crucifixion and the Qur'an*. Like Mourad, Lawson acknowledges that the Koran's presentation of a docetic crucifixion is a problem for interfaith dialogue:

> Obviously, such a doctrinal position serves as a great obstacle separating Muslims and Christians on the grounds of belief. But, more importantly, such belief frankly serves to diminish Islam in the eyes of Christians and so-called 'Westerners' whose cultural identity is bound up, whether they are believers or not, with the axiomatic and unquestionable 'myth' of the death and resurrection of Jesus.[33]

Lawson sets out to remove this doctrinal "obstacle separating Muslims and Christians" by arguing that the Koran does not mean what it literally says about the crucifixion. To accomplish this, he makes use of certain medieval Shia interpretations of this topic.

Lawson begins by conceding that, throughout the centuries, in the past as in the present, most mainstream Sunni and Shia exegetes, along with the vast majority of Muslim believers, have accepted the Koran's repudiation of the crucifixion. But he draws attention to the work of several commentators who belonged to a minoritarian Shia sect known as the Isma'ilis.

One example is the tenth-century scholar Abu Hatim al-Razi, who accepted the reality of Jesus' crucifixion, with the following proviso, as summarized by Lawson: "That which *appeared* to be crucified was precisely the body, what others will refer to as 'the human dimension' (*al-nasut*), while the spirit or true reality of Jesus was 'raised' to his Lord." Lawson also cites some tenth-century Muslim freethinkers who realized that denying a historically certifiable event such as Jesus' crucifixion tended to diminish the intellectual claims of Islam as a coherent, rational, and philosophical system.[34]

---

[32] Ibid., 2:354.
[33] Todd Lawson, *The Crucifixion and the Qur'an: A Study in the History of Muslim Thought* (Oxford: Oneworld Publications, 2009), p. 1.
[34] Ibid., pp. 81–86.

Lawson combines this Isma'ili approach with Koranic surah 3:169 (the same verse used by Mourad—"Do not consider dead those who have been killed in Allah's path") to argue for what he calls a "figurative Docetism". It was only the "body of Jesus" that was crucified, "as distinct from his spiritual and eternal reality that, by its very nature, is invulnerable to suffering and death." This particular Islamic exegesis of the crucifixion, he insists, is compatible with New Testament texts such as the Gospel of John and Paul's Letter to the Philippians.[35]

"Invulnerable to suffering": in a later chapter, I will want to challenge this Islamic claim when we discuss Christian teachings on the Lamb of God and the post-Resurrection marks of Christ's wounds. For now I will note the following:

What is missing from Lawson's account is any recognition that the difference between Islamic and Christian understandings on this issue has to do with much more than simply the reality of the crucifixion as a historical datum. It is also a question of issues that are not adequately addressed in his argument about the crucifixion, just as they are not adequately addressed in Muslim Koran-exegesis: the reality of Christ's *suffering*; the *meaningful, voluntary,* and *salvific* nature of that suffering; and the quality of divine *love* that suffuses this voluntary suffering. This absence is significant but entirely understandable; for suffering, love, and self-sacrifice are nowhere to be found in the Koran in its references to Jesus.

The question of Roman involvement in the crucifixion

Lawson also presents an additional and rather different type of argument to try to prove that Islamic scripture does not deny the crucifixion. When the Koran states, "They did not kill them", the "they" in question are the Jews; and it was the Roman state after all, not the Jewish authorities, that carried out Christ's execution. Lawson remarks that "This argument has been used extensively by modern Christian authors in their attempts to accommodate the Qur'anic and the Gospel accounts of the crucifixion."[36]

[35] Ibid., pp. 4–6, 24.
[36] Ibid., p. 140.

But this argument misses the point Muhammad himself wished to make with these verses. Although the historical distinction made by Lawson (the Roman role in Christ's death) is important, it seems not to have mattered to Muhammad. Nowhere does the Koran ever mention the Romans of Jesus' time. The Koran's statement "They did not kill him" is *not* some interfaith goodwill gesture to excuse Jews from a role in Christ's death. Rather, it dates from a period in Medina when Muhammad had already begun to turn against the local Jews of the region. By the time of his reciting these crucifixion verses, Muhammad had already shifted the *qiblah* (prayer direction) from Jerusalem to Mecca, ordered the expulsion of at least one Jewish tribe (the Qaynuqa') from Medina, and arranged for the assassination of a Jew (Ka'b ibn al-Ashraf) who had composed defamatory poetry about Muhammad.[37]

So, no, these Koranic crucifixion verses were not meant to be conciliatory at all. Instead, Muhammad used these verses to claim that the Jews of Christ's time had failed in what they attempted. In saying this, he wanted to deny them (and, by extension, the Medinan Jews of his own time) the pleasure of a victory they supposedly claimed. Muhammad of the mid-to-late-Medinan period saw Jesus as an anti-Jewish predecessor and proxy for himself; and he used the docetic version of the crucifixion to claim the Islamic Jesus as a winner against anyone who opposed Allah—or Allah's prophets.

Why the Koran—and Muhammad—denied the reality of Christ's crucifixion

Contrary to Lawson and Mourad, I think it is clear that the Koran rejects the notion that Jesus was crucified. I base my argument on how Muhammad viewed Jesus as Allah's messenger in relation to his own self-understanding as a prophet.

First, it is important here to recall that Muhammad understood the Koran not only as a revelation to others but as a comfort and source of encouragement for himself. A number of verses are presented as

---

[37] W. Montgomery Watt, *Muhammad: Prophet and Statesman* (New York: Oxford University Press, 1961), pp. 127–28; 'Ali, *Meaning of the Holy Qur'an*, p. 182.

being directly addressed to him in order to help him through difficult moments. A good example is surah 35:24–25, where Allah speaks to Muhammad: "We have sent you in truth as someone who brings good news and as a warner. Every community in the past has been visited by a warner. And if they call you a liar, well: their own ancestors made the same accusation in the past against the prophets who came to them with clear proofs and signs."

Verses such as these suggest that Muhammad put into perspective his own challenges as Allah's messenger by contemplating what other prophets in bygone times had had to endure. Like Muhammad, his spiritual predecessors—Noah, Abraham, Hud, Salih, Lot, Moses—preached tawhid but were rejected and threatened by those to whom they preached. In each case, Allah intervened with what I call an eleventh-hour rescue: cooling the flames into which Abraham had been pitched; drowning Pharaoh's army; or saving a righteous remnant while destroying foes by flood, earthquake, or a hail of brimstone and fire. As surah 40:51 states, "In truth, we deliver Our messengers and those who believe, both during life in this world and on Judgment Day, the day that witnesses stand forth."

Out of all the prophetic predecessors he admired, Muhammad seems to have identified his own situation particularly closely with that of Jesus. Not only did Jesus preach tawhid and experience rejection, as had earlier prophets. The Koran underlines Jesus' closeness to Muhammad by highlighting Jesus' conflict with the Jews to whom he preached (just like the conflict Muhammad experienced with the Jews of Medina). It notes that Jesus was accused of practicing sorcery (the same accusation that was hurled at Muhammad). And it describes Jesus' disciples as Ansar, "those who help bring about Allah's victory" (the same term the Koran applies to Muhammad's helpers in Medina).

But in embracing Jesus as a predecessor and brother-prophet, Muhammad had to deal with a certain irreducible historical datum: what happened at the end of Christ's life on earth. There was no ignoring the Cross: it loomed too large on the skyline of time. Like the Gnostics, Muhammad could not look away from the crucifixion. As an event, it was simply too well known.

How to resolve this? The Gnostics dealt with the historical reality of the Cross by positing a docetic crucifixion, as we have seen: it only seemed as if Jesus had been nailed to the Cross, but in reality he never suffered.

The Near Eastern sects we examined above, together with the Arabic references in Shahrastani and the Koran's own citations of the Sabians, provide evidence to suggest that Muhammad had heard Gnostic tales of a Christ who escaped death at the hands of his persecutors. We also know from Islamic sources that Muhammad learned from Christians such as Bahira the monk, Quss the preacher, and Jabra the slave swordsmith. From them he would likely have heard the orthodox doctrines of how Christ truly suffered and died a truly redemptive death on the Cross.

Thus Muhammad faced a choice in how to present the crucifixion in his own Koranic preaching. Why did he pick the docetic version? After all, Islam is not a Gnostic faith; on the contrary, it is very much a religion of this world. It is only in the crucifixion that Gnosticism intersects with Muhammad's religion.

Insight into this question can be found by noting that surah 4:157 (the verse on Jesus and his docetic fate) is not the only place in the Koran that mentions crucifixion. I would argue that these other scriptural passages give us some idea of Muhammad's own view of this form of execution.

I have in mind two passages in particular. The first is from the Koran's version of the story of Joseph in Egypt. You may know the tale already from Genesis. After his brothers sell him to a caravan of Ishmaelite slave-traders, Joseph resists the allures of Potiphar's wife, is falsely accused of assaulting her, and is then cast into prison. There he meets two fellow prisoners—Pharaoh's cupbearer and baker—and interprets their dreams for them. The cupbearer's dream is auspicious; Joseph gladdens him with the news that within three days he will be restored to Pharaoh's favor.

But the baker is not so lucky. According to the biblical Book of Genesis, Joseph tells him, "Within three days Pharaoh will lift up your head—from you!—and hang you on a tree; and the birds will eat the flesh from you." The outcome: "He [Pharaoh] restored the chief butler to his butlership, and he placed the cup in Pharaoh's hand; but he hanged the chief baker, as Joseph had interpreted to them" (Gen 40:19–22).

Now let's look at how the Koran (in surah 12:41) modifies the baker's doom. Here is how Joseph interprets the dreams of his fellow inmates: "O my two companions of the prison! As for one of you, well, he will pour wine for his lord. But as for the other: well, he will be crucified, and the birds will eat from his head." And that is all the Koran has to say about the baker.

Crucifixion (a form of punishment not present in the biblical version of this story) is presented here in a way that has nothing positive, heroic, or noble about it. It is merely an outcome allotted to a character who has no more than a bit part in this drama. The baker is a minor throwaway player, consigned to a luckless and wretched fate.

So brutal is this punishment that the Koran commentator 'Abdullah Yusuf 'Ali speculates on what crime the baker might have committed to merit crucifixion: "Perhaps he had been found guilty—perhaps he had been really guilty—of some act of embezzlement or of joining in some palace intrigue, and he was to die a malefactor's death on the cross, followed by exposure to birds of the air—vultures pecking away at his eyes and cheeks."[38] The Koran offers us no explanation; the baker is nameless and disappears from our view.

Even more telling is surah 5:33:

> The punishment for those who wage war against Allah and His messenger, and who strive to spread corruption throughout the land, is that they be killed, or crucified, or have their hands and feet cut off on alternate sides of their bodies, or that they be expelled in exile from the land. That is their shame and disgrace in this life; and in the afterlife they will have a dreadful punishment.

Based on the words of the Koran, words that were spoken and preached by Muhammad himself, we can see how he regarded crucifixion. Muhammad saw it as an appropriate punishment for those guilty of the worst sins (waging war against Allah and His prophet), a fate involving both public humiliation ("shame and disgrace in this life") and the specter of an afterlife of more horrors to come.

Further insight into Islamic scriptural views of crucifixion can be gained by consulting Baydawi's Koran commentary on surah 4:157. Baydawi quotes the boast "We killed the Messiah" and then states: "In claiming this, it is likely that they [the Jews] said this as a form of mockery. Similar to this is 'Your prophet who has been sent to

---

[38] 'Ali, *Meaning of the Holy Qur'an*, p. 560, commentary on Koran 12:41.

you is majnun!'"³⁹ Here Baydawi is quoting the cry of Pharaoh in surah 26:27, an episode where Moses confronts the Egyptians with his Islamic message. Pharaoh's response is to shout that Moses is jinn-ridden.

The implication offered by this Koranic commentary is as follows: to claim Jesus was crucified is akin to claiming a prophet is majnun (a point on which we know Muhammad was particularly sensitive). Each is a form of public insult—as the Koran says, a "shame and disgrace in this life".

Now let's assemble the evidence and review what we have learned about the Koran's presentation of Jesus, crucifixion, and prophethood.

First, Muhammad decreed crucifixion for those who opposed Allah and his prophets.

Second, Muhammad felt a sense of kinship with all the prophets but identified himself particularly closely with the experience of Jesus.

Third, Muhammad viewed his Koranic revelations as a comfort to help him endure periods of rejection and envision a triumphant outcome.

Fourth, Muhammad saw the career path of prophets as one that was crowned with vindication. As surah 10:103 puts it, "In the end, We deliver Our messengers and those who believe."

Given all this, it makes perfect sense that the Koran insists on a docetic crucifixion, denying that Jesus was either crucified or killed. In my opinion, Muhammad would never have preached that the prophet Jesus had truly undergone a form of punishment that Muhammad himself decreed for those who oppose Allah and His prophets.

To sum up: the Koran and the New Testament differ radically in their presentations of Jesus, the crucifixion, and the significance of the Cross. In the post-Koranic era, Islamic theological texts and devotional literature articulated these differences even further, as we will see in the next chapter.

---

³⁹ Nasir al-Din Abu Sa'id al-Baydawi, *Anwar al-tanzil wa-asrar al-ta'wil* (Beirut, Dar al-Kutub al-'Ilmiyah, 1988), 1:247, commentary on Koran 4:157; translated from the Arabic by D. Pinault.

CHAPTER 8

"WHEREVER THE SUN SET, THERE HE WOULD HALT AND PRAY TILL DAWN": JESUS IN THE ASCETIC AND SUFI MYSTICAL TRADITIONS

"We do not want the Garden, and we are not afraid of the Fire": My introduction to Egyptian Sufism

Cairo, summer 1982. Enrolled in an Arabic language course, I found myself with a homework assignment unlike any I had ever had before. Each of us, the instructor told the other students and me on the first day, was to spend our free time researching some aspect of life in Cairo, something that would force us out of the classroom and onto the streets. At semester's end, we would each give a sixty-minute presentation—in Egyptian Arabic—on what we had found.

I raised my hand and asked if I could do something on Cairo's tariqahs (Sufi brotherhoods or associations). "Certainly," grinned the instructor, "if you can find one that will take you in."

It involved two weeks of legwork—making inquiries, making a pest of myself, and exercising my Arabic (which was what our instructor wanted). It meant wandering from Saladin's Citadel to the Muqattam Hills and the City of the Dead, pressing through the crowds from the Tentmakers' Street to the bazaar of Khan al-Khaleeli, pausing at every mosque and saint's shrine I found en route. But I got what I had hoped for: a contact that led to one of the city's tariqahs.

The tariqah in question was an order known as the Burhaniyah. Its master was called Sheikh 'Uthman. Affable and genial, he was not at all put out when I explained I am a Christian ("Not a problem", was all he had to say on that point) and that I wanted to sit in on some of their dhikr rituals (which involve the "recollection" and recitation of the Names of Allah).

He said fine, provided that before I attend any dhikr I first take part in a few nighttime *halqahs* (circles, lectures where students sit gathered around their master).

What stays in my memory from the initial Sufi *halqah* I attended was a comment made to me by two young *murids* (aspirants or novices) who sat beside me while the sheikh lectured. (He had tasked them with answering my questions and keeping me out of trouble—I was the object of many an inquisitive gaze in that crowded hall.)

The comment the two young men made was in response to a question I whispered as we sat at the back of the room. What I said went something like this: *Here we are, two hours into a presentation on the spiritual life. You attend talks like this every Wednesday night. Then every Thursday night you go to the dhikr. You are also encouraged to perform spiritual exercises on a daily basis. All this, on top of the already rigorous ritual life every Muslim is supposed to lead: prayer five times a day; jum'ah (congregational worship) on Fridays; fasting during Ramadan. Tell me: are Sufis simply hyper-worried about making it into heaven?*

At once the *murids* replied, their words almost in unison (which made me think they were repeating something they had learned from Sheikh 'Uthman): "We do not want the Garden, and we are not afraid of the Fire. What we want is just the face of Allah, now, that is all."

At that moment I did not fully appreciate it, but with time I came to recognize that these words provided me with an insight into one of the sources of motivation for Sufis (and for practitioners of other mystical traditions, too, I should think, in religions throughout the world).

Years later, I came upon the same theme in a text that told an anecdote about Rabi'a al-'Adawiyyah. An eighth-century native of Basra (in Iraq), she is one of the most famous saints of the Sufi path. Here is the story:

> One day some friends-of-God [holy men] saw Rabi'a running along with fire in one hand and water in the other. "Lady of the next world, where are you going and what does this mean?"
>
> Rabi'a replied: "I am going to burn paradise and douse hellfire, so that both veils may be lifted from those on the quest and they will become sincere of purpose. God's servants will learn to see him

without hope for reward or fear of punishment. As it is now, if you took away hope for reward and fear of punishment, no one would worship or obey."[1]

We will have reason to recall this burn-paradise/douse-hellfire tale in a subsequent chapter, when we travel with a band of Crusaders to thirteenth-century Damascus. For now, let's consider the message conveyed by Rabi'a and the two *murids* I met in Cairo. To do that, we need to examine what is said about the afterlife in the Koran—especially the details provided by the Koran about the punishments or rewards we should expect.

Let's begin by reading the following passages from Islamic scripture. All these verses are from Meccan surahs, which means that Muhammad's primary audience would have been his Jahiliyah pagan neighbors:

> In truth, the tree of Zaqqum will be the food of sinners. It is like molten brass, and it will boil within their bellies, the way that scalding water boils. Seize him, and drag him, into the middle of the fire of hell! Then pour over his head the torture of boiling water! Taste! You, yes, you, the powerful one, the one with noble ancestry! This is what you used to doubt and quarrel about! (Koran 44:43–50)

Another passage in the Koran provides more details about hell's vegetation and how it functions as an instrument of Allah's wrath:

> The tree of Zaqqum: We made it a punishment for those who do wrong. It is a tree that sprouts from the floor of hell. Its stalks are like the heads of satanic demons. The wicked will eat from that tree and fill their bellies with it. Then they will be given a roiling brew of boiling water; after which they will be returned to hellfire. They had found their forefathers following the wrong path, astray. And then they, too, found themselves hurrying along the same path. (Surah 37:62–74)

Medieval Koran commentators found an earthly analogue to the "tree of Zaqqum", identifying it as "one of the most noxious and

---

[1] Cited in Michael A. Sells, ed. and trans., *Early Islamic Mysticism: Sufi, Qur'an, Mi'raj, Poetic and Theological Writings* (New York: Paulist Press, 1996), p. 151.

bitter shrubs in Tihamah, which Allah has also planted in Gehenna."[2] Tihamah is a place Muhammad's Meccan audience would have known well. It is the coastal plain along the Red Sea shores of Arabia and Yemen, known and dreaded as one of the hottest and most oppressively sun-scorched sites in the Arabian peninsula.

Having to drink water that scalds and burns; making do on a diet of ungiving plants with spiky stalks; journeying forever along an oven-hot "floor of hell". Bedouin travelers knew what it was like to live in such a world. What the Koran presented for Meccan pagans was a recognizable afterlife: tactile, palpable, real.

Also palpable are the Koran's descriptions of the Paradise that awaits Muslim believers (again, I draw here on Meccan surahs):

> As for the pious, they will be in a place safe and secure, among gardens and springs of water. They will be dressed in silk and brocade, facing each other. We will pair them with lustrously dark-eyed houris. They will be able to call for every kind of fruit to be brought to them, as they enjoy an existence of security ... a bounty from your Lord....
>
> They will recline on carpets lined with brocade.... In the gardens will be virgin women who keep their gaze lowered, virgins kept in reserve for the believing men of paradise, virgins never previously deflowered by man or jinn ... like sapphires, like pearls....
>
> The companions of the right hand ... will be seated on elevated seats.... Immortal youths will serve them, with drinking glasses, and pitchers, and cups from a fountain. From this drinking they will experience no hangover or ache. There will be fruit, any kind they want; and the flesh of birds, whatever they desire; and houris with lustrous eyes, like hidden pearls: a reward for what they have done. (Koran 44:51–57, 55:54–58, 56:8–24)

Again, consider Muhammad's original audience: Meccan merchants, pagan Bedouins, accustomed to cycles of scarcity and indulgence, schooled to endure what they had to and binge when they could. Understandable, then, the values we have seen in Jahiliyah poetry: carpe-diem hedonism.

---

[2] Jalal al-Din 'Abd al-Rahman al-Suyuti, *Tafsir al-jalalayn*, ed. Marwan Sawar (Beirut: Dar al-Ma'rifah, n.d.), p. 591, commentary on Koran 37:62. See also Nasir al-Din Abu Sa'id al--Baydawi, *Anwar al-tanzil wa-asrar al-ta'wil* (Beirut: Dar al-Kutub al-'Ilmiyah, 1988), 2:295.

But it would not be accurate to say the Koran frowns altogether on sensuality. Rather, it promulgates what I would call transposed or postponed hedonism. In this life, believers are enjoined to follow a stringently regulated regimen of self-control, including mandated prayer, seasons of fasting, and total abstinence from alcohol. But in the next life, they will enjoy a heaven of sensual delights, depicted in terms that would have been most appetizing to an audience that was all too acquainted with barren scarcity and desert heat. Fruit, flesh, no anxieties about where the next meal would come from; a limitless supply of houris and plenty to drink (but with no morning-after hangovers); gardens and flowing streams. No wonder the color of Islam is the color of Paradise: green.

Post-Koranic pious literature has developed a tradition of elaborating ever more details on what awaits us in the next life. When I lived in the Pakistani city of Lahore, news vendors at various street-side venues sold a popular-format Urdu-language magazine that featured in every issue a column called *Islami safhah* (the Islamic page). The column frequently exhorted readers to be mindful of their mortality. One essay urged us to visualize the imminence of death:

> Every person's [predestined] grave makes a daily announcement: "I am the abode of complete desolation; I am the abode of maggots.... When an evildoer or kafir is buried ... seventy serpent-dragons will begin biting him. They are so poisonous that if even one of them exhales its breath onto the earth, then until the Day of Resurrection no grass or crops will ever grow on that spot. These serpents will bite at him constantly until Judgment Day."[3]

Another *Islami safhah* column described the scorpions Allah has allowed to infest hell as a punishment for sinners: "The testimony of their poisonous power is this: when one of them stings, the denizen of hell will feel the lingering, burning pain of the sting for forty years."[4]

Yet another essay cites a *hadith* (a non-Koranic statement by the prophet Muhammad) concerning a grave robber who repents after

---

[3] Amir Husain, "Qabr ka khawf", *Khofnak Dijast* 4, no. 8 (Lahore: December 2000): 2. Translated from the Urdu by D. Pinault.

[4] Mukhtar 'Ali Parimi, "Dozakh ki ag aur andhera", *Khofnak Dijast* 6, no. 1 (May 2002): 3. Translated from the Urdu by D. Pinault.

the discovery he makes in the tombs he tries to plunder: he comes upon the tortured corpses of sinners. He finds that one corpse has been transformed into a tightly fettered pig; another burns in flames; and a third is pierced with "nails of fire".[5]

Sensual punishments; sensual rewards: from seventh-century Meccan Bedouins to twenty-first-century Pakistani Muslims, such incentives have been inducement enough for many ordinary believers.

But not for the Sufis. "We do not want the Garden", my *murid*-guides told me firmly, "and we are not afraid of the Fire." And we have seen how Rabi'a announced herself ready to burn down heaven and dump a quenching bucket over hell. For the mystics, the prospect of rewards and punishments was gross and materialistic—simply the wrong way to organize one's spiritual life. They wanted more. They wanted, as my Sufi friends said, "the face of Allah".

Waving swords at Satan: Jesus as a guide for Sufi conduct

As a discernible social movement, Islamic mysticism seems to have originated very early in Islamic history, partly as a response to the conquests that created an Islamic empire. You will recall that the prophet Muhammad himself had authorized jihad campaigns against Byzantine territories. The leaders of the Muslim *ummah* after his death, known as the *khulafa' rasul Allah* (successors to Allah's messenger) or caliphs, undertook a series of invasions that subjugated Spain, North Africa, the Levant, Iran, and much of Central Asia and the Indian subcontinent.

The results transformed Islamic society. Plunder and tribute flowed into the caliphate. Infidel prisoners by the thousands crowded the slave markets of Damascus and Baghdad. In such a world, to be a Muslim was to be in the top tier of the social order, ranked above dhimmi Jews and Christians and kafir unbelievers.

The consequent risk: an attitude I would call "I've got Allah in my pocket"—the feeling of belonging to a religion that gave one superior status in this life and priority-access boarding for the next. Such status easily led to complacency and spiritual pride.

---

[5] Shabnam Daoud Shinakeh, "Panj qabron ki chashmdid-e halat ne gonahgar ko tawba par amada kar diya", *Khofnak Dijast* 6, no. 7 (November 2002): 4. Translated from the Urdu by D. Pinault.

Troubled by such trends, Sufis turned to the Koran for solace, sometimes interpreting Koran verses in ways that shifted the surface meaning. An example is surah 5:54: "O you who believe! If any of you becomes a renegade-apostate and turns away from his faith, then Allah will bring forth another people. He will love them, and they will love Him. They will be humble with the believers, and harsh against the infidels, engaging in jihad in the path of Allah."

In its original seventh-century context, this verse addressed a situation that Muhammad confronted in Medina. A number of Muslims had abandoned Islam; some Arabs had become attracted to "false prophets" who competed with Muhammad. Baydawi's commentary on this verse mentions an individual named Musaylimah, who preached to a tribe known as the Banu Hanifah.[6]

According to Ibn Ishaq (Muhammad's earliest biographer), Musaylimah "began to utter rhymes in saj' and speak in imitation of the style of the Koran".[7] (You may recall that saj' is a form of prose rhyme found in both Jahiliyah recitation and Islamic scripture.)

Musaylimah went so far as to hail Muhammad as a brother-prophet. He sent him a letter that began: "From Musaylimah, the messenger of Allah, to Muhammad, the messenger of Allah." Muhammad's reply: "From Muhammad, the messenger of Allah, to Musaylimah, the liar." (Muhammad was not about to share his title with competing claimants.) Ultimately, a Muslim army killed Musaylimah and thousands of his followers (all of them condemned as rebels against the emergent Islamic state) at the battle of Yamama in 632.[8]

In this context, the warning inherent in surah 5:54 is clear. If Muhammad's followers become apostates, Allah will simply produce another community of Muslims, who will wage jihad as intended by Allah and who will be "harsh" enough with infidels to stabilize the ummah.

But apostasy, group loyalty, and communal identity—the issues addressed in the above passage—were not what interested the Sufis about this verse. What transfixed them were the words "He will love them, and they will love Him." Torn loose from their original

[6] Baydawi, Anwar, 1:271, commentary on surah 5:54.

[7] Ibn Ishaq, The Life of Muhammad: A Translation of Ibn Ishaq's Sirat Rasul Allah, ed. and trans. A. Guillaume (Karachi; New York: Oxford University Press, 1968), pp. 636–37.

[8] Baydawi, Anwar, 1:271, commentary on Koran 5:54.

historical context, these scriptural words were reinterpreted by Sufis as a marker of Allah's desire to initiate intimate spiritual relations with individual mystical strivers. "It was this Koranic passage", as Annemarie Schimmel explains in her book *Mystical Dimensions of Islam*, "that provided the Sufis ... with proof for their theories of the mutual love between the Creator and the creature."[9]

With this esotericist reading of surah 5:54 in mind, now is a good moment to pause and attempt a general definition of mysticism, one broad enough to apply not only to Islam and Christianity but to faith traditions throughout the world.

Here is my attempt. *Mysticism is that dimension of religion that has to do with an individual's direct, immediate, and personal experience of the Divine in this life, without having to wait for the next life.*

The emphasis on experiencing the divine presence in this life, rather than the next, would satisfy, I think, the burn-heaven/douse-hellfire enthusiasts we encountered earlier. But let's also note the following. Although mystical experience can be unsought and spontaneous, many adherents of various religions believe such experience can be cultivated, can be induced via a set of spiritual disciplines.

This has led certain Muslims to couple Sufism with what is known as *zuhd*: a life path of asceticism. And for many Sufis of the premodern era, one of the foremost examples of a *zahid* (practitioner of *zuhd* or asceticism) was Jesus, son of Mary. Such a notion is reflected in the description of Jesus that we find in Abu Ishaq Ahmad ibn Muhammad al-Tha'labi's eleventh-century work *Qisas al-anbiya'* (Tales of the prophets):

> Jesus had the habit of walking barefoot. He took for himself no home or personal ornaments. He had no property or clothes, nor did he have any food except what would suffice him for that day. Wherever the sun set, there he would halt and pray until dawn.
>
> He cured the blind and the leper, and with Allah's permission he brought the dead back to life.... He was a *zahid* [ascetic], renouncing this world, desirous of the afterlife, eager to engage in the worship of Allah.

---

[9] Annemarie Schimmel, *Mystical Dimensions of Islam* (Chapel Hill: University of North Carolina Press, 1975), p. 40. See also pp. 25 and 138 of Schimmel's book for further discussion of this verse.

He wandered throughout the earth, until the Jews sought him and wished to kill him. But then Allah raised him up to heaven; and Allah is most-knowing.[10]

Certain portions of this description replicate phrasing we have already encountered in the Koran—Jesus performing miracles "with Allah's permission"; Allah rescuing Jesus by raising him to heaven at the crisis of the docetic crucifixion.

But what strikes me as a Christian reader of Tha'labi is how his sketch of Jesus the barefoot and homeless wanderer recalls famous verses from the New Testament Gospels. "Take nothing for your journey," Christ tells the Twelve, "no staff, nor bag, nor bread, nor money" (Lk 9:3). "Foxes have holes, and birds of the air have nests", observes Jesus, comparing his own life to that of the animals he must have studied on his journeys, "but the Son of man has nowhere to lay his head" (Mt 8:20).

Whether Muslims such as Tha'labi drew directly on the Christian Gospels is uncertain. Manuscripts of Arabic translations of the Bible survive from as early as the mid-ninth century; and certain anti--Christian Muslim polemicists (as we will see in a subsequent chapter) consulted the Bible closely in their attempts to refute Christian doctrine. But when it comes to medieval popular-format works such as *Tales of the Prophets*, it is likely that the author drew on Koranic statements about Jesus (as in the passage we have just read) and combined them with an oral storytelling tradition that blended vivid dramatic elements from the Bible and apocryphal Christian texts such as the Arabic Infancy Gospel.[11]

For many centuries, Sufi authors transmitted anecdotes about Jesus in which he is cited as a model of proper behavior for the aspiring mystical novice. An example can be found in an eleventh-century treatise by a spiritual practitioner named 'Abd al-Karim al-Qushayri. A chapter of his treatise is devoted to *adab* (good manners or courteous conduct), a matter of considerable concern for anyone who

[10] Abu Ishaq Ahmad ibn Muhammad ibn Ibrahim al-Tha'labi, *Qisas al-anbiya' al-musamma 'ara'is al-majalis* (Beirut: al-Maktabah al-Thaqafiyah, n.d.), p. 348; translated from the Arabic by D. Pinault.

[11] Tarif Khalidi, *The Muslim Jesus: Sayings and Stories in Islamic Literature* (Cambridge, Mass.: Harvard University Press, 2001), p. 21.

understands that discipline of heart, mind, and action is a prerequisite for cultivating intimacy with the Divine. (As the scholar Tor Andrae wisely notes in his own study of Islamic mysticism, "Life must not be lived at random.")[12] Here is a sampling of what Qushayri had to say:

> And the essence of good manners in conduct (*adab*) is as follows: the gathering of all the qualities of goodness; and thus *al-adib* (the well-bred man) is one who has gathered into himself the qualities of goodness....
>
> I heard the teacher Abu 'Ali al-Daqqaq—may Allah have mercy on him—say, "Man reaches Paradise through his obedience; but by exercising good manners and courtesy in his obedience, he reaches Allah."....
>
> And Abu 'Uthman said, "When love is sound, then impress on the lover the pursuit of courteous behavior."
>
> And al-Nuri said, "For him who receives no training in courtesy at the proper time, his portion is hateful."
>
> And Dhu Nun al-Misri said, "When the novice ceases his use of good manners, then he returns to where he came from."
>
> With regard to the Koranic verse: "And Job when he called out to his Lord, 'Truly hurt befalls me, and You are the most merciful of the merciful'" (surah 21:83), I used to hear the teacher Abu 'Ali—may Allah have mercy on him—say, "Job did *not* say, 'Have mercy on me!' because he held onto courtesy of speech."
>
> And Jesus behaved the same way, when he said, "If You torment them, then they are Your slaves" (surah 5:118); and when he said, "If I used to say it, then You already know it" (surah 5:116). Jesus did *not* say, "I did not say it," out of regard for proper conduct before the divine Presence.[13]

To illustrate good conduct, al-Qushayri presents two figures known from both the Bible and the Koran: Job and Jesus. What our Sufi author chooses to emphasize about these Koranic figures is speech in which they exercise courteous self-discipline. When Job tells Allah of his suffering, he does not express a direct wish (such

---

[12] Tor Andrae, *In the Garden of Myrtles: Studies in Early Islamic Mysticism* (Albany: SUNY Press, 1987), p. 35.

[13] 'Abd al-Karim al-Qushayri, *Al-Risalah al-qushayriyyah*, 2 vols. (Cairo: Dar al-Kutub al-Hadithah, n.d.), 2:558, 563–564; translated by D. Pinault.

as "Have mercy on me!"), for that would be acquisitive, grabby, and rude.

So, too, with the Son of Mary. Qushayri sympathetically imagines Jesus' state of mind when he is commanded to appear before Allah's throne on Judgment Day (a Koranic passage we have seen earlier). Allah asks Jesus whether he was the one responsible for spreading Trinitarian doctrines on earth. Qushayri uses Christ's response as phrased by the Koran—"If I used to say it, then You already know it"—as a model of *adab* for Sufi novices who might be called to account before their own spiritual masters. A flat-out "No" would seem abrupt and crude; Christ's response is self-diminishing and deferential.

While the above passage from Qushayri uses Jesus to demonstrate proper modes of speech, a thirteenth-century text authored by the Sufi master Najm al-Din al-Kubra shows Jesus interacting with the material things of this world:

> It is said of Jesus, upon him be peace, that he was sleeping, with his head resting upon a brick, when he woke up suddenly from his sleep; and there was the Accursed One by his head. Jesus said to him, "Why have you come to me?" Satan replied, "I covet you." Jesus said, "Accursed One, I am the Spirit of Allah. How are you able to covet me?" Satan replied, "You have taken possession of some refuse of mine, and so I covet you." Jesus said, "And what is that refuse?" Satan replied, "That brick beneath your head." Then Jesus, upon him be peace, hurled the brick at him; and so Satan departed from him.[14]

Immediately after telling this story, Najm al-Din goes on to recount what happened to him personally on one occasion during his own private meditations. While trying to concentrate on his dhikr exercises (recollecting the divine Names), he found himself suddenly distracted by Satan's whisperings. The Sufi records that he thereupon sprang into action. Waving a mystic sword upon which were engraved the words "Allah-Allah", he whirled it against the thoughts crowding in to distract him from meditation.

It seems to me that Najm al-Din established a rough equation with this anecdote. His own combat, in which he made use of spiritual

---

[14] Fritz Meier, ed., *Die Fawa'ih al-Gamal wa-Fawatih al-Galal des Nagm ad-Din al-Kubra* (Wiesbaden: Franz Steiner Verlag, 1957), p. 15; translated by D. Pinault.

weaponry, was analogous to Christ's self-defense in pelting Satan with a brick. Like Jesus, when confronted with temptation, he moved quickly to dispel a dark presence.

Casting away a pillow-brick—the sole comfort, rough as it was, that Jesus had allowed himself in this anecdote—demonstrates that he was a true *zahid*, an ascetic renouncing all the things of this world. The renowned twelfth-century philosopher Abu Hamid al--Ghazali illustrates this motif further in a treatise called *Al-Durrah al-fakhirah* (*The Precious Pearl*). He presents Jesus as someone who subjected himself to a discipline of ever-increasing detachment from the world, stripping himself successively of belongings that others would deem essential:

> Learn a lesson from the Messiah, for it is said that he had no purse at all, that he was dressed in the same woolen garment for twenty years, and that in his travels he had only a small mug and a comb. One day he saw a man drinking with his hand, so he threw the mug from his hand and never used it again. Then he passed by a man running his fingers through his beard, so he threw away the comb from his hand and never used it after that.[15]

Elsewhere in this same text, Ghazali continues this identification of Jesus with austerity and poverty. He states that on the Last Day, Allah will call out as follows to the assembled throngs of those who knew poverty in their earthly life: "Greetings to those for whom the world was a prison!" Then Allah will group them under a banner behind Jesus.[16]

*Christ of the Sufis, Christ of the Cross:
Identical or radically different?*

In 2001, a professor of Arabic and Islamic studies in Beirut named Tarif Khalidi published a book entitled *The Muslim Jesus*. It is a useful

---

[15] Abu Hamid al-Ghazali, *The Precious Pearl*, ed. and trans. Jane Idleman Smith (Missoula, Mon.: Scholars Press, 1979), p. 77.

[16] Ibid., p. 75.

work that gathers together many post-Koranic stories and sayings linked to representations of Jesus as a Sufi and Muslim ascetic.

In his introduction, Khalidi makes a statement that clarifies why he assembled these tales: "Clearly, the mystical and often metanomian branch of any tree of religion is the one that most closely intertwines with the similar branch on a neighboring tree."[17] That is, because mysticism is frequently metanomian—that is, inclined to transcend or ignore mere rules and traditional regulations—it is supposedly an ideal agent for dissolving the doctrinal distinctions that keep religions apart. The mystical limbs of one denominational tree will become fruitfully entwined with the mystical branches of a neighboring denominational growth.

Khalidi then goes on to state, "The Jesus of Islamic Sufism became a figure not easily distinguished from the Jesus of the Gospels."[18] Here he sharpens the focus of his assertion: if mysticism in general can bridge the gap between religions, then the Sufi Jesus in particular can serve as a span linking Islam with Christianity. Thus, underlying this collection of ascetic-Sufi Jesus tales, it seems to me, is apparently an interest in what in Arabic is called *taqrib*—interfaith rapprochement, an attempt to diminish, blur, or dissolve theological distinctions between faiths.

In his book, Khalidi assembles scattered Islamic Jesus-sayings and anecdotes from a thousand-year period ranging from the eighth to the eighteenth centuries. "In referring to this body of literature," he states in his introduction, "I shall henceforth use the phrase 'Muslim gospel'", thereby claiming for this material a thematic coherence that might be comparable to that found in each of the Christian New Testament Gospels.[19] This, too, strikes me as part of an attempt at *taqrib*—in this case, scriptural equivalence: if Christians have gospels, well, so do Muslims, in this case a putative "gospel" consisting of Islamic Jesus-sayings and doings that have been assembled and edited by Tarif Khalidi.

What I would like to do here is evaluate Khalidi's assertion with regard to this "Muslim gospel", namely, whether it is accurate to

[17] Khalidi, *Muslim Jesus*, p. 41.
[18] Ibid.
[19] Ibid., p. 3.

claim, as he does, that "the Jesus of Islamic Sufism became a figure not easily distinguished from the Jesus of the Gospels." To test this, let's look at two recurrent motifs in the ascetic Sufi material gathered in Khalidi's text: Jesus' attitudes toward the world; and Jesus' attitude toward women. Then we will compare these motifs to what we find in Christian Gospel accounts within the New Testament.

Let's begin with a ninth-century Islamic source that claims to depict how Jesus viewed his life with us on earth: "Jesus was asked, 'Teach us one act through which God may come to love us.' He answered, 'Hate the world and God will love you.'"[20]

World hatred in turn generates a code of conduct. Consider the advice and ethical commands attributed to Jesus in various Islamic ascetic texts that Khalidi has brought together in his *Muslim Jesus* volume:

> Jesus said, "What God loves most are the strangers." He was asked, "Who are the strangers?" He replied, "Those who flee [the world] with their faith [intact]."[21]

> Jesus used to tell his followers: "Take mosques to be your homes, houses to be stopping places. Eat from the plants of the wilderness and escape from this world in peace."[22]

> Jesus said, "O disciples, seek the love of God by your hatred of sinners; seek to be near Him by [doing] that which distances you from them; and seek His favor by being angry with them."[23]

The third of these sayings is closely linked in spirit to the attitude expressed in the first two. If you decide to "flee" and "escape" from the messiness of our sinful world, then you will also be tempted to insist on "doing that which distances you" from sinners (who through their actions are still mired in the realm from which you are trying to escape).

Many of the Jesus-sayings gathered by Khalidi link "the world" with the moral risks of being involved with women in any form:

[20] Ibid., p. 118.
[21] Ibid., p. 83.
[22] Ibid., p. 58.
[23] Ibid., p. 57.

Jesus said, "I toppled the world upon its face and sat upon its back. I have no child that might die, no house that might fall into ruin." They said to him, "Will you not take a house for yourself?" He replied, "Build me a house in the path of the flood." They said, "Such will not last." They also asked Jesus, "Will you not take a wife?" He replied, "What do I do with a wife that might die?" ...

Jesus said, "The greatest sin is love of the world. Women are the ropes of Satan. Wine is the key to every evil."[24]

It is reported that the world was revealed to Jesus and that he saw it in the form of a toothless hag covered with every adornment. "How many men have you married?" Jesus asked her. "I cannot count them," the hag replied. "Did they all die before you, or did they all divorce you?" Jesus asked. "Neither, for I killed them all," she replied. Jesus said, "What wretches they are, your husbands that remain! For they do not learn from your former husbands how you killed them one after the other, nor are they on their guard against you."[25]

Aside from such sayings, Jesus also features in stories assembled by Khalidi that involve relations between women and men. One tale begins with Jesus passing by a gravesite, where he sees a man weeping over the recent death of his beautiful young wife. Out of pity, Jesus resurrects her from the grave.

But this does not bring about a happy ending. The young woman abandons her husband and runs off with the first man she sees after her resurrection. As punishment, Jesus strips her of her second life and sends her back to the grave. As for the husband: he vows never to marry again and departs from society to live as a hermit in the wastelands.[26]

Women as faithless runabouts, destroyer-hags, and "ropes of Satan": the Islamic Jesus is made to serve as a mouthpiece for all these misogynistic fears. And fear is truly the operative word here, a fear felt by many men in many different cultures and times with regard to elemental physical realities—sexual attraction; involuntary impulse; the pull of appetite.

Underlying these stories and sayings is an anxiety: losing control over the uneasy empire of bones and blood we call the human body.

[24] Ibid., pp. 86, 109–110.
[25] Ibid., pp. 109–10.
[26] Ibid., pp. 206–8.

And once that happens, how can we possibly focus on seeking the divine Presence? For many Sufi ascetics, the solution was clear. Follow the advice of Jesus: Flee from women; escape from the world.

Given the texts amassed by Khalidi, how accurate is he, then, in his assertion that "the Jesus of Islamic Sufism became a figure not easily distinguished from the Jesus of the Gospels"?

First of all, a concession: I am very willing as a Christian reader of the Gospels to acknowledge that one can find traces of ascetic practice in the Jesus we see in the New Testament. After his baptism in the River Jordan, the Spirit drives him into the wilderness, where he fasts for forty days, lives among the wild beasts, and is tempted by Satan (Mk 1:12–13). And as we think over Jesus' life as recorded in the Gospels, there are other instances as well we could identify as his "fleeing the world".

Consider his behavior in Capernaum. "That evening, at sundown, they brought to him all who were sick or possessed with demons." Jesus spends a long night healing everyone who comes to him. Then, "in the morning, a great while before day, he rose and went out to a lonely place, and there he prayed" (Mk 1:32–35).

I think it is fair to say that healing and tending to the needs of others tired Jesus out (the same effect it would have on any other human being). Recall what happens when the woman afflicted with a hemorrhage is cured by touching the cloak he is wearing: Jesus "[perceived] in himself that power had gone forth from him" (Mk 5:30).

And think of the challenges of healing on the Sabbath: Jesus succeeds in curing a man who suffers from a withered hand, but, in the process, the regulation-minded scribes and Pharisees become "filled with fury" against him. No wonder, then, that thereafter "he went out to the hills to pray; and all night he continued in prayer to God" (Lk 6:6–12).

In this context, it is worth remembering how he reacted after he received the distressing news that Herod had beheaded Jesus' spiritual colleague, John the Baptist. "Now when Jesus heard this," the Gospel of Matthew tells us, "he withdrew from there in a boat to a lonely place apart." His withdrawal is understandable. In the face of violence and fury from the powerful, and incessant demands from the needy and the poor, who would not want to sail away to some "lonely place"?

But the common people heard about his departure, and they followed him "on foot from the towns". And look at what Matthew tells us in the very next verse about Jesus' response as he realizes what is awaiting him back on land: "As he went ashore he saw a great throng; and he had compassion on them, and healed their sick" (Mt 14:13–14).

So, yes, the Gospels show us that Jesus engaged in ascetic practice, praying, fasting, and withdrawing to deserts and mountaintops for solitude. But after each such instance, filled with the Holy Spirit, his strength renewed, Jesus *returned* to the world, in order to serve others.

This differs radically from the injunctions put into the mouth of the Islamic Jesus in the Sufi ascetic literature assembled by Khalidi: Flee the world; escape from this world; "hate the world and God will love you." To realize how profoundly these Islamic ascetic sentiments differ from the message of the Christian Gospels, we need simply recall John 3:16: "For God so loved the world that he gave his only-begotten Son."

But the material cited above suggests another important way in which Khalidi's "Muslim gospel" diverges from the New Testament: the question of how to relate to those who sin. As we have just seen, the Jesus depicted in Khalidi's Islamic sources tells his disciples to please Allah by keeping their distance from sinners, hating them, and being angry with them.

The Jesus of the New Testament, however, actively sought out tax collectors, prostitutes, and other individuals shunned by the upright. In fact, he was comfortable dining with them, regardless of what scandalized onlookers might say (as we can see in Matthew 9:10 and Mark 2:15–16).

Which brings us to the question of Christ's relations with women. The Islamic Jesus whom Sufis looked to as a model is presented as someone who mistrusted women—along with wine—as sources of temptation ("ropes of Satan").

Here again the Christian Gospels differ radically. Jesus was at ease in women's company, whether to heal them or welcome them as co-workers in his ministry. When a woman is caught in adultery, he intervenes compassionately on her behalf, defying the mob-mentality of those who want to stone her. When a local prostitute ("a woman of the city, who was a sinner") weeps over Jesus' feet and wipes them dry with her hair, his dinner host is suspicious and perhaps embarrassed on Christ's behalf ("If this man were a prophet, he would have known who and what sort of woman this is who is touching him"). But Jesus focuses, not on her sins or her outcast status, but on the fact that "she loved much" (Jn 8:1–11; Lk 7:36–50).

His ease with women shows itself, too, in his travels. As he journeyed from town to town, "preaching and bringing the good news of the kingdom of God", Jesus was accompanied not only by the Twelve but also by a number of women, several of whom are identified by name—Mary Magdalene, Joanna (the wife of Herod's steward, Chuza), Susanna, "and many others, who provided for them out of their means" (Lk 8:2–3). And when, separated briefly from his followers and "wearied as he was with his journey", Jesus paused alone at a well to sit and rest, he struck up an extended conversation with a Samaritan woman who approached to draw water. When his disciples found him, "they marveled that he was talking with a woman" (Jn 4:6, 27).

Such interactions were considered shocking in the society of that time; as the *Catholic Study Bible's* commentary points out, "Early rabbinic documents caution against speaking with women in public." Unlike the Jesus of the "Muslim gospel", the Jesus we encounter in the New Testament challenges and defies the norms of male-female relations in his society.[27]

Sunnah of Jesus, Sunnah of Muhammad: Divergent models of conduct?

As we have seen from the above discussion, post-Koranic ascetic Sufi literature contains many references in passing to Jesus, holding him up as a model of conduct for aspirants who seek to discipline themselves spiritually. Thus we can speak meaningfully of a *sunnat 'Isa* (that is, the sunnah or exemplary path of conduct offered by the life of the Islamic Jesus).

At this point, you might usefully object: But wait, Muslims already have an exemplary path of conduct to follow in the sunnah of

---

[27] Donald Senior and John J. Collins, eds., *The Catholic Study Bible*, 2nd ed. (New York: Oxford University Press, 2006), p. 1368, commentary on Luke 8:1–3.

Muhammad. Why did some Muslims—namely, the world renouncers and mystics of Islam—feel the need to create and transmit sayings and anecdotes that generated a sunnah linked to Jesus?

Here it is worth comparing the life-styles of Muhammad and the Jesus of post-Koranic Islamic tradition. Muhammad was a businessman in the caravan trade. The Sufi Christ wanders the earth barefoot, discarding comb and cup and pillow-brick. Muhammad was a mayor, warlord, and religious leader, very much a success in this world. The Sufi Christ flees the world, advising his followers to shun it and hate it. Muhammad accumulated a total of thirteen wives and at least four concubines. The Sufi Christ refuses marriage and is wary of women as distractions and temptations.

In other words, a sunnah of Jesus developed within Islamic ascetic and Sufi traditions precisely because many mystics and world renouncers felt the need for an alternative to Muhammad as a role model, someone to whom they could look as both exemplar and justification for their desired escape from the world. They found this exemplar in Jesus—but a Jesus substantially different from the person we encounter in the Christian Gospels.

To crucify a moth: Docetic motifs in the death of the Sufi martyr Hallaj

Given how radically divergent from Islam's mainstream is Sufism in various ways, it will probably not surprise you to learn that Muslim mystics have been condemned—and sometimes targeted for harsh punishment—at various points in Islamic history down to the present day.

One of the main accusations directed against Sufis is that their focus on divine experience makes them socially irresponsible. This critique is developed in a popular textbook on Islam by Isma'il al-Faruqi (a former professor of religious studies at Temple University in Philadelphia). According to Faruqi, Sufis were among the primary culprits who brought about the decay and collapse of medieval Islamic civilization:

> Engagement in the affairs of society and state, so expressive of the Muslim's consciousness of vicegerency, was slowly abandoned for

contemplative bliss and mystical experience. The Muslims ... withdrew from "history," from the "now," and became preoccupied with eternity and mysticism.... Mysticism dulled the Muslim sense of realism and drew Muslims away from society, from their businesses, even from their families. Instead of pursuing the will of God as law, Sufism (mysticism) taught the Muslim to run after the dream of union with God in gnosis, or "mystical experience."[28]

"The dream of union with God" is exemplified in the life of a celebrated—and notorious—tenth-century Sufi, Husain ibn Mansur al-Hallaj. He wandered for years, from Arabia and Iraq to India and Turkestan, preaching about the priority of inner spiritual states over public communal acts of worship and making ecstatic statements in which he apparently claimed that Allah had taken up residence within his human flesh. Orthodox clerics and caliphal officials abhorred him for his blasphemous public cry *"Ana al-Haqq"*: "I am the Truth" (al-Haqq/"the Truth" is one of the Koranic names or attributes of Allah).

In his writings, Hallaj made poetic use of moth-flame symbolism, imagining himself as a winged creature drawn to the luminous blaze of divine union:

> Until dawn the moth circles about the candle, and then he returns to his companions, reporting to them in the sweetest speech about the state associated with the glow. And in his flight he takes delight in the flickering play of the flame: he longs to reach its perfection....
>
> Not enough for him is its light, not enough is the heat from it. So, finally, he hurls his whole being into it.
>
> Meanwhile his companions await his return and his report to them of what he has seen, since they know he is not one to be satisfied with mere talk passed on by others. But at this very instant he is annihilated, reduced to nothing, made to vanish. There remains of him nothing: body, name, record, fame: gone.[29]

---

[28] Isma'il al-Faruqi, *Islam*, 4th ed. (Beltsville, Md.: Amana Publications, 2007), pp. 77–78.

[29] Arabic text in Louis Massignon, ed., *Kitab al-Tawasin par Abou al-Moghith al-Hosayn ibn Mansour al-Hallaj* (Paris: Librairie Paul Geuthner, 1913), pp. 16–17; translated from the Arabic by D. Pinault. For more on moth-flame imagery in Islamic mystical literature, see David Pinault, *Horse of Karbala: Muslim Devotional Life in India* (New York: Palgrave, 2001), pp. 33–40.

The transcendent and world-defying longing evident in these words is especially poignant, considering what finally happened to this Sufi-moth. The caliphal government condemned Hallaj as a heretic and subjected him to torture and public crucifixion in Baghdad, in accordance with the Koran's prescribed punishment for those who "spread corruption throughout the land" (surah 5:33).

But what the Koran claims about Christ, many Sufis claimed about Hallaj. They insisted that it only looked as if he had been crucified and put to death, whereas in fact Allah had rescued Hallaj alive and substituted someone else in his place on the cross. The scholar Louis Massignon summarizes these claims: "One of Hallaj's disciples maintained that the one who had been executed was an enemy of Hallaj, changed to look like him ... just as in the case of Jesus, son of Mary. Some of them claimed that they had seen him the very next day."[30]

Jesus T-shirts and interfaith outreach: Concluding thoughts on the Sufi Christ

Mosque field trips with my students are always a learning experience, not only for them but for me. One thing I find particularly interesting is to watch how our Muslim hosts package and present the Islamic faith to their undergraduate guests.

When I first began teaching, several decades ago, the approach we encountered sometimes verged on polemics. In 1991, while visiting a mosque in upstate New York, my students and I were handed leaflets entitled *The Invitation: Invite to the Cause of Allah*. The text critiqued what it presented as various troubling aspects of Christianity, with particular attention to the figure of Jesus:

> Another Christian problem: In Christendom, Western scholars write [that] Jesus is portrayed as a celibate person, [a] 33-year-old and yet an unmarried bachelor, all alone at home? Is that normal? [a] healthy portrayal? ask many Christian scholars. How can you honestly emulate

---

[30] Louis Massignon, *The Passion of al-Hallaj: Mystic and Martyr of Islam*, trans. Herbert Mason (Princeton: University Press, 1982), 1:571; see also pp. 561–62 and 589–98.

such a model, a single man, unmarried and unattached to family responsibilities, [who] had no family life, no wife or any children?...

It is not a criticism of Jesus, just a question on role models. Also, embracing Jesus' doctrine of promoting singleness does no good, it only adds to the problems. Singleness (loneliness) leads to all sorts of temptations, problems; psychological imbalances among singles [are] the biggest problem in this society.

Man is not made to be single, [a] mate is created for him. So whether Jesus or Paul or Church, whoever taught "singleness" ... [is] promoting an unhealthy environment.[31]

This leaflet reminded me of how Christ is portrayed in many Sufi texts, as we have seen above ("They also asked Jesus, 'Will you not take a wife?' He replied, 'What do I do with a wife that might die?'"). But I would not say this leaflet's aggressive and overtly polemical approach worked well with my undergraduates. They found it jarring, grating, "kind of insulting", as one of my students said as we drove back to campus.

Fast-forward twenty-five years: 2016, and a field trip to a mosque in the San Francisco Bay area. Among those welcoming us was a smiling young man wearing a T-shirt that read "I'm a Muslim and I♥Jesus." He said he likes the shirt because it shows how much Islam has in common with Christianity; the same people Christians respect, Muslims respect, too. Like Noah, he said, and Abraham and Moses and Jesus.

He meant this as a hospitable gesture, and I honor it for the goodwill he showed us. It is certainly a more courteous approach than handing visitors leaflets describing Christ as "an unmarried bachelor, all alone at home" and asking "How can you honestly emulate such a model?"

And yet of the two approaches, I prefer the latter, because its hammer-blow polemics at least avoid the facile let's-all-hold-hands oversimplifications of an I♥Jesus logo.

In fact, precisely because of such oversimplifications, I make a point of supplementing mosque field trips with classroom readings from Islamic texts that acknowledge the substantive Christological differences between the Muslim and Christian faiths.

---

[31] Musa Qutub and M. Vazir Ali, "Western Feminism Movement Problems vs. Islam's Gender Balance Dynamism", *The Invitation* 9, no. 2 (Des Plaines, Ill., April 1991).

I draw not only on theological texts but also occasionally on Middle Eastern folktales. One example is a story that a folklorist named Hasan el-Shamy heard from a Nubian Muslim in Egypt in the late 1960s. It involves al-Khidr, a legendary spiritual guide and shape-shifter. Al-Khidr has the power to make our wishes come true—but the gifts he bestows turn into tests that probe whether we are worthy of what we have been given.

The story I have in mind involves a robber who comes upon al-Khidr while the latter is disguised as an apparently helpless old man walking alone along a deserted road. The robber plans to attack him, but al-Khidr reveals himself, calls on him to repent, and offers to grant him any wish he likes if he does so. The robber agrees and impulsively says he wants to be a great and learned scholar of all the branches of Islamic knowledge.

Al-Khidr grants this wish, and at once the robber finds he is a master of Koran and *hadith*. Equipped with this sacred learning, he acquires money and prestige; Muslims throng to him for guidance.

Sometime later, al-Khidr returns to see how truly the man has reformed his life. The shape-shifter finds him in a mosque "where the pashas and beys and all big and important and knowledgeable people went. This one was learning new things, and that one was receiving instructions, and this one was receiving interpretations and answers to his questions."

Disguised afresh as "an old man walking with a cane, looking clumsy and not very tidy", al-Khidr humbly asks the robber-turned-scholar if he, too, may ask a question.

Failing to recognize him, the onetime bandit contemptuously shouts, "Do you think I am for the likes of you? I instruct only the very knowledgeable and the very important."

That does it. On the spot, al-Khidr withdraws his gift. And here is what happens to the robber: "Now, after having been saying nothing but the holy and the truthful, he uttered nothing but the blasphemous and the profane. Instead of saying, 'There is no God but Allah,' he started saying, 'Jesus is the son of God.' People gave him a good beating, the like of which he had never seen in his life, and drove him away."[32]

---

[32] Hasan M. El-Shamy, ed., *Folktales of Egypt* (Chicago: University Press, 1980), pp. 128–30.

Here we get a brass-knuckled reminder: Christological distinctions matter. As soon as the would-be scholar made the "blasphemous" and "profane" proclamation about the divine Sonship of Christ, he was no longer fit for Muslim society. I suspect even wearing an I♥Jesus shirt would not have saved him his job.

All of which is to say: claims of shared love for Christ can be misleading. Ask devout Muslims: *Do you pray to Jesus? Do you worship him? Do you acknowledge his crucifixion and its salvific and redemptive value? Do you acknowledge him as God's Son?* You will likely find the answer to all these questions will be: No.

Again: these Christological distinctions matter (as our robber--turned-scholar found out). Putting together a "Muslim gospel", while declaring that the ascetic Sufi Jesus depicted therein is someone "not easily distinguished from the Jesus of the Gospels", is, it seems to me, a well-intentioned but misdirected effort. There are other paths one might follow in the interest of improved Christian-Muslim relations—paths I will explore with you in subsequent chapters of this book.

CHAPTER 9

THE TRUE CROSS TAKEN CAPTIVE: CHRISTIAN-MUSLIM RELATIONS IN THE AGE OF THE CRUSADES

Introduction: An episode from the First Crusade:
The fate of Rainald Porchet

April 1098. For months the Crusader army had been besieging the city of Antioch on the Turco-Syrian frontier. Assaults, nighttime sorties and ambushes, hand-to-hand combat. Then one day, during a lull in the fighting, the Crusaders heard a cry from the battlements and looked up. A priest named Peter Tudebode, who was present as an eyewitness, tells us what they saw:

> The Turks led atop the city's fortress-wall one of our noble knights, a man named Rainald Porchet, whom they had held for a long time in a wretched dungeon. They told him he should address the pilgrims of Christ and have them ransom him for the highest possible price, if he did not want to get his head cut off.
>
> Once he was positioned atop the wall, this is how he addressed our leaders: "My lords! It is as if I am already dead. So I pray you, my brothers: offer nothing for me. But remain steadfast and secure in your faith in Christ and the Holy Sepulchre, because God is with you now and always will be."

Then, the priest tells us, Rainald began shouting information to his comrades below: how many Muslim emirs had been killed, how greatly the city's defenses had been weakened by the siege. At that point, his captors realized their prisoner was not cooperating:

The Turks asked one of their interpreters what Rainald was say-ing. The interpreter said to them, "He is saying nothing good about us!" Whereupon the emir Qasim ordered him to be brought down at once from the wall and said to him through the interpreter, "Rainald, would you like to live a life of honor and enjoyment with us?"

Rainald replied, "How could I possibly live such a life without committing sin?" The emir said, "Deny your God, whom you wor-ship and in whom you believe."

The Turkish leader then told him if he would accept Muhammad and become Muslim, in exchange Rainald would be given gifts of women, gold, silver, horses, "and every other fine thing you might want".

Instead of accepting this offer, the knight knelt and prayed aloud for God to receive his soul. The impatient emir then asked the interpreter what Rainald was saying. "Not in any way", came the explanation, "is he denying his Lord God." Whereupon the Muslim leader, "greatly enraged", had the Christian beheaded on the spot.[1]

I mention this incident because it defies the erroneous and all-too--common appraisals that dismiss Crusaders as "early Western imperi-alists" who, "fueled by fear, greed, and hatred", engaged in "colonial exploitation" because they supposedly sensed "an opportunity to gain territory, riches, [and] status".[2]

Rather than an unprovoked attack on peace-loving Muslim lands, the Crusades were part of a centuries-long back-and-forth struggle, desperate and existential in terms of what was at stake, between two civilizations that were based on distinctly different universalist mis-sionary faiths. Islamic armies had been attacking Christian realms since the seventh century; you may recall that Muhammad himself had authorized assaults on Byzantine territories once he had subdued his Meccan opponents.

Two Syriac Christian accounts from that time provide what are probably the oldest non-Muslim references to the prophet Muham-mad and the early Islamic invasions. One dates from A.D. 637, the

---

[1] Peter Tudebode, *Historia de Hierosolymitano Itinere*, in Jacques-Paul Migne, ed., *Patrologia Latina* (Paris: Frères Garnier, 1880), 155:786; translated from the Latin by D. Pinault.

[2] Rodney Stark, "The Case for the Crusades", *The Southern Baptist Journal of Theology* 20, no. 2 (2016): 9–28. This article does an excellent job of summarizing and disproving inaccu-rate representations of the Crusades.

other from the year 640. Both manuscripts are incomplete. The older of the two is preserved on badly damaged parchment; a number of pages are missing from the other. Nonetheless, they offer us a vivid if fragmentary impression of the brutality of the Islamic conquests of Christian lands:

> Many villages were destroyed through the killing by (the Arabs of) Muhammad and many people were killed. And captives were taken from the Galilee to Bet.... Those Arabs camped by (Damascus)....
>
> About four thousand poor villagers from Palestine—Christians, Jews, and Samaritans—were killed, and the Arabs destroyed the whole region.... The Arabs invaded all Syria and went down to Persia and conquered it. They ascended the mountain of Mardin, and the Arabs killed many monks in Qedar and Bnata. The blessed Simon, the door-keeper of Qedar, the brother of Thomas the priest, died there.[3]

And so it continued. By the late eleventh century, when the First Crusade began, Muslim forces had conquered much of the Near East, North Africa, and parts of Europe such as Spain.

Despite the brutality and massacres (committed by both Muslims and Christians), the Crusades were also characterized—as we have just seen in the death of the knight Rainald—by steadfast religious faith, idealistic self-sacrifice, and generosity of spirit. No prospect of wealth or worldly gain could suffice to explain the Crusades or the sufferings the "pilgrims of Christ" chose to endure.

But do not take my word for it. Ask Salah al-Din Yusuf ibn Ayyub, the twelfth-century Muslim warlord better known to the Crusaders as Saladin. The text survives of one of his appeals for support from fellow Islamic emirs as he organized a jihad against the Crusaders:

> Where is the sense of honour of the Muslims, the pride of the believ-ers, the zeal of the faithful? We shall never cease to be amazed at how the Unbelievers, for their part, have shown trust, and it is the Muslims who have been lacking in zeal. Not one of them has responded to the call, not one intervenes to straighten what is distorted; but observe how far the Franks have gone; what unity they have achieved, what aims they pursue, what help they have given, what sums of money

---

[3] Michael Philip Penn, *When Christians First Met Muslims: A Sourcebook of the Earliest Syriac Writings on Islam* (Oakland: University of California Press, 2015), pp. 24, 28.

they have borrowed and spent, what wealth they have collected and distributed and divided among them! There is not a king left in their lands or islands, not a lord or a rich man who has not competed with his neighbours to produce more support, and rivalled his peers in strenuous military effort.

In defence of their religion they consider it a small thing to spend life and soul, and they have kept their infidel brothers supplied with arms and champions for the war. And all they have done, and all their generosity, has been done purely out of zeal for Him they worship, in jealous defence of their Faith.[4]

"Done purely out of zeal for Him they worship": the Muslim leader who made this remark, notwithstanding his status as a staunch opponent of the Crusaders, understood that what motivated these Christians was religious fervor rather than greed for gold.

"Displayed ... as a reminder of being put to death": The meaning of the Cross in Christian texts from the Crusades

A good way to appreciate the distinctive spirituality of the Crusades is to compare how Crusaders and their Muslim adversaries responded to that most fundamental of Christian symbols: the Cross.

Let's begin with the *Gesta Francorum* (*The Deeds of the Franks*), an early twelfth-century work that offers a close-up portrait of the First Crusade. The anonymous author, a Norman knight in the entourage of Prince Bohemond of Antioch, was a pious layman, a combatant, and an eyewitness of the events he described. As such, he is one of our best sources for understanding the religious world view of the early Crusaders.

Here is how the *Gesta* begins:

When that point in time approached which the Lord Jesus has been indicating for so long to His faithful ones on a daily basis—especially when He says in the Gospel, "If anyone wishes to follow me, let him deny himself and pick up his cross and follow me"—then a powerful

---

[4] Shihab al-Din Abu Shama, *Kitab al-raudatain*, cited in Francesco Gabrieli, ed. and trans., *Arab Historians of the Crusades* (Berkeley: University of California Press, 1984), pp. 214–15.

movement swept through all the regions of France, so that if someone
zealously wished to follow God with a pure heart and mind, and faithfully carry his cross and follow Him, then such a person did not delay
in setting forth swiftly on the path to the Holy Sepulchre.[5]

The words of Jesus quoted here (from Matthew 16:24) appear
frequently in medieval Crusader writings. As the historian Heinrich
Hagenmeyer points out, many twelfth-century Christians understood this Gospel verse as an ancient prophecy foretelling the advent
of the Crusades, in which a multitude of believers would indeed pick
up their crosses and follow Christ's path to Jerusalem.[6]

We see this motif elaborated in the writings of Ekkehard of Aura,
a Benedictine monk and abbot of a Bavarian monastery who traveled
with a band of Crusaders to the Holy Land in the year 1101. Ekkehard quotes a priest named Arnold of Rohes, who preached a sermon
to the assembled Crusaders just before the battle of Joppa:

> You are that blessed and holy people ... who, having left behind
> everything—homeland, family, and worldly goods—have taken up
> your cross every day to follow Christ. On Christ's behalf you have
> handed over your bodies for torture and engaged in combat. And this
> land that Christ has made holy: He has graciously deigned to wash it
> with the blood you have voluntarily sacrificed for Him, and with the
> precious deaths of your brothers, your fellow knights.[7]

Here the preacher uses Luke 9:23 ("Then he said to all, 'If any man
would come after me, let him deny himself and take up his cross daily
and follow me' ") to integrate the Gospel's way of the Cross with the
self-sacrifice of Crusader death in combat.

Ekkehard pursues further the nexus of sacrifice, cross, and crusade in two other passages in his account, where he describes what
it meant to participants to affix to their clothing the insignia of the
Crusade—a cloth cross, sewn to each Crusader's outer garment:

---

[5] *Gesta Francorum: The Deeds of the Franks and the Other Pilgrims to Jerusalem*, ed. Rosalind
Hill (London: Thomas Nelson & Sons, 1962), p. 1.

[6] *Anonymi Gesta Francorum et Aliorum Hierosolymitanorum*, ed. Heinrich Hagenmeyer (Heidelberg: Carl Winter's Universitätsbuchhandlung, 1890), p. 101n2.

[7] Ekkehard of Aura, *Hierosolymita*, in *Recueil des historiens des Croisades: Historiens Occidentaux*
(Paris: Imprimerie Nationale, 1886), 5:34; translated from the Latin by D. Pinault.

Wearing the sign of the cross on their garments, the cross-bearing army displayed this as a reminder of being put to death (*ob mortificationis praeferebat commonitorium*)....

Various individuals bore the sign of the cross on their foreheads or on their clothing or on whatever part of their body had been divinely indicated to them by heaven. Through this mark, they considered themselves to have enlisted in the army of the Lord. Some persons, compelled by a sudden change of heart or led forth by a vision in the night, found satisfaction and peace in leaving behind their worldly belongings, their homes, and their families and sewing to their garments the sign of being put to death (*signumque mortificationis vestibus assuere placuit*).[8]

In both of these Latin passages, the Crusaders' insignia of the cross is described in terms of the word *mortificatio*, as either a "reminder of" (*commonitorium*) or "sign of" (*signum*) "being put to death" (*mortificatio*).

Now this word *mortificatio* is highly charged. It occurs only once in the Vulgate (the Latin Bible used by the Crusaders), specifically in Saint Paul's Second Letter to the Corinthians:

We are ... always carrying in the body the death of Jesus, so that the life of Jesus may also be manifested in our bodies. For while we live we are always being given up to death for Jesus' sake, so that the life of Jesus may be manifested in our mortal flesh. (*Semper mortificationem Iesu in corpore nostro circumferentes, ut et vita Iesu in corporibus nostris manifestetur. Semper enim nos, qui vivimus, in mortem tradimur propter Iesum: ut et vita Iesu manifestetur in carne nostra mortali.*) (2 Cor 4:10–11)

Saint Paul's letters are a good choice for men and women embarking on the hazards of a Crusade (and I say women as well as men, because many a wife and warrior-princess joined in those armed Holy Land pilgrimages).[9] For Paul himself was no stranger to torment: he knew what it was like to be shipwrecked, scourged, stoned, and chased by howling mobs, and all for Christ's name.

---

[8] Ibid., 5:16–19; translated by D. Pinault.

[9] See Christoph T. Maier, "The Roles of Women in the Crusade Movement: A Survey", *Journal of Medieval History* 30, no. 1 (2004): 61–82; Susan Edgington and Sarah Lambert, *Gendering the Crusades* (New York: Columbia University Press, 2002). Of particular interest: the teen Crusader Florine of Burgundy, killed in combat fighting the Turks in the year 1097.

It seems to me likely that Ekkehard had Paul's epistle in mind when he used the word *mortificatio* and that he chose such wording deliberately to bring out the significance of the Crusaders' insignia. It is clear from the preacher Arnold's sermon (cited above) that Christian combatants were encouraged to identify their sufferings with Christ's; and Ekkehard's harking back to the words of Saint Paul—"so that the life of Jesus may be manifested in our bodies"—must have reflected the passionately held feelings of other Crusaders besides himself. As Christ suffered in torment, so should we as His Christian followers; as Christ traveled the road to Calvary and bore the burden of the Cross, so should we travel as pilgrims and each bear our own cross, the instrument of His mortification, on our shoulders. This, Ekkehard implies, is the function served by the Crusaders' insignia: it makes the life of Christ manifest in our mortal flesh.

Characteristic of Crusading spirituality is the way in which it combined the way of the Cross with the concept of pilgrimage. This is reflected in a battlefield speech by Baldwin of Boulogne (later to become the first Crusader king of Jerusalem) to his assembled knights: "We Franks do not fear death but rather wish, as pilgrims of Christ, either to conquer in Christ's name or to die on behalf of Christ."[10]

These motifs are developed more fully in a Latin document called *Dermatii Cujusdam Hiberniensis Proficiscentis Jerusalem Itineraria seu Exhortatoria* (The travel-letter or exhortation of a certain Dermatius of Ireland, who is on his way to Jerusalem). This document is a written plea for food and lodging on the road; Dermatius, a Crusader and pilgrim, carried this note about with him as he traveled on his own to the Holy Land in the year 1117. (We even have the name of the scribe who wrote this *exhortatoria* for him; the note concludes: "And if, with God's assent, I experience your kindness and hospitality, please, I beseech you, pray also for Raimbald of Liège, who wrote this letter and gave it to me as a viaticum for this journey.")

The letter carried by this Irishman makes clear that the city toward which he is traveling is simply the earthly representation of a celestial domain:

[10] Ekkehard of Aura, *Hierosolymita*, pp. 32–33.

Dearest ones, I speak of the spiritual and heavenly Jerusalem.... I urge you to journey to this city and to leave behind Babylon, that is, this world.... You who are pilgrims on this earth, I call you forth from this house of clay to an eternal city....

You see how I have made myself an exile for God; you see that the cross I wear is not just the one on this bit of cloth; no, it is the Cross of Christ I bear. You see that I go to take refuge, not just with the God who is in Jerusalem, but the God who is everywhere, because in fact He is everywhere. Through Him, therefore, I admonish you: take care, to the extent that you are able, to ensure that I do not fail or fall short on this path.[11]

Dermatius' plea for hospitality seeks to draw his hosts imaginatively into his journey: the Jerusalem that is his destination is no more than a sign of the heavenly city that is the true home and destination of us all. His own pilgrimage is a reminder of the spiritual journey that should be undertaken by the hosts who offer him food and lodging: they, too, are called forth from their "house of clay to an eternal city".

So, too, with the insignia sewn on his shoulder. It is not just a "bit of cloth"; it is a symbol and a reminder, linking him with Jesus' Passion, so that, like Christ, he, too, is in temporary exile from his true home, as a traveler on the way of the Cross.

The letter carried by this Irish wanderer provides us with a glimpse of an entire world view. The Crusaders understood things about faith we today may have forgotten. They understood that to be Christian is to be a pilgrim; to be Christian is to make one's life conform—in a physical, tangible, and strenuous way—to the Cross of Christ.

"Regarding this thing as a god was an article of their faith": Muslim understandings of the Cross and Christian worship in the age of the Crusades

To get some sense of how Muslims understood the Cross during the Crusades, let's begin with the memoir of Muhammad ibn Jubayr, a

---

[11] *Dermatii Cujusdam Hiberniensis Proficiscentis Jerusalem Itineraria seu Exhortatoria*, in Migne, *Patrologia Latina*, 155:485–90; translated from the Latin by D. Pinault.

twelfth-century traveler who visited the port of Acre after Christian forces freed it from Muslim rule:

> It is the chief Frankish city in the region of Syria ... and a meeting point of Muslim and Christian merchants from every horizon. Its lanes and streets are very congested and almost too crowded for people to make their way on foot. Unbelief and idolatry are established there. The city swarms with pigs and crosses, impure, greasy, unclean. The whole city is full of filth and excrement. The Franks wrested Acre from the hands of the Muslims in the first decade of the sixth [Islamic] century. All of Islam wept over this loss.... Its mosques have reverted to being churches.[12]

For Ibn Jubayr, as a pious Muslim, two things sum up Acre's condition, now that it is fallen to the Franks: pigs and crosses. Both symbolize a world in disorder. Pork is a forbidden food in Islam; and the medieval "Covenant of Umar", which regulated the status of non-Muslims in Islamic lands, forbade the public display of crosses on Christian churches. (The Covenant also prohibited Christians from carrying crosses in processions or building any new churches.)[13] Pigs on the street; crosses visible to passersby: no wonder the city struck him as "unclean".

For Ibn Jubayr, as for many Muslims from the time of Saladin up through the twenty-first century (as you will see in subsequent chapters), the Cross offered the solution to a problem: how to mock Christianity without insulting the person honored by both Christians and Muslims. You will recall that Islam acknowledges Jesus as a prophet but rejects the doctrine of his salvific death on the Cross. For the Crusader Christians encountered by Ibn Jubayr, the Cross meant the loving self-sacrifice of the Son of God and a reminder that we should make our own life and death conform to this sacrificial model.

But for Muslims such as Ibn Jubayr—for whom the crucifixion meant nothing—the Cross was the symbol of a hated foe. Thus it became part of a vocabulary of mental shorthand for Muslims.

---

[12] Muhammad ibn Ahmad ibn Jubayr, *Rihlat ibn Jubayr* (Cairo: Matba'at al-Sa'adah, 1908), p. 285; translated by D. Pinault.

[13] John L. Esposito, ed., *The Oxford History of Islam* (New York: Oxford University Press, 1999), p. 308.

Doctrinal errors and blasphemies against Allah; social disruption (city streets swarming with pigs) and the inversion of the theocratic order (Christians rather than Muslims in charge): all these things came to a focus in this symbol, so that the Cross, whenever mentioned in an Islamic text of the Crusading era, tended to represent all that was detestable about the Franks. Unsurprising, then, that Muslim sources from that time frequently referred to the Crusaders as "followers of the cross" and "cross-bearing Satans".[14]

At the same time, Muslims understood very well how sacred this symbol was to the enemy they loathed. This helps to explain an incident recorded by the priest Peter Tudebode, whom we met earlier as a participant in the First Crusade. The incident in question occurred in 1099, while the Franks were besieging Jerusalem. Before the final assault, they undertook a barefoot procession around the walls of the sacred city, while the Muslims watching them jeered and grinned from the ramparts. Here is what happened:

> The Saracens standing atop the walls were shouting, clamoring, blowing into horns, and showing every type of derision and contempt with whatever they could find. In addition, they fashioned out of wood a crucifix in the likeness of Christ—Christ who, in His compassion, redeemed the human race through the pouring forth of His own blood.
>
> In order to inflict pain and sorrow while all the Christians below were watching, the Saracens began beating the crucifix with a stick. Then, so as to inflict yet more pain, they banged it against the city wall and broke it into pieces, yelling, "Frangi, ogit salib", which in our language means, "Hey, you Ferenghees, this is a nice cross!" When they saw this, the Christians were afflicted with great sorrow.[15]

Behavior of this kind was not unique. A letter sent to England in 1187 by a Templar knight describes what happened after Muslim

---

[14] 'Izz al-Din ibn al-Athir, *Kamil al-tawarikh*, in *Recueil des Historiens des Croisades: Historiens Orientaux* (Paris: Imprimerie Nationale, 1887), vol. 2, pt. 2, pp. 61–72. In his chronicle (on pp. 62–63), Ibn al-Athir likewise gives a theological tinge to his polemics by referring to the Crusaders as *ahl al-tathlith* (the people of the Trinity) and *ahl al-shirk* (the people of the sin of associating partners with Allah).

[15] Tudebode, *Historia*, in Migne, *Patrologia Latina*, 155:815; translated from the Latin by D. Pinault. The insult voiced by the Saracens appears as *Frangi, ogit salio* in the *Patrologia*. I have emended *salio* as *salib*, since the latter spelling represents the word for "cross" in Arabic.

forces captured the capital of the Crusader kingdom: "Jerusalem, alas! has fallen. Saladin ordered the cross to be cast down from the summit of the Temple of the Lord, and for two days to be carried about the city and beaten with sticks."[16]

Muslim awareness of Christian devotion to this symbol of the crucifixion also appears in connection with the greatest defeat inflicted by Saladin on the Crusaders: the battle of Hattin, in July 1187. Not only did the Muslims take prisoner Guy de Lusignan (ruler of the Kingdom of Jerusalem) and annihilate most of his army; they also captured what they called *al-salib al-a'zam* (the great cross).

This was the True Cross, the instrument of Christ's crucifixion. You will recall from previous chapters how it had been discovered by Saint Helen, how it was captured by the Persians and carried off as a trophy to Iraq, and how the Byzantine emperor Heraclius rescued it and brought it back in triumph to Jerusalem.

During the Crusades, this relic (actually a fragment from the wood of the Cross, encased within a large jeweled cross of gold) reposed within the Church of the Holy Sepulchre. On a number of occasions, culminating with Hattin, the Cross had been paraded and taken into combat. (Some idea of the spiritual force attributed to such an object can be garnered from a twelfth-century description of a cross borne on Crusader campaigns by a bishop named Gerard, which he carried *ad confusionem et obcaecationem Sarracenorum, liberationem vero Christianorum*: "for the confusion and blinding of the Saracens, but for the freeing of Christians").[17]

Here is an Arabic account of the capture of the True Cross at Hattin. The author is 'Imad al-Din al-Katib al-Isfahani, who was a member of Saladin's entourage and one of his personal secretaries as well as an eyewitness of many of the events he recorded:

Topic: the Great Cross (*al-salib al-a'zam*) and how it was captured on the day of the battle [of Hattin, July 4, 1187].

And no sooner was the king captured than the cross of the crucifixion (*salib al-salbut*) was also taken. Without it, the people of idol worship were destroyed.

[16] Stephen Howarth, *The Knights Templar* (New York: Atheneum, 1982), p. 154.

[17] Albertus Aquensis, *Historiae*, in *Recueil des Historiens des Croisades: Historiens Occidentaux* (Paris: Imprimerie Nationale, 1886), 4:550.

When this cross was set up and raised and lifted high, every Christian would kneel and bow down in prostration before it. They claim that it comes from the wood on which, so they claim, the one whom they worship was crucified. Thus they worshipped it and bowed down before it. They had encased it with red gold and crowned it with pearls and jewels. They kept it prepared for their days of great public spectacle and for each season of their holy celebrations.

And when their priests brought it out and their chiefs carried it in procession, they would hurry forward and seek to touch it. Lagging behind in such processions was considered unacceptable.

They considered the capture of this cross a greater loss than the capture of their king and the worst affliction they suffered in this battle. For there was nothing comparable to this cross that they lost, and they had no object of desire other than this.

Regarding this thing as a god was an article of their faith. For them, this *was* in fact their god. They placed their faces in the dirt before it, and their mouths would glorify it with praise. When it was brought forth, they would faint; and they would be dazzled if they caught a glimpse of it. When it made an appearance, they felt as if they would vanish away. If they saw it, they would close their eyes and feel ecstatic longing. They offered their life's-blood for it, and in it they sought comfort.

In fact, they went so far as to shape in its likeness crosses that they worshipped. In their homes, they would humble themselves before these crosses and use them in giving testimony.

So when this great cross was captured, great also was their affliction. Their spines grew feeble, and the number of those who were broken was overwhelming.[18]

Two things strike me at once in reading 'Imad al-Din's account. The first has to do with his summary of Christian beliefs about the True Cross: "They claim that it comes from the wood on which, so they claim, the one whom they worship was crucified." Note how circumspectly he identifies the person on the Cross: "the one whom they worship". 'Imad al-Din carefully avoids using the word "Jesus" or "Christ" or any other name or honorific title recognized

---

[18] 'Imad al-Din al-Katib al-Isfahani, *Kitab al-fath al-qussi fi al-fath al-qudsi*, in *Conquête de la Syrie et de la Palestine par Salah ed-Din*, ed. Le Comte Carlo de Landberg, vol. 1, *Texte Arabe* (Leiden: Brill, 1888), pp. 27–28; translated from the Arabic by D. Pinault.

by Muslims. The effect is to emphasize that *Islamic* belief and Islamic notions of Jesus have nothing to do with *Christian* beliefs and devotional practices related to Jesus, His crucifixion, and the Cross.

Second, despite his doctrinal hostility (characterizing Christians as "the people of idol worship"), 'Imad al-Din's account nonetheless provides the clearest glimpse presented by a Muslim observer that I have ever encountered of what the Cross meant to Christian participants in the Crusades. He emphasizes the dazzlement, fainting, and "ecstatic longing" experienced by those who beheld the True Cross "when it made an appearance". In doing so, 'Imad al-Din conveys something essential about Crusader piety: its down-in-the-dirt emotionalism, its gritty and intensely sacramental quality.

The aftermath of Hattin: What happened to captive members of the Hospitallers and Knights Templar

'Imad al-Din al-Isfahani's account of Hattin does not stop with Saladin's conquest in battle. He records what he personally witnessed in its aftermath. Most Christian captives were ransomed or sold into slavery. But Saladin, he says, singled out for special punishment all the prisoners of war who belonged to the military-monastic orders of the Hospitallers and the Knights Templar. (Another chronicler of the time, 'Izz al-Din ibn al-Athir, explains why Saladin particularly targeted these fighting monks: "They were the fiercest of all the Frankish warriors.")[19]

'Imad al-Din describes what happened next:

Two days after the victory, on Monday morning, on the seventeenth day of the month of Rabi' al-Akhar, he [Saladin] sought out those prisoners who were Templars and Hospitallers (al-Dawiyah wa-al--Isbitariyah). He announced, "I am going to purify the earth of these two unclean races."

He arranged things so that everyone who brought forth a Templar or Hospitaller prisoner was given fifty dinars. So right away, members of the army brought forth two hundred captives.

[19] Ibn al-Athir, cited in Francesco Gabrieli, ed., *Arab Historians of the Crusades* (Berkeley: University of California Press, 1984), p. 124.

He ordered them all to be beheaded. He preferred to kill them rather than enslave them.

In the entourage of the sultan was a large group of religious scholars and Sufis as well as a number of ascetics and those who loathe and renounce the world. And every one of them asked if he could kill one prisoner apiece. Each drew a sword and pushed back his sleeve to bare his forearm.

The sultan sat enthroned. Joy was evident on his face, while the unbelievers scowled and frowned. The soldiers were drawn up on parade, and their emirs stood waiting in a double row.

Among the volunteer executioners were those who sliced neatly and trimly and were acknowledged with thanks. Others lost their taste for the job and said no, so they were excused. There were other volunteers who were ridiculed when they tried to do it, so they were replaced.

And I myself, when I was there, saw some who jeered and laughed with contempt as they did their killing. Others whom I saw were talkative and preachy as they did the job:

And how many vows they fulfilled! And what praise did they earn!

And what rewards did they win forever, with the blood they made flow!

And what piety each of them embraced, with the neck he sliced through!

And how many blades they smeared with blood, for the victory they had preached about in sermons!

And how many spears did they seize, to use against those lions in chains!

And how many fevered temperatures they cured

With all the Templars that they skewered!

(wa-da' daawaahu li-daawi adwaahu)

And how much strength did they give to the leaders whom they strengthened!

And how many banners did they raise high, against the disasters they dispelled!

And how much pagan faith they put to death, so Islam could catch its breath!

And how they demolished the faith that gives partners to Allah,

So that true monotheism could be raised high and taller![20]

---

[20] 'Imad al-Din, Kitab, 1:28–29; translated by D. Pinault.

As a learned bureaucrat, rhetorician, and scribe, 'Imad al-Din had the job of entertaining Saladin with ornamental language celebrating his master's victories. (This was typical of the time. Poets and other composers would compete for cash prizes in reciting their encomia before Muslim warlords.) 'Imad al-Din presented his account in carefully articulated—and extravagantly overwrought—saj' prose rhyme. (In my translation, I try to convey his reliance on assonance and alliteration; I render the Arabic verse *wa-da' daawaahu li-daawi adwaahu* as: "And how many fevered temperatures they cured/ with all the Templars that they skewered!") There is something distasteful—to put it mildly—in seeing this man's pleasure in playing with words as he gloats in recalling the murder of unarmed prisoners.

Disturbing, too, to see "volunteer executioners" eagerly line up (even if some were so unskilled they botched the job) to kill these prisoners—volunteers who were religious scholars and devout ascetics. Such a passage should dispel any fantasy that Sufis can always be counted on to be blissful people of peace.

An ugly business, this massacre of prisoners at Hattin, and a blot on Saladin's reputation. But four years later, as you are about to see, his greatest Frankish opponent will reciprocate with even greater violence, in an outburst that gives us an unexpected last look at the True Cross.

"Not to honor it, but rather to insult it": A final glimpse of the True Cross

The capture of the True Cross at Hattin was not the last time anyone in Christendom saw this relic. Four years later, in the summer of 1191, Richard the Lionheart's forces captured the city of Acre. The Muslim combatants captured by Richard became part of the negotiations he undertook with Saladin: these captives were to be released in exchange for Christian prisoners held by the Muslims along with a large payment of gold and the True Cross. 'Imad al-Din describes the complex haggling and air of mutual distrust that pervaded these negotiations, and in the process he shows us a remarkable moment involving this Christian relic:

And the envoys kept going back and forth, and ever-new exchanges of messages took place. And opinions and desires were gathered and scattered, until one hundred thousand dinars and the prisoners that had been sought and the cross of the crucifixion (*wa-salib al-salbut*) were gathered, so that all of these could be given to the Ifranj on the specified date and the agreed-upon time. And there was disagreement concerning how to implement the handing-over and delivery, and how anyone could trust or rely on the infidels (*al-kuffar*) with regard to taking on the responsibility of this financial burden. . . .

The [Christian] envoys came and saw that the prisoners were present and that the money had been weighed out and was there in full. They [the Christian envoys] thought that the Cross of the crucifixion had been sent to the House of the Caliphate [Baghdad] and so it would not be there. So they asked that it be brought out while they were there as witnesses.

And when it was brought out, they fell to the ground before it and prostrated themselves in worship. And so they confirmed it as witnesses and acknowledged that the conditions had been completely fulfilled.[21]

Then disaster.

Saladin decided to drag out the negotiations, awaiting the approach of a freshly assembled Muslim army that would supplement his own forces for another assault on Crusader-held Acre. The haggling continued in the summer heat; the deadline originally agreed upon expired.

And that was more than the mercurial Lionheart had patience for. Fearful of a trap, frustrated with the whole business, he had his captives killed en masse. 'Imad al-Din tells us what happened next:

The Frankish prisoners were sent back to Damascus to be returned to their owners and the hands of their masters. For they had been gathered from people throughout the realm because of the need there had been for them. So when there was no longer any need for the prisoners, they were returned to their owners.

And the Cross of the crucifixion was returned to the treasury, not to honor it, but rather to insult it and hold it in contempt (*wa-u'ida salib al-salbut ila al-khizanah la lil-i'zaz bal lil-ihanah*). And the wrath of the unbelievers at our keeping the cross was fierce. Day and night, their calamity seemed to them always renewed.

[21] Ibid., 1:371–72.

Both the Greeks and the Georgians expended great efforts to recover it, and they dispatched one envoy after another. But they never found any means to do so, nor did they come upon any devilish way to talk the Muslims into its release.[22]

'Imad al-Din speaks of this Cross as if it were somehow alive and a menace. After all, as he stated earlier, "For them, this *was* in fact their god." As such, it was an enemy and a fit target for mockery and scorn, something to be held prisoner and locked away in a sultan's treasury, "not to honor it," as he triumphantly notes, "but rather to insult it and hold it in contempt." For Muslims of the Crusading era, the Cross, along with the crucifixion it represented, remained what it had been for non-Christians in the time of Saint Paul—foolishness and a stumbling block.

Here a moment's pause for reflection is in order. Other medieval European shrines, of course, claimed to have relics that housed some small portion of the wood of the Cross. (In a subsequent chapter, we will glimpse one such relic when you join me at the battle of Lepanto.) But the object captured at Hattin was unique for its lineage and history—discovered in Jerusalem by Saint Helen, preserved in the Church of the Holy Sepulchre, carried by Crusaders in combat. The incident from the summer of 1191 recorded by Saladin's scribe—where Frankish envoys "prostrated themselves in worship"—was the last time, to my knowledge, that anyone in Christendom had the opportunity to behold and revere the True Cross. After this, it passes from our view.

Postscript: Glimpses of Christian-Muslim friendship in the age of the Crusades

Grim reading, all this—massacres in the name of one's faith; exulting over conquered foes and captured relics. But it is possible to catch sight of another aspect of this era: namely, friendships that spanned the religious divide and intellectual interests that suggested sympathetic engagement with an alien creed—even if that engagement

[22] Ibid., 1:373.

was sometimes tempered with ambivalence. Two examples come to mind, one Muslim, the other Christian.

The first person I have in mind is Usamah ibn Munqidh, a twelfth-century Syrian poet and nobleman who knew Saladin personally. He fought the Crusaders and in times of truce counted some as friends. Near the end of his long life (he lived into his nineties), Usamah composed a memoir I find fascinating for the impressions it offers of the Ifranj he knew in peace and war.

Although he introduces some of his Crusader anecdotes by calling down generic curses on the Franks (for example, "May Allah disfigure them!"), nonetheless Usamah is careful to acknowledge that some of these infidels were better behaved than others. Thus he begins an account about ritual prayer and religious tolerance by stating, "All those who are newly arrived in the land of the Ifranj are coarser and cruder in their conduct than those Franks who have settled in the region and live alongside Muslims."

He then goes on to recall what happened once when he went to al-Masjid al-Aqsa (part of what is known today as Jerusalem's Temple Mount, the ancient site of the Temple of Solomon), which in Usamah's time was under the control of the Crusaders:

> Beside al-Masjid al-Aqsa was a small mosque that the Franks had made into a church. Whenever I went to al-Masjid al-Aqsa, the Templars who were there—and they were friends of mine—would let me enter the little mosque and do the salat (the Islamic canonical prayer) there. One day I entered and did the *takbir* (calling out *Allahu akbar*, "Allah is great") and was just starting my salat when some Frank pounced on me and grabbed me and turned my face toward the East, saying, "*This* is how you are supposed to pray!"
>
> But a group of Templars rushed over and took him and pushed him away from me, and so I returned to my prayer.... Later, they apologized to me and said, "This fellow is a newcomer who just arrived a few days ago from the Frankish realm. This is the first time he has ever seen someone pray who was not facing East."[23]

Christians of the Crusading era typically faced East for their prayers; Usamah ends his anecdote marveling at "that Satan" who

---

[23] Usamah ibn Munqidh, *Kitab al-i'tibar*, ed. Hartwig Derenbourg (Paris: L'École des Langues Orientales Vivantes, 1886), p. 99; translated by D. Pinault.

was so ignorant he did not even know Muslims turn to Mecca to pray.

Another text authored by Usamah tells of how he once visited a site in the vicinity of Nablus said to be the tomb of John the Baptist (a figure honored in both Christianity and Islam). Afterward he noticed a nearby church and out of curiosity entered to see what was going on inside. He found a group of monks facing the East, earnestly engaged in prayer.

"The sight of their piety touched my heart," confesses Usamah, "but at the same time it displeased and saddened me, for I had never seen such zeal and devotion among the Muslims. For some time I brooded on this experience."

What finally cheered him up was a subsequent visit to a Sufi monastery, and, seeing a hundred ascetics at prayer: "This was a reassuring sight, and I gave thanks to Almighty God that there were among the Muslims men of even more zealous devotion than those Christian priests."[24]

Worth juxtaposing with Usamah ibn Munqidh—who had friends among the Crusaders, who was curious about Frankish life even as it triggered decidedly mixed reactions in him (admiration, envy, and competitive religious pride)—is the experience of a thirteenth-century Christian known as Yves le Breton. A Dominican friar, he lived in Outremer (as the French called the Holy Land: "the land beyond the [Mediterranean] sea"), spoke Arabic, and served as an interpreter and envoy for Saint Louis (also known as Louis IX) during the Seventh Crusade.

We know about Yves because of a memoir written by Jean de Joinville, a French knight who took part in this crusade and was a personal comrade of Saint Louis. Joinville wrote his memoir many years later, near the end of his life (a point to which I will return in a moment); but one thing that comes across in his recollections is that he was impressed by Yves le Breton.

Joinville describes him as "an expert in the Saracen tongue" who was given the difficult—and potentially life-threatening—task of going as ambassador to the fortress of Shaykh al-Jabal (the old man of the mountain), otherwise known as the Grand Master of the Order of Assassins (this was a militant Shia sect that warred against both

[24] Cited in Gabrieli, *Arab Historians*, pp. 83–84.

Crusaders and Sunni Muslims). Joinville records in some detail the discussion Yves had with the Grand Master on Islamic theology as understood by the Assassins.

The shaykh presented a doctrine about the transmigration of souls in relation to Abel, Noah, Abraham, and Peter, the disciple of Christ. "On hearing this," Joinville tells us, "Brother Yves pointed out to the Old Man that he was mistaken in this belief and expounded much sound doctrine to him; but the Old Man would not listen." Joinville was no doubt aware of the diplomatic delicacy—and raw courage—it must have required for the Dominican to attempt to correct the Assassin Master on a point of dogma, and to do so without unduly displeasing his host—or jeopardizing his own life. "On his return to us", Joinville says, "the good friar reported all these things to the king"—and I suspect, from the detail provided to us in his memoir, that Joinville himself was present when Yves made his report.[25]

But even more fascinating is Joinville's description of something that happened to the friar when he was sent on another diplomatic mission, this time as an envoy to the sultan of Damascus (and as you read what follows, ask yourself if it reminds you of something you encountered in a previous chapter—hint: our discussion of Sufi mysticism):

> As they were on their way from their lodgings to the sultan's palace Brother Yves caught sight of an old woman going across the street, with a bowl full of flaming coals in her right hand and a flask filled with water in her left.
>
> "What are you going to do with these?" he asked her.
>
> The old woman answered that with the fire she intended to burn up paradise and destroy it utterly, and with the water she would quench the fires of hell, so that it too would be gone for ever.
>
> "Why do you want to do that?" asked Brother Yves.
>
> "Because," said she, "I don't want anyone ever to do good in the hope of gaining paradise, or from fear of hell; but solely for the love of God, Who deserves so much from us, and Who will do us all the good He can."[26]

[25] Jean de Joinville, *The Life of Saint Louis*, in *Chronicles of the Crusades*, ed. and trans. Margaret R. B. Shaw (Harmondsworth: Penguin, 1976), pp. 279–80.

[26] Ibid., p. 274.

Doesn't this sound exactly like the anecdote I shared with you last chapter, about Rabi'a al-'Adawiyyah, the eighth-century Iraqi mystic and the most celebrated woman saint in Sufi history?

The difference here, of course, is that Jean de Joinville presents this, not as a story *about* Rabi'a, but as a personal encounter that the Dominican friar experienced himself: seeing a woman running down the street, a bowl of flaming coals in one hand, a water flask in the other.

But here it is worth knowing that Joinville composed his memoir many decades after the incident, in old age, near the end of his life. And at this moment, you may be thinking the same thing I am: perhaps the French knight misremembered the encounter as he thought back, over the long-gone decades of his life, to his time as a Crusader.

Or, to put it more precisely: perhaps Joinville remembered the story perfectly but forgot the nature of the source. Maybe, after Yves returned from Damascus, what he recounted to his friend was not something he had *seen* on the street but something he had *read* in an Arabic text or *heard* from Sufi storytellers. (And in fact, the water/fire story about Rabi'a was the most famous of the many tales "illustrative of the singlemindedness of her devotion" that circulated in medieval Islam about this celebrated woman mystic.)[27]

As Joinville recalled the story years later, it is unsurprising that he may have displaced this vivid anecdote as he had heard it from Yves, transposing it from something in a manuscript to a face-to-face encounter on the street.

If this speculation is correct, then this suggests to me that the Dominican friar used some of his time in Syria to learn about Islamic mysticism. And, in my opinion, this is an entirely plausible hypothesis. After all, we already know that Yves was conversant with Arabic and interested in Islamic theology. And Joinville's reference to the envoy's meeting with the Old Man of the Mountain suggests that Yves was sufficiently interested in Assassin-Shia theology to engage the Grand Master at length on the doctrine of the transmigration of souls as espoused by that Muslim sect.

The memoirs I have just cited, one by Jean de Joinville, the other by Usamah ibn Munqidh, are valuable for the way in which they

---

[27] Annemarie Schimmel, *Mystical Dimensions of Islam* (Chapel Hill: University of North Carolina Press, 1975), p. 38.

help us see their era in unexpected ways. A pious Muslim, moved by Christian piety; Templar knights, intervening to shield a Muslim friend at prayer; a Dominican friar, intrigued by Sufi teachings but also courageous enough to preach his Christian faith in the castle of the Assassins. Reminders, these moments, that even in an age of Crusade versus jihad, not all was violence and war.

CHAPTER 10

MUSLIM SECTARIANISM AND SUNNI-SHIA COMPETITION FOR THE LEADERSHIP OF GLOBAL ISLAM

Looking back, looking ahead: Some thoughts to introduce this section

Let's review what we have learned together thus far in this book.

We began with the Jahiliyah, noting how pre-Islamic Arabia was home not only to pagan tribes but also to adherents of the Jewish and Christian faiths. You may recall that, as we proceeded to examine the life of Muhammad ibn 'Abd Allah, I emphasized the many contacts—contacts that appear to have been very influential—Muhammad had with individual Christians. As examples, I cited Islamic sources that described Muhammad's early encounters with the preacher Quss ibn Sa'idah, Abu 'Amir the monk, and Jabra the slave swordsmith.

We remarked the shift in tone of Muhammad's Koranic preaching not long after his hijrah from Mecca to Medina. Angry with the pagan Meccans who had rejected him, Muhammad expected a better reception from Medina's Jews and Christians. But when they, too, failed to convert to Islam, Koranic verses denounced them as *mushriks* and kuffar. Meanwhile Muhammad strip-mined biblical tradition for heroic prophets, discarding as heterodox slag whatever did not conform to Islamic tawhid.

Among the biblical figures appropriated by Islam was Jesus himself. But as I pointed out in our study of the Koranic Christ, Muhammad denied Jesus His status as Son of God and second Person of the Trinity. Also rejected was any notion of Jesus' divine Incarnation, salvific crucifixion, or Resurrection from the dead.

Given my own attraction as a Christian to the figure of Jesus, it is unsurprising that in our subsequent examination of Sufism I investigated how Muslim mystics employed Him as a role model for their own norms of conduct. But I took care to indicate how radically this Sufi Jesus—a world-hater, scorning women as the "ropes of Satan"—varied from the Christ of Christian witness.

In our investigation thus far, I have insisted on these substantive differences because of my own disillusionment with attempts by all too many Muslims and Christians on the interfaith dialogue circuit to minimize areas where Islamic and Christian dogma diverge. This shaped the presentation I just gave you of the Crusades. Anyone tempted to go along with the theological-rapprochement crowd need only consider how differently Crusaders and twelfth-century jihadists responded to the presence of the Cross. We have seen how Christian warrior-pilgrims bore this sign proudly "as a reminder of being put to death" in solidarity with the suffering of the Son of God. But their Muslim opponents, recognizing the Cross as symbolic of a doctrinal teaching where the two religions radically disagree, subjected it to mockery and beatings, "to insult it", as one Muslim chronicler gloated, "and hold it in contempt".

In keeping with my belief that studying Islam can help Christians rediscover what is distinctive and uniquely valuable in their own tradition, I will introduce you in an upcoming chapter to Muslim anti-Christian polemics that mock the Jesus of the Christian Gospels. It is a genre with a long history. Such polemics single out for ridicule any notion of Christ's suffering, his human frailties, and his public humiliation via death on the Cross. But as you will come to see, such writings—ranging in date from the eleventh century to the twenty-first—have often been authored by Sunni Muslims who are not only stridently anti-Christian but are also hostile to Sufism and Shiism. In such texts, the authors present New Testament Christology in such a way as to link it with Sufi and Shia teachings—while condemning all three sets of doctrine in the process.

Which means that before exploring these anti-Christian polemicists, I need to introduce you to the Shia form of Islam, to give you a sufficient background for understanding what the polemicists are up to. So let's take a quick look at the origins of Shiism and the significance of Sunni-Shia sectarianism for the stability (or instability) of the Middle East and the larger Islamic world.

"Well, at least you're not Shia": Piety and prejudice on a Pakistani campus

A traditional strength of Islam as it expanded beyond the Arab Middle East in the premodern era was its syncretistic adaptation to local religious traditions, whether in Africa, the Indian subcontinent, or the islands of Indonesia. For centuries, Islamic practice was regionally based, a landscape-oriented faith linked to saints' caves, Sufi tombs, and sacred trees (notwithstanding protests by pious-minded mullahs).

But worldwide socioeconomic changes after World War II profoundly affected Muslim communities. In a rapidly globalizing economy, farmers and other rural workers abandoned the countryside to find work in capitals such as Teheran, Cairo, and Jakarta. The suddenly wealthy Gulf emirates and Saudi Arabia drew labor migrants from throughout South Asia.

Thus—to take one example—hundreds of thousands of Pakistanis migrated to the Arabian peninsula in the 1970s and 1980s in search of jobs. They returned with their earnings, not to their villages of origin, but to urban centers such as Karachi and Lahore. These migrants no longer found so appealing the old regionally based Islam they had once known. Deracinated Muslims, facing the challenges of modernity in unfamiliar city settings, were susceptible to evangelizing by the missionaries of a revivalist and universalist Islam, an Islam based on Koranic scriptural authority rather than on the charisma associated with local saints' tombs or Sufi shrines. The preachers of this revivalist Islam were quick to condemn the traditional folk rituals of the countryside as—depending on the locale—Hindu-tainted, Christian-derived, or simply pagan.

Much of the funding for such preaching came from oil revenues at the disposal of Saudi Arabia's Wahhabi Salafists (adherents of an ideology that has its roots in the Sunni form of Islam). These are followers of a dichotomizing mentality that divides the world into *mu'minin* (believers) and kuffar (infidels, who are to be either converted or combated as enemies). Saudi Arabia's religious authorities have long regarded themselves as the natural leaders of global Islam, citing their role as guardians of the *haramayn* (the "sacred cities" of Mecca and Medina). The Saudi government, as host of the hajj-pilgrimage to Mecca that draws millions every year, has used this opportunity to proselytize fellow Muslims, seeking to shape a unified and standardized Islam that will place all believers under Wahhabi leadership.

But since the late 1970s and the Iranian Revolution, Saudi Arabia has faced ever-increasing competition from a religious ideology long loathed by the Wahhabis and by many other Sunnis. I can best illustrate the depth of this loathing via an anecdote from Pakistan.

Several years ago, while visiting the University of Peshawar in Pakistan's North-West Frontier Province, I was asked by a group of professors about my religious identity (I found out later that all of them were Sunnis). Since I was scheduled to give a guest lecture to their students on Sunni-Shia relations, they thought it appropriate to find out if I was Muslim. "No", I replied. "I'm a Christian."

Silence for a moment. I sensed disappointment. "Well," said one of my hosts, breaking the tension, "at least you're not Shia."

I recall this incident because it reflects a prejudice I have encountered surprisingly often in Pakistan and elsewhere among Islamic communities—the notion that Shias (who make up some 15 percent of the world's 1.6 billion Muslims) are kuffar, that they really are not Muslims at all. This religious bigotry is not new; but in recent years anti-Shia propaganda has circulated among Sunnis with renewed virulence. The reason for this phenomenon has to do, I believe, with a struggle for dominance of the *ummah* (the global community of Islam).

Thirst, suffering, martyrdom: Sacred history and Shia identity

To gain perspective on this struggle, it is helpful to know the historical origins of Islamic sectarianism. Shiism arose in the seventh century because of a political dispute over leadership of the *ummah* after the death of the prophet Muhammad in 632. Most Muslims (those who ultimately became known as Sunnis) supported the principle of election in selecting the caliph (the political title of the prophet's successor). But a minority insisted that the caliphate should be reserved for 'Ali ibn Abi Talib (Muhammad's cousin and son-in-law) and for the offspring of 'Ali and his wife Fatima. Such individuals were known as *Shi'at Ali*, "the adherents of 'Ali." These Shias resented bitterly those Muslim leaders who tried to block 'Ali's bid for the caliphate. In particular, Shias condemned Abu Bakr and 'Umar, the first and second caliphs (who are revered by Sunnis as *al-shaykhayn*, "the two elders"). Shia partisans claimed that Abu Bakr and 'Umar conspired to rob 'Ali of his rightful throne.

'Ali did manage to take power and rule as caliph for five years, only to be murdered in the year 661. Further tragedy befell his descendants. According to Shia belief, 'Ali's elder son Hasan was poisoned by order of the reigning caliph. Thereupon the title of "imam" passed to Hasan's younger brother, Husain ibn 'Ali.

The term "imam" is important for understanding doctrinal differences between Sunnis and Shias. All Muslims use the term to mean "prayer leader", someone who leads a congregation in worship. But most Shias (especially those belonging to the *Ithna-'Ashari* or "Twelver" denomination, which is by far the numerically largest form of Shiism, as well as the state religion of the Iranian Islamic Republic) also use the term "imam" in a more restricted sense to refer to the rightful spiritual leader of the entire *ummah*. Twelver Shias insist the imam must be from the prophet's immediate bloodline and that he is both *ma'sum* (sinless, perfect, and divinely protected from error) and *mansus* (chosen by Allah as leader, thereby avoiding the vagaries of any human electoral process). The first such imam, say Twelver Shias, was 'Ali; the second, his elder son, Hasan; the third, 'Ali's younger son, Husain.

In the year 680, at the urging of Shia partisans in Kufa, Husain set out from Arabia to Iraq to organize a rebellion against the reigning caliph, Yazid ibn Mu'awiyah. Husain was accompanied by the women and children of his household and only a small number of bodyguards and servants.

He never reached his destination of Kufa. Yazid's soldiers intercepted Husain near the river Euphrates at a site called Karbala (which today is revered as Shiism's foremost pilgrimage site). Not wanting Husain to become a martyr and a rallying point for further Shia resistance, Yazid ordered his soldiers to force Husain to surrender and offer the caliph *bay'ah* (an oath of allegiance). So the soldiers besieged Husain and his family, preventing them from reaching food or water. Husain and his family suffered torments of thirst under Iraq's pitiless desert sun. Shia preachers recount these sufferings in vivid detail during annual Muharram observances (Muharram is the Islamic month in which the siege of Karbala occurred).

Finally, Husain chose death rather than surrender. On 'Ashura, the tenth day of Muharram (the high point of the liturgical lamentation calendar for Shias today), Husain died in combat against Yazid's forces. This effectively put an end to Twelver Shia hopes for reclaiming the caliphate.

The usefulness of revulsion: Blood and lamentation

But it was precisely this political failure that generated the rise of Shiism as a distinctive theological tradition within Islam. Shia theologians argued that Husain had foreknowledge of what would happen at Karbala but voluntarily sacrificed himself for the good of the *ummah*. In exchange, Allah granted Husain the power of *shafa'ah* (intercession on behalf of sinners). Preachers I encountered in Pakistan and India recounted legends to the effect that Fatima continues to lament her martyred son even while she resides in Paradise; but she is comforted whenever mourners gather here on earth to remember the Karbala Martyrs. Husain will exert his power of *shafa'ah* on behalf of anyone who joins his mother in mourning and sheds tears in remembrance of Karbala.[1]

Such mourning rituals are referred to by the term *matam*. During Muharram, preachers recount the sufferings of the martyrs with the express purpose of moving their congregations to tears and loud wailing. Each year, in the days leading up to 'Ashura, Twelver Shias hold processions in which they chant *nauhajat* (lamentation poems in honor of Husain and the other Karbala Martyrs) and mark time by rhythmically slapping their chests. In countries such as Pakistan and India, many *matami guruhan* (Shia lamentation associations) go further, arranging public processions in which hundreds of men perform *zanjiri-matam* (self-flagellation involving knives, flails, or chains).

This ritual bloodshed is both controversial and popular. Theologically, *matam* earns practitioners intercession; but from a sociological perspective, it is worth noting that, wherever possible, Shias tend to perform such rituals publicly. One gains access to Husain's favor

[1] David Pinault, *The Shiites: Ritual and Popular Piety in a Muslim Community* (New York: St. Martin's Press, 1992), pp. 19, 123–24.

by having the courage to stand up and be identified as a Shia via conspicuously distinctive rituals. (Under Saddam Hussein's secularist–Ba'athist regime, public Muharram processions were prohibited; but since his fall from power in 2003, and with the subsequent dominance of sectarian factions supported by Iran's Shia government, Iraqi Shias have fervently embraced the public performance of self-scourging.)

We can get some sense of the importance of *matam* by consulting the sixteenth-century Koran commentator Husain Wa'iz al-Kashifi. In his Persian-language devotional work *Rawdat al-shuhada'* (The garden of the martyrs), Kashifi explains the role of physically manifested emotional involvement in the communal remembrance of the martyred imam:

> Weeping as one performs gestures of mourning pleases Allah and is the means by which one attains the Gardens of Eternity. As it has been stated in various writings: "Paradise is awarded to anyone who weeps for Husain or who laments in company with those who weep for Husain"....
>
> "Paradise is awarded" for the following reason, that every year, when the month of Muharram comes, a multitude of the lovers of the Family of the Prophet (*jam'i az muhibban-e Ahl-e Bayt*) renew and make fresh the tragedy of the Martyrs, and they bewail the offspring of the Lord of Prophecy. They enflame their hearts with the fire of sorrowful regret; their eyes stream with tears from the overwhelming extent of their loss.[2]

Especially important to note from Kashifi's text are the words *muhibban-e Ahl-e Bayt*: "lovers of the Family of the Prophet". Kashifi's sixteenth-century phrase is vital to an understanding of how Shiism has differentiated itself from other Islamic denominations. Shia populations have tended to understand themselves as a community that surpasses all others in its love for the Prophet's family and for the descendants of Fatima and 'Ali. Self-scourging rituals are seen as a way of publicly showing this love.

Nevertheless, the bloody forms of *matam* generate widespread revulsion, both among Sunnis and even among some Shias (as will be

---

[2] Husain Wa'iz al-Kashifi, *Rawdat al-shuhada'* (Teheran: Kitab-Forushi Islamiyah, 1979), p. 12, translated from the Persian by D. Pinault.

discussed below). Spurting blood is normally classed in Islamic law as *najis* (ritually polluting), and the extravagant weeping and displays of grief associated with *matam* offend Islamic notions of decorum and self-restraint. Of course, it is precisely this offensive quality of *matam* that makes such rituals socially useful, as a means of defining and demarcating a minority community and safeguarding it from being absorbed by a dominant majority.

The "Hidden Imam" and the purging of the world

One other distinctive Ithna-'Ashari practice should be noted in this context: veneration for the twelfth imam. Ithna-'Ashari Shias believe that in the ninth century, Muhammad al-Muntazar, the twelfth imam, was on the point of being murdered by the reigning Sunni caliph. Allah intervened, however, and protected the imam by causing him to enter *al-ghaybah* (occultation): he became invisible and hidden from his persecutors. The twelfth imam is still alive but will return to usher in Judgment Day, fill the earth with justice, and execute *intiqam* (vengeance, retribution) against all those who have made Shias suffer.

While looking forward to this retribution, Shias are permitted to practice taqiyah (protective dissimulation, pretending to be a Sunni and disguising one's true identity as a Shia for survival's sake while residing among a potentially hostile non-Shia population). To this day, Shia congregational prayers include invocations to Sahib al--zaman (one of the twelfth imam's titles: "the lord of time" or "lord of the age"). When this "Hidden Imam" returns to earth, he will bear the title al-Mahdi (the one who is divinely guided).

Shia Islam and Catholic Christianity: Some similarities— and some significant differences

Lamentation for a martyred sacred figure; devotion to the sorrowing mother of a leader who made a sacrifice of himself; the promise of intercession for the forgiveness of sins; and the hope for the second coming of a Mahdi who will usher in the Day of Judgment: such distinctively Shia practices and beliefs suggest analogues with Christianity, especially the Catholic form of the Christian faith.[3]

Those seeking additional Catholic-Shia parallels could also compare the deployment of emotion and ritual in each tradition. In the fourteenth and fifteenth centuries, Christian confraternities in Germany and Italy sponsored Lenten processions in which *disciplinati* scourged themselves while chanting *laudi spirituali*, "hymns of spiritual praise". (Similar examples in more recent times can be found in the *Penitentes* sodality of New Mexico and the present-day Good Friday flagellant gatherings in the Philippines.)

Eyewitness descriptions of the time give you a sense of what medieval Christian penitential processions were like for the participants, as evidenced in this account from a source known as the "Monk of Padua": "Each of them held in his hands a whip of thongs; and with weeping and groans they flogged themselves fiercely on the back and shoulders to the point of bloodshed. Pouring out fountains of tears, as if with their corporeal eyes they perceived the actual Passion of our Savior, they prayed in tearful song for the Lord's mercy and the help of God's mother."[4]

The monk's account hints at the personal emotional involvement underlying the actions performed in the liturgy: "as if with their corporeal eyes they perceived the actual Passion of our Savior". This emotionally charged mood of imaginative visualization seems to have been actively cultivated. A fourteenth-century source, Hugo von Reutlingen, describes how the spiritual guide of a German confraternity encouraged penitents during their collective self-scourging: *Et magister eorum adhortatur eos ad passionem Christi recolendam* (And their master exhorts them to recall Christ's Passion).[5]

As you and I ponder such practices, we can speculate that perhaps each penitent's faculty of imaginative visualization was further

---

[3] Such themes are explored in James A. Bill and John Alden Williams, *Roman Catholics and Shi'i Muslims: Prayer, Passion, and Politics* (Chapel Hill: University of North Carolina Press, 2002).

[4] Arthur Hübner, *Die Deutschen Geisslerlieder: Studien zum geistlichen Volksliede des Mittelalters* (Berlin: Verlag Walter de Gruyter, 1931), p. 9; translated by D. Pinault.

[5] Paul Runge, *Die Lieder und Melodien der Geissler des Jahres 1349 nach der Aufzeichnung Hugo's von Reutlingen* (Leipzig: Breitkopf & Haertel, 1900), pp. 26–27. This passage is translated and cited at length in David Pinault, "Self-Mortification Rituals in the Shi'i and Christian Traditions", in *Shi'ite Heritage: Essays on Classical and Modern Traditions*, ed. Lynda Clarke (Binghamton, N.Y.: Global Publications, 2001), p. 380.

stimulated by the wording of the devotional hymns sung during the act of self-scourging. One *lauda*, chanted by an Italian group called the *Disciplinati di Gubbio*, was composed in the form of a dialogue, with Jesus speaking directly to the flagellants:

> Shame on anyone who does not bear his cross;
> Harder than stone is the heart of anyone
> Who is not moved to follow me....
> Who will be the penitent to accompany me to the Cross
> And bathe himself in tears while lamenting his sins?[6]

I ask you now to consider the lyrics of Muharram hymns chanted by present-day Shia lamentation associations (the verses cited here are from texts I collected while doing field research with various *matam* groups in the Indian city of Hyderabad):

> Karbala is a jihad; Karbala is steadfastness.
> You [O Husain] have given a message that will endure until
>   Judgment Day:
> The spirit of Karbala, the secret of the world's origin, and
>   the mysteries of creation.
> Hail, beloved Husain, O beloved Husain.[7]

Keep in mind that as such hymns are sung, the assembled congregants and street-side onlookers participate by striking themselves rhythmically (whether with the palms of their hands or with knife or flail) in time to the cadence established by the chant. And note how the ritual itself is referenced in the lyrics from the following hymns:

> This sound of *matam* that echoes forth
> Is the announcement of victory over care and affliction.
> In the victory of truth is the oath made with tears:
> Karbala: no god is there save Allah.

---

[6] Hübner, *Deutschen Geisslerlieder*, p. 9.

[7] Mirza Farid Beg Farid, "Ay Husain jan, ay Husain jan", in *Du'a-ye Fatima: muntakhab-e nauhajat* (Hyderabad: Anjuman-e Ma'sumeen, 1987), pp. 2–3; translated from the Urdu by D. Pinault.

O young men of lamentation,
You embody the prayer of everyone's heart.
Truly, till the gathering of mankind on Judgment Day,
There will continue from breasts this sound of *matam*.

This *matam* is Fatima's prayer;
How could this *matam* be stopped?
This *matam* is a cry of challenge;
Each tear is part of a passionate desire for victory.[8]

The Shia poets who wrote these hymns composed them to be sung in a group liturgical setting. These verses create a sense of immediacy that breaks down the barriers of time: sacred history is not just commemorated; it is made alive and brought into the present. The words not only evoke the long-ago battle of Karbala; they also address the singers directly: "O young men of lamentation. . . ." And these texts likewise focus on the ritual performed by the congregants as well as the heightened feelings generated by the liturgical performance: "This *matam* is a cry of challenge; each tear is part of a passionate desire for victory."

For me, as a Catholic observer of Shia practice, what impressed me when I first witnessed Muharram rituals beginning in the 1980s, in Hyderabad, Ladakh, Lahore, and Chicago, was the presence of structural analogues in the two faiths. Christian *disciplinati* and Shia flagellants: each group pairs collective chant and the percussive use of the body to achieve closeness with a sacred figure who likewise endured a rending and piercing of his flesh. The parallels are certainly noteworthy.

And yet—

It is all too easy and tempting, in the service of interfaith rapprochement, to exaggerate similarities while overlooking substantive disagreements. So let's take note of the following:

Lacking in the Shia mythos is anything corresponding to Easter. The annual lamentation season in Shiism lasts some fifty days, from the first of Muharram through 'Ashura (the tenth of Muharram, when Husain died) and continuing until Chehelom (an observance marking

---

[8] Translated from the Urdu and cited in Pinault, "Self-Mortification Rituals", p. 382.

the fortieth day since 'Ashura and the death of Husain). At all the Muharram rituals I have attended over the years, whether in India, Pakistan, or America, the tone ranges from mournful to indignant. Preachers induce worshippers to weep, as they recall the torments of the Karbala martyrs; they also generate anger and a collective sense of victimhood, as they remind attendees of how the tyrannous caliph Yazid excluded the prophet's grandson from power. At times the presiding mullah will then extend history into the present by denouncing "the Yazids of today". I have heard the label applied to the former shah of Iran, Iraq's Saddam Hussein, the Wahhabis of Saudi Arabia, Zionist Israel, and the United States. Missing from the Shia liturgical calendar is any commemoration of how sorrow is transmuted into joy—joy accompanied by the assurance of redemption—such as is found in Christians' annual celebration of the risen Christ.

Lacking, too, in the Muharram ethos is the Christian emphasis on God's divine love as an element that is intimately bound up with earthly sorrow. In allowing Himself to take on human flesh, the second Person of the Trinity made himself vulnerable to our suffering. The emotion motivating such an act of generosity is made clear in the New Testament, as we see in the Gospel of John (3:16): "For God so loved the world that he gave his only-begotten Son, that whoever believes in him should not perish but have eternal life." This theme continues in the words Jesus offers to His disciples at the Last Supper, at the onset of His Passion on the eve of His crucifixion: "As the Father has loved me, so have I loved you; abide in my love.... These things I have spoken to you, that my joy may be in you, and that your joy may be full. This is my commandment, that you love one another as I have loved you. Greater love has no man than this, that a man lay down his life for his friends" (Jn 15:9, 11–13).

Closely linked to the above is another difference between the Muharram season and Christians' Holy Week: the question of violence. Although Shia preachers emphasize Husain's status as an innocent victim of caliph Yazid's oppression, nonetheless, Husain died fighting in combat. His father 'Ali was famous for killing kuffar and Jews; and Muhammad himself fought in battles such as Uhud, authorized the execution of opponents, and ordered the beheading of various prisoners of war.

But Christian accounts of the Passion remind us of what happened when the disciples tried to defend Jesus in the Garden of Gethsemane.

He told them to put away their swords. He healed the wound of the high priest's servant who had been injured by one of Christ's followers. And then he reminded them all that if he wanted he could pray to His Father and be granted "more than twelve legions of angels" to rout his oppressors (Mt 26:51–53; Lk 22:49–51). As Lamb of God, Jesus chooses the path of nonviolence.

Christians of course have a long history of engaging in violence and fighting for their faith (we have seen this in the Crusades). But that history has been tempered—admittedly, not always with great success—by the awareness of Christ as an exemplar of peace.

Joy; divine love; nonviolence. A fourth element of divergence in commemorations of Christ's sufferings and Husain's has to do with reconciliation and the forgiveness of enemies. Christ on the Cross prays, "Father, forgive them; for they know not what they do" (Lk 23:34).

In place of reconciliation and joy, a very different motif recurs in relation to Muharram. Many Shia theologians and political leaders have interpreted the battle of Karbala and the subsequent history of the persecution of the imams in such a way as to portray Shias as ongoing victims who await the vindication of Judgment Day, when the earth will be violently purged of the unrighteous majority who currently hold power.

Consider, if you will, the following verses from a medieval litany to the Mahdi (remember that according to Twelver Shia belief, the Mahdi is a sinless descendant of Muhammad who will appear on earth to inaugurate the end of time and the beginning of the final judgment): "On that day, you [O Mahdi] will raise high the banner of conquest, and you will see us surround you as you fill the land with your presence.... You will make your enemies taste humiliation and punishment. The arrogant, the violent, those who have denied the truth: all these you will destroy."[9]

The mood of these verses is reflected in an essay by the twentieth-century Iranian political activist 'Ali Shari'ati (d. 1977). The essay, entitled "Thar" (an Arabic word meaning "retaliation", "revenge", or "blood feud"), sets out to explain the significance of one of the Mahdi's honorific titles, al-Muntaqim (the avenger).

---

[9] 'Abbas Qummi, *Mafatih al-jinan* (Beirut: Dar Ihya' al-Turath al-'Arabi, 1970), pp. 535–38; translated by D. Pinault.

"What will he avenge?" announces Shari'ati of the Mahdi. "Everyone says, 'He will avenge the murder of the Sayyid al-Shuhada' [the Lord of martyrs], Husain.' Not at all! He will avenge the *thar* for which the tribe of Cain is responsible."[10]

To understand this view, it is necessary for us to study Shari'ati's vision of the battle of Karbala. " 'Ashura", he argues, "is not a one--and-a-half-day event. It is the issue of the eternity of history." That is, the death of the innocent victim Husain at Karbala comprised the continuation of a historical pattern that had first been articulated with Cain's murder of the innocent victim Abel. "It is then", asserts Shari'ati, "that the bipolarity of human society has begun."

According to this model of history, the "tribe of Cain" (also called by Shari'ati the "tribe of *taghut*", the word *taghut* referring to the pagan idols of the Jahiliyah) has persecuted the "tribe of Abel" since the beginning of time. He identifies Abel's spiritual descendants as "members of the tribe of God" who rise up "in every generation for revenge against the tribe of *taghut*, from whom blood is owed.... After Adam, humanity divides into two tribes, the tribe of *taghut* and the tribe of God, which division Islam has recognized. Without such duality, Islam cannot be understood."

The genius of the prophet Muhammad, Shari'ati concludes, was to substitute religious loyalty for family loyalty and religious vendetta for family feud. Thus Shari'ati elaborates the victim status of Shias in their suffering into a dichotomized world view of conflict and retaliation that will end only with the coming of the Mahdi.[11]

Shari'ati's cosmic vendetta vision has been continued in more recent years by religious-political leaders such as the Ayatollah Ruhollah Khomeini, who undertook to unite the Iranian nation around his *taghut*/Islam dualism. This sense of perennial victimhood is captured by a popular Shia proverb: *Kullu yawm 'Ashura wa-kullu 'ard Karbala* (Every day is 'Ashura and every land is Karbala). The online forum Shiachat.com offers the text of a Muharram sermon from the year 2012 that begins with this proverb and then goes on to give a vision of our twenty-first century as an age that can only be explained by the paradigm of the violent death of Husain: "The Muslim world is

---

[10] 'Ali Shari'ati, "Thar", in Mehdi Abedi and Gary Legenhausen, eds., *Jihad and Shahadat: Struggle and Martyrdom in Islam* (Houston: Institute for Research and Islamic Studies, 1986), p. 260.

[11] Ibid., pp. 256–58.

dominated by Yazids who have pledged themselves to the modern--
day Pharaohs.... There is a long list of tragedies that have befallen
upon [sic] us that can be cited as our present-day Karbala: Bahrain,
Palestine, Afghanistan, Iraq, Syria, Kashmir, Bosnia, Somalia, Pakistan, and Gujarat are but a few."[12]

One final example—this one a personal anecdote—to illustrate
just how different can be Shia and Christian understandings of self--
sacrificial death on behalf of one's faith:

In December 1997, at the invitation of one of my undergraduates,
I gave a lecture at the Shia mosque she attended in Pomona, California. The talk itself, I think, went well enough; but a curious bit of
conversation from that night lingers in my memory.

After the lecture, while I was mingling with attendees, I overheard
two young Shia clerics chatting in Arabic. Not knowing—or perhaps
not caring—that I could understand what they were saying, one said
to the other that Christians have no right to condemn the acts of those
Muslims who undertake 'amaliyat istishhadiyah (martyrdom-seeking
operations). Christians, he continued, have no business referring to
such actions as 'amaliyat intihariyah (suicide operations). I was already
aware that many zealots prefer the term "martyrdom-seeking" as the
Islamically correct way of designating terrorists who strap on a bomb
and blow themselves up in a crowd.

But what really startled me was the reply voiced by the second of
the young mullahs. He agreed with his colleague and then had this to
say (I will not put it in quotation marks, because I do not recall it word
for word; but I certainly remember the gist): *If Muslim martyrs are people who commit suicide, what does that make Christ on that cross Christians
claim he was crucified on? Christians say he knew he would get killed. But he
went ahead anyway. If what they say is true, he committed suicide.*

At that they both laughed.

Khomeinist politics and Iran's bid for leadership of global Islam

The history and rituals that we have just examined together are
worth knowing about because they figure in the increasingly fierce
sectarian polemics linked to the Iranian Islamic Republic's bid for

---

[12] http://www.shiachat.com/forum/topic/235008336.

leadership of global Islam. The regime in Teheran, fully aware of the widespread hostility to Shiism among Sunni populations, has pursued a policy—dating back to the reign of the Ayatollah Khomeini—of downplaying its Shia identity in international pronouncements directed to the general Muslim public. Hence Iran's support for the Palestinian terrorist group Hamas; hence the frequent televised appearances by members of the Iranian leadership featuring maps of Palestine and photos of Jerusalem's Dome of the Rock. Support for Palestinian militancy constitutes an attempt to gain popularity among Sunni Arabs by focusing on shared objects of revulsion: Israel; Zionism; America.

Saudi-based Wahhabi Salafists, eager to derail Iran's drive for leadership, have been reminding Sunnis of precisely those sectarian differences that are most likely to keep anti-Shia sentiment alive. The first of these (and one that Sunni informants referred to angrily, in interviews I conducted in Yemen and Pakistan) involves the centuries--old Shia practice called *sabb al-sahabah* (reviling the Companions). As noted above, Shias to this day fault those companions of Muhammad who blocked 'Ali ibn Abi Talib from the caliphate. Particular blame is placed on the first two caliphs, Abu Bakr and 'Umar.

There are moments when such cursing becomes a communal practice. Muslim colleagues in locales ranging from Lahore to California have told me of occasions when Shia clerics, in mosque sermons to their congregations, have included invocations to Allah to condemn and withhold His mercy from all those individuals who blocked 'Ali's ascent, especially Abu Bakr, 'Umar, and 'Ayeshah (the latter was Muhammad's youngest wife, who after her husband's death became 'Ali's rival for power).

Since Sunnis revere all these figures, this is a particularly sore point. As one Sunni informant in the Yemeni city of Sanaa complained to me of Twelver Shias: "They insult the Companions. They insult 'Ayeshah. They are not Muslims at all." Partly because of this issue, Shias are sometimes derided with the term *Rafidi* (rejectionist, renegade), a pejorative that recurs in present-day anti-Shia polemics.[13]

---

[13] David Pinault, "Sunni, Shia, Zaydi: Religious Identity and Sectarian Proselytizing in Contemporary Yemen", *Journal of South Asian and Middle Eastern Studies*, 33, no. 1 (Fall 2009): 1–19.

The dangling corpse: Sectarian politics in The Thousand and One Nights

"Reviling the Companions" has a long pedigree that can be discerned even in the celebrated medieval collection of stories known as the *Kitab alf laylah wa-laylah* (*The Book of the Thousand and One Nights*). The story I have in mind features the famous 'Abbasid caliph Harun al-Rashid and comes from a nineteenth-century Arabic edition of the *Nights* published in Egypt (a country with an overwhelmingly Sunni population).

Harun wrongly suspects the story's hero—a young man named 'Ala' al-Din (more commonly known in English as Aladdin)—of a crime, has him arrested, and orders him killed. Unknown to Harun, the hero escapes and another prisoner is hanged instead. Thereafter, the caliph announces a desire to see Aladdin's corpse hanging from the gallows. Accompanied by his vizier Ja'far, Harun goes to the execution ground but becomes suspicious when he sees the dangling corpse.

"Then," we are told, "Harun ordered the corpse to be brought down from the gallows. When they brought it down, he found inscribed on the bottoms of its feet the names of the "two sheikhs" [that is, Abu Bakr and 'Umar]. Then Harun said, 'O vizier, Aladdin was a Sunni, and this fellow is a Rafidi!' "[14]

Inscribing these names on the bottoms of one's feet (the point where one comes into contact with the world's legions of unclean things) is a way of reviling Abu Bakr and 'Umar with every step one takes. The assumption underlying this episode, of course, is that only a Shia "Rejectionist" would dishonor the first two caliphs like this. The fact that the storyteller does not bother to explain this suggests how widespread among the Sunni audience of the *Nights* was this perception of Twelver Shia attitudes and behavior. The story may also dramatize Sunni impressions of the doctrine of taqiyah: as a crypto-Shia, this Rafidi outwardly appeared to be an orthodox Sunni; but concealed beneath his feet was his contempt for the "two sheikhs".

---

[14] *Kitab alf laylah wa-laylah*, ed. 'Abd al-Rahman al-Safati al-Sharqawi (Cairo: Bulaq, 1835), 1:437 (Night 265); translated from the Arabic by D. Pinault.

"Standardized Islam" and exporting the Iranian revolution

The second sectarian issue that appears frequently today involves *matam* lamentation rituals during the annual Muharram season. Since 1994, 'Ali Khamenei, Khomeini's successor as supreme leader of Iran, has issued *fatwas* forbidding the public performance of self--flagellation. Khamenei's stated justification? "It is not a question of individual or physical harm," he has argued, "but one of great injuries linked to the reputation of Islam." In forbidding the public performance of bloody *matam*, he has claimed that outsiders might point to this ritual in order to "present both Islam and Shiism as an institution of superstition".[15]

Khamenei's *fatwas* represent a trend currently discernible among competing Shia and Sunni missionaries: the attempt to eradicate traditional regionally based forms of Muslim worship and replace them with a standardized and homogenized version of Islam—a global Islam that would be easier to supervise from one centralized source.

These *fatwas* have encountered considerable resistance. Shias I have visited since the 1990s in Muslim locales in Pakistan and India continue to stage spectacularly bloody public performances of *matam*. They express resentment at what they see as attempts by Iranian outsiders to meddle in local affairs. Sunni polemicists, for their part, regard Khamenei's decrees as a ruse to disguise Shiism's inherently unorthodox and unislamic character and as a tactic to further the Khomeinist policy of *tasdir al-thawrah al-iraniyah* (exporting the Iranian revolution).

Rushing to the Apocalypse?: The theology of the Iranian "Hasteners"

The third sectarian difference that has drawn attention in recent years involves devotion to the twelfth imam. Insurrectionist and militant movements have often invoked this figure. An example is Muqtada al-Sadr's Iraqi Shia militia known as *Jaysh al-Mahdi* (the Mahdi army).

---

[15] For the text of Khamenei's *fatwas*, see David Pinault, *Horse of Karbala: Muslim Devotional Life in India* (New York: Palgrave, 2001), pp. 149, 174–75.

Among the more notorious devotees of the Mahdi in recent years is Mahmoud Ahmadinejad (who was president of the Iranian Islamic Republic from 2005 to 2013). For centuries, many Shias have favored a theological stance known as *intizar* (awaiting, expectation). Rather than wage open war against tyrants and other earthly incarnations of injustice, faithful Shias avoid political confrontations and adopt a quietist position, piously awaiting the Mahdi's appearance among us. But Ahmadinejad belongs to a sect known as the *Ta'jiliyan* (those who bring [something] about quickly, or "the Hasteners").

This sect claims that believers can, through their actions, "hasten" the twelfth imam's apocalyptic return. While serving as president of Iran, Ahmadinejad ended a speech he gave at the United Nations with a prayer for the Mahdi's appearance: "O mighty Lord, I pray to you: hasten the emergence of the promised one, that perfect and pure human being." Ahmadinejad also supervised the rebuilding of the Jamkaran Shrine in southern Teheran (from which the Mahdi will one day arise, according to Twelver belief). In addition, he has claimed to be in frequent personal contact with the "Hidden Imam".[16]

Ahmadinejad's version of "Hastener" theology was explored at the 2009 Herzliya Conference, an annual gathering on Israeli security issues, in a presentation by the researcher Shmuel Bar. Bar remarked that "Ahmadinejad's declared objective ... is to hasten the appearance of the Hidden Imam. This is to be accomplished through the precipitation of a clash of civilizations between the Islamic world and the West."[17]

It should be noted that Iran's political-clerical leadership is divided on this issue. Nevertheless, in light of Iran's drive to acquire nuclear capability and the very real possibility that the Islamic Republic will eventually develop nuclear weaponry, Hastener devotionalism of the kind favored by Ahmedinejad is—to put it mildly—not reassuring. This prospect, of a nuclear-armed and ever-more influential Iran, has

---

[16] Frances Harrison, "Row over Ahmadinejad Imam Beliefs", *BBC News*, February 20, 2008; Charles Colson, "Preparing for the Mahdi", January 19, 2006, http://www.catholic exchange.com; World Net Daily, "Iran Leader's U.N. Finale Reveals Apocalyptic View", September 21, 2006, http://www.wnd.com.

[17] Shmuel Bar, "Iranian Terrorist Policy and 'Export of Revolution'", working paper from the Ninth Annual Herzliya Conference on the Balance of Israel's National Security and Resilience, February 2–4, 2009 (Herzliya, Israel: Institute for Policy and Strategy, 2009).

spurred Saudi Arabia's Wahhabi Salafists to do whatever they can to lessen their adversary's prestige by portraying Iran as "Persian" and Shia, and hence as alien and heterodox in the eyes of Sunni Arabs.

Sunni-Shia polemics and rivalry, from the Palestinian territories to Yemen

Sectarian polemics have also arisen in intra-Palestinian politics (despite the fact that almost all Palestinian Muslims are Sunni). Members of Fatah have taken to taunting their rivals in Hamas by calling them "Shia"—a derogatory reminder of the support given Hamas by Teheran.

Competition between Sunnis and Shias has also become manifest recently in the realm of religious conversion from one denomination to another within Islam. A current arena for such competition is Yemen. The target: a segment of Yemen's population known as the Zaydis. Zaydi religious teachings, although historically derived from Shiism, occupy a doctrinal position that shares features of both Sunnism and Shiism. Zaydis I interviewed in Sanaa (Yemen's capital) in 2009 acknowledged that since the abolition of Yemen's Zaydi Imamate in 1962 and the subsequent diminishment of Zaydi political power, many young Zaydis are ideologically adrift and uncertain of their own communal identity.[18]

Saudi-funded missionaries have succeeded in converting some Zaydis to Wahhabi puritanism. Other Zaydis, however, are drawn to Iran's Khomeinist propaganda. Government sources in Yemen accuse Iran of funding the Houthi rebels in northern Yemen's Saada province, along the Saudi border (the Houthis are militant Zaydis whose leadership comes from the family of Badr al-Din al-Houthi). The Houthis deny that they are funded by Teheran, and they repudiate the claim made by many Yemeni Sunnis that Houthis have secretly converted to the Twelver Shiism that is Iran's state religion.

But Zaydis I met in Sanaa told me that Houthis take inspiration from Iran and Hezbollah and that they like the feeling of joining a worldwide movement, a universal struggle against what are perceived

[18] Pinault, "Sunni, Shia, Zaydi", pp. 12–19.

as satanic forces at loose in the world. A Houthi apologist recited for me the Houthi slogan: *Allahu akbar al-mawt li-Amrika al-mawt li-Isra'il al-la'nah 'ala al-yahud al-nasr lil-islam* (Allah is great. Death to America. Death to Israel. May the Jews be cursed. Victory belongs to Islam.)

Internet web postings offer further perspectives on the situation in Yemen. Twelver Shia missionaries refer to individuals who convert to their form of Islam as *mustabsirun* (those who have become endowed with insight). The Arabic-language website of the pro-Shia *Markaz al-abhath al-'aqa'idiyah* (Office of doctrinal research) offers the personal testimony of former Sunnis and Zaydis who are now listed as *mustabsirun*.

Their backgrounds are varied. One is a journalist; another, a highly educated attorney with wide travel experience. A third is presented as a one-time Wahhabi; a fourth, as an anti-Shia zealot who originally set out to write a book refuting Twelver doctrine. But they have something in common. The website portrays them all as restless spiritual questers, who independently did research on Twelver Shiism and became so impressed with what they learned that they spontaneously became *mustabsirun*.

When I mentioned the *mustabsirun* phenomenon to a Sunni mosque leader I met in Sanaa, he rejected any notion of the sincerity of their conversion, insisting that such individuals were no more than pawns in a Teheran-based plot to take control of Yemen secretly. "The Iranians," he said, "will use these converts as part of their conspiracy to rule our country from afar."[19]

That conversation, and my fieldwork in Yemen, took place in 2009. Since then, the country's sectarian tensions have exploded into open war—a conflict fueled by military support from neighboring regional powers. Houthi rebels have killed civilians and soldiers alike in battles near the Saudi frontier in northern Yemen. The Houthis have also launched ballistic missiles across the border at targets within Saudi Arabia itself. Iran's Islamic Republic denies any attempt to provide arms to Yemen's Houthis.

But investigators from CAR (Conflict Armament Research, an organization based in the UK and funded by the European Union)

---

[19] Ibid., pp. 1–19; David Pinault, "Sunni-Shia Sectarianism and Competition for the Leadership of Global Islam", *Tikkun Magazine*, January/February 2010, pp. 45–47, 73–75.

have proved otherwise. "Committed to working towards under-standing the landscape of illicit weapon flows," the organization's website declares, "CAR investigation teams work on the ground in active armed conflicts. The teams document weapons at the point of use and track their sources back through the chains of supply." In November 2016, CAR teams succeeded in doing just that, uncovering an armaments pipeline that routed weapons from Iran to Yemen via Somalia.[20]

For its part, Saudi Arabia (with logistical support from both the United States and the United Kingdom) has launched airstrikes that have targeted Houthi forces but have also resulted in thousands of civilian casualties. As of 2017, Yemen's proxy-war conflict between Teheran and Riyadh shows little sign of coming to a quick end.[21]

In 2010, I published a magazine article on what I witnessed in Yemen and how sectarian tensions were escalating as Iran and Saudi Arabia maneuvered there for influence. I ended the article with a prediction: "Yemen, it seems, offers a storm warning of what is to come: increasingly polemicized competition between Sunni and Shia ideologues for the leadership of global Islam."[22]

At this moment I think it is fair to say that that storm is now truly upon us.

[20] "Iranian Technology Transfers to Yemen" (London: Conflict Armament Research, 2017), pp. 1–10, http://www.conflictarm.com/about-us.

[21] "King Salman Challenges Foreign 'Menace' in Yemen", December 14, 2016, http://www.Aljazeera.com; "The United States' Bloody Alliance with Saudi Arabia", Washington Post Editorial Board, January 5, 2017.

[22] Pinault, "Sunni-Shia Sectarianism", p. 75.

CHAPTER 11

WEAKNESS AND SUFFERING AS UNGODLIKE: ISLAMIC CHRISTOLOGY AND ANTI-CHRISTIAN POLEMICS AMONG MUSLIM WRITERS FROM THE ELEVENTH CENTURY TO THE TWENTY-FIRST

"Crucified, while he could do nothing about it": Muslim use of biblical verses as anti-Christian propaganda

Very few Muslims I have known have ever read any of the Bible. From their point of view, why should they? The Koran tells believers what to think about Christians, Jews, and the prophets and scriptures they claim. (This highlights a challenge facing those who want to engage in interfaith dialogue: the Bible provides no information to Jews and Christians about Muhammad or the message he preached, whereas most Muslims feel that, thanks to the Koran, they already know what they need to know about the other religions of the Book.)

Throughout Islamic history, Muslim religious authorities have not encouraged their followers to investigate the sacred texts of Judaism and Christianity. But there is one circumstance in which it has been considered permissible for Muslims to read Judeo-Christian scripture. Muslim propagandist Yahiya Emerick, author of *How to Tell Others about Islam*, puts it as follows: "Remember, it is no sin in Islam to examine the Bible if the intention is to glean arguments to show non-- Muslims where they have erred."[1]

It is an attitude with a long pedigree. The logic behind it: to turn Judeo-Christian scripture against the very "people of the Book" who

---

[1] Yahiya Emerick, *How to Tell Others about Islam* (Beirut: Noorart, 2004), p. 77.

honor it, using the Bible as a club with which to smite the beliefs of Jews and Christians. In reading the New Testament with an eye to disproving the divine Sonship of Christ, these Muslim polemicists, in a tradition extending over more than a thousand years, inadvertently reveal—as you are about to see—their own Islamic preconceptions as to what qualities are appropriate or inappropriate for a deity.

An example is 'Abd al-Malik ibn 'Abd Allah al-Juwaini, an eleventh-century Iranian legal scholar and theologian. While living in Baghdad, a city harboring a sizable minority population of Jews and Christians, he wrote a work entitled *Shifa' al-ghalil fi al-tabdil* (The satisfaction of burning thirst concerning the alteration of the scriptures).

In his polemic, Juwaini scornfully identifies what he considers the inconsistencies and logical absurdities to be found in the portrait of Jesus provided by the Christian Gospels of the New Testament:

> Christ possesses, in relation to Allah—may He be exalted and glorified—the highest rank, and he is among the greatest and most revered prophets. But in claiming that he was crucified, along with two thieves who insulted him (or alternatively that one of them insulted him) and said to him, "Save yourself!" while he was unable to do so: well, these claims by the Christian evangelists diminish his rank and his power and make one imagine that he was incapable of accomplishing any miracles at all.
>
> The same applies to the Christian Gospel claims that Jesus was clothed with a crown of thorns and a dyed robe, while men genuflected before him, mocking and insulting him. So, too, with the notion that his mother and his aunt, afflicted with sorrow, saw him crucified, while he could do nothing about it.[2]

The lack of rank and power; helplessness in the face of mockery and insults: as far as Juwaini is concerned, the Christian scriptures themselves prove that Christ could not possibly have been Son of God.

Although Juwaini is willing to exploit biblical verses to assault Christian claims, he also displays a certain cognitive discomfort at peering into Nazarene texts, as is suggested by an anecdote he recounts concerning the prophet Muhammad. Juwaini tells us what happened

[2] 'Abd al-Malik ibn 'Abd Allah al-Juwaini, *Shifa' al-ghalil fi al-tabdil*, in *Textes apologétiques de Guwaini*, ed. Michel Allard, S.J. (Beirut: Dar el-Machreq Imprimerie Catholique, 1968), p. 79; translated from the Arabic by D. Pinault.

when Muhammad discovered one of his own trusted companions
(the future caliph 'Umar ibn al-Khattab) glancing at the Bible:

> I have turned away from expanding on this subject, in citing pas-
> sages from the Torah and the Christian Gospels that provide proofs
> and arguments against the enemy, for the following reason. Once,
> when the Lord of prophets—may Allah's blessings rest upon him!—
> saw 'Umar looking at the Torah, he became angry at him and said:
> "If Moses himself were alive today, he would be incapable of doing
> anything except following *me*." So, for this reason, I myself have not
> pursued any further my own studies of the Torah and the Gospels.[3]

The moral of the story is clear: If Muhammad himself got angry at
seeing a disciple display interest in the Bible, then Muslims in general
should handle the toxic texts of "the enemy" as little as possible—
unless it is for the purpose of disproving Jewish and Christian beliefs.
But such things should be undertaken only by experts who are qualified to deal safely with such toxicity.

"Why have You abandoned me?": A Muslim polemicist's view of Christ's cry from the Cross

One such expert was the renowned twelfth-century philosopher and
theologian Abu Hamid al-Ghazali. Among his many writings is a treatise entitled *al-Radd al-jamil li-ilahiyat 'Isa bi-sarih al-Injil* (The beautiful
refutation of Jesus' divinity through explanation of the Gospel). Like
Juwaini, Ghazali mines the New Testament for scriptural statements
to demonstrate that Christ could not possibly have been divine:

> In the Gospel are verses that indicate the purely human nature of
> Jesus, peace be upon him, and verses that testify that the attribution
> of godhood to him, according to what the Christians claim, is impos-
> sible ... especially concerning a person whose human nature has been
> made evident. The necessities and liabilities of this human nature are
> confirmed, along with the attributes of its personal identity: the exis-
> tence of a nature susceptible to lower appetites; [human] statements
> and utterances; fatigue, exhaustion, and weakness; hunger, thirst, and

---

[3] Juwaini, *Shifa'*, p. 83.

sleep; existence within a woman's womb; and suffering—according to what Christians believe—on the cross.

This suffering on the cross is reflected in the Gospel verse that states: "My God, my God, why have You abandoned me?" [cf. Mk 15:34 and Mt 27:46].

All these things refute the notion of godhood. How could that be denied?[4]

From Ghazali's point of view as a Muslim polemicist, the cry of the crucified Christ—"My God, my God, why have you abandoned me?"—suffices to "refute the notion of godhood". What this Muslim critic fails to remark, however, is that the words voiced in anguish by Jesus constitute the opening verse of Psalm 22—familiar words that any Jew present at the foot of the Cross might well have recognized, words that constituted a prayer to be recited in times of distress.

Certainly the initial portion of this psalm suggests a desperate soul in torment: the psalmist evokes someone who is "scorned by men, and despised by the people". In agony, the speaker moans, "I am poured out like water, and all my bones are out of joint; my heart is like wax" (Ps 22:6, 14).

But the psalm does not end there. The speaker calls on God for help, as any son might call on his father for aid: "But you, O LORD, be not far off! O my help, hasten to my aid!... Save me from the mouth of the lion." And from there the prayer moves toward a conclusion marked by serenity, in a mood of quiet acceptance and praise for God: "All the ends of the earth shall remember and turn to the LORD; and all the families of the nations shall worship before him. For dominion belongs to the LORD, and he rules over the nations. Yes, to him shall all the proud of the earth bow down; before him shall bow all who go down to the dust" (Ps 22:19–21, 27–29).

Golden calf, talking jinn: Ibn Taimiyyah's attack on blasphemous beliefs among Shias, Sufis, and Christians

A very distinctive approach to anti-Christian polemics, involving unflattering comparisons with Shiism, Islamic mysticism, and

---

[4] Abu Hamid al-Ghazali, *al-Radd al-jamil li-ilahiyat 'Isa bi-sarih al-Injil* (Beirut: Dar al-Jil, 1990), pp. 99, 113; translated from the Arabic by D. Pinault.

traditional Arab beliefs about demonic possession, can be found in the writings of the fourteenth-century author Ahmad ibn 'Abd al-Halim ibn Taimiyyah. A Damascus-based professor of Islamic law and a harsh critic of what he regarded as doctrinal excesses in both Shias and Sufis, Ibn Taimiyyah condemned many forms of *bid'ah* (heretical religious "innovation" supposedly introduced after the time of the prophet Muhammad), especially practices involving the veneration of Muslim saints and devotional pilgrimages to their tombs.

An inspiration for the eighteenth-century founder of Wahhabi fundamentalism as well as for many of the most violent Muslim terrorists of the twenty-first century, Ibn Taimiyyah has been cited approvingly in the writings of both Osama bin Laden and Ayman al-Zawahiri (Bin Laden's successor as head of al-Qaeda).[5]

Ibn Taimiyyah was also hostile to the religions of the Book. According to the scholar Mohammed Ben Cheneb, "Islam being sent to replace Judaism and Christianity, it naturally incited ibn Taimiya to attack both of these religions.... [H]e wrote pamphlets against the maintenance or building of synagogues and particularly of churches."[6]

In other words: as people of the Book and practitioners of faiths whose shelf life has long since expired and been replaced by Islam, Jews and Christians are to be tolerated—but that does not mean they should be *encouraged* in their faith in any way. Hence Ibn Taimiyyah's recommendation not to let them maintain or build any places of worship. His view echoes regulations to be found in an Islamic legal document you will recall from a previous chapter: the so-called "Covenant of 'Umar", which mandates various restrictions to be applied to Jews and Christians living under caliphal rule.

Of immediate relevance for our investigation is a lengthy anti-Christian work by Ibn Taimiyyah entitled *al-Jawab al-sahih li-man baddala din al-Masih* (The correct response to those who have altered Christ's religion). There are several passages from this treatise I will share with you now.

The first involves Ibn Taimiyyah's use of the Arabic term *hulul*. The word is derived from a verb that means to descend, befall,

---

[5] See treatises by both Bin Laden and Zawahiri citing Ibn Taimiyyah in *The Al Qaeda Reader*, ed. and trans. Raymond Ibrahim (New York: Broadway Books, 2007), pp. 12–13, 67–68.

[6] Mohammed Ben Cheneb, "Ibn Taimiya", in *Encyclopaedia of Islam*, ed. M. Houtsma, A.J. Wensinck et al., 1st ed. (Leiden: Brill, 1923), 3:422.

alight, or occupy. In medieval theological texts, *hulul* was some-times used to describe the descent from heaven of a divine spirit that takes up residence in a living body of flesh (a concept abhorrent to most followers of Islam). Thus the word is used by some Muslims to render the Christian doctrine of the Incarnation. In various Islamic heresiographical treatises, *hulul* is hurled as an accusation to condemn certain Sufis and Shias for being *ghulat* (doctrinal extremists whose beliefs disqualify them from being considered true Muslims).[7]

The logic underlying the charge of *hulul* is that the errors Christians make in divinizing Jesus are similar to the doctrinal errors made by those Sufis and Shias who divinize their own charismatic and all-too-human leaders. Being tagged a *hululi* (adherent of the blasphemous belief in *hulul*) could precipitate a harsh fate: public torture and execution by order of the caliphate.

Which is what happened to someone we met in an earlier chapter—the tenth-century moth-mystic Hallaj. Drawn to the candle flame of divine union, he cried out in ecstasy *Ana al-Haqq*: "I am the Truth!" (You will recall that al-Haqq, "the Truth", is one of the Koranic names or attributes of Allah.)

Such ecstatic cries led some Muslim authorities to group Hallaj's alleged claims with those made by Christians about Jesus. We can see this at work in the condemnation directed at Muhammad ibn al-Shalmaghani. This was a tenth-century Shia whose teachings were reviled as "an impiety that this accursed man implanted in the heart of these people to prepare them for what he tells them about God's having united with him (*ittahada*), and having infused Himself into him (*halla fihi*), as the Christians say of the Messiah; he converts them to the doctrine of Hallaj, upon whom be God's curse."[8]

Let's see how Ibn Taimiyyah makes use of the notion of divine-descent-into-a-human-body in his anti-Christian polemics:

> Those who believe in the doctrine of *hulul* are among the *ghulat* whom Muslims condemn as infidel *kuffar*. For example, there are doctrinal

---

[7] Louis Massignon, "Hulul", in *Encyclopaedia of Islam*, 3:333.

[8] Louis Massignon, *The Passion of al-Hallaj: Mystic and Martyr of Islam*, trans. Herbert Mason (Princeton: University Press, 1982), 1:318.

extremists who believe in Allah's taking up residence within some of the Shia *Ahl al-bayt* [revered members or descendants of the prophet Muhammad's family]. There are others who believe in Allah's taking up residence within the Sufi sheikhs and spiritual masters.

Thus those among the Shias and Sufis who are infidels accompany the Christians in believing in *hulul*, even if they do not explicitly say, "The Word that has taken up fleshly residence is God the Creator." In any case, they are all repugnant and contradict themselves and each other with their very evident logical contradictions.[9]

According to Ibn Taimiyyah, a recurrent tendency in certain forms of both Shia and Sufi Islam has been to venerate their spiritual leaders as individuals on whom Allah's spirit has descended in such a way as to divinize them. Thus he consigns them to the blasphemous and blighted company of Christians: they are all guilty of "believing in *hulul*". (Of course Ibn Taimiyyah's characterization does not begin to do justice to how Christians themselves conceptualize Christ's Incarnation. But what mattered for this polemicist was to equate heterodox sectarian beliefs in his own community with the doctrines of a faith that all Muslims could agree on condemning as unacceptable: Christianity.)

Attacking Shiism by linking it with Christianity is a tactic that continues to the present day. I was reminded of this on a recent field trip with my undergraduates to a mosque near the campus where I teach, when one of our Muslim hosts handed several of my students complimentary copies of a book entitled *Bearing True Witness*. Published in Saudi Arabia, it is meant for new converts or those considering conversion to the religion of Allah. Its Wahhabi bias is evident in the way it presents the Shia tradition:

> Shi'ite Muslims are just one group of a long list of deviant sects which have chosen to disregard the Sunnah of Muhammad (peace be upon him), to one degree or another, in favor of the teachings of their sectarian leaders. Similar to the Christians who discarded the orthodox teachings of Christ Jesus in favor of the more permissive, though contrary, theology of Paul, the deviant sects of Islam are almost always

---

[9] Ahmad ibn 'Abd al-Halim ibn Taimiyyah, *Al-Jawab al-sahih li-man baddala din al-masih* (Beirut: al-Maktabah al-'Ilmiyah, 2003), 1:459; translated from the Arabic by D. Pinault.

characterized by the error of assigning priority to human teachings which stand contrary to the trustworthy foundation to be found in the Qur'an and Sunnah.[10]

In class the day after our visit, I made a point of talking with my students about how give-away English-language da'wah-texts like this are written so as to undermine not only Shiism but also Christianity here in the West.

But let's get back to Ibn Taimiyyah. After attacking Shia and Sufi "infidels" by grouping them with Christians, he goes on to note how those individuals—such as Jesus—to whom Allah has given the ability to perform miracles are then frequently mistaken as gods by the gullible:

> Many people—no, make that *most* people—are dazzled and fooled by miracles and wonder-working, so that they put their faith in whoever it was that wrought these miracles. Most people believe in such wonder-workers before carefully considering the validity of whatever the wonder-workers claim.
>
> And if they do believe such claims, they also are inclined to believe the Christians in their claims of Christ's godhood. These kinds of people also believe those who make claims about divine incarnation and the union of Allah and men taking place with regard to certain Sufi sheikhs or certain Shias of the *Ahl al-bayt* or others like them from among the people of immorality, depravity, and falsehood....
>
> In the time of Moses, the sons of Israel supposed that the [Golden] Calf was the god of Moses, and so they said, "This is your god, and the god of Moses!"... And the Christians continually say, "Christ is Allah." And among those who belong to the Qiblah [that is, those who pray toward Mecca = Muslims], there are many who make claims similar to "This is your god!" concerning the Sufi sheikhs and the Shia *Ahl al-bayt*.
>
> It has gotten to the point that many leaders among the masters of mystical knowledge and Sufism treat such claims as an assertion of truth and Allah's Oneness. In other words, they claim that the person who declares Allah's Oneness is the same as the One whose Oneness is declared.[11]

[10] Laurence B. Brown, *Bearing True Witness* (Riyadh: Darussalam, 2005), p. 22.
[11] Ibn Taimiyyah, *Al-Jawab*, 1:464.

Here Ibn Taimiyyah describes the beliefs of Christians and heterodox Muslims in terms of a notorious incident from Koranic and biblical scripture. Wayward Israelites built themselves a golden idol and cried out, "This is your god, and the god of Moses!" (surah 20:88, a verse that recalls Exodus 32:3–4: "Aaron ... received the gold at their hand, and fashioned it with a graving tool, and made a molten calf; and they said, 'These are your gods, O Israel....!'"). Just as the children of Israel misdirected their worship to a thing of gold, so, too, claims Ibn Taimiyyah, do Christians and certain Muslims err in proclaiming as Allah a mere human, whether that person is Jesus, a Shia imam, or a Sufi sheikh.

Another mistake Christians supposedly make about Jesus is illustrated with reference to the demons of ancient Arab tradition. This is one of the more intriguing and curious arguments made by Ibn Taimiyyah:

> When people heard the voice of Jesus [as he addressed them in speech], they did not hear a voice that was different from his. But whenever a jinn takes up fleshly residence in a human and makes use of his tongue to speak [wa-al-jinni idha halla fi al-insan wa-takallama 'ala lisanihi], it becomes evident to listeners that this voice is *not* the voice of a human being. And when such a person speaks, he does so in such a way that those present know that this is *not* the speech of a human being.
>
> As for Christ, peace be upon him: nothing was ever heard from him except what was heard from others like him among the prophets. But if the speaker using the tongue of [Jesus'] human nature to say something had been a jinn or maybe an angel, then that would have been evident, and it would have been known that it was not human. So what would it have been like if the speaker had been the Lord of the Worlds? If this had truly been the case, then it would have been much, much more tremendously evident than the occurrence of an angel or a jinn using a man's tongue to speak.[12]

Here Ibn Taimiyyah uses the vocabulary of *hulul* to engage in a bit of alternative sacred history: What if a demon had taken up "fleshly residence" in the Son of Mary? What if Jesus had been majnun? (You may remember from our earlier chapters that Muhammad himself

---

[12] Ibid., 1:476.

had been plagued with doubts about whether he was jinn-ridden or not.)

If Jesus had been majnun, argues Ibn Taimiyyah, onlookers surely would have heard an altered voice as soon as he opened his mouth to preach. Yet they heard nothing unhuman. Hence, so goes our polemicist's Islamic logic, Jesus could not have been even majnun, let alone the divine "Lord of the Worlds".

"His prophets do not have doubts about His promise": *Twenty-first-century Islamic polemical portraits of Christ's Passion and crucifixion*

Recent Muslim polemical works published in Arabic over the last fifteen years share considerable continuity with the themes of anti-Christian treatises from the premodern era.

An example is a book published in Cairo in 2010 by an author named Muhammad Mahmud al-Sayyid. Entitled *Al-Masih bayna al-lahut wa-al-nasut* (Christ between divine nature and human nature), it is prefaced by a decree from the "Islamic Research Academy" of al-Azhar University authorizing the publication of this book and affirming that its contents conform to Islamic doctrine. Given al-Azhar's reputation as the Islamic world's most prestigious place of learning, this makes Sayyid's arguments all the more worth our attention.

In reading this book, I was struck by the author's selective use of Christian Gospel verses concerning Jesus' Passion. Consider Sayyid's presentation of the Agony in the Garden (an event completely missing from the Koran) and the theological conclusions he derives from it:

> On the one hand, Christ never once clearly stated that he would offer himself as a sacrificial expiatory victim, offering himself voluntarily in an act of obedience, acting out of love and generosity, as an offering on the Cross. But, on the other hand, he did in fact clearly and explicitly express his anguish, fear, terror, and lack of satisfaction at the prospect of being crucified or killed. Moreover, he implored, begged, and prayed, with the most intense obstinacy, that Allah deliver him from this fate—that is, death by crucifixion—which his enemies were preparing for him—a kind of killing well known at that time. Hence the Gospel passage: "And going a little farther he fell on his face and

prayed, 'My Father, if it is possible, let this chalice pass from me ...'"
(Matthew 26:39).

"And he said to them, 'My soul is very sorrowful, even to death....'
And going a little farther, he fell on the ground and prayed that, if it
were possible, the hour might pass from him. And he said, 'Abba,
Father, all things are possible to you; remove this chalice from me"
(Mark 14:34–36).... "And being in an agony he prayed more earnestly; and his sweat became like great drops of blood falling down
upon the ground" (Luke 22:44).

"Now my soul is troubled. And what shall I say? 'Father, save me
from this hour'?" (John 12:27).[13]

After this pastiche of Gospel quotations, Sayyid moves in to clinch
his argument (and keep in mind as you read this that al-Azhar University's Islamic Research Academy has approved the doctrinal content of his book):

These clear verses, coming from Christ himself, refusing crucifixion,
desiring deliverance, striving and struggling in prayer, pleading that he
not die on the cross, begging Allah that He might permit this "Hour"
to pass him by: could these verses possibly agree with the [Christian]
doctrine that he offered himself voluntarily for this self-sacrifice, by
his own choice, as an act of love?!... Does his [Christ's] fate in the
Gospels agree with Allah's own word that He would rescue him in his
anguish and answer his prayer?[14]

The last lines quoted above highlight one of the main reasons why
Muslims reject the reality of Christ's crucifixion: they insist that Allah
would have intervened to save him from such a death. This argument appears in another recently published book, this one entitled
Al-Masih wa-al-Islam (Christ and Islam). Its author, al-Sayyid Basim
al-Hashimi, explains in the preface the high hopes he has for what
this text might accomplish:

The method of this book relies basically on textual comparisons [of
Islamic and Christian scriptures].... Therefore, the respected reader

---

[13] Muhammad Mahmud al-Sayyid, *Al-Masih bayna al-lahut wa-al-nasut* (Cairo: Basamat fi
Adhhan al-Athirin, 2010), pp. 274–76; translated from the Arabic by D. Pinault.
[14] Ibid., p. 276.

needs to focus and meditate on the similarities between the textual passages, even if this book contains a conceptual approach that differs from a Christian perspective at certain points, for this book is based on an Islamic approach to these passages....

This work is composed with the idea of rallying readers under the banner of interfaith rapprochement [al-taqrib] among members of the heavenly religions, particularly Muslims and Christians, especially because they constitute the great majority of the world's inhabitants.[15]

Hashimi then juxtaposes Koranic and biblical verses on topics including fasting, the forgiveness of sins and submission to Allah, justice and injustice, Jesus' miracles, and the special status of the Virgin Mary, all with an eye to highlighting similarities between Christianity and Islam. In the midst of this flowing cornucopia display of interfaith goodwill, he "corrects" various points of Christian doctrine along the way—the reality of Christ's crucifixion, his divine status, the notion that he could be *Ibn Allah* (Son of God)—points that happen to be central to Christian belief.

Talk of *taqrib*—interfaith rapprochement; minimizing or erasing doctrinal differences—tends to put me on guard. Marching under this "banner", as Hashimi proposes, strikes me as a mug's game: emotionally unsatisfying and theologically unsound. *Taqrib* does a disservice to both faiths, for it is false to pretend that the differences between Islam and Christianity are not profound. In any case, *taqrib* as Hashimi presents it involves no compromise on the part of Muslims; it simply expects Christians to embrace Islamic interpretations of Christ's life and his Cross.

Which is what comes out in a chapter of Hashimi's book called *Allah ma'a anbiya'ihi* (Allah is with His prophets). Here he positions John 8:28–29 ("Jesus said, ... he who sent me is with me; he has not left me alone, for I always do what is pleasing to him") alongside a carefully chosen pair of verses from the Koran:

> Allah—may He be exalted and glorified—has said: "In truth We will make Our messengers and the believers victorious, both in the life of this world and on Judgment Day, when witnesses of deeds will arise." (Koran 40:51)

---

[15] al-Sayyid Basim al-Hashimi, *Al-Masih wa-al-Islam* (Beirut: Dar al-Mahajjah al-Baida', 2010), pp. 5–6; translated from the Arabic by D. Pinault.

And He, most exalted, has said: "Thereupon We rescue Our messengers and those who believe. Such action is proper and rightful for
Us, that We rescue and deliver those who believe." (Koran 10:103)[16]

The argument made here by Hashimi is the same as what you
just saw presented above by Muhammad al-Sayyid: Allah rescues His
messengers. He makes them triumph, not just in the afterlife, but
in this earthly realm. Hence the cognitive difficulty for Muslims of
accepting Christ's Passion, his anguish and doubts, and especially his
pain-wracked death on the Cross.

The critiques raised by Sayyid and Hashimi are voiced with even
greater vehemence in a book recently published in Beirut entitled
*Hayat al-masih 'Isa ibn Maryam 'alayhima al-salam min manzur islami:
dirasah muqaranah* (The life of Christ Jesus, Son of Mary—upon them
both be peace—from an Islamic viewpoint: a comparative study).
The author, Hanan Qarquti Sha'ban, quotes some of the same Gospel
passages we have seen in Sayyid's study—the Agony in the Garden
and Christ's cry from the Cross—and then cites a commentary on
these verses by a Saudi-influenced traditionalist Koran scholar named
Taqi al-Din al-Hilali:

> Consider the statement of the one who was crucified on his cross [in
> the following Gospel verse]: "Towards the ninth hour, Jesus screamed
> in a loud voice, saying, 'Eli, Eli, lama shabaqtani,' that is, 'My God,
> my God, why have You forsaken me?'"
>
> And Dr. Hilali comments on this text as follows: "This is one of the
> greatest proofs that the person who said these words was no believer in
> Allah, let alone one of Allah's prophets, because Allah does not break
> His promise, and His prophets do not have doubts about His promise."[17]

Two things strike me at once as I read this. The first is the insistence on the emotional invulnerability of Allah's messengers, the
refusal to admit that such persons, in their capacity as humans, could
ever be subject to the very human condition of uncertainty: "His
prophets do not have doubts about His promise."

---

[16] Ibid., p. 48.
[17] Hanan Qarquti Sha'ban, *Hayat al-masih 'Isa ibn Maryam 'alayhima al-salam min manzur
islami: dirasah muqaranah* (Beirut: Dar al-Kutub al-'Ilmiyah, 2004), p. 91. Translated from the
Arabic by D. Pinault.

The second is the peculiar way of referring to Christ as "the one who was crucified on his cross." The author refuses to admit that this "one who was crucified" could truly have been the same man venerated by Muslims as Jesus. "Remove this chalice from me"; "Why have You forsaken me?": a host of such Gospel passages leads Sha'ban to the conclusion: "This is proof of *al-tashbih* having occurred."[18]

The word *al-tashbih* literally means "the act of making something appear similar to something else." *Tashbih* is the gerund derived from the verb that occurs in surah 4:157, where the Koran (as we have seen in previous chapters) dismisses Christ's crucifixion as merely docetic: *walakin shubbiha la-hum* (but it was made to appear so to them). In this theological context, then, *al-tashbih* refers to the Islamic belief that the likeness of Jesus was cast upon another person (often designated as Judas), who was then tortured, crucified, and killed instead of Jesus. Meanwhile, the disguised Jesus, his appearance altered by Allah's command, was supposedly raised up to heaven without experiencing any of this anguish, crucifixion, or death.

The doctrine of *tashbih* underlies another passage in Sha'ban's book, where she cites the work of a Muslim professor of Islamic studies named 'Abd al-Karim al-Khatib:

> In the Gospel it states that the crucified one asked the Jews for something to drink, and so they gave him vinegar mixed with gall. He tasted it but did not drink it down. Then he cried out, "My God, my God, why have you forsaken me?" But all the Gospels declare explicitly that Christ—upon him be peace—fasted and went hungry for forty days and forty nights and that he told his disciples, "I have food of which you have no knowledge."
>
> So how could someone who had the patience and endurance to master thirst and hunger for forty days and nights then turn around and show neediness and expose himself to his enemies as an object of humiliation and contempt on account of merely one day's thirst? This is something not even the lowest and least significant person would do.
>
> So how could such a thing be done by someone who is one of the elite prophets, or someone who—as they claim—is the divine Lord Himself? Therefore, the one who claimed to be thirsty was someone

---

[18] Ibid., p. 92; translated by D. Pinault.

other than Christ, and he was the one who "was made to appear so to them"!

His statement "My God, my God, why have you forsaken me and abandoned me?" is a statement that can be made only by someone who completely lacks any acceptance of the divine Will and any sense of submission to the command of Allah, may He be glorified. But Christ—upon him be peace—is free of any such blemish. Thus the crucified one was someone else.[19]

What characterizes the above passage is something I have seen in many Islamic assessments of the crucifixion: a preoccupation with honor and shame, a feeling that Christ's exalted status is compromised by his becoming "an object of humiliation and contempt". After all, according to this logic, if even "the lowest and least significant person" could manage to make it through "merely one day's thirst", then surely Jesus, as "one of the elite prophets", would never have done what the Christian Gospels claim: he could not possibly have asked for something to drink. When Muslim authors such as Sha'ban exhibit revulsion at the idea of Christ's "neediness", they reveal the radically different ways Islam and Christianity view Jesus and his crucifixion.

The "neediness" of Christ as portrayed in the Gospels is condemned again later in Sha'ban's book, where she once more cites the work of the Koran scholar Hilali:

We see him [Jesus] worshipping his Lord again in the Gospel of Matthew in chapter 14, verse 23, where there appears the following: "And after the group withdrew, he climbed up the mountain, drawing apart in solitude so that he might pray. And when night came, there he was, alone."

Christ—upon him be peace—was praying. Well, to whom was he praying? Was he praying to himself, or to his "Father"? . . .

And Dr. Muhammad Taqi al-Din al-Hilali has commented on this as follows: "If Christ—peace be upon him—were Allah, or a part of Allah, then how could he engage in prayer? For prayer is performed only by a servant who is lacking something and who is in need of Allah's mercy, just as He—may He be glorified!—has said in *surat*

---

[19] Ibid., p. 94; translated by D. Pinault.

Fatir, verse 15 [Koran 35:15]: 'O people! You are the ones who are destitute and in need of Allah. As for Allah: He is the one who is free of all needs [Arabic: al-Ghani] and worthy of praise.'"[20]

Al-Ghani: this is one of *al-asma' al-husna* (the "beautiful names" or divine attributes of Allah). It is a quality that the Koran ascribes repeatedly to its God, as you can see from the following verses:

They have said: "Allah has begotten a son." May He be glorified! He is the One who is free of all needs; everything in the heavens and on earth belongs to Him. (10:68)

And Moses said, "If you become unbelievers—you, and everyone on earth—well, Allah in truth is free of all needs, and worthy of praise." (14:8)

If someone is grateful [to Allah], that benefits his own soul; but if someone is guilty of impious ingratitude: well then, in truth, my Lord is free of all needs and most noble. (27:40)

And as for those who strive and struggle, waging jihad: well, they strive and struggle for the benefit of their own souls; for in truth Allah is free of all needs. He needs nothing from the two worlds. (29:6)

And We gave wisdom to Luqman, [saying]: "Show your thanks to Allah." And as for those who show gratitude: well, they show gratitude for the benefit of their own souls. And as for those who are impiously ungrateful: well, Allah is free of all needs; He is simply to be praised. (31:12)

You get the idea. Allah is invulnerable. He is neither helped nor harmed by whatever we do, whether we behave as pious believers or impious infidels. The sentiment is reinforced by a *hadith* statement in which the prophet Muhammad claimed that Allah Himself stated, "O my servants, you can neither do Me any harm nor can you do Me any good."[21]

Immune to suffering, the Allah of Islamic belief is far removed from the God made flesh who writhes in anguish on the Cross in solidarity with us all.

[20] Ibid., pp. 131–32; translated D. Pinault.

[21] *Sahih Muslim*, bk. 45, *hadith* 70, https://sunnah.com/muslim/45/70. I thank Muhammad Yasir Ali, guest-preacher at the South Bay Islamic Association in San Jose, California, who very kindly supplied the source-reference for this *hadith* after I heard him quote it in a mosque-sermon.

"This inexplicable agony for an inexplicable act
of mercy": Muslim meditations on the Cross
from the interfaith dialogue circuit

The authors I have just cited are polemicists—Muslims who see it
as their job to attack Christianity as a way of asserting Islam's superiority. But what about Muslims who favor interfaith dialogue and
do their best to find points of contact and understanding between
their own religion and Christianity? Even they, it seems, find Christ's
Cross too much to accept.

Consider the case of Ali Merad, an Algerian Muslim author who
in 1980 was invited by Vatican-affiliated scholars to submit a paper
on "Christ according to the Qur'an" for publication by the Pontifical
Institute for Arabic and Islamic Studies. Here are Merad's thoughts
on the crucifixion:

> In the Qur'an, everything is aimed at convincing the believer that he
> will experience victory over the forces of evil which assail and torment
> him and which for a time seem to get the better of his strength and of
> his hope. In such a perspective the death of Christ would have been a
> contradiction of the constant doctrine of the Qur'an. Moreover, this
> hypothesis would have been in disagreement with all the Qur'anic
> facts, referring directly or indirectly to the history of Christ, for Christ's
> death on the Cross would have meant the triumph of his executioners,
> whereas the Qur'an unquestionably affirms their failure....
>
> The Muslim's conviction is therefore strengthened by everything
> he reads in the Qur'an, namely that God does not abandon His own:
> how then could He have abandoned Jesus?... Islam refuses to accept
> this tragic image of the Passion. Not simply because it has no place for
> the dogma of the Redemption, but because the Passion would imply
> in its eyes that God had failed.
>
> Islam rejects the idea of the death of Christ.... Failure to rescue
> Jesus before he was placed on the Cross, denial of his elevation to
> God, would imply a terrible ruin and as it were the collapse of hope.[22]

So, too, with Mona Siddiqui, a British Muslim and a celebrated
professor of Islamic and interreligious studies at the University of

---

[22] Ali Merad, "Christ according to the Qur'an", *Encounter: Documents for Muslim-Christian
Understanding* 69 (November 1980; Rome: Pontifical Institute for Arabic and Islamic Studies),
pp. 14–15.

Edinburgh. Her book *Christians, Muslims, and Jesus* (published in 2013) sympathetically investigates points of contact between two faiths that both honor Jesus—though they honor him in radically different ways.

For me, the most interesting part of her book is its concluding chapter, "Reflections on the Cross". She begins by summarizing Islamic doctrine: "It is true that from the Islamic perspective the cross has little religious significance of either death or suffering, as Jesus' death by crucifixion is largely denied.... In Islam, there is no paschal mystery and Jesus is simply gone."[23]

She then offers a personal reflection: "I conclude this part of my own journey sitting in front of a cross in a local church and wondering what this symbol means to me as a Muslim.... I don't think I have truly reflected on why the cross remains so powerful. Maybe it is unsettling, for it blurs the boundaries between God and humanity."[24]

Thereafter she records what Christian colleagues have shared with her about their faith:

> Some [Christian friends of mine] have tried to convey the experience of suffering and victory on the cross, the agony of Jesus, the wretchedness of humanity, but also the power of love and hope in this redemptive death. All the various meanings of the cross still point to one truth, which is that at the center of the Christian faith is the passion and death of Christ on the cross.... Nothing in Islam compares to this and, if anything, Muslims have either rejected or ignored the significance of the cross.[25]

Siddiqui concludes with her own personal response to Christ's Passion as understood by Christians: "The cross is powerful and the crucifixion is sorrowful. But as I sit here I feel that while the cross speaks to me, it does not draw me in. Its mystery is moving, but I cannot incline towards what it says about a God in form, a God who undergoes this inexplicable agony for an inexplicable act of mercy."[26]

---

[23] Mona Siddiqui, *Christians, Muslims, and Jesus* (New Haven: Yale University Press, 2013), pp. 228, 231.

[24] Ibid., pp. 233–34.

[25] Ibid., pp. 237–38.

[26] Ibid., p. 242.

Christ the Mesopotamian vegetation-god?: A glance at the Tammuzi poets of Iraq

It does not draw me in: a mild-mannered way of voicing Islam's scandalized discomfort with the Cross and all it signifies. But as I recall the readings I myself have done in Islamic literature over the years, I can think of two members of this faith who in their own way were drawn in by the Cross and fascinated by the image of Christ crucified.

I have in mind two twentieth-century Iraqi Muslim poets, Badr Shakir al-Sayyab and 'Abd al-Wahhab al-Bayati. I say "Muslim" but then immediately have to concede that their religious identity was largely a question of background, of family upbringing. Both men at an early age became drawn to secularist thought and Marxist revolutionary ideology. Both were caught up in modernity's claim to "free" mankind from religion; both were seduced by Communism as a substitute for religious faith as a locus of meaning.

Bayati made his socialist hajj to Russia in the late 1950s, serving in Moscow as a cultural attaché representing Iraq's Ministry of Education and giving lectures at the Soviet Academy of Sciences. As for Sayyab: for years he was a devout member of the Iraqi Communist Party. In 1952, when he was in his mid-twenties, Sayyab took part in a Communist-inspired uprising against Iraq's reigning Hashemite monarchy and various targets perceived as agents of Western foreign influence. Among these targets was the U.S. Information Service's American Cultural Center in Baghdad. Demonstrators set fire to the center and its library, burning books and film-reels. To hearten the rioters, the young Sayyab shimmied up a nearby utility pole and from atop this perch bellowed a freshly composed poem attacking the monarchy and the Iraqi government. (His activities and his very public act of rebellion led the government to seek his arrest. Sayyab had to flee Iraq and endure an emotionally wrenching exile from his homeland.) All this was at a time when secular-nationalist and pan--Arab movements fought each other for leadership of the Middle East, before the triumphant emergence of Islamist ideologues in the 1970s and 80s.[27]

---

[27] Elliott Colla, "Badr Shakir al-Sayyab, Cold War Poet", *Middle Eastern Literatures* 18, no. 3 (2015): pp. 247–63.

It was during this moment of mid-twentieth-century secular ideologies that both poets came under the influence of the so-called Tammuzi movement. A literary phenomenon that sought to replace religious loyalties with national pride and Arab cultural identity, the Tammuzi movement revived and repurposed the vegetation-god myths of Mesopotamia and the ancient Levant.

Heavily influenced by the verse of T.S. Eliot (especially his poem "The Waste Land"), Tammuzi poets (notably writers from Syria, Lebanon, and Iraq) encouraged their audiences to rediscover their own pre-Islamic heritage and understand in a new way the old tales of Ishtar, Tammuz, and Adonis. These myths tell of deities and heroes who are slain and mourned but then are raised to new life. The Tammuzi poets wrought from these stories a symbol for the violent subjugation and imminent rebirth of the nations of the Arab Middle East.[28]

This movement involved the secularist appropriation of not only pagan but also Christian motifs. And here is what strikes me as remarkable, from my vantage point as a Catholic Christian scholar of Islam: the Tammuzi poets borrow the story of Jesus, not as it appears in the Koran, but as it is presented in the Gospels—the narrative of a man who truly suffers and dies on the Cross. Only with true death can there be any true prospect of resurrection—the motif that interested the Tammuzis above all. (In this context it is worth noting that the foremost pan-Arab secularist movement of our time is known as *Hizb al-Ba'th*, "the Resurrection Party", to which the Assad dynasty in Syria has adhered for decades.)

Not that the Tammuzis displayed adherence to Christian doctrines of Christ as Son of God. Far from it. But they found Christ useful. Useful for their poems, for their self-image. For them, Christ crucified was simply one image among many in a political repertoire to suggest the idea of a single sensitive soul enduring anguish and, in the process, inspiring an oppressed population.

We can see this at work in a poem by Bayati entitled "Ughniyah ila sha'bi" (A song to my people), where the poet imagines himself in the role of Jesus undergoing crucifixion:

---

[28] David Pinault, "Images of Christ in Arabic Literature", *Die Welt des Islams* 27 (1987): 103–25.

I am here, alone, upon the cross.
They devour my flesh, the men of violence of the
highways, and the monsters, and the hyenas.
O maker of flame
My beloved people
I am here, alone, upon the cross.
The young assail my garden
and the elders revile my shadow,
which spreads its palms out to the stars
that it might wipe away the sorrows
from your saddened countenance.
O my imprisoned people ...
I am here, alone, driving drowsiness
From your exhausted eye
O maker of flame
My beloved people.[29]

Another poem by Bayati is more overt in its political use of Christ.
It is from a collection published in 1968 entitled *Ash'ar fi al-manfa*
(Poems in exile):

And his eyes filled with tears and he said to me:
Jesus passed by here yesterday, Jesus.
His cross: two tree-limbs, green, blossoming.
His eyes: two stars.
His appearance: that of a dove.
His bearing: that of songs.
Yesterday he passed by here
and the garden flowered
and children awoke, abounding in grace
and in the heavens
the stars of night were like bells, like crosses
drowned in my tears—the sorrows were
our way to love and oblivion;
and our green earth in her birth-pains

---

[29] 'Abd al-Wahhab al-Bayati, *al-Majd lil-atfal wa-al-zaytun* (Beirut: Dar al-'Awdah, n.d.),
pp. 27–28; translated from the Arabic by D. Pinault.

weakened by wounds
was dreaming of lilies and the morning,
dreaming of a thousand Jesuses who will bear
their cross in the darkness of prisons
and who will be numerous
and who will give birth
to progeny who will sow God's earth with jasmine
and make heroes and saints
and make revolutionaries.[30]

Let's turn now to Sayyab, who imagines a different moment from Jesus' Passion in his poem "al-Masih ba'da al-salb" (Christ after crucifixion):

Warmth touches my heart.
My blood runs into its moist earth.
My heart is the sun, for the sun pulses with light;
My heart is the earth, pulsing with wheat, and blossoms,
and pure water.
My heart is the water, my heart is the ear of corn:
Its death is the resurrection; it gives life to him who eats.
... I died by fire, darkness scorched my soil,
yet the god endured.
... I died that bread might be eaten in my name,
that they might plant me in due season.
How many lives I shall live!
For in each furrow of the field
I have become a future; I have become a seedling;
I have become a generation of men:
In every man's heart is my blood,
A drop of it, or more.[31]

Sayyab evokes both the Christian Eucharist and the vegetation myths of Tammuz. The poet imagines Jesus as a Mesopotamian fertility god

[30] 'Abd al-Wahhab al-Bayati, *Ash'ar fi al-manfa* (Cairo: Dar al-Katib al-'Arabi, 1968), pp. 50–53; translated from the Arabic by D. Pinault.

[31] Badr Shakir al-Sayyab, *Unshudat al-matar* (Beirut: Dar Maktabat al-Hayah, 1969), p. 129; translated from the Arabic by D. Pinault.

who describes his own heart as an ear of corn and his body as a sacrifice to the crops, ready to enrich the soil "in due season". And in imagery familiar to Christians, Jesus offers himself on the Cross and institutes the commemoration of his sacrifice in the breaking of bread. (The language here recalls John 12:24: "Unless a grain of wheat falls into the earth and dies, it remains alone; but if it dies, it bears much fruit.")

Like Bayati, Sayyab adopts the Christ-role by using the first person "I" and "my" and imagining himself as the slain victim: "My blood runs into its moist earth."

"Christ after Crucifixion" is a poem Sayyab wrote a number of years after his participation in the violence of Iraq's 1952 street-revolt. I cannot help but wonder: As he jotted these Christ-lines, did he think back to his younger self, raised aloft above the rioters, exposed to public view and clinging to a utility pole like a sacrificial offering, shouting defiance at the powers of the world?

What I have translated here are among my favorite verses in modern Arabic. And yet—

As I reread the Tammuzis, I am reminded of a passage from one of Thomas Mann's novels. In *Doctor Faustus*, Mann describes a self-taught amateur researcher, a "dreamer and speculator" named Jonathan Leverkühn. In his makeshift home-laboratory, Leverkühn conducts experiments while lecturing local village schoolchildren. Underlying his experiments is a zeal for the invisible sinews binding the disparate realms of beings that populate our cosmos—a zeal that fuses science and German nature-mysticism.

The narrator of the passage I have in mind is one of the fascinated children who watch Leverkühn in his endeavors. The child marvels at the "pleasure [Leverkühn] found in ice crystals":

> On winter days when the little peasant windows of the farmhouse were frosted, [Jonathan Leverkühn] would be absorbed in their structure for half an hour, looking at them both with the naked eye and with his magnifying glass.... They [the ice crystals] imitated the vegetable kingdom: most prettily of all, fern fronds, grasses, the calyxes and corollas of flowers. To the utmost of their icy ability they dabbled in the organic.[32]

---

[32] Thomas Mann, *Doctor Faustus: The Life of the German Composer Adrian Leverkühn as Told by a Friend*, trans. H. T. Lowe-Porter (New York: Alfred A. Knopf, 1948), p. 18.

The narrator then recalls another of the researcher's experiments, in which he filled an aquarium with water and "sprinkled the sand at the bottom with various crystals; if I mistake not, potassium chromate and sulphate of copper." The results both impressed and troubled the onlookers:

> He had succeeded in making a most singular culture; I shall never forget the sight. The vessel of crystallization was three-quarters full of slightly muddy water ... and from the sandy bottom there strove upwards ... blue, green, and brown shoots which reminded one of algae, mushrooms, attached polyps, also moss, then mussels, fruit pods, little trees or twigs from trees, here and there of limbs. It was the most remarkable sight I ever saw, and remarkable not so much for its appearance, strange and amazing though that was, as on account of its profoundly melancholy nature. For when Father Leverkühn asked us what we thought of it and we timidly answered him that they might be plants: "No," he replied, "they are not, they only act that way. But do not think the less of them. Precisely because they do, because they try as hard as they can, they are worthy of all respect."[33]

Leverkühn then demonstrated to the children that "these growths ... entirely unorganic in their origin" were nonetheless "light-seeking, heliotropic, as science calls it": "He exposed the aquarium to the sunlight, shading three sides against it, and behold, toward that one pane through which the light fell, thither straightway slanted the whole equivocal kith and kin: ... little trees, algae, half-formed limbs. Indeed, they so yearned after warmth and joy that they actually clung to the pane and stuck fast there."[34] .

From my viewpoint as a Christian, what strikes me about the Tammuzi verses I quoted above is that they, too, like Leverkühn's crystals, are "light-seeking, heliotropic"—but the sun to which they are drawn is the passionate light of Christ. How poignant—and how ironic—that the closest I have seen Islamic literature come to an appreciation of Christ's crucifixion and sufferings are these poems by the Tammuzis: authors who in their sensibility are secularist, Communist—and post-Muslim.

[33] Ibid., p. 19.
[34] Ibid., pp. 19–20.

*Exegetical afterthought. One prophet's behavior sheds light
on another's: The question of King David in the Koran*

Just now we have seen a variety of Islamic writings on Jesus, ranging
from Tammuzi musings to anti-Christian polemics. The final point
I would like to investigate with you in this chapter has to do with
Allah's attributes and Koranic notions of decorous and appropriate
behavior in Allah's prophets. Looking at how King David is portrayed in the Koran will offer us another way to understand why
Islam rejects the idea of Christ's death on the Cross.

Allah, as we have seen, is portrayed as al-Ghani, the One who is free
of all needs. Koranic scripture also identifies Him as "the One who
holds complete domination over His slaves" (6:18), "the almighty
conqueror" (39:4), "the One who compels" (59:23). Gracious and
merciful? Absolutely—such traits are asserted repeatedly—but this is
a god who bestows mercy only from a position of unquestioned and
absolute power.

This helps us understand how the Koran depicts Muslim prophets,
who are representatives of Allah's power and authority on earth. Such
a view very much reflects Muhammad's own self-understanding, as
someone who triumphed not only as a prophet but also as a military
commander and civic leader. Hence we find Koranic verses that tell
believers to "obey Allah, and obey the Messenger" (4:59) and that
warn us what will be the violent penalty for those who "wage war
against Allah and against His Messenger" (5:33).

As earthly agents of Allah "the almighty conqueror", it is unsurprising that the prophets are shown in the Koran as ultimate victors.
As noted above, Allah is said to declare, "In truth We will make Our
messengers and the believers victorious, both in the life of this world
and on Judgment Day" (40:51).

Each messenger is considered one link in what is called *silsilat al--
anbiya'*, "the chain of the prophets"; any imputation of dishonor or
weakness to one prophet threatens to dishonor and discredit them
all. In this context, we can see why Muhammad rejected the idea
of Christ's crucifixion and repudiated the notion that he had been
exposed to shame and contempt on the Cross.

Decorum, status, unblemished honor: Islamic scripture's preoccupation with these concerns sheds light not only on the Koranic

Jesus but also on how the Koran portrays King David (whom Islam celebrates as one of Allah's prophets). I have in mind here the story of David and Bathsheba.

Before turning to the Koran's version, let's review how the Bible (in 2 Samuel, chapters 11 and 12) tells the tale. From his palace rooftop, David sees a beautiful woman bathing. He learns that her name is Bathsheba and that she is married to one of David's own soldiers, a warrior named Uriah the Hittite.

Bathsheba's marital status does not stop David; he is a king, and he can have what he wants. She is brought to the palace and becomes part of his harem. Soon she is pregnant by the monarch.

David disposes of any embarrassment by telling his military field commanders as they go into battle against the Ammonites, "Set Uriah in the forefront of the hardest fighting, and then draw back from him, that he may be struck down, and die" (2 Sam 11:14). Sure enough: Uriah is killed in action. End of David's problem.

Well, not quite. For God sends a spiritual counselor named Nathan to David. Nathan is wise enough to know that the best way to reprimand a despot is to take the oblique approach. Nathan approaches David and says he needs advice on how to deal with sheep stealing:

> Nathan ... said to him, "There were two men in a certain city, the one rich and the other poor. The rich man had very many flocks and herds; but the poor man had nothing but one little ewe lamb, which he had bought. And he brought it up, and it grew up with him and with his children; it used to eat of his morsel, and drink from his cup, and lie in his bosom, and it was like a daughter to him. Now there came a traveler to the rich man, and he was unwilling to take one of his own flock or herd to prepare for the wayfarer who had come to him, but he took the poor man's lamb, and prepared it for the man who had come to him." (2 Sam 12:1–4)

Blind to his own failings but quick to spot another's, David gets angry when he hears this report. Self-righteously he declares, "As the LORD lives, the man who has done this deserves to die; and he shall restore the lamb fourfold, because he did this thing, and because he had no pity."

But now Nathan slaps him with his wake-up call: "You are the man." Then Nathan lashes David with a blow-by-blow reminder of the vicious things he has done: "You have struck down Uriah the

Hittite with the sword, and have taken his wife to be your wife, and have slain him with the sword of the Ammonites."

David sees himself for what he is. "I have sinned against the LORD", he admits. He fasts; he clothes himself in sackcloth; he asks God for forgiveness. He is clearly less than perfect.

What about the Koran? In its references to David, it says nothing about Bathsheba, nothing about Uriah, nothing about Nathan. Given its concern with prophetic honor and decorum, this should not surprise us.

But I think we can in fact detect a trace element of the Bible's Bathsheba tale in the Koran. Take a look at the Koranic verses below and see what you think:

> Has the report concerning the litigants reached you? They climbed the wall leading to the king's private quarters. Suddenly they came upon David, and he was alarmed at their presence. They said, "Do not be afraid! We are disputants, and one of us has wronged the other. Judge between us in truth. Do not treat us unjustly, but guide us along the level path. This is my brother. He has ninety-nine ewes, while I have only one ewe. Well, he said, 'Give her to me to look after', and he got the better of me in argument."
>
> He [David] said, "He has wronged you in asking that your ewe be added to his ewes. Many business partners wrong each other, except for those who believe and do good deeds. But few people are like that."
>
> Then David perceived that We had tested him, and so he sought forgiveness from his Lord: he fell and bowed down and repented. And so We forgave him for this. (Koran 38:21–25)

A curious passage, isn't it? The reference to the dispute over the ewe certainly suggests that Muhammad had heard some version of the biblical tale.

But note the difference. The Koran retains mention of two men. One has many sheep, the other only one. Yet Islamic scripture presents this as a story in its own right, not as a parable told by Nathan to catch the conscience of a morally wayward king. The Koran does not indict David for having stolen Bathsheba or arranged for her husband to be killed.

And yet: the Koran follows the Bible's lead in describing David's behavior as that of a man who is suddenly aware he has sinned: "He fell down and bowed and repented." Repented for what? It is unclear. And the reason it is unclear is that missing from the Koran are David's crimes against Bathsheba and Uriah.

Why the omission? I think it has to do with decorum, status, and honor—the same factors that help explain why the Koran rejects the idea that Jesus was ever subjected to humiliation and shame on the Cross. The mentality underlying such concerns is reflected in the Koran commentary on these ewe verses by the twentieth-century scholar 'Abdullah Yusuf 'Ali:

> David was a pious man.... Those who think they see a resemblance to the Parable of the prophet Nathan (2 Samuel, 12:1–17) have nothing to go upon but the mention of the "one ewe" here and the "one little ewe-lamb" in Nathan's Parable. The whole story is here different, and the whole atmosphere is different. The biblical title given to David, "a man after God's own heart," is refuted by the Bible itself in the scandalous tale of heinous crimes attributed to David in chapters 11 and 12 of 2 Samuel, viz., adultery, fraudulent dealing with one of his own servants, and the contriving of his murder. Further, in chapter 13, we have the story of rapes, incest, and fratricide in David's own household! The fact is that passages like these are mere *chroniques scandaleuses*, i.e., narratives of scandalous crimes of the grossest character. The Muslim idea of David is that of a man just and upright, endowed with all the virtues, in whom even the least thought of self-elation has to be washed off by repentance and forgiveness.[35]

Implicit in 'Ali's commentary is the Islamic doctrine that all of Allah's prophets are *ma'sum*, that is, sinless, perfect, infallible, and divinely protected against error. The Pakistani legal scholar Abul A'la Mawdudi has this to say on the moral qualities that are the mark of a true prophet: "His nature and character are so good and pure that in all affairs his attitude is that of truthfulness, straightforwardness and nobility. He never does or utters wrong, nor does he commit any evil. He always inspires virtue and righteousness, and practices himself what he preaches to others. No incident of his life shows that

---

[35] 'Abdullah Yusuf 'Ali, *The Meaning of the Holy Qur'an* (Beltsville, Md.: Amana Publications, 1999), p. 1165n4171, p. 1167n4178.

his life is not in harmony with his ideal."[36] Measured against such standards, the biblical David, who indulges his lust with no thought of consequences, must surely fall short.

But Christianity takes a different approach. Let me illustrate this with an anecdote.

In the early 1960s, as a young Catholic and enthusiastic altar boy (back when the Mass was still in Latin), I was eager to learn about my biblical namesake. Finding out about Bathsheba and Uriah and what David did to them was—to put it mildly—upsetting.

But I was fortunate in being able to consult my older brother Paul (who excelled in Bible-based storytelling). How, I asked him, could someone like King David, who did so many good things, also do what he did to Bathsheba and Uriah?

"It's because we're earthen vessels", he said, and then he read aloud to me from the Second Letter to the Corinthians: "For it is the God who said, 'Let light shine out of darkness,' who has shone in our hearts to give the light of the knowledge of the glory of God in the face of Christ. But we have this treasure in earthen vessels, to show that the transcendent power belongs to God and not to us. We are afflicted in every way, but not crushed; perplexed, but not driven to despair" (2 Cor 4:6–8).

Earthen vessels. My brother went on to explain the image, saying something like this: *In creating us, God works with clay, a humble substance. It can become misshapen but can also be formed into something noble and fine. If even King David could sin—and commit sin in a spectacularly horrible way—and yet be forgiven and reconciled with God, then there's hope for us all.*

As I was at my desk writing this just now, I paused to leaf through my *Catholic Study Bible.* Here is its commentary on 2 Corinthians 4:7: "*In earthen vessels*: the instruments God uses are human and fragile; some imagine small terracotta lamps in which light is carried."[37]

Flame-bearing clay lamps. The light sometimes flickers but never quite goes out.

A good description of King David. Of all of us.

---

[36] Abul Aʻla Mawdudi, *Towards Understanding Islam* (New York: Message Publications, 1997), p. 33.

[37] Donald Senior and John J. Collins, eds., *The Catholic Study Bible*, 2nd ed. (New York: Oxford University Press, 2006), p. 1546.

CHAPTER 12

THE RISEN CHRIST STILL BEARS THE MARKS OF THE CROSS: THOUGHTS ON KENOTIC THEOLOGY IN RESPONSE TO ANTI-CHRISTIAN MUSLIM POLEMICS

Introductory considerations. How not to approach interfaith dialogue: Hans Küng and the attempt to minimize Christian-Muslim differences

Since the Islamic terrorist attacks of 9/11, some Christians have sought to improve relations with Muslims via a form of *taqrib* (interreligious rapprochement), specifically by trying to diminish or erase doctrinal distinctions between the two faiths.

One example is the German Catholic theologian Hans Küng, who in his impressively lengthy book *Islam: Past, Present and Future* argues that "lines lead from the very first Jewish Christianity to the seventh century, indeed to Islam."[1] What fascinates Küng (and, as you will see, some present-day Muslim authors as well) is the notion that early "Jewish Christianity" embodied a doctrinal purity and simplicity supposedly lost in later Trinitarian articulations but then retrieved in the preachings of Muhammad.

Let's explore this theory. The term "Jewish Christians" refers to those early Jewish followers of Jesus who continued to practice circumcision and observe traditional dietary restrictions and other provisions of the Law of Moses. Among their leaders was "James the Just", revered as one of the elders of what was known as the "Church of Jerusalem".

---

[1] Hans Küng, *Islam: Past, Present and Future*, trans. John Bowden (Oxford: Oneworld, 2007), p. 37.

A point of contention among Christians shortly after Jesus' crucifixion and Resurrection was whether Jewish ritual practices should be imposed on converts who were Gentiles. Saint Paul, missionary to the Gentiles of the Roman Empire, strongly objected to any such imposition (a point to which we will return).

After the martyrdom of James in A.D. 62, many of his Jewish-- Christian followers withdrew from Jerusalem across the Jordan River to the vicinity of the Greco-Roman city of Pella, south of the Sea of Galilee. There they formed a variety of faith communities that absorbed doctrinal influences from neighboring sects, some pagan, others Gnostic.

Church Fathers of the second through fourth centuries identified these trans-Jordanian Jewish-Christian populations as Ebionites (God's poor) and noted that they held varying Christological doctrines. Some "accepted the messiahship and divine sonship of Jesus"; others accepted Jesus as a prophet but refused to acknowledge his divinity.[2]

The latter type of Ebionite excited Küng's interest, since such a Christology foreshadows what we find in the Koran. On the basis of what he calls "the affinity between primitive [that is, chronologically early] Christianity and primitive Islam", Küng says such doctrinal similarities should be "utilized for Muslim-Christian dialogue". He then argues:

> Christians should no longer see the Qur'anic understanding of Jesus as Muslim heresy but as a christology with a primitive Christian colouring on Arabian soil....
>
> Faced with Muslims, may Christians still exclusively appeal to the high christology of the Hellenistic councils and make them the sole norm for belief in Jesus as the messenger of God for all the 'children of Abraham'?...
>
> How far are they prepared to take seriously the much more original christology of the Jewish disciples of Jesus and the early Christian communities, as reflected in the Qur'an?[3]

---

[2] Jaroslav Pelikan, *The Emergence of the Catholic Tradition (100–600)* (Chicago: University Press, 1971), p. 24.

[3] Küng, *Islam*, pp. 501–2.

By "the high christology of the Hellenistic councils", Küng is referring—in a surprisingly dismissive way—to the teachings promulgated at the ecclesiastical gatherings of Nicaea (A.D. 325) and Chalcedon (451). These councils resulted in statements of faith emphasizing Christ's nature as fully human but also fully divine, as we know from the Nicene Creed: "born of the Father before all ages, God from God, Light from Light, true God from true God, begotten, not made, consubstantial with the Father."[4]

The lines from Küng quoted above seem to imply that the Nicene Christology of a divine-human Jesus somehow conflicts with the "much more original Christology of the Jewish disciples of Jesus". This "original Christology", with a genealogy extending from James the Just to the Ebionites of trans-Jordan, can then supposedly be retrieved in the Koran.

Proto-Koranic Christology in the Epistle of James?
An attempt at a reply (with help from Paul of Tarsus)

Küng's thesis is cited as an inspiration by the Turkish Muslim journalist Mustafa Akyol in a book published in 2017 called *The Islamic Jesus: How the King of the Jews Became a Prophet of the Muslims*. I have strong objections to Akyol's main argument. But let me say first what I like about his book—and in fact like very much.

In the closing chapter of *The Islamic Jesus*, Akyol builds a case for "what Jesus can teach Muslims today". Repelled by fellow Muslims who are obsessed with imposing sharia law and caliphal government regardless of how much oppression may be entailed, he finds a counterargument in the Jesus of the Christian Gospels. Akyol admires Jesus' criticisms of the Pharisees of first-century Judea, with their fixation on the minutiae of the Law. Addressing twenty-first-century Muslims, Akyol riffs on Jesus' words from the Bible to assert that

---

[4] "Hellenistic" strikes me as an imprecise choice of word; "Hellenized" or "Hellenizing" would have been more accurate. ("Hellenistic" is generally used to refer to Greek culture and history in the Mediterranean world in the time period between the death of Alexander the Great in 323 B.C. and the death of Cleopatra in 30 B.C.) This slip-up is not the translator's fault. The original German edition refers to "die hohe Christologie der hellenistischen Konzilien": Küng, *Der Islam* (München: Piper Verlag, 2004), p. 602.

"the Shariah is made for man" (and not man for the Shariah). Akyol also modifies Jesus' words about the Kingdom of God by reminding Muslims that "the Caliphate is within you."[5]

It is telling that this Turkish author turns for help to the biblical Jesus rather than to the Jesus of the Koran. I have already noted that although Islamic scripture refers to Jesus almost a hundred times, it is usually to condemn Christians for what they believe about him. Thus the Koran insists he is not divine, not the Son of God, not a member of the Trinity or someone who died on the Cross. Amidst all these negatives, the Jesus constituted by the Koran is never fleshed out enough to embody a uniquely distinctive world view. Instead, he is presented primarily as a precursor to the prophet of Islam, his life contours determined by the experiences of the messenger from Mecca. A flickering and barely outlined figure is what we glimpse of Jesus in the Koran, a shadow cast by Muhammad's imagination. No wonder, then, that when the Sufis wanted a Jesus whose conduct they could imitate, they turned to stories derived from the Bible.

Which is just what Akyol does. His application of New Testament Christ sayings to Islamic social problems today is creative. It is an approach far different from that taken by most Muslims with regard to the Bible. So deep-seated is Islamic distaste for Christianity that it sometimes affects the attitude of certain Muslims toward Jesus himself, regardless of his revered doctrinal status as an Islamic prophet.

We see this attitude at work as far back as the Crusades. In A.D. 1144, 'Imad al-Din Zengi, emir of Mosul and Aleppo, announced a jihad against the Christian Ifranj. In response, the court poet Ibn Munir al-Tarabulusi composed verses urging Zengi's son Nur al-Din to wage war against the Crusaders, as he says, "until you see Jesus flee from Jerusalem".[6]

More recently Kamal Nasir (a one-time adherent of the Ba'ath party and, until killed in Beirut in 1973, a member of the executive committee of the Palestine Liberation Organization) articulated what the scholar Stefan Wild describes as "a kind of poetic theology of

---

[5] Mustafa Akyol, *The Islamic Jesus: How the King of the Jews Became a Prophet of the Muslims* (New York: St. Martin's Press, 2017), pp. 206–10.

[6] Cited in Emmanuel Sivan, "Le caractère sacré de Jérusalem dans l'Islam", *Studia Islamica* 27 (1967): 155.

hatred", which Nasir expressed in his poem *Unshudat al-haqd* (the song of hate). According to Nasir, Christian concepts of love and peace are worthless until Palestinian nationalist goals are realized. In this poem, Nasir also addresses a speech directly to the figure of Christ, warning him to get out of Israel if he chooses to identify himself with Western "imperialist" powers: "If you belong to them, Son of Mary, then go back to their dwellings."[7]

In a previous chapter, I have already mentioned an incident when my students and I visited a mosque in New York and our Muslim hosts handed us leaflets featuring the following comments on the biblical Jesus: "In Christendom, Western scholars write [that] Jesus is portrayed as a celibate person, [a] thirty-three-year-old and yet an unmarried bachelor, all alone at home? Is that normal? [a] healthy portrayal? ask many Christian scholars. How can you honestly emulate such a model, a single man, unmarried and unattached to family responsibilities, [who] had no family life, no wife or any children?"[8]

Mustafa Akyol is far more generous in his reply to the Christ of the Gospels. For this I give him credit.

Where we differ is in his understanding of early Christian history. Citing Hans Küng as one of his inspirations, Akyol fixes on those fourth-century Ebionites who accepted Jesus as Messiah but not as Son of God and who denounced Paul as "an apostate from the [Jewish Mosaic] law." Jewish Christians such as these Ebionites, argues Akyol, rejected what he calls "Pauline Christianity" but accepted a Christology that conforms to what is said about Jesus in the Koran.[9]

Akyol goes further. He claims that Ebionite and Koranic Christology can also be found in first-century Judea, among the Jewish Christians who followed the leadership of James. "For both James and his fellow believers at the 'Jerusalem Church,'" asserts Akyol, "this Messiah was not God incarnate but 'the last great Jewish prophet.'"[10]

Akyol voices the astonishment he felt as a Muslim when he first unearthed the Bible's Epistle of James, "buried", as he puts it (there is

---

[7] Stefan Wild, "Judentum, Christentum und Islam in der palästinensischen Poesie", *Die Welt des Islams* 23–24 (1984): 259–97.

[8] Musa Qutub and M. Vazir Ali, "Western Feminism Movement Problems vs. Islam's Gender Balance Dynamism", *The Invitation* 9, no. 2 (Des Plaines, Ill., April 1991).

[9] Akyol, *Islamic Jesus*, pp. 5–6, 50–53.

[10] Ibid., p. 35.

a bit of the *Da Vinci Code* about the way he conveys his discoveries), "toward the final pages of the New Testament".[11]

He tells us what happened when he shared this epistle, with "its implicit divergence from mainstream Christianity and its curious resonance with my Muslim faith", with his fellow believers in Islam: "'This is very similar to the Qur'an,' one of my friends said. 'And there is nothing in it which says that Jesus is the Son of God,' another one noted. 'Are you sure it is from the Christian Bible?'"[12]

From here Akyol contrasts a Jamesian Jewish Christianity with what he calls "Paul's line" of Gentile Christianity. Akyol emphasizes that as a Muslim he cannot accept Paul's Christology (with its faith in a crucified Son of God). Rather, he is at home with what he regards as the proto-Islamic practices of James the Jewish Christian: "The place for prayer for James was the Jewish Temple centered on the Holy of Holies—not a 'church' centered on the cross."[13]

But is Akyol really accurate in claiming that James and the first generation of Jewish Christians differed so radically from Paul by claiming that Jesus was not truly Son of God? I do not think so.

First, let's examine the Epistle of James itself. The editors of the *Catholic Study Bible* note that it is derived from the "genre of *parenesis* or exhortation and is concerned almost exclusively with ethical conduct. It therefore falls within the tradition of Jewish wisdom literature, such as can be found in the Old Testament."[14] As such, this epistle focuses on moral guidance for Christians rather than on doctrine or theology.

But the fact that the author omits a discussion of Christian doctrine does not mean he repudiates it. Quite the contrary. Let's look at the salutation that opens this letter: "James, a servant of God and of the Lord Jesus Christ, to the twelve tribes in the Dispersion: Greeting" (Jas 1:1). Note how James identifies himself: he is a "servant" of "the Lord Jesus Christ".

The word "Lord" is worth lingering on. It is used repeatedly, in both the Hebrew Bible and the Christian scriptures, to designate

<hr />

[11] Ibid., p. 4.
[12] Ibid., p. 3.
[13] Ibid., p. 34.
[14] Donald Senior and John J. Collins, eds., *The Catholic Study Bible*, 2nd ed. (New York: Oxford University Press, 2006), p. 1638.

God; and in the New Testament, this title is applied to Jesus. As Church historian Diarmaid MacCulloch remarks, "All the New Testament writings are written with this consciousness in mind: Jesus is Lord, the word for God."[15]

And in chapter 2 of this epistle, James mentions "the faith of our Lord Jesus Christ, the Lord of glory" (Jas 2:1). For Christian readers, "Lord of glory" is a resonant phrase; it also appears in Paul's First Letter to the Corinthians: "Yet among the mature we do impart wisdom, although it is not a wisdom of this age or of the rulers of this age, who are doomed to pass away. But we impart a secret and hidden wisdom of God, which God decreed before the ages for our glorification. None of the rulers of this age understood this; for if they had, they would not have crucified the Lord of glory" (1 Cor 2:6–8).

And it is precisely this crucified "Lord of glory" that Paul proclaimed as worthy of worship. In Acts (9:20) we hear of how Paul "in the synagogues immediately ... proclaimed Jesus, saying, 'He is the Son of God.'"

The Christology of James' epistle, then, seems to agree with—rather than diverge from—the faith professed by Paul. The evidence suggests both men accepted Jesus as divine.

In that case, where did James and Paul differ? As mentioned earlier, James was leader of the Jewish Christians of Jerusalem; Paul was a missionary to the Gentiles. Paul opposed any imposition of Jewish ritual requirements on Gentile converts to the Christian faith. According to the Acts of the Apostles, "Some men came down from Judea and were teaching the brethren, 'Unless you are circumcised according to the custom of Moses, you cannot be saved'" (Acts 15:1). How Paul felt about such matters can be seen in his Letter to the Galatians:

> For even those who receive circumcision do not themselves keep the law, but they desire to have you circumcised that they may glory in your flesh. But far be it from me to glory except in the cross of our Lord Jesus Christ, by which the world has been crucified to me, and I to the world. For neither circumcision counts for anything, nor

---

[15] Diarmaid MacCulloch, *Christianity: The First Three Thousand Years* (New York: Penguin, 2011), p. 96.

uncircumcision, but a new creation.... Henceforth let no man trouble me; for I bear on my body the marks of Jesus [*ta stigmata tou Iesou*]. (Gal 6:13–17)

The editors of the *Catholic Study Bible* comment as follows about these "marks of Jesus": "Paul implies that instead of outdated circumcision, his body bears the scars of his apostolic labors (2 Cor 11:22–31), such as floggings (Acts 16:22; 2 Cor 11:25) and stonings (Acts 14:19), that mark him as belonging to the Christ who suffered (cf. Rom 6:3; 2 Cor 4:10; Col 1:24) and will protect his own."[16]

Tensions in cultic practice between Gentile and Jewish Christians were addressed at the "Council of Jerusalem" (which took place sometime between A.D. 48 and 50). Paul was there, together with his companion Barnabas. So were James the Just and the apostle Cephas (Simon Peter).

But no sooner had an elated Paul reported on his success in bringing Gentiles to Christ than he faced swift resistance: "Some believers who belonged to the party of the Pharisees rose up, and said, 'It is necessary to circumcise them, and to charge them to keep the law of Moses'" (Acts 15:5).

After much discussion, both James and Peter eventually agreed with Paul's position. Neither circumcision nor the detailed ritual prescriptions of Mosaic Law were to be imposed on Gentile converts. As James put it, "Therefore my judgment is that we should not trouble those of the Gentiles who turn to God, but should write to them to abstain from the pollutions of idols and from unchastity and from what is strangled and from blood" (Acts 15:19–20).

We have Paul's own report on the outcome of the Jerusalem Council. As he says in his Letter to the Galatians, "And when they perceived the grace that was given to me, James and Cephas and John, who were reputed to be pillars, gave to me and Barnabas the right hand of fellowship" (Gal 2:9).

But note this: despite all the disputes about ritual matters, neither Galatians nor Acts makes any mention whatsoever of Christological disputes between these early Church leaders. Now, if James the Just had claimed (as Mustafa Akyol would have us believe) that Jesus was

---

[16] Senior and Collins, *Catholic Study Bible*, p. 1570.

Messiah but not Son of God, would Paul have been willing to challenge the head of the Jerusalem church? I would say: Yes, absolutely.

After all, look at how Paul reacted when Simon Peter seemed to favor imposing kosher dining restrictions on Gentile Christians. Across the centuries we are still singed by the blast from Paul's shotgun-mouth pushback: "But when Cephas came to Antioch I opposed him to his face, because he stood condemned.... When I saw that they were not straightforward about the truth of the gospel, I said to Cephas before them all, 'If you, though a Jew, live like a Gentile and not like a Jew, how can you compel the Gentiles to live like Jews?'" (Gal 2:11–14).

Here we have Paul at his give-'em-both-barrels best: by turns affectionate and irritable, enthusiastic and angered, quicksilver-ready to defend the "truth of the gospel". And if he is willing to confront Peter "to his face" over a point of Mosaic Law and dining, he would certainly be ready to speak out over any questions concerning the status and rank of the Jesus he knows and loves as the Son of God.

When Paul says, "I have been crucified with Christ" (Gal 2:20), he means this in a very fleshly way. Beaten, stoned, whipped, and shipwrecked, afloat on the open sea for a night and a day, he is one man who can truly say he bears the *stigmata tou Iesou*, the "marks of Jesus", on his body (2 Cor 11:24–27).

And Paul lets us know he has withstood all these things because he feels a real solidarity in suffering with that "Lord of glory" who was nailed to a cross. It is a solidarity that gives him the strength to proclaim Jesus as Son of God (as he does in Acts 9:19–20 and Romans 8:1–39).

So if James or any other Jerusalem Christians had ever voiced less than a full acknowledgment of Jesus as divine, you can bet Paul would never have accepted from them the "right hand of fellowship". No, Paul would have raised a roar to rattle roof tiles from Rome to Judea.

Jesus proclaimed as divine Lord: Evidence for a high Christology among the earliest post-Resurrection followers of Christ

But if Mustafa Akyol's argument does not hold up—that the Christology of James and other early Jerusalem Christians is supposedly proto-Koranic—what about Hans Küng, whose work inspired Akyol? After all, as we have seen above, there are passages in Küng's book on Islam that might seem to support Akyol. Küng creates an opposition between "high Christology" (focused on Jesus as divine Son and eternally preexistent Word of God) and "low Christology" (emphasizing his human nature). Küng downplays the "high Christology of the Hellenistic councils" (of the fourth and fifth centuries A.D.) and instead privileges what he calls the "much more original Christology of the Jewish disciples of Jesus", which he sees reflected in Islamic scripture.

Underlying Küng's argument, it seems to me, is a false assumption, namely, that "high Christology" and the acceptance of Jesus as divine are late additions to Christian belief, arriving centuries after the Resurrection as the result of Greek influence.

But, in fact, our earliest surviving textual sources strongly suggest that Küng is incorrect in his assumption. Here I will draw on the work of four New Testament scholars (all of whom I recommend to you): Martin Hengel, Richard Bauckham, Larry Hurtado, and David Wenham. All of them defend the idea of Jesus' divine status as central to the post-Resurrection beliefs of the very first Jewish and Gentile Christians. Bauckham states this position succinctly: "The highest possible Christology—the inclusion of Jesus in the unique divine identity—was central to the faith of the early church even before any of the New Testament writings were written, since it occurs in all of them."[17]

This might seem startling, given the disarray among Christ's disciples after his death. They were scattered, fearful, hiding behind locked doors—typical behavior, we might imagine, after the brutal execution of a cult's leader and what looked like the failure of yet another Messiah movement.

And yet it was precisely among these disheartened followers that there arose a fervent belief in their slain leader as divine Lord. This belief did not take decades, let alone centuries, to develop. As Hurtado demonstrates, this was an "explosively quick phenomenon, a religious development that was more like a volcanic eruption".[18] And this belief in Jesus as Lord was not something his disciples timorously

---

[17] Richard Bauckham, "God Crucified", in *Jesus and the God of Israel* (Grand Rapids, Mich.: Eerdmans, 2008), p. 19.

[18] Larry W. Hurtado, *How on Earth Did Jesus Become a God?: Historical Questions about Earliest Devotion to Jesus* (Grand Rapids, Mich.: Eerdmans, 2005), p. 25.

kept to themselves. Instead, they put their lives on the line to share this belief with others.

What gave them this sudden confidence to defy death itself? Accounts from the New Testament let us know: a direct, immediate, and personal experience of the risen Christ, who breathed into them a sense of peace and clarity of purpose that gave their lives direction and focus. And it was precisely these post-Resurrection appearances of Jesus that caused his disciples to reappraise their memories of his life, reinterpret their Jewish scriptural tradition in light of his rising from the dead, and acclaim him as divine Son of God.

The fact that such reinterpretation and acclamation occurred very swiftly is attested by the career of Saul of Tarsus (later renamed Paul). A fervent Pharisee and violent anti-Christian, the young Saul was present at, and approved of, the stoning of Saint Stephen, which took place within a year or two of Christ's crucifixion. Saul then became one of the leading persecutors of the earliest Christian communities (as attested in Acts 7:54–60, 8:1–3).

Important to remember here is that at this very early stage of its history, the Christian movement was made up almost entirely of Jews. As Hurtado points out, what we see here is a Jewish leader persecuting fellow Jews. "The concern of this devout Pharisee", Hurtado tells us, "appears to have been to protect the religious integrity of his ancestral religion against what he regarded as inappropriate, even dangerous developments manifested in early circles of Jewish believers in Jesus.... [P]rominent among [Saul's] reasons for proceeding against the early Jewish Christians was his outrage over their claims about Jesus and their reverence for him."[19]

In other words, the fact that Saul was so ferociously harassing Christians within a couple of years of Christ's death suggests that even at that early date Christians were proclaiming beliefs about Jesus that Saul found blasphemous. (And the notion that it was beliefs specifically about Jesus and his status that triggered the anger of Saul and other orthodox Jews is reinforced by what happened to Saul on the road to Damascus, as he was on his way to persecute more Christians. He was struck to the ground as light from the sky flashed all around him and a voice demanded, "Saul, Saul, why do you persecute me?"

---

[19] Ibid., p. 34.

[Acts 9:4]. It was the voice of Jesus—Jesus, whom Saul was persecuting, which suggests that Jesus was the focus of the devotion that Saul had found so blasphemously offensive.)

Or, to put it another way: if early Jewish Christianity (as claimed by Mustafa Akyol) had been no more than a lingering post-mortem Messiah remembrance cult, piously honoring Jesus as simply another of God's righteous prophets rather than as divine Son of God, then it would not have been likely to draw the furious attention of watchful Pharisees such as Saul.

Important to remember here is not only that early Christian belief in Jesus' divinity arose largely among Jews, but also that these were Jews living under imperial Roman occupation. They adhered proudly to their monotheistic beliefs and rituals to avoid assimilation in the face of a powerful and seductive polytheistic culture. Thus, when these Jewish disciples had their visual experiences of the risen Jesus—a Jesus who could walk through doors and hail them from the seashore in the light of an early dawn—they sought to make sense of these things in light of the Jewish scriptures that formed part of their own tradition. This, after all, was a tradition that Jesus himself had declared to be fulfilled rather than annulled.

So it is fascinating to see how the very earliest Christian writings integrate the Jewish scriptures with the disciples' firsthand experiences of Christ's death and Resurrection. An example can be found in Paul's Letter to the Philippians. In the passage I have in mind, he is urging the Christians of Philippi to be "of the same mind, having the same love, being in full accord and of one mind". He goes on to say, "Do nothing from selfishness or conceit, but in humility count others better than yourselves. Let each of you look not only to his own interests, but also to the interests of others" (Phil 2:2–4).

To encourage the Philippians to be humbly unselfish and set aside their own narrow interests, Paul instructs them to imitate their divine Lord: "Have this mind among yourselves, which was in Christ Jesus." Immediately thereafter Paul illustrates his point by citing the text of what New Testament scholars agree was an early Christian hymn in popular use for group worship rituals.[20]

---

[20] Martin Hengel, *Studies in Early Christianity* (Edinburgh: T&T Clark, 1995), pp. 379–80; Hurtado, *How on Earth*, pp. 84–85.

Here is Paul's citation of the hymn:

> Christ Jesus,
> Who, though he was in the form of God,
> did not count equality with God
> a thing to be grasped,
> but emptied himself,
> taking the form of a servant,
> being born in the likeness of men.
> And being found in human form
> he humbled himself
> and became obedient unto death,
> even death on a cross.
> Therefore God has highly exalted him
> and bestowed on him the name
> which is above every name,
> that at the name of Jesus
> every knee should bow,
> in heaven and on earth and
> under the earth,
> and every tongue confess that
> Jesus Christ is Lord,
> to the glory of God the Father. (Phil 2:5–11)

Let's note, first, the kind of Christology contained in this hymn. Jesus, prior to becoming man, enjoyed a divine existence "in the form of God". But rather than regarding such status as "something to be grasped", this divine Jesus underwent incarnation and "emptied himself" (in Greek, *heauton ekenosen*, a clause that forms the germinal point for "kenotic" theology, a topic to which we will return). As a divinely self-emptied man, Jesus underwent crucifixion, then exaltation, leading to his recognition with the name of "Lord".

I think you will agree with me: what we have here is very high Christology, indeed. Worshippers singing this hymn were praising Jesus as a divinity who existed "in the form of God" before becoming man, who "emptied himself" of "equality with God" to become man, and who then obediently exposed himself to the agony of crucifixion prior to God's exalting him and bestowing on him the divine title of Lord.

What is startling about this passage is that, in quoting it, Paul feels no need to explain its theology. This divine preexistence/kenosis Christology is not something whipped up by Paul himself. In fact, Paul emphasizes at various points in his letters that his mission is to pass on faithfully the Christian teachings he has learned from others (1 Cor 11:23–26; 1 Cor 15:3–7). Rather, he cites this hymn in passing simply to make the point that the Christians of Philippi should imitate Christ in being self-giving and humbly unselfish. The fact that Paul expresses no need in this letter to explain the hymn's complex Christology implies that his readers were familiar with both the hymn and its content.

Now this is doctrinal content of very early date. Paul wrote his Letter to the Philippians sometime in the mid- to late-50s A.D. But the kenosis hymn quoted by Paul is regarded as considerably older. Hurtado argues that "this passage may be the earliest example that has survived from the very first few decades of the emergent Christian movement."[21] So that when you and I read these words quoted by Paul, of the divine Jesus divesting himself of the "form of God" and humbling himself "in human form", we realize that we are listening in on something special—the words of praise chanted by the earliest Christians as they gathered to worship in the first few years after their Lord's death and Resurrection.

But there is more. Both Bauckham and Hurtado point out that the Philippians hymn uses phrasing from a passage in the Jewish Old Testament, specifically the Book of Isaiah. It is a set of verses in which God himself is quoted as speaking:

> Turn to me and be saved,
>   all the ends of the earth!
>   For I am God, and there is no other.
> By myself I have sworn,
>   from my mouth has gone forth in righteousness
>   a word that shall not return:
> To me every knee shall bow,
>   every tongue shall swear. (Is 45:22–23)

Here God himself declares that every knee shall bend to him and every tongue shall swear by him. It is a stringently monotheistic

---

[21] Hurtado, *How on Earth*, p. 84.

assertion of God's oneness, a passage with which any Muslim might well agree: "I am God; there is no other!"

And yet the Christian hymn quoted in Philippians resonates with echoes of these words: "At the name of Jesus every knee should bow ... and every tongue confess that Jesus Christ is Lord." If you keep in mind that "Lord" (*Kyrios/Adonai*) is a recurrent biblical title of God, then it is clear that the Philippians hymn has incorporated Jesus into the divine Oneness to which, as Isaiah proclaimed, every knee should bend in worship. As Bauckham states, "The Philippians passage is, therefore, no unconsidered echo of an Old Testament text, but a claim that it is in the exaltation of Jesus, his identification as YHWH in YHWH's universal sovereignty, that the unique identity of the God of Israel comes to be acknowledged as such by all creation."[22]

Hurtado describes this ancient Philippians hymn as an example of "charismatic exegesis", whereby the first generation of Jewish Christians, heartened by their vision of the risen Jesus and guided by the grace of the Holy Spirit, studied their own scriptural tradition with fresh appreciation:

> This creative understanding of the Isaiah passage must surely lie behind Philippians 2:9–11, and, indeed, this sort of "charismatic exegesis" of numerous biblical passages likely played a major part in earliest Christian efforts to understand the powerful religious events and experiences that prompted and shaped their faith. Indeed, I suggest that it may have been particularly characteristic of *Jewish-Christian* circles, as they mined their traditional scriptures for insights into God's purposes in Jesus, and also sought to find scriptural justification for their convictions about his significance and status.[23]

In other words, contrary to the claims by Akyol and Küng, it was in fact the earliest Jewish followers of Jesus, and not only the Hellenized Gentiles of the second or third or fourth centuries, who first hailed Jesus as divine Lord and who reinterpreted and paraphrased staunchly monotheistic verses from their own Jewish Bible to justify their acknowledgment of Jesus as God made flesh.

---

[22] Bauckham, "God Crucified", p. 38.
[23] Hurtado, *How on Earth*, pp. 92–93.

Here is one more example of early Jewish-Christian assertions of high Christology, an example that employs the foundational testimony of faith from the Jewish tradition. I have in mind here the prayer known as the *Shema' Israel* (Deut 6:4): *Shema' Israel: Adonai Eloheinu Adonai Ehad* ("Hear, O Israel: The LORD our God is one LORD").

Bauckham reminds us that the declaration of monotheism voiced in this prayer (traditionally recited morning and evening by devout Jews) was essential to Jewish identity and Jewish communal survival in Roman Judea of the first century A.D. He describes the "observant Jews" of this period as "highly self-conscious monotheists" who "saw their worship of and obedience to the one and only God, the God of Israel, as defining their distinctive religious way in the pluralistic religious environment of their time."[24]

Let's see how this foundational prayer of Judaism is employed in Paul's First Letter to the Corinthians (and keep in mind as you read this that Paul was not only a Jew but a highly educated Pharisee who knew his Jewish scripture well): "For us there is one God, the Father, from whom are all things and for whom we exist, and one Lord, Jesus Christ, through whom are all things and through whom we exist" (1 Cor 8:6).

Bauckham comments on this verse as follows:

It is now commonly recognized that Paul has here adapted the Shema' and produced, as it were, a Christian version of it. Not so widely recognized is the full significance of this. . . . Paul has, in fact, reproduced all the words of the statement about YHWH in the Shema' (Deut. 6:4: 'The LORD our God, the LORD, is one'), but Paul has rearranged the words in such a way as to produce an affirmation of both one God, the Father, and one Lord, Jesus Christ. It should be quite clear that Paul is including the Lord Jesus Christ in the unique divine identity. He is redefining monotheism as christological monotheism.[25]

Again, what scholars like Bauckham and Hurtado make clear is that belief in Jesus as divine Lord arose among the earliest post-Resurrection followers of Christ.

[24] Bauckham, "God Crucified", p. 5.
[25] Ibid., pp. 27–28.

But even though this earliest Christology is a high Christology, it is one that is inseparable from a Christology emphasizing the reality of Jesus' humanity and suffering. The same Paul who paraphrased the Shema' to include Jesus in the "unique divine identity" is also the Paul who bases his mission on the very physical anguish undergone by the vulnerable human Christ. As we have seen already, in Galatians Paul says that he bears on his body the stigmatic "marks of Jesus", the scars of floggings that "mark him as belonging to the Christ who suffered".

Emboldened in faith by what he has endured, Paul goes even further to say, with the kind of audacity that characterizes the closest and most demanding of divine friendships: "I have been crucified with Christ; it is no longer I who live, but Christ who lives in me; and the life I now live in the flesh I live by faith in the Son of God, who loved me and gave himself for me" (Gal 2:19–20).

The New Testament scholar David Wenham offers an insightful speculation concerning an incident from Christ's Passion that might have helped inspire Paul to write what we have just read. You may already know that one of Paul's comrades in his travels was Luke, author of both the Acts of the Apostles and the Gospel that bears his name. It is in Luke's Gospel that we find the story of Dismas, the criminal who was executed alongside Christ. Wenham says:

> Luke in his gospel includes the story of the penitent thief who was crucified with Jesus: the thief admitted his wrongdoing, and, although a sinner worthy of death, is promised a place in paradise by Jesus (Luke 23:40–2). It is a story that would have appealed to Paul—as illustrating the saving love of Jesus on the cross for sinners; it could just conceivably have contributed to his reflections on being 'crucified with Christ' (2.20).[26]

So powerful are these images—of Dismas on the cross alongside Jesus, gasping words of contrition and finding himself forgiven; of Paul "crucified with Christ", who loved him and gave up his life for him—that they continue to generate acts of sacrificial love to this day.

[26] David Wenham, *Paul and Jesus: The True Story* (Grand Rapids, Mich.: Eerdmans, 2002), pp. 62–63.

We find an example in the memoir of Nabeel Qureshi, a devout young American Muslim who became attracted to Christianity and embraced Jesus as divine Lord. He describes the emotional tumult he felt as his love for Christ led to his estrangement from his Muslim family and friends. But he finds the strength to persevere in his conversion: "Would it be worth it to pick up my cross and be crucified next to Jesus?... Being forever bonded to my Lord by suffering alongside Him? A million times over, yes!"[27]

This, then, is the Christology we find in our earliest Jewish--Christian texts: one that acknowledges Christ as divine Lord while also celebrating the love that led him to be nailed in anguish to a cross. We will return to this below as we explore "self-emptying" in the theology of kenosis.

Jesus the jihadist?—Some twenty-first-century Muslim views of Christ as a sectarian militant

Overlap with Mustafa Akyol's Christology can be found in the writings of another Muslim author, Reza Aslan, author of *Zealot: The Life and Times of Jesus of Nazareth*. Rather than accept the Christian belief that Jesus' original disciples quickly recognized him post-Resurrection as their divine Lord, Aslan imputes such high Christology to foreign pagan influence and a later wave of believers. He writes of "a new crop of educated, urbanized, Greek-speaking Diaspora Jews ... many of them immersed in Greek philosophy and Hellenistic thought", who were the ones responsible for supposedly turning Jesus into "a Romanized demigod".[28]

But what really captivates Aslan in his book on Jesus is the idea that the Nazarene was a violent Zealot, one among many sectarian militants who fought to overthrow Roman rule in Judea by force. Aslan does this by dismissing Gospel passages where Jesus preaches forgiveness and love and then taking very literally verses

[27] Nabeel Qureshi, *Seeking Allah, Finding Jesus: A Devout Muslim Encounters Christianity* (Grand Rapids, Mich.: Zondervan, 2016), p. 253.

[28] Reza Aslan, *Zealot: The Life and Times of Jesus of Nazareth* (New York: Random House, 2013), p. 171.

that seem to legitimize violence. Thus, the first Gospel verse quoted in his book is Matthew 10:34 ("I have not come to bring peace, but a sword").

How Aslan understands these words becomes clear from his summary of Luke 22:36–38 ("He said to them ... 'Let him who has no sword sell his cloak and buy one....' They said, 'Lord, look, here are two swords.' And he said to them, 'It is enough.'"). Aslan's retelling makes it sound as if Christ is taking inventory of his arsenal before launching a terrorist attack. In this spirit, Aslan pictures Jesus' subsequent arrest in the Garden of Gethsemane as a "brief but bloody tussle" that demonstrates Jesus' militant intentions as a Zealot—the kind that takes power by the sword.[29]

The problem with this interpretation is that it gives insufficient attention to other things Jesus said and did that night. Immediately after saying, "Let him who has no sword sell his cloak and buy one", Jesus adds, "For I tell you that this Scripture must be fulfilled in me: 'And he was reckoned with transgressors'" (Lk 22:37). Here he is quoting Isaiah 53:12, which is part of the Old Testament chapter prophesying the fate of God's suffering Servant. Isaiah tells us what befalls the Servant and how he responds to violence:

> He was oppressed, and he was afflicted,
>   yet he opened not his mouth;
> like a lamb that is led to the slaughter,
>   and like a sheep that before its shearers is silent....
> And they made his grave with the wicked....
> By his knowledge shall the righteous one, my servant,
>   make many to be accounted righteous;
>   and he shall bear their iniquities....
> Because he poured out his soul to death,
>   and was numbered with the transgressors;
> yet he bore the sin of many,
>   and made intercession for the transgressors. (Is 53:7–12)

The fact that Jesus is quoting the suffering Servant passage from Isaiah in this context should make us cautious about taking the sword

---

[29] Ibid., p. 78.

verse literally. Such caution in fact is shown by the commentators of the *Catholic Study Bible*, who interpret Jesus' words as follows: "In contrast to the ministry of the Twelve and of the seventy-two during the period of Jesus ..., in the future period of the church the missionaries must be prepared for the opposition they will face in a world hostile to their preaching.... The disciples ... take literally what was intended as figurative language about being prepared to face the world's hostility."[30]

So: literal or figurative, this sword talk? The test comes immediately thereafter, in Gethsemane. The soldiers seize Jesus. Peter, impulsive as usual, takes his sword and slices off the ear of Malchus, slave of the high priest.

At this point, a true Zealot might well be expected to urge his followers on: more sword work, more violence. Instead: Jesus rebukes Peter, tells him to put away his sword, and heals the slave's wound. Hardly the profile of a militant (Mt 26:51–54; Lk 22:49–51; Jn 18:10–11).

But Aslan's Zealot notion finds a grotesque echo in the Internet propaganda circulated by the Islamic State (the terrorist group otherwise known as ISIS). In the summer of 2016, their online magazine (entitled *Dabiq*) featured a special issue attacking Christianity and those who believe in Christ as divine Lord and Savior. The issue's title: "Breaking the Cross". (Such breakage is regarded as one of the marks of successful Muslim conquests.)

Like other Muslims, followers of ISIS claim Jesus as a member of their faith. But their image of him is tailored to suit their own violent agenda; and they are happy to make use of the Bible in the process:

> Even Jesus, whom the Christians have titled the "Prince of Peace," is recorded in their scripture as saying, "Do not think that I have come to bring peace to the earth. I have not come to bring peace, but a sword" (Matthew 10:34). There is also Jesus' order to his followers of being armed, as it is said, "And let the one who has no sword sell his cloak and buy one" (Luke 22:36).... However, despite these clear references to violently applying the Law of the Lord, Christians have cast aside such commandments and instead have followed papal decrees

---

[30] Senior and Collins, *Catholic Study Bible*, p. 1396.

and the sermons of priests—showing that their love for men is greater than their love for the Creator of men.[31]

ISIS also makes use of an Islamic legend to the effect that Jesus will return to earth as a lieutenant of the prophet Muhammad in the time preceding Judgment Day:

> What follows is part of the mission to break the cross, to crush the false notions of Christianity to which millions of people ignorantly adhere.... It shall be shown that the true religion of Jesus Christ is a pure monotheistic submission—called Islam—and that when he returns in the final days, the Messiah will adhere to the Law of Muhammad—may Allah bless him and keep him safe—and wage jihad for the cause of Allah.[32]

Jesus as a cross-breaking Muslim: jihad-talk like this demonstrates what truly interests the Islamic State. Since ISIS-militants themselves show they do not value compassion or love, it is unsurprising—though tragic—that they fail to find these things in Christ.

Thinking about the Trinity: Muslim polemics and a Christian response

On a field trip some years ago to the Muslim Community Association, a mosque complex located just a few miles from Santa Clara University's campus, my students and I were handed a leaflet provocatively entitled *Who Invented the Trinity?*

Beneath the title was a cartoon of what was supposed to be a Church Father, who sat at a writing table, quill in hand, as he rubbed his chin in perplexity. Above his head was a thought balloon illustrating the doctrine that perplexed him: "God the Father is one ... plus God the Son equals one ... plus God the Spirit equals one. Let's see ... one plus one plus one equals one. Hmm ... maybe I should use the egg analogy—shell, yolk, and white; or maybe I can use the

---

[31] "Breaking the Cross", *Dabiq*, issue 15, Shawwal 1437/July-August 2016, p. 79. Accessed online via https://clarionproject.org. The Clarion Project is a site that tracks radical Islamist activity worldwide.

[32] Ibid., p. 49.

water, ice, and vapor analogy; or Father, Son, and Husband. This is so confusing—it does not fit. It's a mystery."[33]

The leaflet also quotes a few lines from the Trinitarian affirmations in the Athanasian Creed ("We worship one God in Trinity, and Trinity in Unity ... for there is one Person of the Father, another of the Son, another of the Holy Ghost") and then comments on this Christian doctrine as follows: "Let's put this together in a different form: one person, God the Father + one person, God the Son + one person, God the Holy Ghost = one person, God the What? Is this English or is this gibberish?"

The leaflet invites us to jeer at the doctrine, swipes at Paul of Tarsus (a favorite villain in Islamic rhetoric) as the culprit who "lay the groundwork" for Trinitarianism, and then makes the following boast: "While Christianity may have a problem defining the essence of God, such is not the case in Islam. 'They do blaspheme who say: Allah is one of three in a Trinity, for there is no god except One God'" (Qur'an 5:73).

In a previous chapter I mentioned how Muslim propagandists have sometimes used the mosque field trips I have organized as a chance for *da'wah* (Islamic missionary proselytizing). *Who Invented the Trinity?* was a classic example of *da'wah* of the not-so-subtle kind: crass, anti-Christian, "in your face", as one of my undergrads put it.

But nonetheless useful, even if not quite in the way intended by the *da'wah*-crowd. Once we were back in the classroom, my students referred to the leaflet as they asked me questions about Christian beliefs in the Trinity, a doctrine that has intrigued and puzzled many—believers and skeptics alike—over the centuries. Let me use the opportunity to review some of the points I have explored with my students.

And I will confess right away, speaking for myself as a Christian, that I lack the Muslim leafleteer's confidence in "defining the essence of God". Yet the experience of teaching courses on Islam and the Koran—to say nothing of the challenge of living and working as a Christian in Muslim countries—has given me the occasion to reflect on the Trinity in ways that might be of interest.

---

[33] Aisha Brown, *Who Invented the Trinity?* (Chicago: Institute of Islamic Information and Education, n.d.).

First, when introducing this topic in the classroom, I have my undergrads review what they have already learned about theological attitudes among the pagan Arabs of the Jahiliyah and ancient Greeks such as Euripides. Prevalent in such societies was the assumption that of course the gods exist—how could one deny their existence, given the way unseen but palpable forces press in on us from all sides in the world around us?

But these divine forces are capricious. Unpredictable in their behavior, they can help us on a whim but are often indifferent and even cruel if we happen to catch their attention. Given this reality, we have to learn to live as if the gods do not care.

What distinguishes the three Abrahamic religions from ancient Arabian paganism is not just a monotheistic belief in one god but also the conviction that this god is benevolent. The vital importance of this conviction is emphasized by the American philosopher and psychologist William James. In his study of individuals who have had direct personal encounters with the Divine, James offers the following insight about that aspect of life we call "religious experience":

> The only thing that it [religious experience] unequivocally testifies to is that we can experience union with *something* larger than ourselves and in that union find our greatest peace.... Meanwhile the practical needs and experiences of religion seem to me sufficiently met by the belief that beyond each man and in a fashion continuous with him there exists a larger power which is friendly to him and to his ideals.[34]

William James is right, I think: it matters urgently to us created beings not only that there exists "something larger than ourselves" but also that this "larger power" wishes us well. This is what was lacking in Jahiliyah religion, and this is the common trait we find in Judaism, Christianity, and Islam: a god who is benevolent.

The Abrahamic God is not only benevolent but relational as well. He takes the initiative in extending himself to us; and in the Bible such initiatives are sometimes expressed in the vocabulary of revelation and covenant. We see this at work when God appears to

---

[34] William James, *The Varieties of Religious Experience* (Harmondsworth: Penguin, 1983), p. 525.

Abraham. The Book of Genesis (15:5) tells us that the Lord "brought him outside and said, 'Look toward heaven, and number the stars, if you are able to number them.' Then he said to him, 'So shall your descendants be.'"

The Lord brought him outside: this phrasing wonderfully conveys the warmth of intimacy in a moment of divine-human encounter.

Benevolence, divine initiative, personal encounter: these things help us approach the Christian notion of the Trinity. Contrary to what Muslim *da'wah*-leafleteers might claim, this doctrine did not originate with fourth-century Church Fathers rubbing their chins and arbitrarily picking a number to quantify God. As theologian Paul Tillich reminds us: "Trinitarian monotheism is not a matter of the number three. It is a qualitative and not a quantitative characterization of God. It is an attempt to speak of the living God, the God in whom the ultimate and the concrete are united."[35]

"The ultimate and the concrete": God as infinite mystery; but also: God as a presence that makes itself approachable and manifest, in response to the hunger felt by created beings for a Divinity to whom they can draw near.

Vital to the doctrine of the Trinity is the assumption that God senses and responds to this hunger we feel and that God will meet us somehow in moments of divinely initiated convergence. Thus, argues Anglican theologian Paul Collins, "The Christian claim that God is both three and one is rooted in the perceived human experience of and encounter with the divine, in the life and ministry of Jesus of Nazareth."[36]

In other words, the doctrine of the Trinity arose first and foremost out of the direct personal experience of devout Jews who encountered God in the person of Jesus Christ. As you and I have already seen, these Jews were staunch monotheists; nonetheless, their experience of the crucified and risen Christ led them to incorporate him into the divine Unity via a rereading of their own scriptural tradition.

Collins approaches the origin of Trinitarian doctrine by emphasizing what he calls "a threefold differentiated understanding of

[35] Cited in Paul M. Collins, *The Trinity: A Guide for the Perplexed* (London: T&T Clark, 2008), pp. 3–4.
[36] Ibid., p. 4.

encounter with divine mystery." He links this to early Christian exegesis of the Jewish Bible: "The interpretation of the encounter with divine mystery as something that suggests or requires an understanding that the divine is differentiated may be traced to the Hebrew Scriptures."[37]

In other words, Trinitarianism implies that God is one but triadically differentiated. The seeds of this doctrine can be found in the Bible itself, not merely in theological speculations centuries after the time of Christ.

If the Christian notion of God as Father hints at the divine qualities of the Divine as loving creator and infinite mystery, then in the initial books of the Old Testament we also find reference to something distinct from, but intimately bound to, the Father. I have in mind here *ruach Elohim*, "the Spirit of God", that moved over the waters at the beginning of creation (Gen 1:2).

Ruach, ruh, pneuma, spiritus: in Hebrew, Arabic, Greek, and Latin, respectively, these words mean not only "spirit" but also "wind" and "breath". For the ancient cultures associated with these languages, the word "spirit" denoted a Being at work in our world, life-giving and palpable, invisible but real.

We see the various connotations of *spiritus* at work in the related words "respiration" and "inspiration". We breathe in life-giving air; and when we are infused with Spirit, we feel fresh life, direction, and purpose.

In Trinitarian terms, "spirit" is a way of talking about God's agentive aspect, God's relational force, perceptible, effective, and real: God's ongoing and active presence in our world throughout time. From remote antiquity, the Spirit was perceived as something that moved between heaven and earth, breathing upon us, giving us fresh hearts, winging between realms seen and unseen.

No wonder the human imagination has often pictured this force in the form of a bird. Hindu scripture refers to Spirit as "the wandering swan everlasting".[38] The New Testament offers us a kindred image in Mark's description of Jesus' baptism in the River Jordan (1:10–11): "And when he came up out of the water, immediately he saw the

---

[37] Ibid., pp. 10–11.
[38] *The Upanishads*, trans. Juan Mascaró (London: Penguin, 1965), p. 135.

heavens opened and the Spirit descending upon him like a dove; and a voice came from heaven: 'You are my beloved Son; with you I am well pleased.'"

Thus already in Mark, the oldest of the four Gospels, we see the beginnings of early Christian articulations of God as Trinitarian: Father, Son, and Holy Spirit.

But the baptism in the River Jordan is by no means a static tableau. Consider what happens next in Mark's Gospel (1:12–13): "The Spirit immediately drove him out into the wilderness. And he was in the wilderness forty days, tempted by Satan; and he was with the wild beasts; and the angels ministered to him."

There is nothing tentative or impalpable here about the Spirit. It did not simply invite or suggest; it *drove* Jesus out into the wasteland, for his time of fasting and trial. It is a force in its own right. Powerful and imperious, it is something that, once it descends upon us (as the disciples found out at Pentecost), can be overwhelmingly transformative.

If "Father" conveys God's infinite mystery and power, and "Spirit" his agentive force at work in the world throughout history, what about the second Person of the Trinity? Here we come to that aspect of the Divine which most sharply differentiates Christianity from Judaism and Islam. Of course it is impossible in a brief discussion to do justice to this concept. For now I will say something about three key terms: Word, Son, and Lamb.

The evangelist John speaks of Jesus as God's "Word". Centuries before John's time, however, the term was also employed in the Old Testament, where it designates the expression of the divine Will. We can see this at work in the Book of Isaiah, where the prophet attributes the following speech to the Lord God:

> For as the rain and the snow come down from heaven
>   and do not return there but water the earth,
> making it bring forth and sprout,
>   giving seed to the sower and bread to the eater,
> so shall my word be that goes forth from my mouth;
>   it shall not return to me empty,
> but it shall accomplish that which I intend,
>   and prosper in the thing for which I sent it. (Is 55:10–11)

Isaiah's verses imply a certain autonomy and personhood in this Word that proceeds from the Lord: it goes forth, accomplishes God's will, and achieves the ends that prompted its mission. "The divine is differentiated", is how Collins characterizes the Trinity; and we get some sense of this in these lines from the Old Testament.[39]

The Word can also be described as God's communication and definitive revelation; it functions as an unveiling, a glimpse of the nature of the infinite mystery. John's Gospel tells us that the Word became flesh and dwelt among us; which means that in this Word-- made-flesh, in the life of Jesus Christ, we have our best chance of perceiving something of what God is like. The Anglican archbishop Michael Ramsey expressed this beautifully: "God is Christ-like, and in Him there is no un-Christlikeness at all."[40]

But this Word-made-flesh, the second Person of the Trinity, is also described as God's divine Son. And as a son, he displays the filial trait of obedience: he fulfills the Father's will, regardless of the cost to himself.

We see this quality in the New Testament's Letter to the Hebrews (5:8): "Although he was a Son, he learned obedience through what he suffered; and being made perfect he became the source of eternal salvation to all who obey him."

He learned obedience through what he suffered. This verse opens the door for us to be initiated into the mystery of kenotic theology, a topic we will explore in the next section of this chapter.

But for now let's look at one more quality of the Trinity's second Person. In the first verses of his Gospel, the evangelist John reveals the following: "In the beginning was the Word, and the Word was with God." What we learn here is that Christ-as-Word, the second Person of the Trinity, has existed from all eternity. (This doctrine helps us understand why the closest analogue to Christianity's Jesus in Muslim belief is not Muhammad but the Koran. For, according to Islamic doctrine, the Koran—Allah's eternal word—has, like the Christ of the New Testament, existed from before all time.)

---

[39] My discussion of the second Person of the Trinity as divine Word draws on the entry in *The New World Dictionary-Concordance to the New American Bible* (New York: World Publishing, 1970), pp. 739–41, s.v. "Word".

[40] Quoted in John V. Taylor, *The Christlike God* (London: SCM Press, 2004), p. x.

But the Christian God's eternal Word—unlike Allah's Koranic communication—is a divine Person; and as such it has agency and has been active in all eternity.

Active in what way? This teaching is conveyed via the image of the Trinity's second Person as Lamb of God. As a Catholic Christian, I am reminded of the Jewish origins of this image every time I attend Mass on the night of the Easter vigil. That is when the liturgical readings recall for us how the Israelites were saved from the angel of death as they prepared to flee Egypt:

> It is truly right and just ... to acclaim our God invisible,
>   the almighty Father,
> and Jesus Christ, our Lord, his Son, his Only Begotten.
> Who for our sake paid Adam's debt to the eternal Father,
> and, pouring out his own dear Blood,
> wiped clean the record of our ancient sinfulness.
> These, then, are the feasts of Passover,
> in which is slain the Lamb, the one true Lamb,
> whose Blood anoints the doorposts of believers.[41]

But in identifying Jesus with this Passover lamb of Exodus, Saint John's Apocalypse says of Christ that he is "the Lamb that was slain from the foundation of the world" (Rev 13:8; KJV). The eternally sacrificial quality of Christ-as-Lamb is reinforced in Christian scripture by the First Letter of Peter: "You know that you were ransomed from the futile ways inherited from your fathers, not with perishable things such as silver or gold, but with the precious blood of Christ, like that of a lamb without blemish or spot. He was destined before the foundation of the world but was made manifest at the end of the [ages] for your sake" (1 Pet 1:18–20).

Destined before the foundation of the world: the implications of this teaching are explored by Catholic theologian Hans Urs von Balthasar. He describes God's gift to the world in the form of the Son's Incarnation and Passion as something that was "always intended.... This

---

[41] This passage is from the liturgical readings for the Catholic Easter Vigil, in the periodical *Magnificat* 19, no. 1 (Holy Week 2017): 216.

self-giving in our fallen world was intended soteriologically from the outset."[42]

But if Christ-as-Lamb is eternally part of the Trinity and has been mysteriously present since "before the foundation of the world", then this implies something about the self-sacrificial nature of God as understood by Christians. Von Balthasar provides insight into this notion when he discusses what he calls the "eternal exteriorization of God" (that is, the eternal self-gift that the three divine persons make to each other independently of the world. Precisely this eternal and absolute self-giving in the Triune Deity makes possible the graciously free extension of himself outward into the world):

> What is at stake, at least in a perspective of depth, is an altogether decisive turn-about in the way of seeing God. God is not, in the first place, 'absolute power', but 'absolute love', and his sovereignty manifests itself not in holding on to what is its own but in its abandonment—all this in such a way that this sovereignty displays itself in transcending the opposition, known to us from the world, between power and impotence. The exteriorisation of God (in the Incarnation) has its ontic condition of possibility in the eternal exteriorisation of God—that is, in his tripersonal self-gift.[43]

The point to emphasize here is that the "tripersonal self-gift" described by von Balthasar is "eternal", that is, something that has always been characteristic of the Triune God, rendered visible in the person of Christ-as-Lamb.

Another Christian theologian, William Placher, conveys to us what we learn about God through the revelation of God's nature in the form of a man who gave himself as a sacrificial offering:

> God could, I suppose, have appeared among us as a seventy-foot high angel with glowing wings ... rather than [as] a wandering Jewish teacher.... In Jesus of Nazareth, however, we encounter God *in human form*.... In encountering him [i.e., Jesus], we encounter God. Now if God's primary characteristic were almighty power, then

---

[42] Hans Urs von Balthasar, "Mysteries of the Life of Jesus", in *The Von Balthasar Reader*, ed. Medard Kehl, S.J., and Werner Löser, S.J. (New York: Crossroad, 1982), p. 144.

[43] Hans Urs von Balthasar, *Mysterium Paschale: The Mystery of Easter*, trans. Aidan Nichols, O.P. (San Francisco: Ignatius Press, 1990), p. 28.

this would be impossible: the crucified rabbi could not be the self-revelation of God. But if God is, first of all, love, then, odd as it might seem, God is *most* God in coming to us in the form of a servant for the sake of our salvation.[44]

Let's catch our breath here a moment in our Trinitarian exploration and review what we have discussed. The first Person as loving Father and infinite mystery; the second as communicative Word, obedient Son, and self-sacrificing Lamb; the third as God's agentive force at work in the cosmos.

An immediate acknowledgment: what I have written here is inadequate, no more than a sketch. Still it is worth the attempt. As Thomas Aquinas so wisely said, "Though our lips can only stammer, we yet chant the high things of God."[45]

And if such stammering causes my students to become intrigued by the Trinity, if it starts them thinking about what is unique and irreplaceably precious about Christian doctrine, then maybe that is a worthwhile start.

Contemplating a Christ "crucified in weakness" in the light of kenotic theology: Rediscovering the God-made-flesh who suffers

I alluded earlier to kenotic theology, an approach to the mystery of Christ that is based on the New Testament verses we encountered above from Paul's letter to the Christians of Philippi. These verses state that, in becoming man, the eternal Christ "emptied himself" and became humbly obedient, even to the point of death on a cross.

Kenosis is worth our attention because it helps us appreciate what is unique in Christianity's veneration of Jesus. It is not enough to say that Christians worship a god made flesh. God-men, after all, can be found in other faiths. Think of Egypt's divine pharaohs, each of them revered as a "son of Ra", the sun-god. Think of the towering sandstone statues of Ramses, built so as to overawe, to stun into submission with the threat of divine violence.

[44] William C. Placher, *The Triune God: An Essay in Postliberal Theology* (Louisville: Westminster John Knox Press, 2007), p. 44.

[45] Cited in ibid., p. 17.

No, what makes Christianity unusual is that the enfleshed god we worship is a god who suffers. Kenosis gives us new ways of thinking about the duophysite reality of Christianity—that he was not only divine but also fully human, with all that this human condition entails by way of trials and torments of the flesh.

In describing the self-emptying of the eternal Christ, Paul links this kenosis to death on a cross. The centrality of this salvific event is reinforced in Paul's preaching: "For I decided to know nothing among you except Jesus Christ and him crucified" (1 Cor 2:2).

And it is precisely this reality of a self-emptied and crucified Christ—"who loved me and gave himself for me", as Paul says (Gal 2:20)—that makes the New Testament's Christ so radically different from the Jesus of Islam. In denying the crucifixion, the Koran also misses the opportunity to develop a Christology of suffering. The Christ of the Koran never weeps, never shows self-doubt or fear. The Koranic Christ presents to us the flat emotionless tone of a tiled arabesque: admirable, but remote.

To judge from the students I have taught, many Christians are unfamiliar with kenotic theology and the spiritual insights it provides. I am not the only instructor to have encountered this challenge in the classroom. Gordon Fee, an emeritus professor of New Testament studies at Regent College in Vancouver, reminisces about his own pedagogic experiences:

> Historically, holding both realities about Jesus together [i.e., his divine and human nature] has not been easy to do, as I discovered during a quarter-century of teaching a Life of Jesus course in two major evangelical theological schools. Over the years, I found that many students had great difficulty coming to terms with the historical Jesus as a *truly* human person. Evangelical students tended regularly to hold a kind of naive docetism, where Jesus appeared as a real person, but who was God in such a way that it superseded anything truly human about him except for the accidents of his humanity—basically his bodily functions: eating, talking, sleeping, and so on....
>
> The other place where this struggle comes to the fore for the students is in the final lecture on Jesus' messianic self-consciousness, in which I argue that the evidence suggests that this is something Jesus actually learned about himself through the work of the Holy Spirit.

This, after all, is clearly the perspective of Luke's two-volume work: that he actually grew through the enabling work of the Spirit.[46]

One important service kenosis performs is to dislodge in us the notion we might have of God's impassibility—that is, the idea that God is impervious to passion and to the anguish undergone by created beings. I referred earlier to an insightful book by John Taylor entitled *The Christlike God*. Worth quoting, with regard to the issue of divine impassibility, are the following comments by the missionary educator Timothy Yates, who wrote the preface to Taylor's text:

> The title of the book came from Archbishop Michael Ramsey ...: 'God is Christ-like and in Him there is no un-Christlikeness at all.'... In relation to the understanding of God, [Taylor] believed that a large-scale demolition of the prevailing view held by most Christians was required. For too many [Christians], this [image of God] was of an Olympian figure, described classically as 'impassible', detached therefore from human sufferings, of whom was also predicated an 'almightiness' expressed in the capacity to do anything at will. Against this idol, as he judged it to be, could be juxtaposed the figure of Christ 'crucified in weakness', whose historical manifestation as suffering redeemer provided a glimpse into the eternal being of God as 'the Lamb slain from the foundation of the world'.... It is the Christ of the cross who reveals the nature of God.[47]

In other words, if the nature of God is such that he is willing to expose himself to wounding—if he is willing, as Paul tells us (2 Cor 13:4), to be "crucified in weakness"—then suffering is no longer something that separates us from God. Instead, solidarity in experience binds together the enfleshed Deity and created beings. As the philosopher Stephen Evans puts it in his discussion of kenosis, "Jesus ... has chosen to endure the human situation in the same way that all of us must."[48]

[46] Gordon D. Fee, "The New Testament and Kenosis Christology", in *Exploring Kenotic Christology: The Self-Emptying of God*, ed. C. Stephen Evans (Vancouver: Regent College Publishing, 2010), pp. 25–27.

[47] Taylor, *Christlike God*, p. x.

[48] C. Stephen Evans, "Introduction: Understanding Jesus the Christ as Human and Divine", in Evans, *Exploring Kenotic Christology*, p. 7.

But this solidarity in experience does not last only for the thirty-three years of Jesus' time on earth. His post-Resurrection appearance to the disciples proves otherwise. When he appears to them after the crucifixion, his body still bears the five wounds—to his hands, feet, and side—of the Cross. The sight of this reality is enough to make the doubting Thomas cry out and acclaim him as "my Lord and my God!" (Jn 20:28) These wounds constitute an experience, a memory, that Christ takes into eternity.

Thomas has not been the only one to exclaim at the sight of the nail marks. The last time I had my students read aloud in class the post-Resurrection accounts in John, an undergraduate sitting at the back of the room (an individual inclined more to somnolence than sentience) suddenly sat up and said, "Eeeww." When I asked him to elaborate, he said he had not realized that the risen Christ still had the marks of the crucifixion on him. He said the idea was "gross", and he added something to the effect of: *I thought those marks would be gone. I thought he would be all healed or something, like it never happened.*

Like it never happened: but the point of Thomas' encounter with the lance and nail marks, as I tried to explain to my undergrads, is that it really did happen. The reality of Christ's suffering was messy, like our own human lives. And the persistence of those wounds in the risen Christ suggests that kenotic vulnerability and kenotic openness to our fleshly situation continue as ongoing characteristics of the second Person of the Trinity.

Von Balthasar emphasizes this point: "One must realize what theological depth of meaning gets expressed with the showing of the wounds on the risen One: that the state of being sacrificed during the passion has positively entered into and is taken up into the henceforth eternal state of Jesus Christ."[49]

Kenotic Christology, then, involves what von Balthasar calls "affective theology": that is, contemplation of the subjective dimension of the Incarnation, what it was like for Christ himself to undergo enfleshment and fully taste the fears, anxieties, and joys of the human condition—experiences, which, much like the five wounds, must also have left a psychic mark on him.[50]

---

[49] *Von Balthasar Reader*, pp. 145–46.
[50] Von Balthasar, *Mysterium Paschale*, pp. 37–38.

But in order to join us fully in our earthly condition and fully know the fears and sufferings created beings face, the Word-made-- flesh must have been subject to nescience, emptying himself of the divine quality of omniscience. After all, someone who is omniscient, who already understands everything and completely knows the divine plan and has the reassurance that everything will work out, cannot completely experience the terrors of doubt and confusion that assail us throughout our life. This is the point made by the Jesuit theologian Jacques Dupuis:

> What human knowledge did Jesus have?... The Word, incarnate in kenosis, did not possess during his earthly life the perfection (*teleiosis*) [a Greek term that carries the meaning of completed "accomplishment" or "fulfillment"] (cf. Heb 5:9) that became his in his resurrection. Surely, some human perfections must be affirmed in Jesus because of his personal identity as the Son of God. On the other hand, not only does his human nature remain human, but his human existence in kenosis implies voluntarily assumed imperfections.[51]

Dupuis presents us with a further implication of kenosis, namely, that Jesus was not born with complete knowledge or understanding of his messianic mission. This understanding grew in Jesus in the course of his life on earth, as Dupuis explains:

> Furthermore, Jesus' self-awareness and immediate vision of the Father are liable to grow and be subject to development.... Jesus' humanity is subject to the laws of human psychology and spiritual activity. As self-awareness grows through the exercise of a person's spiritual activity, so too Jesus' human self-awareness as Son and the accompanying vision of the Father grew from the early years through the mature age of his public mission. Jesus' awareness of his messianic mission and of the way in which he was to fulfil it also grew accordingly, from his baptism in the Jordan, where he became identified with God's suffering Servant, down to Jerusalem, where he faced his impending death on the cross....
> Nothing indicates or requires that Jesus was aware of his divinity or had the vision of the Father from the moment of the incarnation....

---

[51]Jacques Dupuis, S.J., *Who Do You Say I Am?: Introduction to Christology* (Maryknoll, N.Y.: Orbis Books, 1994), p. 119.

Jesus learned from people, from events, from nature, from experience. In his experiential knowledge he shared the ordinary condition of human beings.[52]

In other words, kenotic theology takes seriously the duophysite doctrine that Christ was fully human as well as divine and thus in many essential ways subject to the "ordinary condition of human beings". Kenosis helps us make sense of what happened (as reported in Mark's Gospel) when the "woman with a hemorrhage" approached Jesus for healing in a crowd. Here is where von Balthasar's "affective theology" comes in handy: this Gospel passage suggests the subjective dimension of what it was like for Jesus to be pressed and harried by people desperate for a cure:

There was a woman who had had a flow of blood for twelve years, and who had suffered much under many physicians, and had spent all that she had, and was no better but rather grew worse. She had heard the reports about Jesus, and came up behind him in the crowd and touched his garment. For she said, "If I touch even his garments, I shall be made well." And immediately the hemorrhage ceased; and she felt in her body that she was healed of her disease. And Jesus, perceiving in himself that power had gone forth from him, immediately turned about in the crowd, and said, "Who touched my garments?" And his disciples said to him, "You see the crowd pressing around you, and yet you say, 'Who touched me?'" And he looked around to see who had done it. (Mk 5:25–32)

If we take this passage seriously (and if we do not make the mistake of dismissing it as mere docetic playacting on the part of Jesus), then, from a kenotic perspective, it makes sense that Jesus would not have known who it was that touched him in the crowd. But the evangelist also tells us that at the moment of contact, Jesus felt that "power had gone forth from him." This sentence can be taken as alluding to the miraculous divine force within him; but it also hints at the notion that healing the sick took a very human psychic toll on him. Mark's account suggests that Jesus' healing ministry drained him at times—an impression confirmed, as you may recall from a previous chapter, by

---

[52] Ibid., p. 123.

other Gospel accounts of how, after healing and preaching, he would withdraw to hilltops and deserted places for solitary prayer.

Reinforcing this impression is John's reference to Jesus' travels just prior to his meeting with the Samaritan woman. Making his way on foot through Samaria, exposed to a hot midday sun, Jesus came upon a well and paused to sit there and rest. He was, as John tells us, "wearied ... with his journey" (Jn 4:6). Again, kenotic theology reminds us to take such details seriously. The incarnate second Person of the Trinity, like other human beings, experienced the limitations of corporeal existence. Travel tired Christ, just as it would tire any of us.

What is intriguing about such scriptural passages is that the four evangelists—all of whom acknowledged Christ's divine Sonship—did not shy away from including incidents about him that highlighted his human nature and creaturely limitations. The Jesuit Dupuis offers an insightful comment on these New Testament accounts:

> Above all, it is necessary to turn to the Gospels to see how the apostolic tradition understood the humanity of Jesus. The Gospel tradition testifies not only to astonishing perfections of Jesus' humanity, but also to obvious imperfections: his nescience, temptation, the agony in the garden, the cry on the cross. Such Gospel indications are all the more trustworthy because they could seem to raise difficulties for the faith in Jesus Christ that the Gospel tradition meant to communicate.[53]

The "difficulties" to which Dupuis refers, of course, are difficulties acknowledged openly by Paul (in fact, he glories in them): "But we preach Christ crucified, a stumbling block to Jews and folly to Gentiles" (1 Cor 1:23). The divine Son embraced by Christians as God made flesh is also someone who truly wept, truly knew human weakness from the inside, truly died on the Cross.

And it is precisely the "difficulties" enumerated by Dupuis that have drawn the contempt of Muslim polemicists. It is as if Paul, with his sharp words on foolishness and stumbling blocks, foresaw the kind of insults and objections that would come from followers of a religion that refuses to recognize a Christ "crucified in weakness".

[53] Ibid., p. 120.

You will recall some of these Islamic objections from the previous chapter. Juwaini mocked the notion of a Christ who was help-
lessly crucified "while he could do nothing about it"; the polemicist
said that such Gospel accounts of Jesus' humiliating death "diminish
his rank and his power". Ghazali was bothered by New Testament
verses that indicated "the existence of a nature susceptible to lower
appetites". Hilali contrasts the self-doubt of the Christian Gospels'
Christ with the supposed self-assurance of Allah's messengers: "His
prophets do not have doubts about His promise." Hilali also finds
foolish the idea of Jesus praying to the Father. Prayer shows one to
be needy, and how could someone who is divine exhibit this trait?
Allah, he reminds us, is al-Ghani: "the one who is free of all needs".
And Khatib laughs at the idea of the crucified Christ confessing he is
thirsty: "How could someone ... show neediness and expose himself
to his enemies as an object of humiliation and contempt on account
of merely one day's thirst?"

But, armed with the insights of kenotic Christology, we can simply reply, Yes, the Christ we worship is a Christ crucified in weakness. Yes, the Christ we worship is far different from an Allah who is
"free of all needs".

Rather than proving Jesus was not divine, the New Testament
verses that are so mocked by Muslims simply illuminate a deity radically at odds with anything Koranic scripture dared conceive: a God
who so loves our world that he entrusts to us a Son who suffers
among us in weakness and self-emptying love.

And like the thief Dismas, we can take comfort in the thought
that, on the bloodstained horizon of our own crucified lives, we are
nailed up there alongside Christ.

*"Even now ... this thirst persists": Catherine of Siena's
vision of the crucified Christ*

In looking at the writings of certain great saints and thinkers of the
Catholic tradition, I am struck by how frequently the things condemned by Muslim critics are precisely what inspire fervent Christian
devotion.

Here is one example to show what I mean. I am thinking of John
19:28 and the words uttered on the Cross by the Son of God: "Jesus

... said ..., 'I thirst.'" You have already read the Islamic criticism that finds repulsive the idea of a god that shows weakness and neediness. Muslim polemicists contrast such traits, as we have seen, with an Allah that is free of all needs.

Now consider the letters written by the fourteenth-century mystic and philosopher Catherine of Siena. In an exhortation sent to the abbot Giovanni di Gano da Orvieto, she has this to say about the "grace that comes in abundance to those who hunger and long for God":

> We develop such a hunger on the wood of the most holy cross. For there we find the Lamb slain and opened up for us with such hungry desire for the Father's honor and our salvation that it seems he cannot effectively show by his bodily suffering alone all that he longs to give.
>
> It seems this is what he meant when he cried out on the cross, "I am thirsty!" as if to say, "I have so great a thirst for your salvation that I cannot satisfy it; give me a drink!" The gentle Jesus was asking to drink those he saw not sharing in the redemption purchased by his blood, but he was given nothing to drink but bitterness. Ah, dearest father, not only at the time of the crucifixion, but later and even now we continue to see him asking for this kind of drink and showing us that his thirst persists.[54]

Saint Catherine develops the theme of persistent divine thirst in another letter:

> Learn from gentle First Truth [one of Catherine's names for Jesus], who dies in his hunger and thirst for our salvation. It seems this spotless Lamb cannot be satisfied: on the cross, saturated with humiliation, he cries out that he is thirsty. Though he was physically thirsty, his thirst of holy longing for the salvation of souls was greater.
>
> Oh wonderful boundless charity! It seems it wasn't enough that you gave so much in surrendering yourself to such torments! You wanted even more. And love was the reason for it all. I'm not surprised, because your love was infinite and the suffering was finite. So the cross of desire was greater than the physical cross.
>
> I recall the good gentle Jesus explaining this once to a servant of his. When she saw in him both the cross of desire and the physical

---

[54] *The Letters of St. Catherine of Siena*, ed. and trans. Suzanne Noffke, O.P., Letter 66 (Binghamton: SUNY, 1988), 1:210.

cross, she asked, "My dear Lord, which was worse for you, the physical pain or the pain of desire?"

He responded kindly and sweetly, "My daughter, have no doubt
... holy desire has no bounds. This is why I carried the cross of holy
desire."[55]

Catherine's mystical experiences of a thirsting Christ have allowed
her to break the barriers of time. As the theologian Mark Mc-
Intosh says in his study of von Balthasar's kenotic Christology, "For
the saints the gospel narratives become a threshold over which the
believer may pass prayerfully into the original and eternal presence
of the saving events themselves."[56] In Catherine's intimate conversations with the "spotless Lamb", past and present fuse into an everlasting Now.

"Consumed by this abominable thirst": A French poet evokes Christ's torment on the Cross

The thirsting Christ is likewise the subject of a meditation by the
twentieth-century French Catholic poet Paul Claudel. And like
Catherine of Siena, Claudel undertakes his contemplation in a way
that reminds me of what von Balthasar calls affective theology, mys-
tically entering into Christ's own subjective experience on the Cross:

> Between heaven and earth, Jesus—deprived here below of the love
> and trust of these people He came to save, deprived on high of dwell-
> ing with His Father—emits this cry, this astonishing groan: I THIRST!
>
> God is thirsty! Thirsty, in the midst of this world He has made,
> this creation that has received from Him everything it has by way of
> existence, for which He constitutes the goal and the reason for being.
> Thirsty, he gazes about and realizes—not in a detached and calmly
> philosophical way, but with a gut-twisting pain of the most urgent
> and immediate kind—that there is nothing there for Him.
>
> He created the world, and the world refuses Him a drop of water.

---

[55] Ibid., 2:114.

[56] Mark A. McIntosh, *Christology from Within: Spirituality and the Incarnation in Hans Urs von Balthasar* (Notre Dame: University Press, 1996), p. 17.

A little water, the only thing in the world that is free, that one would not refuse to a wounded animal, to a sick dog: mankind—either faithless or powerless—refuses to give this to its Creator and Savior.

Let's visualize Jesus consumed by this abominable thirst, jaws open, tongue swollen and hanging between his teeth. "I THIRST!" If Voltaire or Renan [famous French skeptics] ask us: "Where is your God?," well, this is what we have to show them....

Here is the condition to which love has reduced the Second Person of the Trinity. Look at this thirst he endures that nothing can quench.... Look at this feast he has so eagerly desired to share with us.[57]

In this last sentence Claudel evokes a statement by Christ to his disciples at the Last Supper: "I have earnestly desired to eat this Passover with you before I suffer" (Lk 22:15). Eager desire to share a meal: a heartfelt confession from an incarnate God who prizes intimacy over majesty.

Claudel goes on to link Christ's thirst on the Cross with an earlier moment in his earthly life, when he comes upon the Samaritan woman: "He is seated beside the well, near these deep waters, but he needs the charity of this unheeding sinner to bring the water to his lips.... Such, then, is this thirst that is felt by the Crucified One, this thirst that draws Him to the world."[58]

Claudel's contemplation of these Gospel texts reveals a God-made-flesh that lets himself become needy: dependent on the good will of the Samaritan woman, "this unheeding sinner", a sinner who stands in for all of us.

What Claudel and Catherine of Siena show us, in their meditations on the divine longings and desires experienced by Jesus, is a basic bedrock truth. Christianity is a faith where God makes himself kenotically open to weakness and wounding. Such a God differs radically from Islam's Allah, who is advertised in the Koran as majestically "free of all needs". It would be a mistake to follow the lead of Hans Küng and Mustafa Akyol in trying to minimize these differences in the name of a well-intentioned but profoundly wrongheaded theological rapprochement.

---

[57] Paul Claudel, *Un Poète Regarde la Croix* (Paris: Gallimard, 1935), pp. 118–19; translated from the French by D. Pinault.

[58] Ibid., pp. 120, 129.

Such a rapprochement would come at too high a price. It would deprive us of the insights derived from the vision of Christ thirsting on the Cross: the vision of a self-emptying God who makes himself vulnerable out of love for this world he has entered.

Don John's crucifix at Lepanto—and a bravura rescue by his monkey

Paul Claudel and Catherine of Siena, in their fervent devotion to a weak and wounded Christ, exemplify exactly the kind of Christian worship that disgusts pious-minded Muslims. We see this distaste reflected in the writings of the Pakistani scholar Fazlur Rahman. (He taught for many years at the University of Chicago as a "Professor of Islamic Thought".)

Rahman dismisses what he calls "Western critics" of Islam's "pugnacious" prophet Muhammad, especially those who frown at Muhammad's use of violence to conquer in Allah's name. Islam's Muhammad was a worldly success; Christianity's Jesus was, in the eyes of Muslims such as Rahman, an unworldly idealist and failure. Hence Christians, according to Rahman, are uncomfortable with religious leaders who triumph here on earth. Such "Western critics" of Muhammad, claims Rahman, are "addicted ... to pathetic tales of sorrow, failure, frustration and crucifixion."[59]

To which I myself have to plead (in the company of Catherine, Claudel, and Saint Paul): Guilty as charged. But what Rahman scorns as "pathetic tales" are precisely the source of hope and strength for us Christian "addicts".

We can see this source of strength at work in the year 1571 at the naval battle of Lepanto. Here Catholic forces defeated the much larger Turkish fleet assembled by the Ottoman sultan Selim of Istanbul. This was not just a clash of political or economic rivals but a head-on collision of cultures, with all of European civilization as the prize.

[59] Fazlur Rahman, *Islam* (Chicago: University Press, 1974), pp. 16–19. See also the unflattering fictionalized portrayal of Christ in the novel *Children of Gebelawi* by the Egyptian Muslim novelist Naguib Mahfouz.

Lepanto was understood at the time by both sets of adversaries as part of an ongoing religious war between Christianity and Islam. This perception is confirmed by the Turkish historian Onur Yildirim, who in his analysis of caliphal documents from this era cites the following decree. It was issued by the Ottoman court in the name of the reigning sultan to proclaim the Turkish assault on the Christian fleet:

> When the news about the infidels' intention to attack became known by everybody, here the *ulema* (religious scholars) and all the Muslim community found it most proper and necessary to find and immediately attack the infidels' fleet in order to save the honor of our religion and state, and to protect the Land of the Caliphate, and when the Muslims submitted their petition to the feet of my throne I found it good and incontestable. I remain unshakeable in my decision.[60]

Yildirim assesses this decree as follows: "As the language of the document suggests, the Ottomans from the beginning saw the confrontation as one between two faiths, reciprocating in this regard the motivations of the architects of the Holy League, Pope Pius V and the Spanish king Philip II."[61]

In this publicly proclaimed conflict of Muslims versus Christian "infidels", each side trumpeted its religious identity. As the three hundred Ottoman galleys rowed westward through the Mediterranean along the coast of Greece, they were led by the flagship *Sultana*, which hoisted aloft a gargantuan green pennant from Mecca. Its surface was embroidered with gold calligraphy proclaiming the name of Allah repeated some thirty thousand times.

Confronting this threat was the twenty-four-year-old military commander Don John of Austria. The flag that flew from the mast of his warship *Real* was a gift from Pope Pius: the Holy League's battle standard. It featured a blue banner showing Christ on the Cross. It seems to me appropriate, in what was both a religious and civilizational war, that the Christian fleet displayed the one image that best

---

[60] Onur Yildirim, "The Battle of Lepanto and Its Impact on Ottoman History and Historiography", in Rossella Cancila, ed., *Mediterraneo in armi (secc. XV-XVIII)* (Palermo: Quaderni Mediterranea, 2007), p. 541.

[61] Ibid., p. 541.

sums up the radical difference between Caliphate and Christendom: Jesus on the Cross, Christ "crucified in weakness", present at Lepanto to inspire those who fought in his name.

And, in fact, this image was present everywhere among the Christian warships. Consider this description, compiled from the accounts of surviving eyewitnesses, of the moment before the two armadas clashed:

> The Christians preserved complete silence. At a certain signal a crucifix was raised aloft in every ship in the fleet. Don John of Austria, sheathed in complete armour, and standing in a conspicuous place on the prow of his ship, now knelt down to adore the sacred emblem, and to implore the blessing of God on the great enterprise which he was about to commence. Every man in the fleet followed his example, and fell upon his knees. The soldier, poising his firelock, knelt at his post by the bulwarks, the gunner knelt with his lighted match beside his gun. The decks gleamed with prostrate men in mail. In each galley, erect and conspicuous amongst the martial throng, stood a Franciscan or a Dominican friar, a Theatine or a Jesuit, in his brown or black robe, holding a crucifix in one hand and sprinkling holy water with the other.[62]

Spiritual protection had been part of this expedition from the beginning, as described by the Catholic writer Christopher Check:

> Pius V had granted a plenary indulgence to the soldiers and crews of the Holy League. Priests of the great orders ... were stationed on the decks of the Holy League's galleys, offering Mass and hearing confessions. Many of the men who rowed the Christian galleys were criminals. Don John ordered them all unchained, and he issued them each a weapon, promising them their freedom if they fought bravely. He then gave every man in his fleet a weapon more powerful than anything the Turks could muster: a Rosary. On the eve of battle, the men of the Holy League prepared their souls by falling to their knees on the decks of their galleys and praying the Rosary.[63]

---

[62] Sir William Stirling-Maxwell, *Don John of Austria, or Passages from the History of the Sixteenth Century 1547–1578* (London: Longmans, 1883), 1:408.

[63] Christopher Check, "The Battle that Saved the Christian West", *Catholic Answers*, March 1, 2007, http://www.catholic.com.

Surviving documents also tell us of a Christian talisman that protected the Holy League's commander at Lepanto—a talisman derived from a sacred object you and I last glimpsed in the time of Richard the Lionheart. For in the midst of the battle, Don John wore on his chest, beneath his golden armor, a relic given him by Pope Pius: "a large *Lignum Crucis*, enclosed in a silver reliquary flanked by angels". *Lignum Crucis*, "the wood of the Cross": this was a sliver taken from the True Cross, obtained from the Crusader kingdom sometime before Saladin's forces captured the Cross itself in the twelfth century.[64]

Some of the sacred images distributed to the crew even entered into combat:

> A Spanish Capuchin, an old soldier, had tied his crucifix to a halbert, and, crying that Christ would fight for his faith, led the boarders of his galley over the bulwarks of her antagonist; after using his weapon manfully, he returned victorious and untouched. An Italian priest, with a great gilded crucifix in one hand and a sword in the other, stood cheering on his spiritual sons, unharmed in the fiercest centre of the arrowy sleet and iron hail.[65]

Another anecdote involves a small crucifix belonging to Don John, which had been his since his boyhood days in the Spanish castle of Villagarcia de Campos. It came to him from his uncle, along with the story of how "Don Luis, single-handed, had fought a band of Moors in southern Spain and had snatched the Sacred Image from the bonfire onto which they had thrown it." Visible from that bonfire was "the black charring all down one side of the rudely carved Figure and the wooden cross", but Don John kept it with him on his travels, and he had it now at Lepanto.[66] Before battle commenced, he fixed the Villagarcia crucifix on the mast of his ship, below the blue banner of the League, and knelt there for a moment's prayer.

He had brought on board another source of personal comfort: a pet marmoset, named Monecilla (little monkey). It, too, played a role. As the opposing flagships closed in combat, the *Real* was assaulted by

---

[64] Margaret Yeo, *Don John of Austria* (New York: Sheed & Ward, 1934), pp. 214, 227; Luis Coloma, S.J., *The Story of Don John of Austria* (London: John Lane, 1912), pp. 274–75.

[65] Stirling-Maxwell, *Don John*, 1:426.

[66] Yeo, *Don John*, pp. 3–4.

volleys fired by Turkish archers. Eyewitnesses recalled later that Don John's treasured crucifix had become a target: "The Villagarcia Crucifix had been hung on the mast above the cabins. Arrows had struck all round it, then one had pierced the wood of the Cross, another below the left breast. Monecilla had dashed up the rigging, chattering with fury, had pulled out the arrows, broken them with paws and teeth and flung them into the sea."[67]

The contemporary chronicler Geronimo de Torres y Aguilera hailed the monkey's bravura feat as "one of the evident signs of God's mercy to the Christians".[68] Another historian's account mentions an additional accomplishment of this creature in combat: "Even Don John's pet marmoset was seen to join the fight—running across the deck to pick up a live grenade, and drop it in the sea."[69]

But in the confusion of battle—ships aflame, cannons firing, smoke blinding friend and foe—Don John lost sight of the beast. He could not look for it until nightfall, after victory had been won and the shot-torn green-and-gold Meccan flag of Allah had been captured. The Catholic biographer Margaret Yeo evokes the scene:

> It was five o'clock when the battle was over. Great black clouds were piling up in the west and the sea was beginning to heave ominously. Obviously the sunny day with its favouring wind was to be succeeded by a night of storm. Don John gave orders to put about and made for the port of Petala a few miles to the north.
>
> The scene of the battle was a terrible sight. The sea, red with blood, was covered with débris of oars, rigging, plunder, and floating bodies. The glare of burning galleys reflected the stormy sunset, which touched the low hills too with the hues of fire and blood....
>
> Don John went down to his cabin. The cut on his ankle which he had not even noticed in the excitement of battle was still bleeding and had begun to ache. He felt glad to have shed his blood, even in so small a way, during the day which had been crowned by the triumph of Christ over Mahomet.
>
> Up above, the flicker of lightning showed torn sails, splintered bulwarks, bloody decks piled with corpses. Down here, in the yellow

[67] Ibid., pp. 233–34.
[68] Stirling-Maxwell, Don John, 1:426.
[69] Jack Beeching, The Galleys at Lepanto (New York: Charles Scribner's Sons, 1982), p. 214.

light of the silver lamp, swinging with the roll of the ship, all was quiet. The tattered green Standard of the Prophet lay across a chair. The monkey was curled on the bed, fast asleep. Don John knelt before the charred Crucifix, back in its usual place.[70]

No wonder his marmoset was worn out and fast asleep. Dousing Ottoman fire bombs; breaking arrows aimed at the crucified Christ: a pretty good day's work. I would be proud to do half as well in defense of the Cross as that monkey at Lepanto.

[70] Yeo, *Don John*, pp. 231–32.

CHAPTER 13

CHRISTIAN SURVIVAL IN MUSLIM SOCIETIES TODAY: EGYPT, YEMEN, PAKISTAN

Yes, a religious war: Facing facts after yet another Islamist terror strike

Palm Sunday service, Saint George's Church, Nile Delta, Egypt. Priests and choir, robed in white, singing hymns: a congregation celebrating Christ's entrance to Jerusalem.

Then an explosion and a flash. Dozens dead and wounded. Blood spatters the floor, the palm fronds, the marble pillars of the church.

This was just one of a pair of suicide bombings directed against Egypt's Christians on that April Sunday in 2017. Terrorists of the Islamic State proudly took responsibility: "The Crusaders and their apostate followers must be aware that the bill between us and them is very large, and they will be paying it like a river of blood."[1]

Crusaders: enemies of Islam marked with the sign of the Cross. Apostate: a word frequently used by Islamists to label anyone who falls away from the true faith and hence deserves death. ISIS applies this stigma to justify the murder of Muslims (such as security guards) who try to protect Christians and get killed in the process.

Pugnacious terms like these are common on the Islamic State's website and in its online publications. They repeatedly cite Koranic verses and the violent acts of the prophet Muhammad himself as he fought non-Muslims and subjugated pagans, Jews, and Christians in establishing Islamic rule in seventh-century Mecca and Medina.

---

[1] Quoted in Joe Sterling, "ISIS Claims Responsibility for Palm Sunday Church Bombings in Egypt", April 10, 2017, http://www.cnn.com.

But rather than take seriously the motivation explicitly claimed by Muslim terrorists, many well-meaning Christians are squeamish about recognizing the blatantly faith-based character of ISIS-inspired attacks such as these.

We may be reluctant to say we are in a religious war, but ISIS has no such qualms. It sees its actions as rooted in the exemplary life of the prophet of Islam, a figure revered by both Sunni and Shia Muslims as *ma'sum*—sinless, infallible, and perfect—and hence as someone whose actions must be imitated.

The reluctance of many Christians to acknowledge the religious dimension of Islamist terror can be seen in the response to what happened on July 26, 2016, at a Catholic church in Normandy in the parish of Saint-Étienne-du-Rouvray. A pair of young ISIS militants stormed the church and butchered an eighty-five-year-old priest named Jacques Hamel. His death took place at the altar as he celebrated the sacrifice of the Mass.

The response by Pope Francis? His Holiness refused to link Islam with violence in any way: "If I have to talk about Islamic violence, I have to talk about Christian violence. Every day in the newspapers I see violence in Italy, someone kills his girlfriend, another kills his mother-in-law, and these are baptized Catholics."[2]

Of course this comment fails to distinguish between violence committed by someone who happens to belong to a religion and violence committed specifically *in the name of* that religion.

In 2016, a Jesuit from Egypt named Samir Khalil Samir, an outstanding Catholic scholar of Islam, met with Pope Francis in Vatican City to address the question of Islam and violence. Here is a summary from the *New York Times* of what happened when this Egyptian priest tried to inform Pope Francis about certain troubling and deeply embedded features of Islam:

Before the meeting, Father Samir sent the pope articles he had written noting that the Quran contained both peaceful and violent passages.

When Father Samir broached the topic, he said the pope countered that his experiences with an imam in Argentina left him with the

---

[2] Quoted in Jason Horowitz, "Taking Message to Egypt, Pope Faces Difficult Test", *The New York Times*, April 28, 2017, p. A6.

impression that Islam was peaceful and that he viewed his mission as re-establishing good relations with Muslims.

Father Samir said he gently countered that he himself could not be blind to the negative aspects of Islam, that both needed to be considered, but that the pope seemed to have little interest in the subject. "So he simply passed to other things," Father Samir said in an interview, adding that "his knowledge of Islam is limited to the nice discussions he had with the imam."[3]

Pope Francis may reject any connection between Islam and violence. But the Coptic Christians I have met in Egypt in recent years know very well they are the targets in a religious war. They know the goal of ISIS and other Islamist groups is to crush Christianity in Egypt. They know these Islamists will convert, kill, or expel every Copt they can. They know these Islamists want to reduce any Copts that remain to subjugated status in a sharia-ruled state.

And the Copts I have met in Egypt deal with all this by understanding the challenges they face in explicitly religious terms. They turn to an ancient vocabulary of persecution and martyrdom that links their twenty-first-century faith to what Egypt's first Christians endured almost two millennia ago in the time of the Roman Empire.

In what follows I will discuss the things I learned from Coptic informants in my most recent visit to Egypt several years ago, at the beginning of the short-lived "Arab Spring".

"Ready to be martyrs": Coptic Christians in Egypt claim their ancient heritage

My sharpest memory from Cairo was what my driver said: *al-Masih biygarribna*—"Christ is testing us." I had hired Sami to drive me around the city. But as soon as I saw the *washma* on his wrist—a faded tattoo in the shape of a cross—I knew he was a Copt, a member of Egypt's Christian minority, a community that predates the Muslim presence by centuries.

---

[3] Ibid.

Since the early 1980s, I had been to Egypt many times—as a student of Arabic, as a researcher, as a tour guide on Nile cruise boats—but this visit in 2012 was my first time back since the onset of the "Arab Spring" and Egypt's Lotus Revolution.

As we drove, Sami told me about the persecution Copts are enduring at the hands of Egyptian Salafists—those Muslims who want an Islamist government in which the harshest interpretations of sharia law are privileged at the expense of both non-Muslims and progressive-minded Muslims. "Things had been less worse for us under Mubarak", he said. Hosni Mubarak, Egypt's authoritarian ruler until his ouster in the revolution, had suppressed Islamist radicals. But now, said Sami, the Salafists feel bold enough to burn churches, incite anti-Coptic riots, and call openly for the expulsion of Christians.

I told him the statistics: in 2011 and 2012, since the revolution's onset, over 100,000 Copts had fled Egypt. "Well, I am not going to leave", he insisted. "Christ is testing us. I tell my friends to stay. Christ could end this suffering, this trial, at any time. How will you feel, I tell my friends, if you are in Canada instead of Egypt when Christ returns?"

I pondered this apocalyptic thought as we skirted Tahrir Square—the scene of recurrent confrontations between demonstrators and Egypt's military—and passed the blackened ruins of the Institute of Egypt. French scholars had founded the Institute after Napoleon Bonaparte's invasion in 1798. Its archives held centuries-old maps, books, and manuscripts—a priceless treasure.

But in December 2011, when government forces on nearby rooftops shot at demonstrators in the street, protesters retaliated by throwing firebombs at the soldiers. Some of the projectiles fell short. The resultant fire destroyed most of the building and much of the collection. In January 2012, Sami told me, Muslim and Christian volunteers collaborated in salvaging charred volumes from the ruins.

But what lingered in my mind was the observation voiced in the Arabic-language newspaper *al-Ahram* by the Egyptian poet and commentator Kamal 'Arafah. He compared the destruction of Cairo's Napoleonic Institute to the ancient burning of the Library of Alexandria and the Mongols' obliteration of Baghdad's learning centers in the thirteenth century. Labeling Egypt's fire-bombers "Mongols of chaos", 'Arafah added, "I felt pain when I saw in the videos and pictures the cries of *Allahu akbar* (Allah is great) and *La ilaha illa Allah* (there is no god except Allah) coming from young men and women while the Institute of Egypt was burning—young men and women who were ignorant of the extent of the loss bleeding from the heart of Egypt."[4]

When I mentioned 'Arafah's commentary to Sami, he said he, too, found disturbing the linkage of religious sloganeering and violence. He reverted to what we had been discussing earlier: Salafist persecution of the Copts. "I'm staying. I'm not leaving my country. I'm not going to do what the Salafists want me to do." He added that in the aftermath of recent attacks on Christian churches, when he and his Coptic friends assemble for prayer, they have the feeling, "We're ready to be martyrs. We're ready to be with Christ, to live with Christ." Not martyrs in any violent sense, he insisted, but in the sense of giving witness.

The motif of martyrdom recurred as we drove south to Masr al--Qadima, "Old Cairo", one of the city's most ancient neighborhoods and a center of Coptic culture. We visited my favorite church in Old Cairo: al-Kanisah al-Mu'allaqah, "the suspended church", so called because it was constructed atop the remains of a fortress dating to the Roman Empire.

I knew the place well. As a grad-school Arabic-language student several decades ago, I came here on weekends for prayer services and for the pleasure of hearing chanted Coptic, a language that is the linguistic descendant of the tongue of the pharaohs.

Some things were as I remembered: walls with ebony and ivory inlay, worshippers lighting candles before relics and icons of the saints. Vendors by the entrance offered holy cards and painted images of Catherine of Alexandria and Barbara of Heliopolis, saints who were tortured and killed for their faith.

But there was something new: tables in the church courtyard, where men sold copies of two newspapers aimed at a Coptic Christian readership—*Nida' al-watan* (An appeal to the nation) and *al-Katiba*

---

[4] Kamal 'Arafah's comment was cited in Mahmud Fu'ad, "Ma lam yaf'alhu al-a'da' fa'alahu al-abna'", *al-Ahram* (Cairo), December 26, 2011, http://www.ahram.org.eg/Print .aspx?ID=120407.

al-Tibiya (The Theban legion). *Nida' al-watan* featured a front-page red-lettered headline: "In Memory of the Maspero Martyrs—Who Was It that Ran Over and Killed Innocent Copts?" The question referred to a notorious incident in October 2011, when armored military vehicles rammed and crushed dozens of Christians who had gathered in a Cairene locality known as Maspero to protest the burning of Coptic churches. The article referred scornfully to a government inquiry into the Maspero killings that dragged on inconclusively for months.

Beneath these words was another headline: "The Blood of the Martyrs Cries out from the Darkness, and the Tears of the Copts Will Not Dry. But Our Lord Is Present."[5] A photomontage accompanied this text—a crowd of wailing women at Maspero, horror and shock in their eyes; and the face of Jesus, his head bowed beneath a crown of thorns. Suddenly the distant days of Catherine and Barbara felt very close at hand.

Sami saw me studying the juxtaposed images—Maspero/Christ—and commented, "They are side by side because the two are similar."

The *Theban Legion* newspaper also was forthright in addressing contemporary religious and political issues that Copts must confront. A front-page article reported on the frustration felt by Christians and liberal-minded Muslims at the results of Egyptian parliamentary elections, which brought to power Islamist and Salafist parties.

This article, by a priest named Matthias Nasr Minquriyus, asserted that this frustration did not stem from the prospect of political domination by Muslims, "since, after all, this has been the situation for some fourteen centuries". (Such a statement simply acknowledges an enduring political reality: Egypt has been under Muslim control—aside from brief intervals of French and British rule—since the Arab conquest in the seventh century.)

Rather, wrote Father Minquriyus, Christians and liberal Muslims fear the destruction of "what remains of the Egyptian identity of Egypt" because of the emergent entente between the local "radical extremist current" and "foreign Wahhabi ideology, which is imported from a region from which we are separated by only a body

[5] "Fi dhikra shuhada' Masbiru: man qatala wa-dahasa al-aqbat al-abriya'?" *Nida' al-watan* (Cairo), November 25, 2011, p. 1.

of water that can easily be traversed."[6] (Here the writer was referring to Saudi Arabia, on the eastern shore of the Red Sea.)

Another *Theban Legion* article warned that the Salafists' goal is to "transform the so-called 'Arab Nation' into the 'United Islamic States', whereby Egypt will become merely one province among many that will be governed entirely by a caliph who rules via Allah's sharia."[7]

This concern about the loss of Egypt's identity is reflected in the *Theban Legion*'s website. The site explains that the newspaper borrows its name from a revered third-century band of martyrs—an Egyptian military unit that refused to worship the gods of the Roman Empire and, instead, chose death rather than surrender its Christian identity.

The website articulates two goals in particular. The first is "to offer support for victims, the subjugated, and the oppressed and to prop-agate the spirit of giving Christian witness and providing the means for nonviolent struggle". The second is "to rebuild Christian Coptic identity by rejecting claims of being part of an Arab identity and by developing Egyptian cultural awareness".[8]

The *Theban Legion*, in fact, rejects Arab identity—a relatively recent importation, a "mere" fourteen centuries old—in favor of a much more ancient legacy: a pharaonic tradition that dates to the fourth millennium before Christ. The *Theban Legion* newspaper I bought had a cultural heritage page featuring illustrations of both Christian icons and a jeweled scarab-god talisman from the tomb of Tutankhamun.

Since the beginning of the Arab Spring in 2011, Copts have also asserted their ancient Egyptian heritage in public protests. March-ers commemorating Christians killed in clashes since the revolution's onset staged a demonstration near the Coptic Cathedral in Cairo's Abbasiya neighborhood. The demonstrators bore aloft large Chris-tian crosses but also wore "pharaonic-style" gowns ornamented with ankhs—hieroglyphic symbols of eternal life. And in January 2012, marchers in Tahrir Square carried a replica of a giant obelisk—another survival from Egypt's past—on the capstone of which was inscribed:

---

[6] Matthias Nasr Minquriyus, "Misriyatuna aqwa", *al-Katiba al-Tibiya* (Cairo), December 2011, pp. 1, 5.

[7] "Al-Wilayat al-muttahidah al-islamiyah", *al-Katiba al-Tibiya* (Cairo), December 2011, p. 10.

[8] "Al-Katibah al-Tibiyah: man nahnu". Accessed May 16, 2012.

"Dedicated to the souls of the martyrs of the Maspero Youth Coalition and the Theban Legion."[9]

Such symbolism offers a reply to those Salafists who call for Islamic government and the subordination of Copts or their expulsion from Egypt. My driver put it this way: "We've been here forever. We're true Egyptians. We belong here."

Hidden prayer in Yemen: A memory of Christian endurance in Sanaa

But Egypt's Copts are far from alone in facing persecution from Muslims as they struggle to keep their identity as Christians. Similar threats are active throughout the Islamic world—as I will show you now in sharing my experiences in Yemen.

Keep in mind as you read what follows that I wrote most of it shortly after my return to the States from Yemen's capital in 2009. Since then, a years-long proxy war between Iran and Saudi Arabia—involving air strikes, street fighting, and suicide-bomb attacks by local militants—has killed thousands and reduced to ruins historic buildings in Sanaa and in Yemen's other ancient cities.

A site where Christ once wandered: traces of vanished Christianity in an Arabian stronghold of Islam

Christians in Sanaa, the capital city of Yemen, cannot pray in church. They must congregate in secret in their homes, and Yemeni Muslims are monitored by government agents to ensure they do not attend. During a recent visit to the country, I attended many clandestine services and watched with admiration as beleaguered Christians gathered to practice their faith in a hostile environment.

Unfortunately, the plight of Christians in Yemen is not unique. In Iraq, Saudi Arabia, Iran, and other countries in the Muslim world,

[9] Charles Levinson and Matt Bradley, "Egyptians Show Mix of Jubilation, Anger to Mark Anniversary", *The Wall Street Journal*, January 26, 2012, pp. A1, A10; André Aciman, "After Egypt's Revolution, Christians Are Living in Fear", *The New York Times*, November 20, 2011, pp. 6–7.

freedom of worship is severely restricted, and the number of Christians has dwindled. The values of pluralism and diversity are dismissed in favor of a strict adherence to Islamic law, whereby any visible Christian presence is frowned on as an attempt at evangelization. Yemen is emblematic of an Islamic culture that fails to see the spiritual growth that can come from encounters with people of other faiths.

Yet if you know where to look as you explore the streets of Sanaa, you can find traces of ancient Christian worship in this city at a site known as the Qalis.

Finding it takes work. Walk through the alleys of Sanaa's *Souq al-Milh* (salt market) until you reach the eastern edge of the walled Old City. You will have to ask as you go toward the Qalis (the name comes from the Greek word *ecclesia*). No placards or street signs announce the site.

But fifteen centuries ago, it was something splendid. King Abrahah, a Christian from Ethiopia, ordered a church for pilgrims built in Sanaa, within sight of the desert hills of Mount Nuqum.

Abrahah's building site was linked to a Christian Arabian legend. Jesus is said to have wandered from the Jordan River to Yemen. According to the legend, Jesus reached Sanaa and paused there to pray, during his time of wilderness fasting and spiritual trials before beginning his public ministry.[10]

The Qalis was built to dazzle. The thirteenth-century Muslim geographer Yaqut ibn 'Abd Allah al-Rumi described the church as it looked in Abrahah's time: pulpits of ivory and ebony, crosses of silver and gold, walls of stone taken from the palace of Bilqees, the queen of Sheba. Abrahah hoped the Qalis would rival Mecca's Ka'ba shrine as a venue for pilgrims.[11]

But with Islam's triumph, the church was looted, its pillars plundered to build Sanaa's Great Mosque. The wasteland around the deserted Qalis, reported Yaqut, became the lair of lions, snakes, and demonic jinns.

---

[10] Daniel McLaughlin, *Yemen* (Guilford, Conn.: Globe Pequot Press, 2007), p. 85; Cor Dijkgraaf, "Renovaties in de ouden Stadskern van Sana'a, Yemen", *Bulletin KNOB* (Netherlands) 88 (1989): 6.

[11] Yaqut ibn 'Abd Allah al-Rumi, *Mu'jam al-buldan* (Beirut: Dar Sadir, 1957), 4:394–396, s.v. "Qalis".

What is left is marked by a seven-foot-high circular wall that segregates the site from modern Sanaa. Climb this wall—as I did during a visit in May-June 2009—and you will gaze down onto a pit that plunges twenty feet below street level. Today it is a garbage dump, its surface littered with tires and plastic bottles.

A huge fig tree grows wild from the pit. Its branches brush the top of the wall. As I stared, I saw sparrows flit among the leaves. A feral cat—heir to Yaqut's lions—stalked something through the trash.

"Here, in a Muslim country, we do not take our Christianity for granted": House-church gatherings in Sanaa

Yet Christian worship persists in twenty-first-century Yemen, in the form of clandestine "house church" gatherings (most typically held on Friday mornings, the Muslim day of congregational prayer and a time when everyone is free from work). I attended a number of such services while in Sanaa. They take place discreetly, in rooms and private homes throughout the capital. All the gatherings I attended were small—sometimes as few as three or four persons, never more than twenty-five.

But what they lacked in numbers they made up for in fervor. The services featured singing, clapping, cries of petition, and prayers of thanksgiving for the companionship of Jesus. "Here, in a Muslim country, we do not take our Christianity for granted", as one participant I interviewed said. "Here, with these small communities, meeting 'underground', the original spirit of Christianity can be revived."

All the worshippers I met were foreigners and long-term residents—nurses, teachers, and physicians; supervisors of aid projects involving water management, literacy, or public health. Some came from Europe or America; but most were from Nigeria, the Philippines, Indonesia, Korea, India, or East Africa. Very much a reflection, I thought, of the dynamic and expanding Church that is the future of Christianity.

Given this variety—I encountered charismatics, evangelicals, and fundamentalists of various denominations—some tension was inevitable. When I identified myself as a Catholic, one self-described "born--again believer" replied that she, too, used to be Catholic but now was a true Christian. My host that evening immediately reminded everyone that we all ought to focus on our shared devotion to Christ.

Such a focus is appropriate, given the challenges facing Christians in Yemen. This is especially true for would-be converts in the Yemeni population at large. The government does not prohibit foreigners from Christian worship in private homes but monitors gatherings to ensure no Yemenis attend. Muslim religious authorities and government officials do everything they can to discourage conversion from Islam.

I heard of cases where young Muslim men—apparently commissioned by the Yemeni government—posed as potential converts and approached Christian foreigners to see if the latter would engage in proselytizing. In one recent instance, a Christian Ethiopian resident of Sanaa—a refugee and day-laborer—gave an Arabic text of the New Testament to a Yemeni who feigned interest in the faith. The result: three months in jail for the Ethiopian, followed by deportation from the country.

Consequences can be far harsher for Yemenis with a real desire to convert. In a culture where religious identity is equated with loyalty to family, clan, and nation, conversion from Islam is seen as treason, a threat to Yemen's communal identity. Hence, what one Muslim cleric described to me as *al-khawf min al-tansir*, "the fear of Christianization" (*tansir* comes from the root *nasrani*, "Nazarene").

While in Sanaa, I heard of numerous cases where young Muslims caught flirting with the "Nazarene" faith were arrested, imprisoned, and made to reaffirm their allegiance to Islam. Others suffered beatings and even worse violence at the hands of their own families— "the only way," as one American informant told me, "in an honor/shame society, for a father to erase the stain of shameful behavior on the part of his children."

Jewish martyrs in Yemen: The death of Moshe Yaish Youssef Nahari

Would-be Christians are not the only Yemenis to suffer religious persecution. Yemen used to have a substantial Jewish community. This minority population had existed there for thousands of years;

local traditions linked it to the time of King Solomon. With the creation of Israel in 1948, however, anti-Jewish riots erupted throughout the Arab world, and most of Yemen's Jews fled to the newly established Jewish state.

Now only a handful of Jewish families remain, and many of them have had to leave their villages and take refuge in Sanaa in the wake of death threats by local militant Muslim groups that dominate many rural areas. (Terrorists accuse the Jews of being "agents of Zionism".)

A notorious case—an incident in December 2008—involved Moshe Yaish Youssef Nahari, a resident of Raydah, a village in northern Yemen. Confronted on the street by an armed individual who called on him to embrace Islam, Nahari refused to abandon his Jewish faith and was murdered on the spot.

"Fight against those who do not believe in Allah": *Anti-Christian violence in Muslim countries worldwide*

Violent hostility to non-Muslim religious minorities is at work in other Islamic countries as well. In Iraq in recent years, terrorists have used death threats against indigenous Christians in Mosul and elsewhere in northern Iraq to extort payment of what is known as the jizyah. This is the discriminatory tax imposed on "people of the Book"—Jews and Christians living under Islamic rule—in accordance with chapter 9, verse 29 of the Koran: "Fight against those who do not believe in Allah ... from among the people of the Book, until they pay the jizyah and have been humiliated and brought low."

Enforced during the height of Islamic political power in the days of the caliphate, collection of the jizyah was abandoned by secularizing governments of the modern Middle East. But some of today's Islamist movements view the jizyah as a marker of the resurgence of Islam.

For years, Paulos Faraj Rahho, archbishop of Mosul's Chaldean Catholic community, had made jizyah payments to local militants on behalf of his diocese's Christians. Finally, as the security situation in Iraq improved, he refused any further payments. The result: in

February 2008, he was kidnapped and murdered. Eventually a member of al-Qaeda in Mesopotamia was convicted of the crime. Under such pressure, as of May 2017, some 80 percent of Iraq's Christian population has fled the country since the toppling of Saddam Hussein's government in 2003.[12]

In June 2009, colleagues of mine in Pakistan notified me of analogous recent developments in their country. Under the leadership of Lawrence John Saldanha, Catholic archbishop of Lahore, the National Commission for Justice and Peace (NCJP), Pakistan's leading human rights organization, has been vigilant in documenting abuses against religious minorities and other victims of sectarian violence. The NCJP brought to my attention the following two cases in particular.

In April 2009, Christian day-laborers residing in an impoverished part of Karachi known as Khuda ki Basti found warnings chalked on the walls of their neighborhood: "The Taliban are coming.... Be prepared to pay jizyah or embrace Islam." When the Christians registered their defiance by erasing the threats, ethnic Pashtuns resident in Karachi attacked the neighborhood, killing an eleven-year-old boy and injuring several men and women. The assailants torched homes and set fire to copies of the Bible.

The NCJP also noted that in Pakistan's Tribal Areas (notably Orakzai and Khyber Agency), a group calling itself *Lashkar-e Islam* (The army of Islam) has begun imposing the jizyah on local minority populations of Christians, Sikhs, and Hindus. Nearby in Pakistan's North-West Frontier Province, the *Tehrik-e Taliban-e Pakistan* (the Pakistan Taliban movement) has likewise targeted non-Muslims. At Saint Mary's School in Sangota (in the Swat Valley, where government troops have battled the Taliban for control), the school's classrooms, convent, and chapel were destroyed. Statues of the Buddha in the vicinity were also reportedly desecrated.

Whether in Pakistan, Iraq, or Yemen, such events point to an underlying issue: how Muslim-majority societies choose to view the existence of religious diversity in their midst.

[12] Maria Abi-Habib, "Christians Are Leaving the Middle East", *The Wall Street Journal*, May 13, 2017, pp. A1–10; Andrew E. Kramer, "For Iraqi Christians, Money Bought Survival", *The New York Times*, June 26, 2008, http://www.nytimes.com.

*A church in Sanaa—or even in Mecca?: The question
of religious pluralism in twenty-first-century Islam*

Which brings us back to the lack of churches in the city of Sanaa.
Some years ago, in an exchange between Saint John Paul II and Ali
Abdullah Saleh, president of Yemen, the pope asked President Saleh
to permit the construction of a church in Yemen's capital. The president promised he would see to it. That was years ago. Nothing ever
came of the promise. (And—given the current reality of Yemen's
ongoing forever-war—it is uncertain whether anything ever will.)

This recalls analogous dealings between the Vatican and Saudi
Arabia (a nation lacking any churches, despite the presence of well
over one million foreign Christian workers). In the 1990s, the Italian government had permitted the construction of a Saudi-financed
mosque (one of the largest in Europe) in Rome, a short distance from
Vatican City. Mosques in Rome make sense, given the large number
of Muslims resident there.

In a November 2007 meeting with Saudi monarch King Abdullah,
Pope Benedict XVI noted that the Gulf state of Qatar permitted the
building of a church consecrated to the Blessed Virgin Mary. Pope
Benedict asked that Saudi Arabia similarly permit the construction of
a Christian place of worship within the kingdom.

So far, nothing has come of the request, except for this reply by
Saudi religious scholar Anwar Ashiqi: "It would be possible to launch
official negotiations to construct a church in Saudi Arabia only
after the Pope and all the Christian churches recognize the prophet
Muhammad."[13] So much for reciprocal recognition of the universal
right to freedom of worship.

I raised this issue—President Saleh's broken promise and the lack
of churches in Sanaa and Saudi Arabia—in a conversation in June
2009 with a Sunni imam in Yemen's capital. An affable individual in
his early thirties, this imam directs a mosque in Sanaa and is known as
a hafiz (someone who has learned by heart the entirety of the Koran).

When I pointed out the disparity—mosques in Rome, no churches
in Sanaa—he said this struck him as right. Islam, he stated, is *al-din*

---

[13] Alexander Smoltczyk, "Saudi Church Project Runs into the Sand", *Der Spiegel Online*,
April 16, 2008, http://www.spiegel.de.

al-niha'i (the final, definitive religion). But Christianity and Judaism, he said, were religions from the past, outdated and superseded. "They may be permitted to exist," he continued, "but they shouldn't be allowed to propagate." A church in Sanaa might attract Yemeni Muslims, thereby facilitating *al-tansir*: the propagation of the Nazarene faith. Better, he said, to keep Yemen as nearly as possible 100 percent Muslim.

What this imam articulated was an attitude I encountered in all too many conversations in Sanaa: a resistance to religious pluralism. By pluralism I mean the notion that spiritual paths alternative to one's own have value; that these alternatives have something to teach us, even as they challenge us by their difference; and that our own religious identity and spiritual life are deepened by the self-reflection triggered in the encounter with diversity.

But such encounters happen best in settings where freedom of worship can flourish. In hindering the construction of Christian churches, countries like Yemen impoverish their own Islamic faith.

Christ crucified everywhere: Christian martyrdom under Pakistan's blasphemy law

But it is not only in Yemen that Muslims oppress Christians and thereby impoverish their own faith. I see something similar at work in Pakistan today. A good example—as you will see for yourself in what follows—has to do with a piece of Pakistani legislation that is designed to safeguard the honor of Islam's final prophet.

"We will not spare blasphemers": The killing of Salman Taseer

March 2017: thousands of pilgrims thronged to a shrine on the outskirts of Islamabad to honor the memory of a twenty-six-year-old Muslim on the first anniversary of his death. They hailed him as a "hero" and "martyr" and "holy warrior of Islam".

The holy warrior in question was a government security guard named Malik Mumtaz Qadri. His job had been to serve as a bodyguard for Salman Taseer, the governor of Punjab province. The reason the pilgrims hailed Mumtaz Qadri: he had murdered the man he was assigned to protect. And the reason the crowds called Qadri a martyr: he had been sentenced to death and hanged because of this crime.

Despite this act of violence and betrayal of trust, when Qadri first appeared in court, he was showered with rose petals by mobs of onlookers who approved of his shooting Governor Taseer. After Qadri's execution, his funeral procession became the occasion for violent protests by supporters who applauded his action and condemned the government for hanging him. They denounced Salman Taseer as an apostate from Islam who deserved his death.

And the reason for shooting Taseer? Mumtaz Qadri was angry that the governor had criticized Pakistan's notorious "blasphemy law" (Ordinance 295 B-C, which mandates life imprisonment for desecrating the Koran and death for dishonoring the prophet Muhammad). Governor Taseer had also spoken out in defense of a Christian woman named Aasiya Bibi. She has been imprisoned for years and sentenced to death on the flimsy basis of blasphemy accusations lodged by Muslim neighbors who had quarreled with her.

Pilgrims at Qadri's newly constructed shrine in 2017 were not shy in voicing their admiration for his act of violence and their support for the harshest possible application of the blasphemy law. Muslims at the site who were interviewed by *Washington Post* reporters made it clear that to question the viability or worth of Ordinance 295 was to smear the honor of Muhammad himself. One visitor justified Qadri's action as follows: "What he did was for the love of our prophet.... When someone insults our prophet, we cannot bear it. It is a matter of inexpressible emotions."[14]

Among the speakers addressing the crowds at Qadri's shrine was an influential Islamist preacher named Hanif Qureshi, who had publicly called for the murder of Governor Taseer. Now, with Taseer dead and his killer's corpse entombed beneath a giant green-tiled dome (green, the color of Islam's paradise), the preacher boasted of how popular Mumtaz Qadri has become among Muslims throughout

[14] Pamela Constable and Shaiq Hussain, "Pakistani Capital under Tight Security While Muslim Devotees Honor Man Who Assassinated a Liberal Governor", *The Washington Post*, March 1, 2017.

Pakistan: "Today there are millions of Qadri lovers, and there are many children named after Qadri, but there are none named after Salman Taseer or the apostate Asia Bibi.... The government tried to stop the people from participating in this gathering, but they cannot stop us forever. We will not spare blasphemers."[15]

Since Qadri's execution in 2016, many Pakistani Islamists have honored his memory by staging marches and protests that involve clashes with the police, throwing stones, and setting fires. They have also presented the government with a list of demands: the official recognition of Qadri as a "shaheed" (Islamic martyr); the execution of the imprisoned Christian woman Aasiya Bibi; the immediate imposition of the death penalty on all other persons alleged to have dishonored the prophet Muhammad; and the expulsion from Pakistan of members of the Ahmadiyyah denomination (a sect that is widely persecuted in Muslim countries for its belief that there can be prophets after the time of Muhammad).

What is terrifying about Ordinance 295 are the abuses built into this piece of legislation. A progressive-minded politician from Pakistan's National Assembly whom I interviewed in Islamabad listed what he called three substantive legal problems with this law. First, no evidence is required when filing a blasphemy complaint. The word of anyone claiming to be a witness is enough. Second, the alleged blasphemer is arrested and imprisoned as soon as the complaint is lodged. Defendants often remain in jail for months awaiting trial. Third, plaintiffs can make false accusations with little worry of punishment or any other legal repercussion.[16]

"I believe in my religion and in Jesus Christ": The crimes of Aasiya Bibi

Unsurprising, then, that this ordinance is often used to provide a high religious gloss for low-minded personal grudges. Take the case

---

[15] Ibid.

[16] For more on Pakistan's blasphemy ordinance, see David Pinault, *Notes from the Fortune-Telling Parrot: Islam and the Struggle for Religious Pluralism in Pakistan* (London: Equinox Publishing, 2008), pp. 38–58.

of Aasiya Bibi, the imprisoned Christian whom Governor Taseer had tried to defend. A Catholic from a rural district in the Punjab, she made a hardscrabble living harvesting fruit on fields belonging to local farmers. The Muslim women she worked with subjected her to sporadic harassment, telling her she should convert to Islam. She shrugged it off.

Until the day of the water quarrel. That was the day when, under a hot noontime sun, she paused in her harvest-work in the field and walked to a nearby well. She drew a bucket of water from the well and then used an old metal cup lying beside the well to ladle a drink for herself from the bucket. Thereafter she refilled the same cup and offered a drink to one of her fellow fruit-pickers.

That is when the trouble started. One of the women bellowed that this well water was now undrinkable and "dirtied" because a Christian had put her lips to it. A cry went up from the quickly forming crowd of Muslim workers: "You should convert to Islam to redeem yourself for your filthy religion."

Aasiya Bibi would do no such thing. Instead, she said: "I'm not going to convert. I believe in my religion and in Jesus Christ, who died on the Cross for the sins of mankind. What did your Prophet Muhammad ever do to save mankind? And why should it be me that converts instead of you?"[17]

Outspoken and feisty: a true braveheart. But she paid a price for her courage. Beaten with sticks, dragged through the village streets by an angry jeering mob, she was then flung into jail and charged with insulting the prophet of Islam. In accordance with Pakistan's blasphemy law, a judge sentenced Aasiya to death by hanging, while crowds hailed the sentence with cries of *Allahu akbar!*

That was in 2010. Since then, courageous attorneys—themselves under threat for pleading her case—have appealed this verdict and tried to save her from hanging. Eight years later, Aasiya Bibi is still in jail, still under sentence of death, and still awaiting the outcome of her latest appeal to Pakistan's highest court.

But there has been one hopeful development. In September 2017, European legislators drew attention to Aasiya's plight by nominating

[17] Asia Bibi and Anne-Isabelle Tollet, *Blasphemy: A Memoir: Sentenced to Death over a Cup of Water* (Chicago: Review Press, 2013), p. 21.

her for the Sakharov Prize, the European Union's most celebrated human-rights award.

Meanwhile, Islamist preachers promise that if she is ever released, crowds of the faithful will carry out the death sentence themselves.[18]

"Only a cross and a prayer book in his pockets": On the martyrdom of Javed Anjum

Aasiya Bibi's case is far from unusual. Pakistani advocacy groups such as the Catholic National Commission for Justice and Peace have argued for years that the nation's blasphemy law violates the spirit of Pakistan's own constitution. The commission's annually published *Human Rights Monitor* quotes Article 20 of the Constitution of Pakistan: "Every citizen shall have the right to profess, practice and propagate his religion." The *Monitor* documents numerous recent examples of how Pakistani Christians and other non-Muslims have been subjected to violence in retaliation for refusing to convert to Islam.[19]

One brutal instance from among many: the case of Javed Anjum. On May 2, 2004, this eighteen-year-old Catholic set out on foot to visit family members in a nearby Punjabi village. Along the way he paused to drink water from a tap outside the Jamia Hassan madrasa (Islamic school) in the district of Toba Tek Singh. Confronted by some of the seminary students and accused of being non-Muslim, he refused to deny his faith and instead confirmed that, yes, in fact he was Christian.

Things turned ugly fast. With the assistance of one of the madrasa's teachers, the students detained Javed by force and accused him of trying to steal the school's water pumps and faucets. They kept him locked up for five days, beating him with iron pipes and trying to force him to recite the Islamic creed professing allegiance to Allah and Muhammad.

---

[18] Madeeha Bakhsh, "Trial of Blasphemy Accused Asia Bibi 'Likely' to Resume in June", *Christians in Pakistan: Voice of Pakistani Christians*, April 21, 2017. Madeeha Bakhsh, "Asia Bibi Nominated for EU's Sakharov Prize", *Christians in Pakistan: Voice of Pakistani Christians*, September 14, 2017. Both articles are available on the website http://www.christiansinpakistan.com.

[19] Emmanuel Yousaf Mani, ed., *Human Rights Monitor 2006: A Report on the Religious Minorities in Pakistan* (Lahore: National Commission for Justice and Peace, 2006), p. 23.

The young Christian refused, insisting on adhering to his faith. After five days of torture, the madrasa students dumped him at a police station, calling him a thief. A week later he died of his injuries.

The *Monitor*'s report includes a photo of Javed Anjum from his student days: a handsome young man who looks right into the camera, poised, proud, and self-aware. The *Monitor* provides another photo as well, showing a rally by Christian protesters in Lahore denouncing his religiously motivated murder. One protester carries a placard shaped like a black tombstone. The tombstone reads: "Javed Anjum. Age: 18. Profession: Student. Crime: *Ghair Muslim Hona* (being non-Muslim)."[20]

Crime: being non-Muslim. This ironic and bitter comment highlights a recurrent motif in Pakistani Islamist politics: an inability to tolerate religious diversity.

Since Javed's death, the Pakistani bishop Joseph Coutts has spoken out at international gatherings on religious freedom, drawing attention to Javed's martyrdom and praising him as "the youth who was killed for refusing to deny Christ".[21]

Family and friends remember Javed now for "the solidity of his faith". Bishop Coutts says of this teen that "only a cross and a prayer book were found in his pockets when he died."[22]

A cross in his pockets; killed for refusing to deny Christ. I cannot help remembering the words of Paul, another martyr killed giving witness to his faith—faith in a God who suffers in solidarity alongside us: "I have been crucified with Christ" (Gal 2:20).

One need spend only a short time in Pakistan to see Christ crucified everywhere.

"Islam is in danger": Siege mentality and the popularity of Pakistan's blasphemy law

For years critics have pointed out that Ordinance 295 B–C has been used as a way to hound Christians and other religious minorities in

---

[20] Ibid., pp. 22–23.
[21] "Pakistani Bishop: 'Don't Forget Javed Anjum, Killed for Refusing to Deny Christ'", June 7, 2006, http://www.Asia News.it.
[22] Qaiser Felix, "Killers of Catholic Youth, Javed Anjum, Sentenced", June 3, 2006, http://www.Asia News.it.

Pakistan. But no government to date has dared to repeal this blasphemy law. In my own visits to Pakistan, I have seen why. The law is simply too popular.

Judging from interviews in both the Punjab and localities in Pakistan's North-West Frontier such as Peshawar, I would say the blasphemy ordinance is widely accepted by many Muslims because it is seen as a useful weapon for the defense of Islam.

A Muslim professor in Peshawar explained to me that when rumors of blasphemy or Koran desecration circulate, many mosque preachers warn their congregations that *Islam khatar mayn hay*: "Islam is in danger." This sense of endangerment comes from a widespread perception among Pakistani Muslims that they are a beleaguered minority.

Surprising, since 97 percent of Pakistan's population is Muslim. But it makes sense if we take into account the feeling many Pakistanis have that they are overshadowed and threatened by neighboring India—which is not only much bigger than Pakistan but overwhelmingly Hindu. Hinduism is perceived by many Pakistani Muslims as fundamentally inimical to Islam.

For many Pakistanis, what keeps their country from being swallowed up is its Islamic identity, symbolized by reverence for the Koran and devotion to the prophet Muhammad's honor. Ordinance 295 is popular because it is seen as safeguarding both of these.

And in a country that was founded as a homeland for the subcontinent's Muslims and that is officially known as an "Islamic republic", to be Christian is to be susceptible to the charge that one's patriotism and national loyalty are somehow deficient. Christians become recurrent targets.

Yet Pakistan's Christian community has proven to be resilient. In 2002, I attended a Palm Sunday service in Lahore's Cathedral of the Resurrection, shortly after terror attacks on churches in Islamabad and Bahawalpur. Only a few foreigners were in attendance: some Africans, a few Brits. But there were hundreds of local Christians, more than I had ever seen at this church in previous visits.

The sermon that morning began with a familiar tale, how Jesus' entry into Jerusalem became a path that led to the Cross. But then the sermon became explicitly topical. The preacher spoke openly of the Islamabad and Bahawalpur massacres. "We don't know if such acts will continue," he told the assembled worshippers, "but we have to remember we are not walking this path alone." Christ, too, journeyed along this road, as did his early followers.

And Christ journeys now, he said, with the members of this congregation. "This is what enables us to endure any persecution."

"At risk of paralysis": The wide-ranging harm inflicted by Pakistan's blasphemy law

Most of the individuals I interviewed in Pakistan about the blasphemy law preferred to remain anonymous. This is understandable, given the volatile politics surrounding Ordinance 295.

One exception was Lawrence Saldanha, the Catholic archbishop of Lahore. When I interviewed him in 2005 in his office in Lahore's cathedral, he was the president of Pakistan's Catholic Bishops' Conference. He was also at the forefront of a controversial movement to repeal Ordinance 295's harsh penalties for blasphemy against the Koran and Muhammad. He was fighting for the repeal, he told me, because this harmful ordinance—which is worded so as to encourage slander against anyone designated an "enemy of Islam"—has provided a legal rationale for inciting interreligious violence and the persecution of minorities.

But Christians are not the only ones who suffer because of Pakistan's blasphemy law. The Catholic Bishops' Conference has pointed out that 50 percent of the individuals imprisoned under Ordinance 295 are Muslim. They were denounced as apostates by fellow Muslims—whether out of religious zealotry or sheer opportunism—on charges of questioning the Koran or showing insufficient reverence for the prophet Muhammad's legacy. The remaining 50 percent of those imprisoned are Christians, Hindus, and Ahmadis. (The latter are legally classified in Pakistan as non-Muslims even though they themselves claim Islam as their identity.)

After being charged under 295 B–C and publicly identified as having "insulted the faith", dozens of people in recent years have been snatched from the authorities by angry mobs and dragged through the streets and beaten to death. Most of these victims of extrajudicial brutality are Muslim. Those labeled "apostates" and "traitors" to

Islam are regarded with far more hatred, and as far worse, than mere non-Muslims.

The fact that Muslims use Ordinance 295 to indict fellow Muslims points up the larger harm inflicted on Pakistan as a whole by this legislation. A Lahore-based Muslim intellectual told me. "295 makes it impossible to think out loud about Islam freely. We're at risk of paralysis, both as a nation and as a religious tradition."

For the good of all its citizens, it is time for Pakistan to repeal its blasphemy law.

CHAPTER 14

ISLAM, CHRISTIANITY, AND PRE-ISLAMIC TRADITIONS: PLURALISM VERSUS INTOLERANCE IN THE INDONESIAN ARCHIPELAGO

What lies coiled in the coffer: My introduction to local forms of faith in East Java

My host paused with his hand on the lid as we stood before the long wooden box. "Are you ready", he asked, "to see the 'shawl' of Mbah Jarik?" What awaited me in that container was a glimpse of Indonesia's ancient Muslim traditions—traditions that are syncretistic, animist-tinged, tolerant of other faiths, and very much under attack today by puritanically minded Islamists.

Mbah Jarik (the name means "Grandma Sarong" in Javanese) is the *penunggu* (literally, the "watchman" or, more generally, the "resident guardian spirit") of a neighborhood called Kampong Candi Badut in the east Javanese city of Malang. The "shawl", I knew, was an animal that had been captured in the woods on the edge of the kampong: an area known for its fresh-water spring, steep forested ravine, thick bamboo groves, and numerous snakes that emerge at night to hunt for prey.

I nodded in response to my host's invitation, and he removed the box's lid. Coiled inside lay a ten-foot-long python. My guide enthused over its color, rippling waves of white, black, and chocolate brown. "Like the patterns on a shawl", he explained.

As we spoke, the snake suddenly opened its eyes. This was one garment that was very much alive.

"*Ular ini*", I was told, "*adalah hewan peliharaan Mbah Jarik*": This snake is Mbah Jarik's pet. Villagers bring this python offerings of fresh flowers and chickens. The flowers are for honoring the *roh*, or resident spirit with which the animal is associated. (The spirits are nourished as they inhale the flowers' pleasing fragrance.) The meat is for satisfying the snake's more substantive appetites.

Several villagers told me of dreams in which they saw Mbah Jarik "wearing her shawl": appearing to the dreamer with a python draped about her neck. Informants explained to me that *penunggu--penunggu* such as Mbah Jarik typically take up residence in trees (often banyans) situated in the liminal area between village and forest. Like other nature spirits, Mbah Jarik will protect the locality's human community as long as humans show her honor by doing no unnecessary violence to the kampong's river, vegetation, or wildlife. (When I asked about the propriety of caging a snake, my hosts said Mbah Jarik would let it escape back into the jungle if it were not treated respectfully.)

I was told of one recent incident where a *tukang* (manual laborer), eager to cut as much wood as possible with a chainsaw, carelessly sliced into a stand of sacred *bambu kuning* (yellow bamboo). When I located and interviewed this man, he told me of a dream he had experienced the night after his transgression: he was back in the sacred grove with his chainsaw, but in the dream he sliced into a beehive.

Immediately an angry Mbah Jarik stood before him, while the bees swarmed in a loud buzz above her. She cried out, "Attack him, my children!", and he ran and ran, pursued by the bees, until he awoke in a sweat. The next morning he visited Pak Warto, keeper of Mbah Jarik's "pet", and paid for special offerings to be given the python as a visible demonstration of his repentance for the harm he had done to the spirit's forest dwelling.

Pak Warto, the python's keeper, is also the *orang ketua*, or headman, of Kampong Candi Badut. The neighborhood's population is almost entirely Muslim; but the locality's most famous monument, Candi Badut, is an eighth-century Hindu temple. Still visible, as one tours the site, are the remains of statuary such as a multi-armed figure of the warrior goddess Durga.

What I found especially intriguing about this site is that it is still very much in use—by the Muslims of the local kampong. Pak Warto—village headman, python-minder, and intermediary between the communities of humans and nature spirits—visits this temple to make offerings whenever a moment of crisis arises in the kampong.

One of the persons who taught me about the shrine at Candi Badut was a Javanese Catholic priest named Tomas Hatmoko. As we toured the site together, Father Tomas said something that lingered in my thoughts: "These villagers know that over a thousand years ago, holy people lived and prayed here and left a lingering influence that makes this a special sacred place."

Wildlife protected by tree spirits: The "palace cave" in the forest of Alas Purwo

To this day, pre-Islamic temples and sacred forests throughout east Java attract worshippers of many faiths. At such sites, I have met Javanese Catholics, Hindus, and Muslims. Villagers pray before certain trees where indwelling spirits expedite their petitions to God.

Traditional Indonesian Islam, in other words, is highly syncretistic—which is one reason why this Southeast Asian country is my favorite place for fieldwork. Home to the world's largest Muslim population, it legally acknowledges the practice of five faiths: Islam, Hinduism, Buddhism, Confucianism, and Christianity (Protestantism and Catholicism are each individually recognized). Your KTP (Kartu Tanda Penduduk, or national identity card) indicates to which of the five you belong. Leaving the space blank (or requesting an alternative designation—"agnostic", say, or "atheist") is not an option.

The majority of Indonesians (over 85 percent) are Muslim, many of them adherents of a tolerant form of Islam that blends Sufi mysticism with the region's Hindu-Buddhist legacy and the kind of animist nature rituals I saw at Candi Badut. When my Javanese friends found out about my fascination with the region's still-surviving forms of ancient worship, they recommended Alas Purwo as a good place to find them.

Alas Purwo (the name means "primordial forest") is one of the most secluded locales on the island of Java, situated in the far southeastern corner of the island. Comprising savannah grasslands, mangrove swamps, oceanfront beach, and thickly forested jungle, Alas Purwo is many hours' drive, and a world away, from the turmoil of urban centers like Jakarta.

In the summer of 2014, I was lucky enough to go to Alas Purwo. My goal was to visit Goa Istana, the "Palace Cave", a hilltop grotto within this forest that for centuries has been used for meditation by ascetic practitioners.

My guide and I walked along a path that led past thickets of towering bamboo. Macaques and *lutung-lutung* (leaf monkeys) leapt from branch to branch in the trees overhead. Above us soared a sea eagle. I glimpsed a peacock in the brush. Rangers we encountered (the government has declared Alas Purwo a national park) showed us camera--trap photos of other residents more commonly glimpsed at night: leopards, *kuching hutan* (jungle cats), and pangolins (scaly anteaters).

This impressed me. On islands like Sumatra and Borneo, poachers have trapped every creature they can and shipped many—especially pangolins—to China, to feed that country's ever-expanding appetite for animal body parts associated with Chinese traditional medicine.

Why, I asked, have so many animals survived here in Alas Purwo?

Because, my guide explained, this place is considered *angker* (eerie, haunted).

He saw he had my interest and continued. Alas Purwo, he said, is full of *penunggu* (a word you will recall from Candi Badut): guardian nature spirits that inhabit the tallest and noblest of the trees that surrounded us everywhere along the trail. These spirits sense the intentions of those who enter this forest, he said, and if people enter with bad intentions, well: *mereka berputar-putar dan tidak pernah keluar* (They will go round and round and never get out). The result, he concluded, is that poachers are afraid to come here and harm the wildlife.

By now we had reached our goal. Worn steps led us uphill past statues of club-bearing guardian demons. As its name suggested, the "Palace Cave" was spacious. Once our eyes adjusted to the dark, we saw blankets and matting spread out on the ground; and seated quietly within the cave was a group of five men.

Not at all put out by the intrusion, they welcomed us warmly. One, a friendly man in his forties named Sri Wijoyo, explained they had come on foot from Surakarta (in central Java: the journey had taken a month) to meditate here and acquire *kesaktian* (mystical power, "by means of which", said Wijoyo, "we can help the many people who need help").

I asked what religion they belonged to. "Islam KTP," they replied (Islam, according to their identity cards). But they also thought of themselves as members of *agama Jawa primitif* (Java's primordial faith, that is, Javanese animism). They had been *bertapa* (secluding themselves as hermits) here for several weeks already, Wijoyo said, and in that time they had met fellow pilgrims who had come to the Palace Cave from various parts of Bali and Java, some of them Muslims, others Hindus or Christians. But all honored this site.

We chatted for hours (amid occasional distractions—bats flitting by in the gloom and marauding monkeys that snatched a bag of food). Wijoyo outlined what Javanism meant to him: prioritizing contemplative quiet over noisy display, the "*halus*" (the refined and the spiritual) over the "*kasar*" (that which is coarse or crude). Javanists, he said, prefer coexistence to confrontation, and they revere the many points in the island's landscape where cosmic forces are made manifest, no matter what religion may be officially associated with these sites.

These manifestation points include not only caves but also mountaintops and ancient temples. One of the most famous of these ancient shrines is called Candi Panataran; and despite the fact that it is a sacred Hindu site, the worshippers who cluster there today (as you will see below) include not only Hindus but also Muslims, Christians, and Javanese animists.

The four watchmen atop the volcano: A visit to Panataran Temple

"The Holy Ghost", explained the woman who had been afflicted by a curse, "took possession of this site long before the Hindus or the Muslims arrived." A chance chat at an ancient shrine in East Java gave me insights into Indonesia's tradition of religious pluralism—and the emergent puritanism threatening that tradition.

It began with a visit to the ruined thirteenth-century temple complex of Candi Panataran, located at the foot of the still-active volcano known as Gunung Kelud. As I wandered the site, schoolchildren toured the shrines. The girls' uniforms included Islamic veils that kept their hair modestly covered. On a stage nearby, preparations were underway for a nighttime shadow-puppet play and Javanese gamelan concert.

Panataran is a remnant of the pre-Islamic past—its walls writhe with carved monkey gods in combat with demons from the Hindu

Ramayana epic—but most Javanese Muslims today regard this place as part of their heritage.

Panataran was part of the Majapahit Empire, a realm based on the island of Java that ruled from Sumatra to New Guinea and combined the religions of Hinduism and Buddhism with local animistic faiths. Although eventually overwhelmed by Muslim conquerors in the fifteenth and sixteenth centuries, the Majapahit kingdom is still recalled proudly by the Javanese today for its onetime political dominance that prefigured the rise of Indonesia. And the most palpable traces (both architectural and spiritual) of the island's pre-Islamic heritage are in the eastern part of Java, for it was here that many non-Muslims fled in the face of Islamic conquest.

More intriguing than the temple carvings was something pointed out to me by Mas Bayu, the Javanese friend with whom I wandered the site. Visible inside one of the shrines was a young woman who sat alone and immobile on the stone floor, apparently absorbed in meditation or prayer. *To whom or what is she praying?*, I wondered.

A turn in the weather allowed me to ask. Two hours into the visit, a storm made my friend and me run for cover under a plastic awning propped up on poles near a perimeter wall. The monsoon drove other visitors to join us. "Do you recognize her?" asked Mas Bayu, and he nodded at one of the newcomers—the young woman we had seen seated in the shrine.

Not at all put out by questions from a rain-soaked foreigner, the woman (she gave her name as Veronica) explained she came here often. Troubled for much of her life with bad health because of a hereditary family curse, one day she felt the impulse ("called" or "summoned" was how she put it) to come to Panataran. Here she met a *dukun* (a Muslim holy man or healer) named Muhammad who happened to work as a custodian at the site. And in fact the healer joined us under the awning a few minutes after her arrival; so the two of them answered our questions.

When she mentioned that her *dukun* had instructed her to pray here frequently because of the curative powers of Panataran, I asked Veronica about her religious identity. "Javanese Catholic", she explained, and she said her Christian faith did not preclude her praying at this site. The Roh Suci (Holy Ghost) chose Panataran as its residence before the world was created, centuries before the Majapahit kingdom; and it was the Holy Ghost's aura that drew first Hindus and—subsequently—Muslims to this spot.

Muhammad the healer had his own explanation. When I asked how he effected his cures (and he works with many clients), he explained that he invokes *empat penunggu*, the "four watchmen" or guardian spirits that—according to local belief—reside atop the nearby volcano.

I could not resist inquiring how he squared such invocations with the Islamic monotheistic insistence on God's absolute oneness. Of course, Allah is unique in his sovereignty, he agreed, "but Allah is on His throne, and He uses *wakil-wakil* (representatives, substitutes) for immediate dealings with men in this world."

The difference in religious nomenclature troubled neither Veronica nor Muhammad. "*Dia membuka pintu gaib*", she said reverently of her healer: "He opens the door of the unseen."

Through that door I had glimpsed this much: a Muslim guru invoking mountain spirits and counseling a Christian woman to practice meditation at an ancient Hindu site. This creative blending of faiths is still strong in Java (especially in the eastern end of the island), but it is increasingly under attack today, as I was soon to learn.

On a subsequent visit (I was lucky enough to go to Panataran several times), I studied the iconography still visible on many of the shrines at this site. Intact and undamaged on the walls are old carvings of goddesses, devils, and winged serpent deities.

As I walked about, the thought came to me: Imagine how long a place like this would last in today's Afghanistan or the war-battered Iraqi-Syrian domain of the newly formed Islamic State caliphate. Whether it is the giant statues of the Bamiyan Buddhas or the tombs of Shia and Sufi saints, the Taliban and Islamic State have destroyed wherever they can both non-Islamic monuments and Muslim sanctuaries deemed heretical.

I voiced this thought to a worshipper I met at Panataran, a young man who identified himself as a Muslim but who also revered the shrine's resident *penunggu*. He said he was well aware that militantly minded preachers in Indonesia talk constantly of "Islamicizing" Java.

But maybe it could work in the other direction, he mused. Maybe people like himself, Muslims who were also adherents of the island's "primordial faith", could exert some influence.

Kami mau menjawakan Islam, he said: "We would like to 'Javanize' Islam."

To which I could only reply: Amen, friend. Amen.

But it is not only Java's pluralist tradition that makes Indonesia my favorite place in the Islamic world. It is also because it was in East Java I first had the chance to help animals that had been rescued from wildlife traffickers. This volunteer work led to some strange adventures. Now is a good moment to tell you that story.

Interfaith collaboration in Indonesia: Responding to animal suffering at a wildlife rescue center on the island of Java

Sewing up the torn paw of a Javanese leaf monkey, with the help of an Indonesian veterinarian, might seem an untried and unexpected form of interfaith dialogue. But for me it proved productive.

The setting for this encounter was a wildlife rescue center in the hill country of East Java, where I first worked as a volunteer in 2007. The organization that runs this center is called ProFauna Indonesia.

Rosek Nursahid, an Indonesian Muslim biologist and the founder of ProFauna, established this nongovernmental organization in 1994 to counter the illegal trafficking in wildlife that has increased in recent years as the logging industry reduces the available woodland habitat in Java, Sumatra, Kalimantan (Indonesian Borneo), and West Papua (the Indonesian part of New Guinea). The rate of deforestation has accelerated because of expanding foreign markets.

Many people are aware of illegal logging in Indonesia. Less well-publicized is the tragedy suffered by Indonesia's wildlife as a consequence of such activities. Poachers—who find their access facilitated by roads carved through the jungle by the logging corporations' bulldozers—net thousands of members of endangered species, from pangolins to orangutans.

Some of these captive animals are sold as pets to Indonesian households. Others are trafficked all over the world, but the foremost market is Communist China. Members of its emergent middle class display limitless appetites for animal body parts that are believed to have special powers in traditional medicine or as aphrodisiacs.

Under Rosek Nursahid's leadership, ProFauna has fought to stop this trade.

Rosek's approach is twofold: activism (rescuing animals, spurring the government to enact and enforce Indonesian environmental laws, and—when necessary—confronting animal traffickers) and education (holding classes and workshops at the camp for students, teachers, government officials, and other members of the Indonesian public). ProFauna's founder considers especially important the ecology camps it runs for Indonesian children. "By educating them in environmental awareness and respect for animals," he told me in one of several conversations we had, "we are investing in the next generation."

As a volunteer, I was integrated into the daily round of chores linked to the care and rehabilitation of the animals at the center: preparing food, cleaning out cages and habitats, and interacting directly with the animals inside their habitats. Aside from learning, in this immediate and direct way, what ProFauna does to rehabilitate animals and prepare them for reentry into the wild, I benefited from the opportunity to interact with Indonesian ProFauna staff members of diverse backgrounds. I learned from Muslims, Hindus, and Christians what it means to be a person of faith who is also committed to environmental stewardship. And as the only foreigner in the camp, I drew plenty of attention and had my share of questions to answer.

One of the most emotionally challenging tasks I faced involved visits to *pasar burung* (bird markets, where in fact all kinds of animals are sold) in Denpasar and the port of Surabaya. In these cities as elsewhere throughout the archipelago, protected species are sold by traffickers to the highest bidder. In conjunction with ProFauna members, who wished to expose such dealers, I presented myself as a foreign buyer.

In these markets, it helps to have a strong stomach. Thousands of animals are crammed into cages in hot airless sheds. One enclosure held sparrows that had been spray-painted with metallic hard-gloss purples and reds.

"Why do this to them?" I asked.

"To draw customers", was the reply.

Another enclosure held a magnificent serpent eagle confined to a cage so small it could neither stand nor flex its wings. A dealer amused himself trying to force a banana down its throat. The bird refused with a fierce, unyielding toss of its head.

Nearby, a dozen monkeys watched as we passed. Each was chained by the neck. Their eyes commanded attention. Plain to see were all too recognizable emotions—dejection, anger, despair. *Mereka sesungguhnya menderita*, said the ProFauna staffer at my side: "They really do suffer."

They really do suffer. This truth stayed with me as I sorted my notes for a lecture back at the ProFauna rescue center. (Rosek had arranged for me to give a workshop and discussion on the topic of "Perspectives offered by world religions on wildlife and environmental issues".) ProFauna staff and officials from the Indonesian government's Department of Forestry attended. In addition, members of the local Muslim, Hindu, Buddhist, and Christian communities were invited to participate.

Representatives of each religion took turns responding to the points I presented. This was followed by a general discussion on how each faith can contribute insights to environmental issues. Among the topics we discussed: the morally problematic sense of overlordship and entitlement that Christians and Muslims have often derived from their readings of scripture. A point of agreement among all those present was the need for religious educators to emphasize mankind's responsibility for environmental stewardship.

In my discussion, I noted how in recent years some Muslim writers (notably the Iranian scholar Kaveh Afrasiabi and the Malaysian human rights activist Farish Ahmad Noor) have called on members of their faith to embrace environmentalism as a topic that concerns Muslims as both a global and Islamic issue. Noor acknowledges that for too long many Muslim thinkers have been preoccupied with collective-identity agendas and a defensive-siege mentality that have precluded interfaith cooperation on global crises.[1]

Too often, Muslim scholars—like some of their Abrahamic kin in the Christian community—have regarded the environment in

---

[1] See Farish A. Noor's discussion of "Globalization, the Environment, and the Future of Us All", in *Progressive Muslims: On Justice, Gender, and Pluralism*, ed. Omid Safi (Oxford: Oneworld, 2003), pp. 331–32. See also Kaveh Afrasiabi, *Mahdism, Shiism, and Communicative Eco-Theology* (Charleston, S.C.: CreateSpace, 2015).

terms of the simplistic formula: Submission to God entitles the faithful to exploitative mastery over the earth. Taken to its extreme, this triumphalism results in an adversarial and manipulative attitude toward nature.

But resources—often overlooked—for countering such trends exist within the Islamic tradition, especially in Sufi mysticism. The contemporary Iranian-American scholar Seyyed Hossein Nasr argues that "Nature in Islamic spirituality is ... not the adversary but the friend of the traveler upon the spiritual path." He sees in nature an invitation to meditate and behold the "signs of Allah" in the created world. Nasr uses this as the basis for proposing an Islamic theology of environmental stewardship.[2]

His imagery of the spiritual traveler accords well with the long-standing Christian conception of men as pilgrims: we should take a contemplative rather than exploitative approach to the world through which we journey.

But in my talk, I also emphasized points where Christianity and Islam sharply differ. I discussed Abraham Joshua Heschel's Jewish theology of the "divine pathos" and how the *shekhina* (God's presence, manifested among us on earth) voluntarily experienced exodus and exile along with the Israelites. Jürgen Moltmann Christianized this theology via the concept of a "crucified God". Moltmann's is a kenotic theology that emphasizes the divine quality of empathetic suffering, a suffering entered into freely by a God who desires ardently to experience a loving solidarity with the world he brought into being.[3]

In my presentation, I outlined how Heschel and Moltmann's thought has been applied in recent years to environmentalist concerns. Theologian Mark Wallace argues that, just as Christ's crucifixion constituted a "terrifying event of loss and suffering within the inner life of God-self", so, too, does God continue today to suffer in the Trinitarian Person of the Holy Spirit. "The Spirit is Christ-like or cruciform", says Wallace, "because she suffers the same violent

---

[2] Seyyed Hossein Nasr, ed., *Islamic Spirituality: Foundations* (London: Routledge & Kegan Paul, 1987), p. 345.

[3] Jürgen Moltmann, "The Crucified God", *Theology Today* 31, no. 1 (April 1974): 6–18. For an introduction to Heschel's thought, see Michael A. Chester, *Divine Pathos and Human Being: The Theology of Abraham Joshua Heschel* (Portland, Ore.: Mitchell, 2005).

fate as did Jesus—but now a suffering not confined to the onetime event of the cross, insofar as the Spirit experiences daily the continual degradation of the earth and its inhabitants."[4]

The Javanese Buddhists in my audience had no problem with all this. They responded with tales from the Jatakas (stories of the Buddha's earlier incarnations): how a prince was so moved with pity for a starving tigress and its cubs that he offered his own body as food; how the Buddha in various cycles of existence took the form of wild animals, who sacrificed their lives to ease the suffering of others.[5]

Some Muslims at the workshop evinced discomfort with the notion of divine vulnerability. After all (as you will recall from previous chapters), the Koran characterizes Allah as "the Mighty", "the Conqueror", and "He who is free from any wants or needs"—names that are far from Christian incarnational notions of a wounded Spirit or crucified God.

Where we overcame our theological differences was in our shared work at the camp, with the forest animals that had been rescued from the poachers and smugglers' markets. For several days, I helped Dr. Wulan, a skilled veterinarian and a devout Muslim, who always wore her hair carefully covered in a headscarf as she worked in her surgery. One day we treated a Sumatran gibbon whose skin was infested with parasites; the next we sutured a leaf monkey's torn foot. (Within forty-eight hours, the sutures tore open, forcing us to stitch the wound again, so this was one monkey's paw with which I became well acquainted.)

I was impressed by the care Dr. Wulan took in reassuring these creatures, stroking their fur, talking to them gently, and doing what she could to ease their very evident fear. Her actions reminded me of *hadiths* (sayings attributed to Muhammad) in which the prophet of Islam encouraged Muslims to lessen the suffering of animals.[6]

---

[4] Mark I. Wallace, "The Wounded Spirit as the Basis for Hope in an Age of Radical Ecology", in *Christianity and Ecology: Seeking the Well-Being of Earth and Humans*, eds. Dieter T. Hessel and Rosemary Radford Ruether (Cambridge, Mass.: Harvard University Press, 2000), pp. 51–72.

[5] For an example of Jatakas involving the Buddha's self-sacrifice on behalf of animals, see "The Bodhisattva and the Hungry Tigress", in *Buddhist Scriptures*, ed. and trans. Edward Conze (London: Penguin, 1959), pp. 24–26.

[6] Richard C. Foltz, *Animals in Islamic Tradition and Muslim Cultures* (Oxford: Oneworld, 2006), pp. 17–27.

For Allah is also known as gracious and merciful—and these are attributes of God on which both Muslims and Christians can agree.

"Just preaching and good counsel": A close-up encounter with the Islamic Defenders Front

But on a subsequent visit to ProFauna's camp, in 2011, I heard how this Indonesia I had learned to love—its wildlife and forests, its nature worship and pluralism—was coming under attack. The attack was being launched by an Islamist group that was altogether new to me. It is known by the acronym FPI, I was told. The letters stand for *Front Pembela Islam*: the "Islamic Defenders Front".

The FPI arose in conversation one evening in the camp as I shared a late-night supper with Rosek Nursahid. We sat on the open-air dining room veranda as a December monsoon rainburst lashed the thatched roof overhead. I told Rosek of my recent visit to Panataran Temple and my encounter with the healer who invoked the *penunggu* spirits of Mount Kelud.

He replied by telling me of the many shrines he has seen in rural Java that are consecrated to local *penunggu*. The shrines are built beside trees such as the giant *pohon beringin* (banyan) where the *penunggu* are believed to reside. There is a longstanding custom of villagers revering the banyans and praying before these trees, in the belief that the indwelling spirit will expedite petitions to Allah.

But the tragedy is that this folk custom has drawn the anger of the Islamic Defenders Front. Rosek described how FPI members have launched a campaign of intimidation, raiding villages at night, cutting down trees associated with *penunggu* veneration, and denouncing worshippers as kuffar (infidels).

Such tactics are characteristic of the FPI. The group began in 1998, as the dictatorial Suharto regime's "New Order" disintegrated and Indonesia's emergent democracy opened up space for long-suppressed Islamist movements. The group's website announces its purpose: *Pelayanan ummat dan pembela agama* (Service to the community of believers and defense of the faith). A flashing headline on the website proclaims, "Allah is our goal; Muhammad is our model; the Koran is our guiding text"—a statement that echoes Article 5 of the Covenant of Hamas (the Gaza-based Palestinian group that arose from Egypt's Muslim Brotherhood). The FPI's website statement concludes: "Jihad is our path of struggle; a martyr's death is our hope."

The Islamic Defenders Front interprets such struggle as a campaign to Islamicize Indonesian society, with the long-term goal of imposing sharia law throughout the nation. FPI members first gained national attention for their vigilante attacks on nightclub customers, prostitutes, and *bancis* (a term used to categorize transvestites and members of Indonesia's gay and transgender communities). An Indonesian friend described to me her disgust at seeing televised news footage of FPI puritans harassing a *banci* while the victim begged for mercy: "They were not just trying to enforce some moral code", she recalled. "They were trying to inflict as much humiliation as possible."

The Defenders Front won further notoriety in June 2012 by protesting a Lady Gaga concert that was scheduled for Jakarta. Indonesian fans had purchased over 50,000 advance tickets to see the American popstar perform. But threats of violence by FPI leaders forced her to cancel the show. Adherents of the Defenders Front marched through the capital's streets holding signs that proclaimed, "O Allah, protect me from the temptation of Satan Gaga, the accursed!"[7]

The FPI casts a wide net. Its members engage in violence against adherents of the Ahmadiyyah, a sect widely loathed in Muslim countries for their belief that prophecy did not end with the seventh-century death of Muhammad. FPI militants frequently target churches and warn of the nation's imminent "Christianization". In 2011, FPI members were sentenced to jail terms of only a few months after being convicted of stabbing a pastor of the Batak Christian Protestant Church and severely beating worshippers at an outdoor prayer service in Bekasi, West Java. Criminal penalties for such assaults tend to be minimal; the national government in Jakarta fears being seen as unfriendly to Islam.[8]

It was not until 2012 that I myself had a direct and up-close encounter with this militant group. For in October of that year, while visiting friends at ProFauna's wildlife rescue center, I received a kind

---

[7] Maria Natalia, "FPI Demo Tolak Lady Gaga di Mabes Polri" ("Islamic Defenders Front Demonstration at Police Headquarters Rejects Lady Gaga"), *Kompas*, May 25, 2012, http://www.Kompas.com; translated from the Indonesian by D. Pinault.

[8] "Bekasi Assault on a Protestant Church: Mild Sentences for Islamic Leaders", *Asia News*, February 24, 2011, http://www.AsiaNews.it.

of summons-via-text-message from the Islamic Defenders Front. Its adherents had heard of my interest in tree shrines, guardian spirits, and other "deviant" forms of the faith. I was told the local FPI leader wanted me to come to his headquarters so he could chat with me in person. He would tell me what was and what was not truly part of Islam.

A chance too good to be missed—but my friends did not want me to go. They were scared and told me I should be, too. (In fact, I was—but I was also adrenalinated by the prospect of fresh data.) These FPI people, they warned me, are quick to quarrel, quick to fight.

But, in the end, I went—and so did four of my Javanese friends. Safety in numbers.

And, in fact, it all went more or less fine. The FPI authority in question was one Habib Abdullah, and we met at the group's regional headquarters in his home in the East Javanese city of Malang.

The first thing he wanted me to know was that although he was Jakarta-born, nonetheless he came from fine Arab stock: his family had its origins in the Arabian peninsula and the town of Tarim in the Hadramaut valley of southern Yemen. This, he said with satisfaction, gave him a certain status—which I could see from how his followers fawned over him. (This exchange reminded me of Joseph Conrad's East Indies tale *Lord Jim* and a character from this novel named Sherif Ali. Claiming Arab lineage and descent from the prophet Muhammad, Sherif Ali creates a religious movement—partly charismatic, wholly piratical—and gathers a band of armed followers. With these men he terrorizes the island of Patusan.)

Once we had all complimented Habib Abdullah on his genealogy, I asked him to talk about how he saw the FPI's mission. "If people commit sins in private," he replied promptly, "it is between them and Allah. But we focus on things people do in public, activities that give a bad example and corrupt the community." This, he added, was all part of *al-amr bi'l-ma'ruf wa'l-nahy 'an al-munkar* (the promotion of virtue and the prevention of vice, a Koranically derived expression that the Taliban also love to cite).[9] He took evident pleasure in quoting the phrase in Arabic.

---

[9] Koran 3:104, 3:114, 9:71, 9:112. For the Taliban's use of the phrase, see Ahmed Rashid, *Taliban: Militant Islam, Oil and Fundamentalism in Central Asia* (New Haven: Yale University Press, 2000), p. 217 (which provides "a sample of Taliban decrees relating to women and other cultural issues").

Habib gave me an example of how the FPI prohibits vice. During the most recent Ramadan season (a time meant for heightened piety), a man was selling liquor at a shop not far from a mosque in Malang. (Indonesia differs from other Muslim-majority nations like Saudi Arabia in permitting the sale of alcohol.) A group of FPI enforcers went to his shop and offered the vendor what Habib Abdullah smilingly described as *dakwah dan nasihat* (preaching of the Islamic message and offering of good counsel). After a scolding and warning, he said, they stripped the man's shop of liquor and confiscated all his bottles.

How did the vendor take all this, I wondered aloud.

Another smile from Habib: *Ya dia mengakui bahwah dia bersalah*— Oh, he admitted he was wrong.

But didn't that amount to intimidation and violence?

Not at all, came the reply. Just preaching and good counsel.

Which, Habib Abdullah went on to say, was exactly what the FPI tried to offer when its enforcers targeted nightclubs in Jakarta and other Javanese cities and told the proprietors their activities were unislamic and they should shut down. It was only when the nightclub owners and customers resisted this "good counsel", he said, that fighting broke out. He claimed his followers fought only in self-defense—something fully permitted by the Koran.

Same thing, he said, with the *waria*. (*Waria* is a slang term derived from *wanita-pria*: "woman-man" or "she-male".) Also with the *bancis*. (The word is applied to people who are gay, transgender, or transvestite.) "When we go on patrol and find them on the street," said Habib, "we try to explain to them there should be no overlap between men and women in their roles, rights, and responsibilities. Homosexuality should not be permitted. It should be forbidden." How men and women dress, how they behave: the boundaries, he said, should be clear. "We only use force with these people", he added, "if we have to."

And as for tree spirits and these other things in which I was interested: "Of course we are all required", he said, "to believe in the world of the unseen. The Koran makes that clear." It only becomes a problem, he explained, when ignorant folk start worshipping trees as if there is some sort of god inside. "That violates tawhid. That is when we have to intervene."

The FPI leader remained in a jovial and expansive mood through-out the interview—until I spoiled things right at the end.

Aware that I am a Catholic, Habib Abdullah decided to wrap up our talk by assuring me Christians will have a "protected status" as dhimmis once sharia becomes the law of the land.

But what about pluralism, I asked. What about affording equal protection for all Indonesia's faiths, rather than forcing a sharia system on everyone? What about the idea that members of different faiths in a pluralistic society might have something to learn from each other?

Pluralism, he said sharply, is something the FPI rejects. Religions other than Islam might be tolerated under sharia, but that does not mean they have anything to offer. The irritation was plain to hear in his voice. "Catholics and Protestants and so on will have their place in our system," he warned, "but it will be a subordinate place. They will be safe as long as they do not cross any lines."

And that was when my friends decided it was time to break off our chat and bid our host goodbye.

The Koran verse that snared a Christian candidate: The Islamic Defenders Front and Indonesia's blasphemy law

If you want proof of how powerful the FPI has become, just look at how it managed to disrupt Jakarta's 2017 election campaign for the post of district governor.

The conflict flared in 2016 at the beginning of the campaign season with a comment by Jakarta's governor, Basuki Tjahaja Purnama (better known by his nickname "Ahok"). He is a controversial politician who hoped for reelection on the strength of his record in office. Respected for his personal integrity and determination to help the poor and combat corruption in government, Ahok is nevertheless reviled by Indonesian Islamists for his religious affiliation and ethnic identity. He is a Christian, serving as leader of the capital city in a country that is over 85 percent Muslim. And he is a member of Indonesia's ethnic-Chinese minority population, a community that for generations has been the target of sporadic persecution and pogroms.

Compounding tensions is the fact that Ahok staunchly defends "Pancasila", the foundational set of principles guiding Indonesia since independence in the aftermath of World War II. Notably, Pancasila includes the concept of religious pluralism and equal legal standing for all Indonesians belonging to any of five officially recognized faiths—Islam, Christianity, Buddhism, Hinduism, and Confucianism. Pancasila offends Islamists who want the nation to become a state ruled by sharia law (in which case Islam would enjoy privileged status as Indonesia's premier religion). They have been vigilant in looking for an opening to cripple Ahok (and thereby weaken Ahok's ally, President Joko Widodo).

Their opening came in a speech Governor Ahok gave in 2016 to Muslim voters on the island of Java. Ahok referred to a verse from the Koran (chapter 5:51) that had been frequently quoted by his political opponents. Here is what the verse commands the Muslim faithful to do: "O you who believe! Do not take the Jews and Christians as friends and allies. They are friends and allies only of each other. And any of you who becomes their friend thereupon becomes one of them."

This Koran verse dates from the later Medinan period of the prophet Muhammad's career. It expressed his growing frustration with those Jews and Christians who resisted his Islamic message. The hermeneutical issue for exegetes today is whether the hostility in this verse should be extrapolated to apply to all Jews and all Christians for all time.

Many Indonesian Muslims clearly think it should. Throughout Jakarta's 2016–2017 electoral campaign, Islamist preachers repeatedly told their congregations that this verse forbids Muslims from voting for Christians in any leadership position that might result in non--Muslims ruling over the followers of Allah.

Ahok fought back in a spirited riposte. Speaking to a group of Javanese Muslims in September, he argued that Islamic religious figures were deliberately misleading voters in using verse 5:51 as a club with which to beat him.[10]

This was all his enemies needed. They fanned a flame of anger: a Christian has the nerve to say he knows better than the Muslims what Islam's holy book really says.

---

[10]Joe Cochrane, "Blasphemy Verdict Shows 'Rot' in Indonesia, Legal Experts Say", *The New York Times*, May 12, 2017, p. A8.

Typical is the demand posted on social media by Habib Rizieq (the national director of the Islamic Defenders Front): *Segera tangkap Ahok karena hina al-Qur'an*: "Have Ahok arrested right away, because he has insulted the Koran!"

FPI leader Habib Rizieq is very much the product of hardline ideology imported from the Arab Middle East. He attended both King Saud University in Riyadh and the Jakarta-based Institute for the Study of Islam and Arabic. The latter organization was established by Saudi Arabia (in fact, Saudi funding provides free tuition for all Indonesian students enrolled at the institute). For the past several decades, the Wahhabi kingdom has paid for the building of hundreds of mosques and *pesantren* (Islamic boarding schools) throughout Indonesia.[11] The purpose of this largesse: to "purify" the world's most populous Muslim nation of its longstanding tradition of syncretistic tolerance and replace this with a homogenized and standardized form of Islam that is subject to guidance by Saudi Arabia. And the Salafist thinking underlying this kind of Islam advocates enmity for Shias, Sufis, Jews, and Christians.

Wahhabi-style intolerance was on display at a mass rally organized by the FPI in December 2016. "Let's defend our religion", Rizieq urged the crowd of some 200,000 Muslims, telling them to "stop all forms of religious blasphemy and put all violators on trial."[12] (Indonesia's blasphemy law, which dates to 1965 and the era of President Sukarno, mandates a penalty of up to five years' imprisonment for public statements expressing disrespect or contempt for religion. Cases that come to court generally involve perceived insults against the religion of Islam.)

The result: amidst the mounting public outcry that built over a period of months, Ahok was put on trial, convicted of blasphemy against Islam, and in May 2017 sentenced to two years' imprisonment. Unsurprisingly, he also lost his election bid for governor. The winner was a Muslim candidate who had openly courted the support of the Islamic Defenders Front.

---

[11] Krithika Varagur, "Saudi Arabia Is Redefining Islam for the World's Largest Muslim Nation", *The Atlantic*, March 2, 2017, http://www.theatlantic.com.

[12] Agence France-Presse, "200,000 Indonesian Muslims Protest against Christian Governor", December 2, 2016, http://www.DailyMail.com.

So: a big win for the FPI and for Saudi-financed forms of Islamist intolerance.

The losers: not only ex-Governor Ahok, but also all who honor Pancasila, pluralism, and religious coexistence—traditions that are still attractive, but that are proving to be all too evanescent.

Two tombs: Garuda-wing mosque, terrorists' turf

The tensions between Indonesia's rival ideologies—pluralism and violent Islamism—can be felt at two sites only a few miles from each other, on the northeast coast of Java. One is a quiet rural shrine to a sixteenth-century saint. The other dates to the twenty-first century— and it honors a pair of militants who planted bombs in nightclubs.

The first site is a mosque called Sendang Duwur, and I visited it for the first time in 2011. Spectacularly situated atop a hill with a commanding view over the countryside, Sendang Duwur is famous for the pre-Islamic influences at work in its elaborately figured gateway. Above the lintel is carved Mount Mahameru: the cosmic mountain, home of deities, the axis connecting earth with heaven. Massive wings of volcanic stone sprout from the wall: the wings of Garuda, the eagle-human hybrid that bears the god Vishnu through the sky. And the doorway through which you pass to enter the mosque is flanked by a pair of sinuous serpentine creatures reminiscent of ancient Indian *nagas*, the snakes that fight Garuda in Hindu myth.

This Garuda-wing mosque is by no means shunned by today's Javanese Muslims. Many come as pilgrims to the tomb of Nur Rahmat, a Muslim saint who is buried within the shrine. On my visits there, I noticed clusters of pilgrims posing for photos of themselves beside the winged gateway.

I chatted with the shrine's custodian, Pak Suayb, and asked about the gateway's carvings. According to *orang-orang tua* (old folks) who live in the vicinity, the two *nagas* flanking the door are *penjaga-penjaga*, guardians of the mosque and its worshippers.

And what were wings doing on a mosque gateway?

This generated a wealth of replies. First, Pak Suayb recited a legend. This mosque had originally been located far away, in a different part of Java. The holy man, Nur Rahmat, admired its beauty so much he asked the sultan who owned the mosque if he could have it. The sultan replied with a challenge: If you can find a way to transport the mosque to your home, you can have it. Whereupon Nur Rahmat prayed to Allah, and in the course of a single night the mosque grew wings of stone and flew to its present location.

But the custodian offered other explanations as well. Some say Nur Rahmat himself carved the mosque with wings and snakes so Hindus would be attracted to Islam. Wings symbolize the ability to go everywhere; as a universal religion, so can Islam.

Pak Suayb saved his most interesting speculation for last. Gifted with the ability to foretell the future, Nur Rahmat shaped the gateway in the form of eagle wings because he knew that one day a new nation would arise that would take Garuda as the symbol of its national identity. And, in fact, the Garuda eagle is the dominant motif in Indonesia's national coat of arms today. And that coat of arms, he reminded me, bears the symbols of Pancasila: unity in religious diversity.

Witness though it is to the legacy of Javanese diversity, the shrine of Sendang Duwur nonetheless reflects the social trends at work today in Indonesian Islam. Inside the shrine, where worshippers crowd close to the saint's tomb, a large sign carries a warning: "Pray only to Allah!" Saudi-influenced visitors, I was told, had insisted on posting the sign, to deter any prayers that might conflict with tawhid.

As I was leaving, the custodian's son, a friendly young man in his late teens, pointed from our hilltop to the village below. He directed my attention to a tower just visible in the distance. Not far from there, he said, is the hometown, and the tomb, of Amrozi.

I knew whom he meant. Amrozi Nurhasyim, a member of the militant group Jemaah Islamiyah, was executed for his role in the 2002 Bali nightclub bombings that killed over two hundred tourists and Indonesians. "And now", he said, "some Muslims go as pilgrims to his grave." (I learned later that Amrozi's brother Ali Ghufron—who also was executed for his role in the attack—is buried alongside him at the same site.)[13]

---

[13] Kathy Marks, "Bali Bombers Buried as Muslim Martyrs", *The Independent*, November 10, 2008, http://www.independent.co.uk.

His father quickly added, "The people who go there are *kasar* (coarse or crude). They never come here. And", he concluded, "the pilgrims who come here never go there."

Garuda-wing mosque; terrorist's tomb. Both were in reach of this perch.

The following year, in 2012, I returned to the region and sought out the village (it is called Tenggulun) where the two brothers are buried. Just as the custodians at the Garuda-wing mosque had told me, the brothers' graves have become a pilgrimage site. When I arrived, I saw many young Muslim men idling in the shade under the trees by the burial ground.

One of the young men proved to be Amrozi's nephew. Conversation with him led to an invitation to visit his family's home. There I met two of the Bali Bombers' older brothers, Ja'far al-Shadiq and Hajji Muhammad Chozin. The brothers are influential in Tenggulun and the surrounding region. Besides being hajj guides (leading groups of Indonesian pilgrims annually to Mecca), they also are senior instructors at a local *pesantren* (Islamic boarding school).

I spoke for hours with Hajji Muhammad during a hot, waterless Ramadan afternoon. He identified himself explicitly as a Wahhabi, claiming proudly that Wahhabism is the only form of Islam that is "free of any influence from culture" and that comes directly from the seventh-century prophet of Islam himself. (He made no mention of the fact that Wahhabism has its own cultural context and historical moment of origin, a moment that came well after the time of the prophet Muhammad: the mid-eighteenth century, when the reformer Ibn 'Abd al-Wahhab began preaching in central Arabia.)

Hajji Muhammad Chozin condemned the folk Islam I had been investigating (with its tree spirits and sacred snakes) because of what he called its "contamination" by Javanese culture—by pre-Islamic Hinduism, Buddhism, and animism. Such contamination, he complained, taints all too many Muslim practices in Java.

Unsure what kind of response I would get, I asked his opinion of the Bali bombing for which his two younger brothers had been executed. He not only admitted their responsibility and leadership roles in this act of terrorism but expressed pride in their actions.

I asked how he as an Islamic scholar and educator could justify such violence. In reply he cited the Koranic phrase that had been quoted to me by a district leader of the Islamic Defenders Front: "the promotion of virtue and the prevention of vice". Hajji Muhammad emphasized that the "prevention of vice" should be accomplished peacefully if at all possible; violence is only a last resort, in the case of repeated rejections of Allah's message.

Which led him to the 2002 Bali bombings engineered by his younger brothers. The nightclubs targeted in these blasts were sinkholes of vice, and their proprietors had disregarded all warnings, all preachings.

And of what, precisely, I asked, had the disco dancers been guilty?

"*Mereka berpesta*", he replied promptly: "They were partying." Such actions, he explained, violated sharia and Islamic scripture, which explicitly condemn frivolous behavior.[14]

(The accusation reminds me of a seventh-century historical figure we discussed in a previous chapter—al-Nadr ibn al-Harith, a Meccan storyteller and rival of the prophet Muhammad. He, too, was accused of frivolousness—specifically, reciting "frivolous tales, to distract people from the path of Allah". In retaliation, the Koran threatened him with "a painful punishment", which in fact was later inflicted on him by Muhammad.)[15]

Accompanying me on this visit to Tenggulun was a good friend, a young Javanese Muslim who managed to maintain his courtesy and deference to Hajji Muhammad throughout our interview. But as soon as we left, my friend voiced his bitterness at how this Islamist ideology threatens to destroy the traditional Java he loves.

But Java is not the only island where Indonesia's pluralist traditions are threatened. Come away with me now to northern Sumatra, where you can get a taste of sharia law in a town called Banda Aceh.

The crucifix on Mecca's front porch: Christian survival under sharia law in the Sumatran province of Aceh

We were just murmuring a low-profile grace before dinner, at an Italian restaurant expats favor in Banda Aceh, when the evening call

---

[14] The Koranic term is *lahw* (frivolousness, amusement, distraction). See, for example, surahs 6:32, 29:64, and 62:11. The latter verse provides a biographical glimpse of moments when Muhammad's intended audience failed to listen properly to his message: "But when they see a bit of business or frivolous distraction, they scatter in pursuit of it and leave you standing there." Palpable here is his frustration with this inattentiveness.

[15] Koran 31:6.

to prayer, loudspeaker-strong, blared from a nearby mosque. It gave our pizza slices a certain savor.

Aceh is best known for the tsunami that drowned this coastal region in December 2004. But I was there, on a visit in November 2016, because of Aceh's other claim to notoriety. It is the only province of Indonesia to have implemented sharia law.

Perched on the northwest tip of Sumatra, Aceh is that part of Indonesia located closest to the Middle East and Arabia. Hence its traditional nickname, Serambi Mekkah: "Mecca's front porch". It was from Aceh that Islam began its conquest of the islands of the East Indies in the thirteenth century; and it was from Aceh that many Muslim pilgrims sailed to Mecca to make the hajj.

Led by GAM (*Gerakan Aceh Merdeka*: "the Free Aceh Movement"), Acehnese Islamists fought a brutal civil war for decades against Indonesia's national government, trying to secede from a Muslim-majority country they condemned as insufficiently pious.

The tsunami forced a halt in the violence. GAM signed a peace deal with Jakarta in 2005 that gave Aceh considerable autonomy. As a result, Aceh remains part of Indonesia but is unique in having a sharia--based local government. At first, Islamic law applied only to Muslims; but recently it has been extended to all non-Muslims in Aceh.

I began my visit in Aceh's capital, the port city Banda Aceh, to glimpse what life is like under sharia. My first stop was the Baiturrahman Mosque, the city's chief place of worship. I picked a moment between prayer times.

But no sooner had I entered the perimeter than guards intercepted me to ask me my religion. Once I identified myself as Christian, they told me non-Muslims are forbidden to set foot within the mosque. Take your photos from a distance, I was told; and as soon as the muezzin's cry proclaimed the next round of worship, I would have to vacate the grounds altogether.

Baiturrahman is one of several mosques in the city where the most high-profile part of Aceh's sharia is executed: public canings after Friday prayers. The sentence is imposed on those found guilty of gambling, drinking, or sexual violations such as *khalwat* (inappropriate proximity, as when unmarried couples are caught holding hands).

Now that Aceh's sharia law has been extended to non-Muslims, it is not only Islamic believers who must beware. In April 2016, a sixty-year-old Christian woman was subjected to dozens of lashes. (She had allegedly sold alcohol.)[16]

Acehnese Muslims I asked about sharia said the worst part of caning is not the pain but the prospect of public shame. When the scourging takes place, they say, there are your neighbors from the mosque, holding up their smartphones, recording your disgrace.

And as for those Muslims who try to opt out of Friday prayers: they may find themselves confronted by uniformed members of Wilayat al-Hisbah (the "Ministry of Public Morals", known by its acronym WH, pronounced "Way-Ha" in Indonesian). WH enforcers approach Muslims they see in the street at Friday prayer times and exhort them to get themselves to the nearest mosque.

WH vigilantes also target young women at traffic stops, waving over females on motorbikes if they are insufficiently veiled or wearing jeans deemed too tight for Muslim tastes. They will be plucked from their bikes and made to change to "modest dress" before they are allowed to proceed.

But Islamic vigilance is directed especially at anyone who might become a *murtadd* (an apostate or spiritual renegade). Aceh's sharia law prohibits Muslims from abandoning their faith and converting to another religion. In Banda Aceh, I heard stories of teens caught reading a Bible or searching online for information on Christianity.

In some cases, anxious parents put their spiritually restless children in a *pesantren* (Islamic boarding school), *supaya dimurnikan*, as one Acehnese informant told me: "so they can be purified" and undergo Islamic reeducation.

Muslims who persist in their attraction to Christianity face even harsher consequences: ostracism and job loss, beatings, and death threats. Some ex-Muslims flee to Jakarta or cities in Sumatra beyond the reach of Aceh's Islamic law. Others remain but keep their Christian faith hidden.

Hypersensitive wariness characterizes the attitude of many Acehnese Muslims toward non-Muslims in their midst. An American Christian teacher I met in Banda Aceh told me her English lessons are sometimes interrupted by students who complain that when

---

[16] Agence France-Presse, "Christian Woman Caned in Indonesia's Aceh Province for Selling Alcohol", *The Straits Times* (Singapore), April 13, 2016, http://www.straitstimes.com.

she writes the letter "t" on the board, she is actually propagating the sign of the Cross as part of a secret plot. *Kristenisasi umat Islam*, it is called: "bringing about the Christianization of the Muslim community".

"Acehnese Muslims are afraid of the Cross": this comment was offered to me by a thoughtful young Muslim lecturer I met at Banda Aceh's UIN (Universitas Islam Negeri: the National Islamic University). He told me that conspiracy theories about forced Christianization flourish in part because so much of Aceh is religiously segregated. Very few Acehnese Muslims know any Christians or have any Christian friends.

And Aceh's politicians seem content to have things this way. "Very few people in the government here", the UIN lecturer told me, "have any interest whatsoever in tolerance or pluralism." Many of these politicians are ex-GAM fighters and remain militantly Islamist in their orientation.

But anti-Christian attitudes and sharia-mindedness have negative effects for Muslims, too. Another young lecturer I interviewed at UIN (I will call her "Nabeela" rather than use her real name)—a devout Muslim who goes about scrupulously veiled—told me what happened when she recently taught a course on gender issues in contemporary society.

Since all her students were Muslim, she decided to introduce an interreligious perspective by taking them to a local church in Banda Aceh. There the pastor spoke with them frankly about the challenges Christian denominations face as they respond to concerns involving women and their role in today's world.

The Muslim students attending this talk reacted favorably. But such was not the case with many of their families or with the local Acehnese Muslims who found out about this field trip.

"They heard I had taken Muslim youth to a church", said Nabeela, "and that I had let a Christian talk to them. And that was enough to make people think I was a *murtadd* who wanted to make other Muslims lose their faith as well and turn into Christians."

The result: threats against Nabeela and her family and demands that the university fire her. She was suspended from teaching, and, fearing for her own safety, she hurried to Jakarta and lived there quietly for three months. Eventually, as she explained to me, UIN allowed her to teach again—but with the understanding there would be no more field trips to churches.

Overwhelmingly Islamic as it is, Banda Aceh nonetheless also includes a downtown neighborhood called Peunayong that is exceptional for its religious diversity. Peunayong is the city's Chinatown: since at least the nineteenth century, Chinese immigrants have settled there as merchants and shopkeepers. (And it should be noted that ethnic Chinese Indonesians have been the sporadic targets of communal violence in recent decades, in Banda Aceh, Jakarta, and other parts of the Archipelago.)

In Peunayong, I found old Hindu and Buddhist temples, along with several *gereja-gereja resmi*—longstanding "official churches" that are licensed by Aceh's government to hold religious services. One such place of worship, the Catholic Sacred Heart Church, dates to the 1920s and Dutch colonial times. Pastors I interviewed explained that their congregations are tolerated as long as they do not evangelize or encourage Acehnese Muslims to convert.

But faith has a way of slipping past government control. Besides the "official" places of worship, Peunayong has many unlicensed "underground" Christian congregations: recently emergent house-church communities where small gatherings of a few dozen believers at a time will meet. (Some of the illegal services I attended were in private homes; one was crowded into a small upstairs office at the back of a garage.)

Aceh's government tries to crush Christian growth by refusing to issue permits for building new churches. But these underground groups need no churches to thrive.

Some congregations consist of expats from Australia and the States; others, ethnic Chinese Indonesians or collections of Christian Sumatrans and Javanese. They pray, share food, and read from the Bible. To judge from my visits, all these groups seem to favor verses from Saint Paul's epistles that instruct the faithful on how to survive persecution and stay strong.

One gathering I visited particularly stays in my mind—a youth group called *Menara Doa Kristen* (the tower of Christian prayer), where teens described what it is like to be a young Christian in Aceh. Some go to schools in outlying villages where they are the only non-Muslims in the classroom. They are often bullied because of their religious identity. Their Muslim classmates—and often their teachers, too, I was told—tell them their Bible is false and their religion is wrong.

This reflects a trend I noticed: Christian populations in rural Aceh face even harsher treatment than they do in the province's capital city. In October 2015, mobs in Aceh's Singkil district burned down three churches. Thousands of Christians were forced to flee the region.[17]

I spent my last day in Aceh at Sacred Heart Church. The place was packed, every pew full. Mass began with a procession to the altar: priests striding slowly, acolytes bearing candles. Leading them all was a young girl. Proudly she held high a crucifix, big and bronze.

After Mass, worshippers approached me to chat. "This place we live, you know they call it Mecca's front porch", one said. For Christians, he said, life in Aceh is not easy. "But we come here," he continued, "and we see the Cross, and then we know we can keep going."

[17] Hotli Simanjuntak and Apriadi Gunawan, "Thousands Leave Aceh after Church Burnings", The Jakarta Post, October 15, 2015, http://www.thejakartapost.com.

CHAPTER 15

CONCLUDING THOUGHTS:
CONFRONTING *DA'WAH*—AND
PROMOTING THE TRUTH
OF CHRIST CRUCIFIED

In the last two chapters, I shared my personal experiences in Indonesia, Pakistan, Yemen, and Egypt, so as to provide you with some sense of the struggle for survival experienced by Christians in these Muslim-majority countries.

My plan now is to begin the final chapter of this book by taking you with me to an altogether different venue—the continent of Europe and cities such as Paris that are home to sizable Muslim populations. Our guide for the first stage of this journey will be a scholar named Gilles Kepel, author of impressive studies on Islamic militancy. I will draw your attention to a topic mentioned by Kepel that I think should particularly concern Christians in America (and in the West at large): Islamic *da'wah* (missionary efforts) targeting unchurched Christian youth.

Islamist preaching in a "de-Christianized" Europe:
Lessons—and a warning—for American followers of Christ

For some months in the early 1970s, I made a hand-to-mouth living playing music in a restaurant on the coast of Normandy. The guitarist I performed with was an Algerian Muslim from Paris. One night between sets, somehow the topic of prayer came up, and I asked him what his mosque in Paris was like. He laughed and said he never went. Mosques were just all-but-empty places where a few old men sat about.

Not anymore. As Gilles Kepel reports in his insightful new book *Terror in France: The Rise of Jihad in the West*, these days mosques from Paris to Toulouse are often occupied beyond capacity for Friday worship, so that nearby streets and even supermarket parking lots are filled with rows of men doing their prostrations in prayer. This phenomenon—often decried by National Front politician Marine Le Pen—is an example of what Kepel calls Islam as an "irrepressible marker of identity in the banlieues" (the impoverished and largely Muslim neighborhoods on the periphery of many cities in France).[1]

Kepel's book is the product of numerous face-to-face interviews in such neighborhoods, combined with careful study of Islamist websites and the ideological texts that have inspired the latest generation of Muslim jihadists. I will read anything by Kepel I can get my hands on; he is by far Europe's greatest Orientalist. (Despite the use of this word as a slur by the Edward Said crowd, I mean it as a compliment; an Orientalist is simply a scholar of Islam who happens to be non-Muslim—a member of a centuries-old discipline that combines language study with textual exegesis and on-the-ground observation of cultures from northwest Africa to southeast Asia.)

An outspoken defender of *laïcité* (the version of secularism sponsored by the French government, whereby all forms of religion are excluded from the public sphere), Kepel has been the target of death threats by adherents of the Islamic State. The New York Times correspondent Robert Worth has reported on Kepel's visits to Villepinte prison in northern France, where he engages in debates on Islam with imprisoned members of ISIS. Such debates draw crowds of Muslim onlookers; in a country where 8 percent of the population is Islamic, fully half the penitentiary inmates nationwide are Muslim. *Terror in France* describes French prisons as "incubators" where young Muslim convicts, doing time for robbery, assault, or drug dealing, are indoctrinated by hardened terrorists so that their unfocused anger is channeled into a vocation of Islamist violence. In his debates with ISIS spokesmen, Kepel

---

[1] Gilles Kepel, *Terror in France: The Rise of Jihad in the West* (Princeton, N.J.: Princeton University Press, 2017), p. 14.

challenges their scriptural interpretations, quoting the Koran in fluent Arabic and inviting listeners to consider less destructive ways of being Muslim.[2]

Kepel's book is thick with details of the year-by-year growth of militant Islam in *Département Quatre-Vingt-Treize* ("District 93", the historic Seine-Saint Denis region) and other localities in metropolitan France where immigrant Muslims have settled over the past sixty years.

He outlines the "three waves of jihad" that have characterized militant Islam over the past several decades. The first arose in the 1980s and 1990s and ranged from Afghanistan and Algeria to Bosnia and Egypt. It entailed all-out war that engulfed whole populations. Ultimately it failed, because of the indiscriminate way *mujahideen* killed civilians and combatants alike. The result: militants could not get the support they needed from local Muslims to install sharia government.

Kepel's summary tallies here with my own experience of Egypt in the 1990s. I visited the Valley of the Kings shortly after al-Gama'ah al-Islamiyah (the "Islamic Group", led by Ayman al-Zawahiri of later al-Qaeda notoriety) massacred several Egyptians and dozens of foreign tourists at Queen Hatshepsut's temple in 1997. The local Muslims I interviewed in the aftermath complained how this terror strike had crippled Egypt's tourist industry. Jobs vanished for thousands of tour guides and souvenir sellers.

What Kepel calls second-wave jihadism was led by al-Qaeda and targeted American interests worldwide. It featured top-down organization, agents recruited directly from Middle Eastern countries, and meticulously planned operations that required months (if not years) of preparation. This second wave crested in 2001 with the Islamic terrorist attacks of September 11.

Kepel alerts us to the features that make jihadism's third wave (which we face today) so different from what has gone before. Rather than use militants from abroad, groups like ISIS recruit locally born French Muslims for what Kepel calls "a jihadism of proximity, based on a network-based system penetrating the enemy societies to be

---

[2] Robert F. Worth, "The Secularist", *The New York Times Magazine*, April 9, 2017, pp. 32–39, 56–65.

overthrown from the bottom up rather than from the top down". He identifies the factors that make young Muslims vulnerable in the banlieues: high unemployment; lingering discrimination linked to the bitter legacy of French colonial Algeria; and a complete break in world view between today's Muslim youths and the hard-scrabble older generation of North African immigrants who worked diligently to build a new life for themselves in France.[3]

Compounding the problem are the many Salafist missionaries, now established throughout France, who are lavishly funded by sources in Saudi Arabia and the Gulf. Their message is one of *l'Islam intégral*—an all-encompassing form of the faith. Listeners are told they have only one identity, as Muslims, and only one loyalty, to the *ummah*—the worldwide community of believers originally founded by the prophet Muhammad. Militant Salafist preaching in France rejects the notion of Muslim integration into French society and despises Christians, Jews, and secular Muslims alike as *kuffar* (infidels against whom one should wage jihad).

The force multiplier for this message is of course the Internet. Anyone who feels estranged from the *laïcité* of contemporary France can retreat into the world of social media, where ISIS stands ready to befriend those who are astray. What is startling is how attractive ISIS' message is for many *Français de souche* (native-born non-Muslim French citizens of European ancestry). A disproportionately high number (30 percent or more) of the ISIS adherents who have flocked to the Syrian-Iraqi caliphate are recent converts to Islam.[4]

Why the attraction? Here is my own sense of the crisis. Secular Western nations are home to plenty of individuals who are spiritually adrift but full of unfocused energy and eager for meaning—eager, in fact, to give themselves to an all-encompassing cause (an impulse that at heart is profoundly religious).

Hence the occasional occurrence of skinheads turning to Islam. I recently saw on the website *Stormfront* a lengthy statement posted by a Muslim proselytizer inviting neo-Nazis to join the religion of Allah. (The response thread showed that most white-nationalist readers found the idea highly unappealing, but the arguments used by the

---

[3] Kepel, *Terror*, pp. 18–23.
[4] Ibid., pp. 2–3.

preacher suggest a stratagem to tap a vein of anger at a consumerist society in which many individuals feel lost.)[5]

For some idea of what attracts many young people to ISIS, watch the YouTube video of a seventeen-year-old Australian who pledged allegiance to the caliphate in 2014. Surrounded by a frowning bearded throng of black-clad men with guns, he shouts *Takbir!* (The cry summons Muslims to declare the greatness of Allah.) Instantly his new friends all bellow *Allahu akbar.*[6]

Where else can a teen get such a rush of violent power? In today's culture of competitive identity politics, embracing Islam is a fast--track way of going from the plain-vanilla dullness of "white privilege" to the thrilling and coveted status of aggrieved and irascible victim.

Kepel does not linger on the following point, but his profiles of ISIS converts indicate that many come from thoroughly unchurched backgrounds in what he calls a "de-Christianized" Europe.[7] Which brings us to the question: What insights can American Christian readers take away from *Terror in France?*

The situation of Muslims in the United States is—thankfully—vastly different from what Kepel documents in France. Compared with French Muslims, their American co-religionists are more affluent, better educated, and far more closely integrated into American society. Although the threat of Islamic terror is always present—as attested by the Boston Marathon bombing, San Bernardino, Orlando, and Fort Hood—the level of lethal alienation among Muslims in the United States is nowhere near as high as it is in France.

But what concerns me more is *da'wah*: proselytizing by Muslim evangelists here in the States. Like Christianity, Islam is a missionary faith. As a Catholic who teaches courses on Islam at a Catholic Jesuit university, I am reminded of this every time I take my students on field trips to local mosques. I know from in-class surveys that most of

---

[5] Mohammed Abdullah (online pseudonym), "Would You Ever Convert to Islam?" *Stormfront: Opposing Views Forum,* December 1, 2008, http://www.stormfront.org/forum /t547801/. See also Amy B. Wang, "A Neo-Nazi Converted to Islam and Killed 2 Roommates for 'Disrespecting' His Faith, Police Say", *The Washington Post,* May 23, 2017.

[6] Dave Rubin, "New ISIS Spokesman—an Australian Teen—Issues Warning", *The Rubin Report,* October 22, 2014, http://www.youtube.com/watch?v=aQ9gWebjRuU.

[7] Kepel, *Terror,* p. 70.

my undergrads are from nominally Christian families but have only the vaguest sense of what Christian faith and life are about.

When they witness Friday mosque prayer, many are dazzled—and attracted—by the spectacle of worshippers packed shoulder to shoulder and prostrating in unison. In conversations after our visit, the comments they make reveal that their mosque trip is the first time they have sensed the deep satisfaction that can come from the collective performance of ritual. So unchurched, so unfamiliar with their own tradition are these students that—by their own account—many have never even attended a Mass.

What this says to me is that the American Catholic community needs to do much more to reevangelize young Christians. If we do not attend to their hunger, others most certainly will.

Violent Bible, peaceful Koran?: The dangers of false equivalence

From time to time, students excitedly draw my attention to knock-'em-on-the-head clickbait headlines like this: "'Violence More Common' in Bible than Quran, Text Analysis Reveals". The article beneath that particular headline describes how some computer engineer used "text analytics software" to argue that "killing and destruction occur more frequently in the Christian texts than the Islamic."[8]

Articles like this seem motivated by a strongly polemical agenda. This is especially blatant in a piece by Sheila Musaji, founding editor of an online newsletter called The American Muslim. Entitled "Throwing Stones at the Qur'an from a Biblical Glass House", the article criticizes Christians who condemn acts of brutality that are committed in the name of Islam. Musaji's argument can be summarized in this sentence from her essay: "Those carrying out these attacks on the Qur'an must be unaware that there are many verses in the Bible that can be considered violent and warlike."[9]

True enough. As a student of the Crusades, I know there have been times when Christians especially favored such verses. When the

---

[8] Samuel Osborne, "'Violence More Common' in Bible than Quran, Text Analysis Reveals", The Independent, February 9, 2016, http://www.independent.co.uk.

[9] Sheila Musaji, "Throwing Stones at the Qur'an from a Biblical Glass House", The American Muslim, March 20, 2007, http://www.theamericanmuslim.org.

Knights Templar gathered for meals in their monastery-castles in the Holy Land, one of these "monks of war" would have the job of reading aloud scripture to the diners. Their favorite passages from the Bible: tales of conflict and conquest from the books of Joshua and Maccabees.[10]

Nonetheless "violent Bible" arguments like the one quoted above from *The American Muslim* seem to me to serve the function— whether unintentionally or deliberately—of furthering the cause of Islamist *da'wah*. The logic here is that biblical violence equals (and hence cancels out) all the violence found in the Koran. Having thus reassured uneasy Christians that there supposedly are not any systemic problems in the Islamic faith, Muslim missionaries can go about the business of packaging Islam as a religion of peace.

But such arguments about biblical and Koranic violence strike me as an example of false equivalence. The reductionist approach of authors like Musaji loses sight of important differences between Islamic and Christian beliefs about their respective scriptures. Let's review those differences here.

Islamic doctrine proclaims the Koran to be eternal and uncreated; as such it is supposedly atemporal and beyond the limiting contexts of human history. Moreover, no human writer is involved. Allah is believed to be the Koran's author; Muhammad was simply the Koranic revelation's recipient and transmitter. Hence the special difficulty, throughout Islamic history, for any Muslim who wishes to question the authority or wisdom of Koranic verses. "Slay the unbelievers wherever you find them", commands the Koran; easy enough for the faithful to regard this verse as being just as obligatory for them as it was for Muhammad. Reformers who have tried to limit the validity of Koran verses by reminding Muslims of the text's original seventh-century context sometimes find themselves in danger.

That is what happened in the 1980s to the Sudanese reformer Mahmoud Mohamed Taha. He critiqued the Koran's Medinan verses promulgating slavery, the subordination of women, and the subjugation and killing of non-Muslims. These verses, he argued, were appropriate for the prophet's time but out of date in the twentieth

[10] Desmond Seward, *The Monks of War: The Military Religious Orders* (St. Albans: Paladin, 1974), pp. 35–37.

century. Instead, priority should be given to the chronologically earlier Meccan verses that emphasize universal human dignity. Sudanese law should be reformed accordingly. The result: Taha was condemned as an apostate and the Islamist government of the Sudan had him hanged in Khartoum in 1985.[11]

The Islamists killed Taha because they did not want anyone challenging the Koran's traditional status. Uncreated, atemporal, devoid of human authorship: you can see how imputing such traits to Islamic scripture makes it all the harder for believers to rethink the rules proclaimed in this text.

A moment's reflection will show how different is Christians' understanding of the Bible. Jews and Christians acknowledge that the authorship of the Bible is human (albeit inspired by the Holy Spirit); in fact, the Bible is the cumulative product of multiple authors over a period of centuries. As such, it is the record of our ongoing attempts to discern the divine Will and understand how best to relate to God.

The chronologically earlier portion of these attempts is the Old Testament—which, as the "violent Bible" polemicists admit, contains most of the passages in Christian scripture referring to warfare and slaughter. This is important. For Christians, Jesus' message of reconciliation and self-sacrificial love serves as a counterweight to Old Testament verses that seem to advocate violence.

Differences between Christianity and Islam are compounded by the fact that the prophet Muhammad—who both preached and practiced the Koran's verses of violence—is revered by Muslims as *ma'sum*. The term refers to a sacred figure who is honored as sinless, infallible, perfect, and divinely protected from error. And because he is sinless and perfect, Muhammad's sunnah (exemplary life-style) is to be imitated by all faithful followers of Islam.[12] Militant Muslims

---

[11] See Mahmoud Mohamed Taha, *The Second Message of Islam* (Syracuse: University Press, 1987). Taha's intellectual legacy has been continued by his student Abdullahi Ahmed An-- Na'im. See Na'im's essay "Shari'a and Basic Human Rights Concerns", in *Liberal Islam: A Sourcebook*, ed. Charles Kurzman (New York: Oxford University Press, 1998), pp. 222–38.

[12] For an introduction to the doctrine of Muhammad as *ma'sum*, see Annemarie Schimmel, *And Muhammad Is His Messenger: The Veneration of the Prophet in Islamic Piety* (Chapel Hill: University of North Carolina Press, 1985), pp. 56–59. This doctrine seems to have originated among the Shias and then gradually shaped Sunni popular devotion as well. See Dwight M. Donaldson, *The Shi'ite Religion: A History of Islam in Persia and Iraq* (London: Luzac & Company, 1933), pp. xxv–xxvi. The twelfth-century Sunni philosopher Abu Hamid al-Ghazali

I met in my overseas research occasionally told me they considered themselves superior to Muslims in America. American Muslims, they complained, were tainted by Western notions like democracy and pluralism, whereas the militants scrupulously imitated Muhammad in destroying enemies of the faith.

"What if the Koran isn't perfect?": Challenges to Islam from within the Islamic tradition

Luckily today there are individuals who have grown up within the Islamic tradition but have been brave enough to challenge these bedrock Muslim beliefs. One, Ayaan Hirsi Ali, is a self-declared apostate. She chastises well-meaning people in Europe and the United States who refrain from saying anything that might be construed as negative about the prophet of Islam: "The *communis opinio* seems to hold that questioning or criticizing a holy figure is not polite behavior, somehow not done." Instead, she advocates addressing what she calls "the core issue of the debate, which is Muhammad's example". Muslims and non-Muslims must be free to question Muhammad's status as *ma'sum*.[13]

Another courageous critic is the feminist Irshad Manji, who has chosen to remain a Muslim even as she challenges essential components of her faith. Read the following passage from her book *The Trouble with Islam Today*, and you will understand why Manji, like Hirsi Ali, has been the target of numerous death threats by angry Islamists: "Far from being perfect, the Koran is so profoundly at war with itself that Muslims who 'live by the book' have no choice but to choose what to emphasize and what to downplay.... The Koran's

---

accepts this doctrine as a given in his autobiographical treatise *al-Munqidh min al-Dalal* (That which rescues from going astray): "Not every teacher is appropriate; rather, it is absolutely necessary to have a teacher who is sinless and infallible.... Our infallible and sinless teacher is Muhammad, peace and blessings be upon him" (*Mu'allimuna al-ma'sum huwa Muhammad 'alayhi al-salat wa-al-salam*). See Ahmad Shams al-Din, ed., *Majmu'at rasa'il al-Imam al-Ghazali* (Beirut: Dar al-Kutub al-'Ilmiyah, 1988), pp. 49–50; translated by D. Pinault. For an English translation of the entire treatise, see W. Montgomery Watt, *The Faith and Practice of al-Ghazali* (Chicago: Kazi Publications, 1982).

[13] Ayaan Hirsi Ali, *The Caged Virgin: An Emancipation Proclamation for Women and Islam* (New York: Free Press, 2006), pp. 173–74.

perfection is, ultimately, suspect.... What if the Koran isn't perfect? What if it's not a completely God-authored book? What if it's riddled with human biases?"[14]

Such questions are unacceptable, of course, both for well-meaning but squeamish non-Muslims and for *da'wah* missionaries who seek to discourage hard thinking and hard questions about Islam. They prefer to blur the differences between the Koran and the Bible on tough issues like violence and holy war so as to facilitate their own attempts to convert unchurched Christians to Islam.

The failure to ask such necessary hard questions about Islam does Muslims no favor. And it is no help to us Christians, either. When we do not speak out as Manji and Hirsi Ali do, when we fail to point out the problematic aspects of Islam, then we are at risk of unconsciously furthering the proselytizing work that is done by Islamist missionaries. Blurring the substantive differences between the two religions amounts to inadvertent *da'wah*. As Christians, we should not do this. Our own faith offers treasures that should never be obscured.

Concluding thought: "He took on the weakness and ordinariness of man, and He hid Himself": Augustine and Thomas Merton on the uniqueness of the biblical Christ

Reflecting on the journey of faith he underwent in his teens and twenties, Saint Augustine in his *Confessions* writes about the time he spent studying the teachings of the pagan "Platonists". He compares their thought with biblical doctrine. Like Christians, he says, the ancient philosophers tell of an eternal God who is the creator of the world. Like Christians, they speak in their treatises of God as divine Light and as communicative Word.

But when it comes to the doctrine of kenosis, of divine Incarnation, of the crucifixion of the God-Man: "Of this", says Augustine, "no mention was made in these books [of the Platonists]."[15] In other

---

[14] Irshad Manji, *The Trouble with Islam Today: A Muslim's Call for Reform in Her Faith* (New York: St. Martin's, 2003), pp. 36, 45.

[15] Augustine, *Confessions*, trans. Maria Boulding, O.S.A. (New York: New City Press, 2014), bk. 9, no. 13—9, no. 14, pp. 169–70.

words, his study of Greek philosophy sharpened Augustine's sense of what is distinctive about the biblical world view and what can be found only in the truths of Christianity.

So, too, for me. Rereading the *Confessions* as I wrote the chapters of the book you now hold in your hands reminded me of my own spiritual education. For it was the study of Islam that helped me to a fresh appreciation of the Catholic Christian heritage and identity I embrace.

The more I have read the Koran—with its characterizations of Allah as al-Ghani (the One who is free of all needs and wants), *al-Qahhar* (the all-conquering Subduer), *Sari' al-'iqab* (the One who is quick to punish), and *al-Shadid al-'iqab* (the One who is harsh in punishment)—the more I have become aware of things I can find only in my own tradition.

For example: I was twelve when I first discovered the works of the Trappist monk Thomas Merton (*New Seeds of Contemplation*, left about on the kitchen table by my older brother). But it was only many years later, after I had studied Islamic scripture, that I rediscovered Merton and renewed a sharp sense of what it is I love about the Christian faith. Listen now as the monk meditates on the divine kenosis:

> The Lord would not only love His creation as a Father, but He would enter into His creation, emptying Himself, hiding Himself, as if He were not God but a creature. Why should He do this? Because He loved His creatures, and because He could not bear that His creatures should merely adore Him as distant, remote, transcendent and all powerful. This was not the glory that He sought, for if He were merely adored as great, His creatures would in their turn make themselves great and lord it over one another....
>
> So God became man. He took on the weakness and ordinariness of man, and He hid Himself, becoming an anonymous and unimportant man in a very unimportant place.[16]

In this book of mine you are reading now, I have focused especially on Christ. I have done this because I believe the varying understandings of Jesus in Islam and Christianity reveal the radical differences between the two faiths.

[16] Thomas Merton, *New Seeds of Contemplation* (Norfolk, Conn.: New Directions, 1961), pp. 292–93.

On the one hand, Islam's denial of divine Sonship, crucifixion, and Trinity means: a god who may be just and merciful, yes, but also a god who is free of all needs, who is invulnerable and impervious to the sorrows of the world he created.

On the other hand, in Christianity we find a god who takes the risk of Incarnation, who exposes himself to weakness and ridicule, who suffers in solidarity with all created beings.

To be enfleshed—a condition we share with the God-made-- Man—is to expose oneself to suffering. But our consolation as Christians is knowing that even as we suffer—as Paul so piercingly reminds us—we are crucified alongside Christ.

GLOSSARY

agama Jawa primitif: "Java's primordial faith": an Indonesian term referring to the animist tradition on the island of Java.

ahl al-kitab: "People of the Book", a term applied especially to Jews and Christians.

Ahmadi, Ahmadiyyah: Islamic sect widely persecuted in Muslim countries for its belief that there can be prophets after the time of Muhammad.

Ansar: "Those who help provide victory": residents of Medina who supported Muhammad after his hijrah from Mecca.

'asabiyah: Group solidarity, tribal loyalty.

'Ashura: Tenth day of the month of Muharram, the day on which Husain ibn 'Ali (revered by Twelver Shias as the third imam) was killed at Karbala (A.D. 680). 'Ashura is the focal point of the annual Muharram lamentation rituals commemorating the death of Husain and the other Karbala martyrs.

al-asma' al-husna: "The beautiful names" (Koran 7:180) or divine attributes of Allah.

ayat al-sayf: The Koranic "sword verses" (such as 9:5) authorizing violence, especially warfare against unbelievers in defense of Islam.

banat Allah: "The daughters of Allah": Jahiliyah goddesses whose worship is condemned in Koran 53:19–23.

banci: A person who is a member of Indonesia's gay and transgender community.

bay'ah: Oath of allegiance.

bertapa: To live as a hermit and devote oneself to spiritual practices. (The word is derived from the Sanskrit *tapas*: religious disciplines of austerity and renunciation.) The practice is a shared tradition among Indonesia's various faith traditions, often involving meditative seclusion in Java's forests, mountaintop retreats, and ancient shrines.

bid'ah: Heretical religious "innovation", supposedly introduced after the time of the prophet Muhammad.

caliph: A word derived from *khalifat rasul Allah*, "the successor of Allah's messenger": the political leader of the Islamic *ummah* after the death of Muhammad.

Chehelom: Fortieth day after 'Ashura (the date of Husain ibn 'Ali's death), the occasion of commemorative lamentation ceremonies in Shia communities.

al-Dahr: Time, as a destructive force. According to the heroic code of conduct among the Jahiliyah Arabs, al-Dahr sets the limits to human efforts and determines the end of life for all created beings.

da'wah: "Summons, call, invitation". As a religious term, the word is used in two ways: to refer to the moment in A.D. 610 when Muhammad felt himself summoned to preach Islam as Allah's prophet; and to refer to Islamic proselytizing in general, when Muslim missionaries encourage individuals to convert to Islam.

dhikr: Sufi rituals that involve the "recollection" and recitation of the Names of Allah.

dhimmi: Non-Muslim "protected persons", typically Jews and Christians living under Islamic rule who are allowed to retain their faith in exchange for acknowledging Muslim suzerainty and paying the jizyah (the discriminatory tax referred to in Koran 9:29).

dukun: Spiritual healer (Indonesia).

al-Fatihah: The opening: chapter 1 of the Koran.

fatwa: Decree by a Muslim authority on a specific topic relating to Islam and contemporary life.

al-Ghani: "The One who is free of all needs and wants": a Koranic name or attribute of Allah.

al-ghaybah: "Occultation, concealment": a term used to describe the twelfth imam, believed by Shias to have been kept alive by Allah since the ninth century. This "Hidden Imam" will return at a divinely chosen moment to trigger the end of time and final Judgment.

ghulat: Doctrinal extremists whose beliefs disqualify them from being considered true Muslims.

hadith: A "report" or "account", specifically a description of things said or done by Muhammad.

hafiz: A Muslim who knows the entire Koran by heart.

hajj: Pilgrimage to Mecca.

halqah: Circle, lecture, where students gather to sit around their masters.

halus: Refined, graceful, characterized by delicacy of taste and behavior (a term used on the island of Java to identify praiseworthy comportment and spiritual attainments).

hanif: A term used to describe denominationally unaffiliated monotheists during the time of the Jahiliyah, that is, individuals who broke with the religious traditions in which they had been raised and who ventured forth on their own as solo spiritual questers to encounter the true God. The word hanif is applied to Abraham in the Koran (3:67).

al-Haqq: The Truth, as a Koranic name or attribute for Allah.

haramayn: Sacred cities of Mecca and Medina.

hijrah: Muhammad's exodus from Mecca to Yathrib/Medina in A.D. 622. Since Muhammad's time, the term has also been understood paradigmatically: following the prophet's example, many Muslims have abandoned cities and countries they deem insufficiently Islamic to emigrate to a new setting where they can establish a pure community that will truly conform to Allah's law.

hulul: "Descent" from heaven of a divine spirit into a living body; used at times as an accusation against Sufis and Shias accused of being extremists and not true Muslims.

hululi: Adherent of blasphemous belief in *hulul*.

Ifranj: Franks; inhabitants of Western Europe. In medieval Arabic texts, the term is commonly used by Muslim chroniclers to identify the Crusaders.

imam: In its simplest meaning, one who leads a congregation in prayer; the word is used in this sense in both Sunni and Shia Islam. The term is additionally used in Shiism, however, to designate the members and descendants of Muhammad's family who were the rightful spiritual and worldly heirs of the prophet's authority and hence were the true leaders of the Muslim community.

Injil: Gospel, good news; an Arabic term derived from the Greek *Evangelion*. The term is used in the Koran to refer to the revelation given by Allah to Jesus Christ.

intizar: Awaiting, expectation—a term used to describe a quietist stance of avoiding political confrontation with the powers
of this world as one awaits patiently the return of the Hidden
Imam as the Mahdi.

'Isa: The Arabic term used in the Koran and other Islamic texts to
identify Jesus.

Jahiliyah: Pre-Islamic tradition in pagan Arabia.

jihad: "Struggle, striving", whether exertions to purify oneself
spiritually or violence in defense of Islam directed against
unbelievers.

jinn: Nature-spirit, associated especially with remote and unpop-
ulated wasteland-sites. Such beings were both venerated and
feared during the Jahiliyah. Islam retains the belief in jinns but
demotes them in rank. Like humans, they have been created by
Allah; and like humans, they must choose whether to submit to
Allah's will and become Muslims.

jizyah: Annual discriminatory tax imposed on non-Muslim "people
of the Book" (usually understood as Jews and Christians) living
under Islamic rule.

kafir; pl.: kuffar: Unbeliever.

kasar: That which is coarse and crude; a term used in Javanese Islam
to identify undesirable behavior or ways of thought.

lawh mahfuz: The heavenly "preserved tablet" (Koran 85:22) on
which the words of Islamic scripture have been inscribed for
all eternity.

madrasa: A "place of study" or school; in traditional Islam, an institution where individuals study the Koran, sharia, and other
branches of Islamic knowledge.

al-Mahdi: One who is divinely guided; a title of the Twelfth Imam.

majnun: Possessed by a jinn.

al-Masih: Christ or Messiah; an Arabic title used in the Koran to refer
to Jesus.

ma'sum: Sinless, infallible, perfect, divinely protected from error.
Sunni and Shia Muslims concur in regarding all of Islam's
prophets as *ma'sum*. Additionally, Twelver Shias ascribe this
quality to Muhammad's daughter Fatima and the twelve imams
of Muhammad's family and descendants whom Shias revere as
the *ummah*'s rightful spiritual leaders.

matam: Mourning rituals, a term used especially in Shia Islam to identify lamentation rituals in honor of the Karbala martyrs.

matami guruhan: Shia lamentation associations.

mufti: Cleric trained in sharia who issues *fatwas*.

Muharram: The first month in the Islamic calendar. It is also the month in which the siege of Karbala and the death of Husain ibn 'Ali occurred; for this reason it is the season in which Shia Muslims perform lamentation rituals in honor of the Karbala martyrs.

mujahid; pl.: *mujahideen* or *mujahidin*: One who strives; holy warrior.

mullah: One educated in sacred theology and Islamic law: a Muslim religious authority.

mu'minin: Believers.

munafiqun: Hypocrites.

al-Muntaqim: Honorific title of the Mahdi: "the Avenger".

murtadd: An apostate or spiritual renegade.

mushrik: Someone who ascribes partners to the sole true god.

mustabsirun: "Those who have become endowed with insight": Twelver Shia name for converts to the Shia form of Islam.

najis: Ritually unclean.

Nasrani; pl.: Nasara: Nazarenes; the word used by the Koran to designate Christians.

nauhajat: Lamentation poems in honor of Husain ibn 'Ali and other Karbala Martyrs.

penunggu: "Watchman", a guardian nature spirit that in Java and other islands of the Indonesian archipelago takes up residence in trees and protects sacred forests.

pesantren: Islamic boarding school.

Peshitta: Syriac text of the Bible.

qiblah: Direction faced in Islamic prayer.

Rabb al-Ka'bah: Lord of the Ka'ba; early title of Allah.

Rafidi: Rejectionist, renegade; a term of derision sometimes used in reference to the Shias.

Sahib al-zaman: "Lord of time"; one of the titles of the Twelfth Imam.

saj': Arabic prose rhyme.

salat: Mandatory five-times-a-day prayer.

Sayyid al-Shuhada': Lord of the Martyrs: Husain ibn 'Ali.

Serambi Mekkah: "Mecca's front porch", a honorific title for Aceh
    derived from its geographic proximity to the Arabian peninsula.

shafa'ah: Intercession on behalf of sinners.

shahadah: The Islamic testimony of faith.

shaheed: Islamic martyr.

sha 'ir majnun: Poet possessed by a jinn (cf. Koran 37:36).

sharia: Divine law, made manifest to mankind by Allah through the
    Koran and applied to Islamic society by the religious scholars
    who elaborate the legal and moral precepts encoded in Scripture.

al-shaykhayn: "The two elders", an honorific title used by Sunni
    Muslims to refer to Abu Bakr and 'Umar, the first and second
    caliphs after Muhammad.

shaytan/shayatin: Satan, Satans.

shirk: "Associationism": the sin of associating divine partners with
    Allah.

shurat: "Vendors"; what the Kharijites called themselves, inspired by
    Koran 9:111: those who "sold" their lives to Allah in exchange
    for the rewards of Paradise.

Sufi: Adherent of the Islamic form of mysticism.

sunnah: Customary or habitual behavior that is regarded as exemplary.
    During the Jahiliyah, the term designated the traditional prac-
    tices of ancestors to be followed by members of a given tribe. In
    Islam, sunnah indicates the sayings and doings of Muhammad,
    which have universal validity and are to be imitated by all faith-
    ful Muslims.

surah: Koran chapter.

tafsir: Koran commentary.

taghut: Pagan idols of the Jahiliyah.

tahrif: The willful distortion and corruption of a sacred scripture.

takbir: The action of voicing the cry Allahu akbar: "Allah is great!"

al-tansir: Propagation of the Nazarene (Christian) faith.

taqiyah: Protective dissimulation: hiding one's true religious identity
    and making an outward show of conformity with a dominant
    majority one secretly opposes. This practice is associated espe-
    cially with Twelver Shiism, where religious authorities have
    deemed this concealment both permissible and spiritually meri-
    torious for Shias who fear persecution by hostile Sunnis or other
    populations.

taqrib: Interfaith rapprochement—the attempt to diminish theological or doctrinal distinctions between faiths (e.g., Islam and Christianity) or between denominations (e.g., Sunni and Shia forms of Islam).

tariqah: Sufi association or brotherhood.

al-tashbih: Act of making something appear similar to something else. The term appears in discussions by Muslim exegetes of the docetic crucifixion presented in Koran 4:157. In this theological context, *al-tashbih* refers to the Islamic belief that the likeness of Jesus was cast upon another person, who was tortured, crucified, and killed instead of Jesus.

tawaf: Ritual circumambulation.

tawhid: "The assertion of oneness": monotheistic belief in Allah.

thar: Retaliation, revenge, blood feud.

ummah: Community of believers.

wudu': Ritual ablution.

zahid: Practitioner of *zuhd*, or asceticism.

zakat: Almsgiving or charity tax: one of the five Pillars of Islam.

zanjiri-matam: Self-flagellation: a popular (and controversial) ritual practice during the annual Muharram lamentation season.

BIBLIOGRAPHY

Abdullah, Mohammed (online pseudonym). "Would You Ever Convert to Islam?" *Stormfront: Opposing Views Forum*, December 1, 2008. http://www.Stormfront.org/forum/t547801/.

Abedi, Mehdi, and Gary Legenhausen, eds. *Jihad and Shahadat: Struggle and Martyrdom in Islam*. Houston: Institute for Research and Islamic Studies, 1986.

Abi-Habib, Maria. "Christians Are Leaving the Middle East." *The Wall Street Journal*, May 13, 2017, pp. A1–10.

Abu Tammam Habib ibn Aws al-Ta'i. *Diwan al-Hamasah*. With a commentary in Arabic by Imam al-Bara'. 4 vols. Cairo: Bulaq, 1878.

Académie des Inscriptions et Belles-Lettres. *Recueil des Historiens des Croisades: Historiens Occidentaux*. 5 vols. Paris: Imprimerie Nationale, 1886.

———. *Recueil des Historiens des Croisades: Historiens Orientaux*. 5 vols. Paris: Imprimerie Nationale, 1887.

Aciman, André. "After Egypt's Revolution, Christians Are Living in Fear." *The New York Times*, November 20, 2011, pp. 6–7.

Agence France-Presse. "Christian Woman Caned in Indonesia's Aceh Province for Selling Alcohol". *The Straits Times* (Singapore), April 13, 2016. http://www.straitstimes.com.

———. "200,000 Indonesian Muslims Protest against Christian Governor." *DailyMail.com*, December 2, 2016.

Ahmad, Mansur, and Husain A. Nuri. *Islamic Studies: Level 5*. Columbus, Ohio: Weekend Learning, 2012.

Akyol, Mustafa. *The Islamic Jesus: How the King of the Jews Became a Prophet of the Muslims*. New York: St. Martin's Press, 2017.

'Ali, 'Abdullah Yusuf. *The Meaning of the Holy Qur'an*. Beltsville, Md.: Amana Publications, 1999.

Allard, Michel, S.J., ed. *Textes apologétiques de Guwaini*. Beirut: Dar el-Machreq Imprimerie Catholique, 1968.

Andrae, Tor. *In the Garden of Myrtles: Studies in Early Islamic Mysticism*. Albany: SUNY Press, 1987.

————. *Mohammed: The Man and His Faith*. New York: Harper Torchbooks, 1960.

Anjuman-e Ma'sumeen. *Du'a-ye Fatima: muntakhab-e nauhajat*. Hyderabad: Maktab-e Turabia, 1987.

Arberry, A.J. *The Koran Interpreted*. New York: Collier Books, 1955.

Asia News. "Bekasi Assault on a Protestant Church: Mild Sentences for Islamic Leaders". February 24, 2011. http://www.AsiaNews.it.com.

————. "Pakistani Bishop: 'Don't Forget Javed Anjum, Killed for Refusing to Deny Christ'". June 7, 2006. http://www.Asia News.it.com.

Aslan, Reza. *Zealot: The Life and Times of Jesus of Nazareth*. New York: Random House, 2013.

Augustine. *Confessions*. Translated by Maria Boulding, O.S.A. New York: New City Press, 2014.

Badawi, El-Said, and Martin Hinds, eds. *A Dictionary of Egyptian Arabic*. Beirut: Librairie du Liban, 1986.

Bakhsh, Madeeha. "Trial of Blasphemy Accused Asia Bibi 'Likely' to Resume in June". *Christians in Pakistan: Voice of Pakistani Christians*, April 21, 2017. http://www.Christiansinpakistan.com.

Balthasar, Hans Urs von. *Mysterium Paschale: The Mystery of Easter*. Translated by Aidan Nichols, O.P. San Francisco: Ignatius Press, 1990.

————. *The Von Balthasar Reader*. Edited by Medard Kehl, S.J., and Werner Löser, S.J. Translated by Robert J. Daly and Fred Lawrence. New York: Crossroad, 1982.

Bar, Shmuel. "Iranian Terrorist Policy and 'Export of Revolution'". Ninth Annual Herzliya Conference on the Balance of Israel's National Security and Resilience, February 2–4, 2009. Herzliya: Israel: Institute for Policy and Strategy, 2009, pp. 1–24.

Barrett, Devlin, and Pervaiz Shallwani. "Terrorism Charges for Bomb Suspect". *The Wall Street Journal*, September 21, 2016, pp. A1–A2.

Bauckham, Richard. *Jesus and the God of Israel*. Grand Rapids, Mich.: Eerdmans, 2008.

al-Bayati, 'Abd al-Wahhab. *Al-Majd lil-atfal wa-al-zaytun*. Beirut: Dar Al-'Awdah, n.d.

————. *Ash'ar fi al-manfa*. Cairo: Dar al-Katib al-'Arabi, 1968.

al-Baydawi, Nasir al-Din Abu Sa'id. *Anwar al-tanzil wa-asrar al-ta'wil*. 2 vols. Beirut: Dar al-Kutub al-'Ilmiyah, 1988.

Beeching, Jack. *The Galleys at Lepanto*. New York: Charles Scribner's Sons, 1982.

Ben Cheneb, Mohammed. "Ibn Taimiya." In *Encyclopaedia of Islam*, edited by M. Houtsma, A.J. Wensinck et al., 3:421–23. Leiden: Brill, 1923.

Bibi, Asia, and Anne-Isabaelle Tollet. *Blasphemy: A Memoir: Sentenced to Death over a Cup of Water*. Chicago: Review Press, 2013.

Bill, James A., and John Alden Williams. *Roman Catholics and Shi'i Muslims: Prayer, Passion, and Politics*. Chapel Hill: University of North Carolina Press, 2002.

Breaking the Cross. Issue 15 of *Dabiq* (online publication of the Islamic State/ISIS), Shawwal 1437/July–August 2016. Accessed online via http://www.clarionproject.org.

Broadway, Bill. "Divining a Reason for Devastation". *The Washington Post*, January 8, 2005, p. B09.

Brown, Aisha. *Who Invented the Trinity?* Chicago: Institute of Islamic Information and Education, n.d.

Buchanan, Robert. *Notes of a Clerical Furlough, Spent Chiefly in the Holy Land*. London: Blackie & Son, 1859.

Burton, Richard F. *The Book of the Thousand Nights and a Night*. 17 vols. London: Burton Club for Private Subscribers, n.d.

Catherine of Siena, Saint. *The Letters of St. Catherine of Siena*. Edited and translated by Suzanne Noffke, O.P. 2 vols. Binghamton, N.Y.: SUNY, 1988.

Check, Christopher. "The Battle that Saved the Christian West". *Catholic Answers*, March 1, 2007. http://www.Catholic.com.

Cheikho, Louis, S.J. *Anis al-julasa' fi sharh diwan al-Khansa'*. Beirut: al-Matba'ah al-Kathulikiyah lil-Aba' al-Yasu'iyin, 1895.

————. *Kitab shu'ara' al-nasraniyah fi al-jahiliyah*. 4 vols. Cairo: Maktabat al-Adab, 1982.

Chester, Michael A. *Divine Pathos and Human Being: The Theology of Abraham Joshua Heschel*. Portland, Ore.: Mitchell, 2005.

Claudel, Paul. *Un Poète Regarde la Croix*. Paris: Gallimard, 1935.

Cochrane, Joe. "Blasphemy Verdict Shows 'Rot' in Indonesia, Legal Experts Say." *The New York Times*, May 12, 2017, p. A8.

Colla, Elliott. "Badr Shakir al-Sayyab, Cold War Poet". *Middle Eastern Literatures* 18, no. 3 (2015): 247–63.

Collins, Paul M. *The Trinity: A Guide for the Perplexed*. London: T&T Clark, 2008.

Coloma, Luis, S.J. *The Story of Don John of Austria*. London: John Lane, 1912.

Colson, Charles. "Preparing for the Mahdi". January 19, 2006. http://www.catholicexchange.com.

Conflict Armament Research. "Iranian Technology Transfers to Yemen". London: Conflict Armament Research, 2017, pp. 1–10.

Constable, Pamela, and Shaiq Hussain. "Pakistani Capital under Tight Security While Muslim Devotees Honor Man Who Assassinated a Liberal Governor". *The Washington Post*, March 1, 2017.

Conze, Edward, ed. *Buddhist Scriptures*. London: Penguin, 1959.

Dijkgraaf, Cor. "Renovaties in de ouden Stadskern van Sana'a, Yemen". *Bulletin KNOB* (Netherlands) 88 (1989): 6.

Donohue, John J., and John L. Esposito. *Islam in Transition: Muslim Perspectives*. 2nd ed. New York: Oxford University Press, 2007.

Doughty, Charles M. *Travels in Arabia Deserta*. 3rd ed. 2 vols. London: Butler & Tanner, 1921.

Dugger, Celia W. "Pakistani Sentenced to Death for Blasphemy". *The New York Times*, August 20, 2001.

Dupuis, Jacques, S.J. *Who Do You Say I Am?: Introduction to Christology*. Maryknoll, N.Y.: Orbis Books, 1994.

Edgington, Susan, and Sarah Lambert. *Gendering the Crusades*. New York: Columbia University Press, 2002.

El-Shamy, Hasan M., ed. *Folktales of Egypt*. Chicago: University Press, 1980.

Emerick, Yahiya. *How to Tell Others about Islam*. Beirut: Noorart, 2004.

Esposito, John L., ed. *The Oxford History of Islam*. New York: Oxford University Press, 1999.

Euripides. *Heracles Mainomenos*. Translated by Philip Vellacott. Harmondsworth: Penguin Classics, 1984.

———. *Hippolytus*. Translated by David Grene. Chicago: University Press, 1966.

Evans, C. Stephen, ed. *Exploring Kenotic Christology: The Self-Emptying of God*. Vancouver: Regent College Publishing, 2010.

al-Faruqi, Isma'il. *Islam*. 4th ed. Beltsville, Md.: Amana Publications, 2007.

Felix, Qaiser. "Killers of Catholic Youth, Javed Anjum, Sentenced". June 3, 2006. http://www.AsiaNews.it.com.

Ferguson, Everett. *Backgrounds of Early Christianity*. 2nd ed. Grand Rapids, Mich.: Eerdmans, 1993.

"Fi dhikra shuhada' Masbiru: man qatala wa-dahasa al-aqbat al--abriya'?" *Nida' al-Watan*. Cairo, November 25, 2011, p. 1.

Foltz, Richard C. *Animals in Islamic Tradition and Muslim Cultures*. Oxford: Oneworld, 2006.

Fu'ad, Mahmud. "Ma lam yaf'alhu al-a'da' fa'alahu al-abna'". *Al--Ahram* (Cairo), December 26, 2011. http://www.ahram.org.eg /Print.aspx?ID=120407.

Gabrieli, Francesco, ed. and trans. *Arab Historians of the Crusades*. Berkeley: University of California Press, 1984.

Gaustad, Edwin S. *Roger Williams*. New York: Oxford University Press, 2005.

al-Ghazali, Abu Hamid. *Al-Radd al-jamil li-ilahiyat 'Isa bi-sarih al-Injil*. Beirut: Dar al-Jil, 1990.

―――. *The Precious Pearl: A Translation from the Arabic*. Translated by Jane Idleman Smith. Missoula, Mont.: Scholars Press, 1979.

Gibb, Hamilton. "Pre-Islamic Monotheism in Arabia". *Harvard Theological Review* 55, no. 1 (1962): 268–80.

Gibbon, Edward. *The Decline and Fall of the Roman Empire*. 2 vols. New York: Heritage Press, 1946.

Ginzberg, Louis. *The Legends of the Jews*. 7 vols. Philadelphia: Jewish Publication Society of America, 1942.

Greenfield, Daniel. "Nidal Hasan on Anwar al-Awlaki". *Front Page Magazine*, August 1, 2013. http://www.frontpagemag.com.

Griffith, Sidney. "Al-Nasara in the Qur'an: A Hermeneutical Reflection". In *New Perspectives on the Qur'an: The Qur'an in Its Historical Context 2*, edited by Gabriel Said Reynolds, pp. 301–22. London: Routledge, 2011.

Hagenmeyer, Heinrich, ed. *Anonymi Gesta Francorum et Aliorum Hierosolymitanorum*. Heidelberg: Carl Winter's Universitätsbuchhandlung, 1890.

Haleem, Muzaffar, and Betty Batul Bowman. *The Sun Is Rising in the West: New Muslims Tell about Their Journey to Islam*. Beltsville, Md.: Amana Publications, 1999.

Harnack, Adolf von. *Marcion: The Gospel of the Alien God*. Durham, N.C.: Labyrinth Press, 1990.

Harrison, Frances. "Row over Ahmadinejad Imam Beliefs". *BBC News*, February 20, 2008.

al-Hashimi, al-Sayyid Basim. *Al-Masih wa-al-Islam*. Beirut: Dar al-- Mahajjah al-Baida', 2010.

Hengel, Martin. *Studies in Early Christianity*. Edinburgh: T&T Clark, 1995.

Hill, Rosalind, ed. and trans. *Gesta Francorum: The Deeds of the Franks and the Other Pilgrims to Jerusalem*. London: Thomas Nelson & Sons, 1962.

Hirsi Ali, Ayaan. *The Caged Virgin: An Emancipation Proclamation for Women and Islam*. New York: Free Press, 2006.

Horowitz, Jason. "Taking Message to Egypt, Pope Faces Difficult Test". *The New York Times*, April 28, 2017, p. A6.

House, Adrian. *Francis of Assisi: A Revolutionary Life*. Mahwah, N.J.: Hidden Spring/Paulist Press, 2001.

Howarth, Stephen. *The Knights Templar*. New York: Atheneum, 1982.

Huart, Claude. "Ibn Daisan". In the *Encyclopaedia of Islam*, edited by M. Houtsma, A.J. Wensinck et al. 1st ed. Leiden: Brill, 1993. Reprint.

Hübner, Arthur. *Die Deutschen Geisslerlieder: Studien zum geistlichen Volksliede des Mittelalters*. Berlin: Verlag Walter de Gruyter, 1931.

Hurtado, Larry W. *How on Earth Did Jesus Become a God?: Historical Questions about Earliest Devotion to Jesus*. Grand Rapids, Mich.: Eerdmans, 2005.

Husain, Amir. "Qabr ka khawf". *Khofnak Dijast* 4, no. 8 (Lahore: December 2000): 2.

Ibn al-Kalbi, Abu Mundhir Hisham ibn Muhammad. *Kitab al-asnam*. Edited by Ahmad Zeki Basha. Cairo: Imprimerie Nationale, 1914.

Ibn Ishaq. *The Life of Muhammad: A Translation of Ibn Ishaq's Sirat Rasul Allah*. Edited and translated by Alfred Guillaume. Karachi: Oxford University Press, 1968.

Ibn Jubayr, Muhammad ibn Ahmad. *Rihlat ibn Jubayr*. Cairo: Matba'at al-Sa'adah, 1908.

Ibn Kathir, Abu al-Fida' al-Hafiz. *Al-Sirah al-nabawiyah*. Edited by Ahmad 'Abd al-Shafi. 2 vols. Beirut: Dar al-Kutub al-'Ilmiyah, n.d.

Ibn Munqidh, Usamah. *Kitab al-i'tibar.* Edited by Hartwig Derenbourg. Paris: L'École des Langues Orientales Vivantes, 1886.

Ibn Qutaybah, Abu Muhammad 'Abd Allah ibn Muslim. *Kitab al-
shi'r wa-al-shu'ara'.* Edited by Hasan Tamim and Muhammad
'Abd al-Mun'im. Beirut: Dar Ihya' al-'Ulum, 1987.

Ibn Taimiyyah, Ahmad ibn 'Abd al-Halim. *Al-Jawab al-sahih li-man
baddala din al-masih.* 2 vols. Beirut: al-Maktabah al-'Ilmiyah,
2003.

Ibrahim, Raymond, ed. and trans. *The Al Qaeda Reader.* New York:
Broadway Books, 2007.

al-Isbahani, Abu al-Faraj. *Kitab al-aghani.* Edited by Ahmad al-
Shinqiti. 21 vols. Cairo: Matba'at al-Taqaddum, 1905.

James, William. *The Varieties of Religious Experience.* Harmondsworth:
Penguin, 1983.

Jonas, Hans. *The Gnostic Religion: The Message of the Alien God and the
Beginnings of Christianity.* Boston: Beacon Press, 1963.

Kanso, Heba. "Symbol of ISIS Hate Becomes Rallying Cry for Christians." *CBS News,* October 20, 2014. http://www.cbsnews.com
/news/for-christians-symbol-of-mideast-oppression-becomes
-source-of-solidarity.

al-Kashifi, Husain Wa'iz. *Rawdat al-shuhada'.* Teheran: Kitab-Forushi
Islamiyah, 1979.

al-Katib al-Isfahani, 'Imad al-Din. *Kitab al-fath al-qussi fi al-fath al-
qudsi.* In *Conquête de la Syrie et de la Palestine par Salah ed-Din,*
edited by Le Comte Carlo de Landberg. Leiden: Brill, 1888.

Kelley, Nicole. *Knowledge and Religious Authority in the Pseudo-
Clementines: Situating the "Recognitions" in Fourth-Century Syria.*
Tübingen: Mohr Siebeck, 2006.

Kenney, Jeffrey T. *Muslim Rebels: Kharijites and the Politics of Extremism in Egypt.* New York: Oxford University Press, 2006.

Kepel, Gilles. *Terror in France: The Rise of Jihad in the West.* Princeton,
N.J.: Princeton University Press, 2017.

Khalidi, Tarif. *The Muslim Jesus: Sayings and Stories in Islamic Literature.*
Cambridge, Mass.: Harvard University Press, 2001.

Khan, Muhammad Muhsin, ed. *Sahih al-Bukhari.* 9 vols. Ankara:
Hilal Yayinlari, 1978.

Kidd, B.J. *The Churches of Eastern Christendom from A.D. 451 to the
Present Time.* London: Faith Press, 1927.

Kramer, Andrew E. "For Iraqi Christians, Money Bought Survival." *The New York Times*, June 26, 2008, nytimes.com.

Küng, Hans. *Islam: Past, Present and Future*. Translated by John Bowden. Oxford: Oneworld, 2007.

Lamb, Harold. *Swords from the West*. Lincoln: University of Nebraska Press, 2009.

Lane, Edward William. *Arabic-English Lexicon*. London: Williams & Norgate, 1863.

Lawrence, T. E. *The Home Letters of T. E. Lawrence and His Brothers*. Edited by M. R. Lawrence. New York: Macmillan, 1954.

Lawson, Todd. *The Crucifixion and the Qur'an: A Study in the History of Muslim Thought*. Oxford: Oneworld Publications, 2009.

Levinson, Charles, and Matt Bradley. "Egyptians Show Mix of Jubilation, Anger to Mark Anniversary". *The Wall Street Journal*, January 26, 2012, pp. A1, A10.

Lewis, Bernard. *The Arabs in History*. Rev. ed. New York: Harper & Row, 1966.

Lieu, Judith M. *Marcion and the Making of a Heretic: God and Scripture in the Second Century*. Cambridge: University Press, 2015.

Lucian of Samosata. *The Works of Lucian of Samosata*. Translated by H. W. Fowler and F. G. Fowler. 4 vols. Oxford: Clarendon Press, 1905.

Lyall, Charles James, ed. *A Commentary on Ten Ancient Arabic Poems*. Calcutta: Dar al-Imarah, 1894.

———. *Translations of Ancient Arabian Poetry*. London: Williams & Norgate, 1930.

MacCulloch, Diarmaid. *Christianity: The First Three Thousand Years*. New York: Penguin, 2011.

Maier, Christoph T. "The Roles of Women in the Crusade Movement: A Survey". *Journal of Medieval History* 30, no. 1 (2004): 61–82.

Mani, Emmanuel Yousaf, ed. *Human Rights Monitor 2006: A Report on the Religious Minorities in Pakistan*. Lahore: National Commission for Justice and Peace, 2006.

Manji, Irshad. *The Trouble with Islam Today: A Muslim's Call for Reform in Her Faith*. New York: St. Martin's Press, 2003.

Mann, Thomas. *Doctor Faustus: The Life of the German Composer Adrian Leverkühn as Told by a Friend*. Translated by H. T. Lowe-Porter. New York: Alfred A. Knopf, 1948.

Marks, Kathy. "Bali Bombers Buried as Muslim Martyrs". *The Independent*, November 10, 2008. http://www.independent.co.uk.

Mascaró, Juan, trans. *The Upanishads*. London: Penguin, 1965.

Massignon, Louis. "Hulul". In *Encyclopaedia of Islam*, edited by M. Houtsma, A.J. Wensinck et al., 3:333. Leiden: Brill, 1923.

———, ed. *Kitab al-Tawasin par Abou al-Moghith al-Hosayn ibn Mansour al-Hallaj*. Paris: Librairie Paul Geuthner, 1913.

———. *The Passion of al-Hallaj: Mystic and Martyr of Islam*. Translated by Herbert Mason. 4 vols. Princeton: University Press, 1982.

al-Mas'udi, 'Ali ibn Husain. *Muruj al-dhahab*. Edited by C. Barbier de Meynard. 9 vols. Paris: l'Imprimerie Nationale, 1874.

Mattson, Ingrid. *The Story of the Qur'an: Its History and Place in Muslim Life*. Oxford: Blackwell, 2008.

Mawdudi, Abul A'la. *Towards Understanding Islam*. New York: Message Publications, 1997.

McClure, M.L., and C.L. Feltoe, eds. and trans. *The Pilgrimage of Etheria*. London: Society for Promoting Christian Knowledge, 1919.

McIntosh, Mark A. *Christology from Within: Spirituality and the Incarnation in Hans Urs von Balthasar*. Notre Dame: University Press, 1996.

McLaughlin, Daniel. *Yemen*. Guilford, Conn.: Globe Pequot Press, 2007.

Meier, Fritz, ed. *Die Fawa'ih al-Gamal wa-Fawatih al-Galal des Nagm ad-Din al-Kubra*. Wiesbaden: Franz Steiner Verlag, 1957.

Merad, Ali. "Christ according to the Qur'an". *Encounter: Documents for Muslim-Christian Understanding* 69 (November 1980). Rome: Pontifical Institute for Arabic and Islamic Studies.

Merton, Thomas. *New Seeds of Contemplation*. Norfolk, Conn.: New Directions, 1961.

Migne, Jacques-Paul, ed. *Patrologia Latina*. 221 vols. Paris: Frères Garnier, 1880.

Minquriyus, Matthias Nasr. "Misriyatuna aqwa". *al-Katiba al-Tibiya* (Cairo), December 2011, pp. 1, 5.

Moltmann, Jürgen. "The Crucified God". *Theology Today* 31, no. 1 (April 1974): 6–18.

Morony, Michael G. *Iraq after the Muslim Conquest*. Princeton: University Press, 1984.

Mourad, Suleiman A. "Does the Qur'an Deny or Assert Jesus's Crucifixion and Death?" In *New Perspectives on the Qur'an*, edited by Gabriel Said Reynolds, pp. 349–57. London: Routledge, 2011.

Muir, Sir William. *The Life of Mahomet from Original Sources*. 3rd ed. London: Smith, Elder, & Co., 1894.

Musaji, Sheila. "Throwing Stones at the Qur'an from a Biblical Glass House". *The American Muslim*, March 20, 2007. http://www.theamericanmuslim.org.

al-Nabighah al-Dhubyani. *Diwan al-Nabighah al-Dhubyani*. Edited by Muhammad Abu al-Fadl Ibrahim. Cairo: Dar al-Maʻarif, n.d.

al-Nadim. *The Fihrist of al-Nadim: A Tenth-Century Survey of Muslim Culture*. Edited and translated by Bayard Dodge. 2 vols. New York: Columbia University Press, 1970.

an-Naʻim, ʻAbdullahi Ahmed. "Shariʻa and Basic Human Rights Concerns." In *Liberal Islam: A Sourcebook*, edited by Charles Kurzman, pp. 222–38. New York: Oxford University Press, 1998.

Nasr, Seyyed Hossein, ed. *Islamic Spirituality: Foundations*. London: Routledge & Kegan Paul, 1987.

Natalia, Maria. "FPI Demo Tolak Lady Gaga di Mabes Polri". *Kompas* (Jakarta), May 25, 2012. http:www.Kompas.com.

Osborne, Samuel. "'Violence More Common' in Bible than Quran, Text Analysis Reveals". *The Independent*, February 9, 2016. http://www.independent.co.uk.

Parimi, Mukhtar ʻAli. "Dozakh ki ag aur andhera". *Khofnak Dijast 6*, no. 1 (Lahore, May 2002): 3.

Parrinder, Geoffrey. *Jesus in the Qur'an*. London: Sheldon Press, 1965.

Pelikan, Jaroslav. *The Emergence of the Catholic Tradition (100–600)*. Chicago: University Press, 1971.

Penn, Michael Philip. *When Christians First Met Muslims: A Sourcebook of the Earliest Syriac Writings on Islam*. Oakland: University of California Press, 2015.

Penrice, John. *A Dictionary and Glossary of the Koran*. London: Curzon Press, 1873.

Petronius. *The Satyricon of Petronius*. Translated by William Arrowsmith. Ann Arbor, Mich.: University of Michigan Press, 1962.

Pickthall, Mohammed Marmaduke. *The Meaning of the Glorious Koran*. New York: New American Library, n.d.

Pinault, David. *Horse of Karbala: Muslim Devotional Life in India.* New York: Palgrave, 2001.

———. "Images of Christ in Arabic Literature". *Die Welt des Islams* 27 (1987): 103–25.

———. *Notes from the Fortune-Telling Parrot: Islam and the Struggle for Religious Pluralism in Pakistan.* London: Equinox Publishing, 2008.

———. "Self-Mortification Rituals in the Shi'i and Christian Traditions". In *Shi'ite Heritage: Essays on Classical and Modern Traditions,* edited by Lynda Clarke, pp. 375–388. Binghamton, N.Y.: Global Publications, 2001.

———. *The Shiites: Ritual and Popular Piety in a Muslim Community.* New York: St. Martin's Press, 1992.

———. "Sunni-Shia Sectarianism and Competition for the Leadership of Global Islam". *Tikkun Magazine,* January/February 2010, pp. 45–47, 73–75.

———. "Sunni, Shia, Zaydi: Religious Identity and Sectarian Proselytizing in Contemporary Yemen". *Journal of South Asian and Middle Eastern Studies* 33, no. 1 (Fall 2009): 1–19.

Placher, William C. *The Triune God: An Essay in Postliberal Theology.* Louisville: Westminster John Knox Press, 2007.

al-Qaradawi, Yusuf. "Suicide Bombers Are Martyrs." July 24, 2003. http://www.memri.org.

Qarquti Sha'ban, Hanan. *Hayat al-masih 'Isa ibn Maryam 'alayhima al-salam min manzur islami: dirasah muqaranah.* Beirut: Dar al-Kutub al-'Ilmiyah, 2004.

Qummi, 'Abbas. *Mafatih al-jinan.* Beirut: Dar Ihya' al-Turath al-'Arabi, 1970.

Qureshi, Nabeel. *Seeking Allah, Finding Jesus: A Devout Muslim Encounters Christianity.* Grand Rapids, Mich.: Zondervan, 2016.

al-Qushayri, 'Abd al-Karim. *Al-Risalah al-qushayriyyah.* 2 vols. Cairo: Dar al-Kutub al-Hadithah, n.d.

Qutub, Musa, and M. Vazir Ali. "Western Feminism Movement Problems vs. Islam's Gender Balance Dynamism". *The Invitation* 9, no. 2 (Des Plaines, Ill.): April 1991.

Rahman, Fazlur. *Islam.* Chicago: University Press, 1974.

Rahman, Jamal. "Making Peace with the Sword Verse". http://www.yesmagazine.org/blogs/interfaith-amigos.

Reda, Yasser. "Countering the Pontiff of Terror". *The Wall Street Journal*, August 24, 2016, p. A13.

Reynolds, Gabriel Said. "Alternate Ending: Lebanese Christians and a Muslim Film about Jesus". *Commonweal*, February 18, 2011. http://www.commonwealmagazine.org.

————, ed. *New Perspectives on the Qur'an: The Qur'an in Its Historical Context 2*. New York: Routledge, 2011.

————. *The Qur'an and Its Biblical Subtext*. London: Routledge, 2010.

Ritner, Robert Kriech. *The Mechanics of Ancient Egyptian Magical Practice*. Chicago: Oriental Institute, 1993.

Roberts, Alexander, Sir James Donaldson, and Arthur Cleveland Coxe, trans. *The Arabic Infancy Gospel of the Savior*. http://www.gnosis.org/library/infarab.htm.

Robinson, James M., ed. *The Nag Hammadi Library in English*. Rev. ed. San Francisco: Harper Collins, 1990.

Rorate Caeli. "Nun: The Sign of Genocide". July 19, 2014. http://www.rorate-caeli.blogspot.com/2014/07/nun-sign-of-genocide.html.

Rubin, Dave. "New ISIS Spokesman—an Australian Teen—Issues Warning". *The Rubin Report*, October 22, 2014. http://www.youtube.com/watch?v=aQ9gWebjRuU.

Rudolph, Kurt. *Gnosis: The Nature and History of Gnosticism*. San Francisco: Harper & Row, 1983.

Runge, Paul. *Die Lieder und Melodien der Geissler des Jahres 1349 nach der Aufzeichnung Hugo's von Reutlingen*. Leipzig: Breitkopf & Haertel, 1900.

Sabah, Zaid. "Sabian Sect Keeps the Faith". *USA Today*, September 28, 2007.

Safi, Omid, ed. *Progressive Muslims: On Justice, Gender, and Pluralism*. Oxford: Oneworld, 2003.

Sandars, N.K., trans. *The Epic of Gilgamesh*. Harmondsworth: Penguin Books, 1964.

al-Sayyab, Badr Shakir. *Unshudat al-matar*. Beirut: Dar Maktabat al-- Hayah, 1969.

al-Sayyid, Muhammad Mahmud. *Al-Masih bayna al-lahut wa-al-nasut*. Cairo: Basamat fi Adhhan al-Athirin, 2010.

Schimmel, Annemarie. *And Muhammad Is His Messenger: The Veneration of the Prophet in Islamic Piety*. Chapel Hill: University of North Carolina Press, 1985.

————. *Mystical Dimensions of Islam*. Chapel Hill: University of North Carolina Press, 1975.

Sells, Michael A., trans. *Desert Tracings: Six Classic Arabian Odes*. Hanover, N.H.: Wesleyan University Press, 1989.

————, ed. and trans. *Early Islamic Mysticism: Sufi, Qur'an, Mi'raj, Poetic and Theological Writings*. New York: Paulist Press, 1996.

Senior, Donald, and John J. Collins, eds. *The Catholic Study Bible*. 2nd ed. New York: Oxford University Press, 2006.

Seward, Desmond. *The Monks of War: The Military Religious Orders*. St. Albans: Paladin, 1974.

al-Shahrastani, Abu al-Fath. *Kitab al-milal wa-al-nihal*. Edited by Muhammad Sayyid Kilani. 2 vols. Cairo: Maktabat Mustafa al-Babi, 1976.

Shams al-Din, Ahmad, ed. *Majmu'at rasa'il al-Imam al-Ghazali*. Beirut: Dar al-Kutub al-'Ilmiyah, 1988.

Shanfara. *Qasidat lamiyat al-'Arab*. With a commentary in Arabic by Mahmud ibn 'Umar al-Zamakhshari. Istanbul: Matba'at al-Jawa'ib, 1883.

al-Sharqawi, 'Abd al-Rahman al-Safati, ed. *Kitab alf laylah wa-laylah*. 2 vols. Cairo: Bulaq, 1835.

Shaw, Margaret R. B., ed. and trans. *Chronicles of the Crusades*. Harmondsworth: Penguin, 1976.

Shinakeh, Shabnam Daoud. "Panj qabron ki chashmdid-e halat ne gonahgar ko tawba par amada kar diya". *Khofnak Dijast* 6, no. 7 (Lahore: November 2002): 4.

Shnizer, Aliza. "Sacrality and Collection". In *The Blackwell Companion to the Qur'an*, edited by Andrew Rippin, pp. 159–71. Oxford: Blackwell Publishing, 2006.

Siddiqui, Mona. *Christians, Muslims, and Jesus*. New Haven: Yale University Press, 2013.

Simanjuntak, Hotli, and Apriadi Gunawan. "Thousands Leave Aceh after Church Burnings." *The Jakarta Post*, October 15, 2015. http://www.thejakartapost.com.

Sisto, Christine. "A Christian Genocide Symbolized by One Letter". *National Review*, July 23, 2014. http://www.nationalreview.com /article/383493.

Sivan, Emmanuel. "Le caractère sacré de Jérusalem dans l'Islam". *Studia Islamica* 27 (1967): 149–82.

Smoltczyk, Alexander. "Saudi Church Project Runs into the Sand." *Der Spiegel Online*, April 16, 2008. http://www.spiegel.de.

Snyder, Graydon F. *Ante Pacem: Archaeological Evidence of Church Life before Constantine*. Macon, Ga.: Mercer University Press, 1985.

Stark, Rodney. "The Case for the Crusades". *The Southern Baptist Journal of Theology* 20, no. 2 (2016): 9–28.

Sterling, Joe. "ISIS Claims Responsibility for Palm Sunday Church Bombings in Egypt." April 10, 2017. http://www.cnn.com.

Stirling-Maxwell, Sir William. *Don John of Austria, or Passages from the History of the Sixteenth Century 1547–1578*. 2 vols. London: Longmans, 1883.

Stokes, Anson Phelps, ed. *Church and State in the United States*. 3 vols. New York: Harper & Bros., 1950.

al-Suyuti, Jalal al-Din 'Abd al-Rahman. *Tafsir al-jalalayn*. Edited by Marwan Sawar. Beirut: Dar al-Ma'rifah, n.d.

Tacitus. *The Annals*. Edited and translated by A.J. Church and W.J. Brodribb. London: Macmillan & Co., 1906.

Taha, Mahmoud Mohamed. *The Second Message of Islam*. Syracuse: University Press, 1987.

Taylor, John V. *The Christlike God*. London: SCM Press, 2004.

al-Tha'labi, Abu Ishaq Ahmad ibn Muhammad ibn Ibrahim. *Qisas al-anbiya' al-musamma 'ara'is al-majalis*. Beirut: al-Maktabah al--Thaqafiyah, n.d.

al-Tha'alibi al-Nisaburi, Abu Mansur 'Abd al-Malik ibn Muhammad. *Kitab thimar al-qulub fi al-mudaf wa-al-mansub*. Edited by Muhammad Abu Shadi. Cairo: Matba'at al-Zahir, 1908.

Varagur, Krithika. "Saudi Arabia Is Redefining Islam for the World's Largest Muslim Nation." *The Atlantic*, March 2, 2017. http://www.theatlantic.com.

Vasiliev, A. A. *History of the Byzantine Empire 324–1453*. 2 vols. Madison: University of Wisconsin Press, 1973.

Wallace, Mark I. "The Wounded Spirit as the Basis for Hope in an Age of Radical Ecology". In *Christianity and Ecology: Seeking the Well-Being of Earth and Humans*, edited by Dieter T. Hessel and Rosemary Radford Ruether, pp. 51–72. Cambridge, Mass.: Harvard University Press, 2000.

Watt, William Montgomery. *The Faith and Practice of al-Ghazali*. Chicago: Kazi Publications, 1982.

————. *Muhammad: Prophet and Statesman*. New York: Oxford University Press, 1961.

————, and M. V. McDonald, eds. *The History of al-Tabari*. Vol. 7: *The Foundation of the Community*. Albany: SUNY Press, 1987.

Wehr, Hans, and J. Milton Cowan, eds. *A Dictionary of Modern Written Arabic*. 3rd ed. Ithaca, N.Y.: Spoken Language Services, 1976.

Wenham, David. *Paul and Jesus: The True Story*. Grand Rapids, Mich.: Eerdmans, 2002.

Wild, Stefan. "Judentum, Christentum und Islam in der palästinensischen Poesie". *Die Welt des Islams* 23–24 (1984): 259–97.

Witztum, Joseph. "Joseph among the Ishmaelites: Q 12 in Light of Syriac Sources". In *New Perspectives on the Qur'an: The Qur'an in Its Historical Context 2*, edited by Gabriel Said Reynolds, pp. 425–48. London: Routledge, 2011.

Worth, Robert F. "The Secularist". *The New York Times Magazine*, April 9, 2017, pp. 32–39, 56–65.

Wüstenfeld, Ferdinand, ed. *Kitab sirat rasul Allah*. Göttingen: Dieterichsche Universitäts-Buchhandlung, 1860.

Yaqut ibn 'Abd Allah al-Rumi. *Mu'jam al-buldan*. 5 vols. Beirut: Dar Sadir, 1957.

Yeats-Brown, Francis. *The Lives of a Bengal Lancer*. New York: Bantam, 1946.

Yeo, Margaret. *Don John of Austria*. New York: Sheed & Ward, 1934.

Yildirim, Onur. "The Battle of Lepanto and Its Impact on Ottoman History and Historiography". In *Mediterraneo in armi (secc. XV-XVIII)*, edited by Rossella Cancila, pp. 533–56. Palermo: Quaderni Mediterranea, 2007.

al-Zamakhshari, Mahmud ibn 'Umar. *Al-Kashshaf 'an haqa'iq al-tanzil*. 4 vols. Beirut: Dar al-Ma'rifah, n.d.

Zawadi, Bassam. "Prophet Muhammad (peace be upon him) and the Satanic Verses". http://www.Answering-Christianity.com /bassam_zawadi/satanic_verses.htm.

BIBLICAL INDEX

KORANIC INDEX

GENERAL INDEX